Studies in modern capitalism · Etudes sur le capitalisme moderne

The new international division of labour

Studies in modern capitalism · Etudes sur le capitalisme moderne

This series is devoted to an attempt to comprehend capitalism as a world-system. It will include monographs, collections of essays and colloquia around specific themes, written by historians and social scientists united by a common concern for the study of large-scale long-term social structure and social change.

The series is a joint enterprise of the Maison des Sciences de l'Homme in Paris and the Fernand Braudel Center for the Study of Economies, Historical Systems, and Civilizations at the State University of New York at Binghamton.

Other books in the series
Pierre Bourdieu: *Algeria 1960*
Andre Gunder Frank: *Mexican agriculture 1521–1630: transformation of the mode of production*
Immanuel Wallerstein: *The capitalist world-economy*
Henri H. Stahl: *Traditional Romanian village communities*
Ernest Mandel: *Long waves of capitalist development*
Peter Kriedte, Hans Medick, Jürgen Schlumbohm: *Industrialization before industrialization*
Calgar Keyder: *The definition of a peripheral economy*
Maurice Aymard (ed.): *Dutch capitalism and world capitalism/Capitalisme hollandais et capitalisme mondial*
Bruce McGowan: *Economic life in Ottoman Europe*

This book is published as part of the joint publishing agreement established in 1977 between the Fondation de la Maison des Sciences de l'Homme and the Press Syndicate of the University of Cambridge. Titles published under this arrangement may appear in any European language or, in the case of volumes of collected essays, in several languages.

New books will appear either as individual titles or in one of the series which the Maison des Sciences de l'Homme and the Cambridge University Press have jointly agreed to publish. All books published jointly by the Maison des Sciences de l'Homme and the Cambridge University Press will be distributed by the Press throughout the world.

The new international division of labour

Structural unemployment in industrialised countries and industrialisation in developing countries

FOLKER FRÖBEL, JÜRGEN HEINRICHS
AND OTTO KREYE

Max Planck Institute, Starnberg

Translated by Pete Burgess

Cambridge University Press
Cambridge
London New York New Rochelle Melbourne Sydney

& Editions de la Maison des Sciences de l'Homme
Paris

Published by the Press Syndicate of the University of Cambridge
The Pitt Building, Trumpington Street, Cambridge CB2 1RP
32 East 57th Street, New York, NY 10022, USA
296 Beaconsfield Parade, Middle Park, Melbourne 3206, Australia
and
Editions de la Maison des Sciences de l'Homme
54 Boulevard Raspail, 75270 Paris Cedex 06

English translation first published 1980
First paperback edition 1981

Printed in Great Britain at the University Press, Cambridge

Library of Congress catalogue card number: 78-72087

British Library Cataloguing in Publication Data

Fröbel, Folker
The new international division of labour. –
(Studies in modern capitalism = Etudes sur le capitalisme moderne, ISSN 0144-2333)
1. Textile industry – Germany (West)
2. Unemployment
I. Title II. Heinrichs, Jürgen III. Kreye, Otto
IV. Die neue internationale Arbeitsteilung.
English V. Series
331.13'7877 HD9863.5

ISBN 0 521 22319 9 hard covers
ISBN 0 521 28720 0 paperback

Contents

Tables

Abbreviations

AG	Aktiengesellschaft (joint stock company)
BfA	Bundestelle für Außenhandelsinformation (Federal Foreign Trade Information Office)
DEG	Deutsche Entwicklungsgesellschaft (German Development Company)
DIW	Deutsches Institut für Wirtschaftsforschung (German Institute for Economic Research)
EC	European Community
EEC	European Economic Community
EFTA	European Free Trade Area
FAO	Food and Agriculture Organisation (a United Nations Agency)
FAZ	*Frankfurter Allgemeine Zeitung* (German daily newspaper)
GATT	General Agreement on Trade and Tariffs
GmbH	Gesellschaft mit beschränkter Haftung (German limited liability company)
IATA	International Air Transport Association
IfO	Ifo-Institut für Wirtschaftsforschung, Munich
ILO	International Labour Office
IMF	International Monetary Fund
ISIC	International Standard Industrial Classification of All Economic Activities
ITT	International Telephone and Telegraph
KD	Knocked-down vehicles
KG	Kommanditgesellschaft (limited partnership)
LDC	Less developed countries
OECD	Organisation for Economic Cooperation and Development
SITC	Standard International Trade Classification
UN	United Nations
UNCTAD	United Nations Conference on Trade and Development
UNIDO	United Nations Industrial Development Organisation

Foreword

In this book the authors argue that a new international division of labour is superseding the traditional international division of labour. This process is bound to have far-reaching consequences for the working and living conditions of people in all parts of the world.

In the introduction of the thesis the tendency towards a new international division of labour is established theoretically; Parts I to III bring together empirical evidence for the thesis. The special character of these empirical investigations has caused the authors to dispense with explicit references to pertaining literature; instead a broader selection and more thorough analysis of the systematically collected and evaluated data was given preference. In order to facilitate an immediate appreciation of the data, numerous texts are cited in the original and foreign-language citations have been translated into English.

The source materials which underly the investigations have been supplied by countless institutions all over the world. This was possible only because of the cooperative spirit of the approached companies', institutes', public authorities', etc. staff on the one hand, and of the staff of the Max Planck Institute for Research in the Conditions of Life in the Scientific-Technical World on the other hand, all of which have contributed to this study over several years. To all of them the authors are heavily indebted.

The present book is a slightly shortened English version of the German original. For some more technical details readers are encouraged to consult the German version. No attempt has been made (except for a few details) to update the statistics and the argument in the light of newer data because such minor improvements would not affect the main thesis and its empirical backing.

Last but not least our thanks go to our friend Pete Burgess who took care of the English translation far beyond the call of duty.

Starnberg, 1 May 1979

Introduction

1 • The new international division of labour in the world economy

Two fundamental issues confront corporate management in 1977. They are:
- the probability that the post-war era of unusual rapid economic expansion is over, and
- the probability that the post-war era of unprecedented world economic and political cooperation is coming to an end.

The world's departure from these patterns could force companies into the most radical and painful reassessments of their plans and strategies in living memory...Growth, translated into improved living conditions, has...become one of the basic expectations of all the world's citizens, including the poorest. These assumptions clearly must now be challenged. The recent world recession will, hopefully, prove to have been merely an extremely severe one, but 1977 may reveal the recession as the sign-off of an exceptional period in world economic history. Within many nations, the tensions from a prolonged era of no or low growth could ultimately prove explosive...The turmoil within and between nations resulting from the frustration of mass expectations would, in many instances, bring revolution and war to the fore.[1]

A blueprint for a new economic era published today outlines profound changes in life-styles that will be needed over the next five years to put capitalist societies back on the track for sustained economic growth. The most significant change is a shift away from the consumer-oriented growth that has marked the post-war period to a model more akin to the Communist bloc countries with the emphasis on improving and expanding plant and equipment. This shift would be achieved in part through a reduction in real wages and limits on the growth of living standards. One of the major tools to effect these changes would be a sustained level of unemployment well over post-war norms although below the record level seen in the just ended recession...The author of this blueprint is the secretariat of the Organisation for Economic Cooperation and Development, the economic clearing house for the 24 largest industrialised states outside the Communist bloc...[The OECD notes] 'that it would be tempting to consider a more favourable

1. Business International Corporation, *Business International – Weekly Report to Managers of Worldwide Operations*, 7 January 1977, p. 1.

scenario... Unfortunately, there are few grounds for believing that this is a realistic alternative unless economic policies prove much more effective than in the past.'[1]

1.1 The phenomenon

Business International is one of the world's largest business consultancy firms. The OECD is the supranational institution which was established by the Western industrialised countries for the purpose of observing and coordinating their economies. What is the empirical evidence of recent changes in the world economy which has induced these two institutions to proffer such gloomy forecasts?

In the Western *industrialised countries* the rate of unemployment has reached its highest level for many years. In 1975 the official rate of unemployment, which always understates the real volume of unemployment, averaged 5% for the OECD countries (USA = 8.5%, Japan = 1.9%, Federal Germany = 4.7%) and has remained at this high level with no indications that it will decrease. The number of people in OECD countries officially registered as unemployed has hovered around the fifteen million mark since 1975 and there is no reason to suppose that it will fall in the immediate future.

An increasing number of the industrial branches of the OECD countries are reporting declining output, overcapacities, short-time working and mass redundancies. For example, the garment, textile and synthetic fibres industries in the most highly industrialised countries have, almost without exception, drastically cut back the production of their respective products at the traditional manufacturing sites as production there is becoming increasingly less competitive in the world market. Employees in many branches of industry are threatened with redundancy and the devaluation of their professional skills – victims of spreading automation and, in particular, of the recent leap forward in the rationalisation of the production process made possible by technical developments in the electrical engineering industry, especially the shift from electromechanical to electronic components in the production both of consumer goods and components to be used in other sectors of the economy.

Domestic investment in the largest industrialised countries (USA,

1. 'Changes in West life-styles expected. OECD sees tough capitalist road ahead' in *Herald Tribune*, 28 July 1976; cf. OECD, *Economic Outlook*, 19 July 1976, Special Supplement, 'A growth scenario to 1980'.

Japan, Federal Germany, France, United Kingdom) has not only been stagnating but has even fallen in Japan and Federal Germany as a proportion of gross national product in the first half of the 1970s. In the face of the decreasing profitability of domestic investments, companies in the OECD countries have expanded and justified their policy of investment directed towards rationalisation on the grounds that they cannot expect any change in the current trends for the foreseeable future. In many countries the increase in the share of domestic investment which has been directed towards rationalisation schemes over recent years has resulted in a substantial loss of local jobs, without any reduction in productive capacity.

By contrast, *foreign* investments originating from the Western industrialised countries have been steadily increasing for a number of years. An ever-increasing share of these investments is flowing into the developing countries. Foreign investment for the purpose of industrial relocation is gaining in importance, both that undertaken in industrialised countries, as well as in developing countries.

Stagnating output, short-time working and mass redundancies in numerous countries do not, however, necessarily reflect the fates of individual companies. On the contrary, many companies, both large and small, from the industrialised countries are expanding their investments, production capacities and employment abroad, especially in developing countries, whilst their investments, production capacities and employment at home are stagnating or even declining.

The primacy given to investment for rationalisation instead of for expansion in the Western industrialised countries implies increased 'mobility' for workers. More and more workers are losing not only their jobs but also their acquired profession as a result of rationalisation schemes. They are thrown onto the labour market where, because they lack relevant qualifications or training, they are obliged to sell their labour-power as unskilled or semiskilled workers at considerably worse terms than before. Given the rapid changes in the specifications and qualifications demanded of the labour-force by current economic developments and the concurrent increase in occupational 'mobility', it is hardly surprising that the rationale and usefulness of professional training is becoming more and more questionable, and that companies are increasingly cutting back on comprehensive programmes of industrial training. More and more workers are being forced to make rapid and psychologically exhausting adjustments to the changing demands of the labour market – changes which are both abrupt and more or less unforeseeable.

In addition, the Western industrialised countries are experiencing a long-term fiscal crisis of the state. High unemployment and short-time working have forced the state to increase its expenditure, while at the same time the state's tax receipts have fallen because high unemployment has reduced the revenue from personal taxation and the threat or reality of industrial relocation has reduced the ability of the state to tax private companies. It is becoming more and more difficult to provide adequate funds for public pension and health programmes. Outlays on social services are being cut, while at the same time higher social security contributions and taxes threaten employees with a decrease in real incomes. On the other hand, the state has been compelled to provide grants, loans and tax concessions to private business on an increasing scale, hoping that this will stimulate domestic investment, reduce the rate of unemployment, and thus avert the danger of potentially explosive social tensions. This policy of curbing real wages and of promoting the so-called growth industries by official massive backing from the state has nonetheless so far failed to yield any noticeable success in making domestic industrial sites attractive again. 'The horses have been led to the water, but are refusing to drink.'

These economic, social and political problems in each of the Western industrialised countries are occurring in the context of world-wide higher turnovers and profits by individual companies. The annual reports of most large companies show that, even in the years of the world recession, these companies have been operating very successfully.

A remarkable contrast then exists between the success of individual private companies and the failure of the economic policies of the industrialised countries to attain their declared principal policy aim, namely the reduction in unemployment. The panacea of the last few decades, high rates of growth in gross national product, no longer appears to be available. In fact, whether the extensive elimination of unemployment is seriously the prime objective of the economic policies of the industrial nations is far from certain when one considers the OECD 'scenario' cited at the beginning of this chapter. One cannot avoid the question: Are the politicians simply incapable, or have the structures of national economies recently undergone such profound changes that the present problem of chronic unemployment is simply so much more intractable than formerly? We shall return to this question later.

The number of un- and underemployed in the *developing countries* is even greater: they constitute an enormous mass of people who are either not at all or only partially integrated as productive labour into the so-called modern sector. This reservoir of potential labour amounts to hundreds of millions of workers. It is an oversimplification to say that it is the traditionally bad living conditions in underdeveloped countries which produced an ever-increasing flow of people seeking work and incomes from the countryside into the cities, the potential sites of the industry which can grant these things. Paradoxically the cause must be looked for in the modernisation of agriculture which can only attain its declared goal of increasing food production by the destruction of small subsistence farming, the traditional modest basis of survival for large sections of the rural population who are then forced to migrate to the cities where they are not usually able to obtain an income sufficient to provide them with a decent living.

The contemporary slums and similar poverty-stricken districts of the underdeveloped countries' cities are overcrowded with these landless rural immigrants. (By 1970 population statistics from at least ten cities in the so-called Third World showed that more than a million people in each of them were living in such areas.) Transformed into proletarianised wage workers they are forced to seek employment regardless of the level of remuneration and under the most inhuman conditions merely to ensure their sheer physical survival. They constitute a nearly inexhaustible source of the cheapest and most exploitable labour in the underdeveloped countries.

This vast industrial reserve army of extremely cheap labour feeds a process of industrialisation which can be observed in many contemporary developing countries. But this process of industrialisation rarely absorbs any significant proportion of the local labourforce. It is oriented to production for export, as the purchasing power of the mass of the local population is too low to constitute an effective demand on the local market for the products of the country's own industry. The markets supplied by the industrialisation of the developing countries are therefore predominantly overseas, primarily in the traditional industrial countries.

This process of export-oriented industrialisation in developing countries is not only highly dependent on foreign companies but also extremely fragmented. Only very rarely do developing countries end up with the establishment of reasonably complex industrial branches (e.g. textile and garment industry in some cases complemented by synthetic fibre production). And even in the very few developing countries where such centres of partial industrialisation have been established there are no signs that they are being supplemented by a wider industrial complex which would enable them to free themselves eventually from their dependency on the already industrialised countries for imports of capital- and other goods, and for the maintenance of their industrial installations.

However, in the overwhelming majority of developing countries not even the beginnings of this partial industrialisation process can be observed, that is, a process which would at least serve to develop a few individual branches of industry. Instead, industrial production is confined to a few highly specialised manufacturing processes: inputs are imported from outside the country, are worked on by the local labour-force in 'world market factories' (for example, sewing, soldering, assembling and testing) and are then exported in their processed form. In other words, these world market factories are industrial enclaves with no connection to the local economy except for their utilisation of extremely cheap labour and occasionally some local inputs (energy, water and services for example), and are isolated from the local economy in almost all other respects. The labour-force recruited for production in these industrial enclaves is equipped with the necessary training in a period that rarely lasts for more than a few weeks, is exploited for a time-span which is optimal for the companies, and is then replaced by a newly recruited and freshly trained labour-force. Under such conditions there is no such thing as a skilled labour-force, or, at best, the skills which the workers do acquire are very minimal. Likewise there is no observable transfer of technology, despite the euphoric claims made by firms which relocate their manufacturing processes in the developing countries. The technology which is employed in these world market factories is not only in most cases quite simple, but also dependent on the expertise of foreign specialists and managers. This technology is often quite useless for the development of any form of industrialisation which would serve the basic needs of the local population.

So far export-oriented industrialisation has failed to achieve any improvement in the social conditions of the mass of the populations of the developing countries, not even as far as their most fundamental needs such as food, clothing, health, habitation and education are concerned. Nor can any improvement be expected in the foreseeable future. Quite the opposite – the social tensions and struggles between the tiny privileged minority which benefits from export-oriented industrialisation, and the vast majority of the population which derives no benefits from it will intensify in the future. It is such predictable developments as these which have occasioned Business International to take account of war and revolution in many countries. The increasing militarisation of the so-called Third World is a clear indication that increasingly overt and repressive force is needed to prevent the violent eruption of social tensions. South Africa, Chile and Thailand are but three especially well-known examples of military repression – but there are very many others. The 'preventive counter-revolution', to use an expression coined by Herbert Marcuse, is well under way in most parts of the so-called Third World (and not only there).

After decades and centuries of the underdevelopment of the so-called developing countries the recent export-oriented industrialisation of these countries offers but faint hope that that living standards and conditions of the mass of their populations will undergo any substantial improvements in the foreseeable future. Moreover there is no reason to assume that the main goal of the policies pursued by the governments of many developing countries is, in fact, the improvement of the material conditions of the mass of their populations. But even in those developing countries whose governments appear to be actively pursuing this goal, little progress can be discerned, except in very rare instances. Again, are the politicians of these developing countries simply incapable, or are the economic and social structures of the developing countries – the stark contrast between élite and masses, and debilitating economic dependency – so rigid that the goal of improving the living standards of the masses of the populations is unattainable under present circumstances? We shall come back to this question also.

Even the most superficial description of the *world economy* in the 1970s cannot be confined to a consideration of the situation of the industrialised countries on one hand, and of the developing countries on the other, each looked at in artificial isolation. (The 'socialist' countries will be taken into account in our study only inasmuch as they are also integrated into the world market.) The world economy is not simply the sum total of national economies, each of which functions essentially according to its own laws of motion, with only marginal interconnections, such as those established by external trade. These national economies are, rather, organic elements of one all-embracing system, namely a world economy which is in fact a single world-wide capitalist system. As our cursory survey has already shown, the structural changes in individual national economies are interrelated within this single world economy and mutually determine one another.

The most striking manifestation of the world economy is international trade. Well over 15% of all commodities and services which are produced every year in Western industrialised and developing countries enter international trade, and this percentage has been steadily increasing for at least the last fifteen years. Recognition of this fact is a first step towards understanding the increase of world-wide economic interpenetration.

The industrialised countries handle 70% of international trade and the developing countries only 20%. Seventy per cent of exports from both developing and industrialised countries are destined for industrialised countries and only 20% for the developing countries. In other words, whereas the foreign trade of the industrialised countries is mostly with each other, the foreign trade of the developing countries is mostly with the industrialised countries, and not their fellow developing countries. Recognition of this fact is a first step towards understanding the economic dependency of the developing countries on the industrialised countries.

The developing countries' exports to the industrialised countries still consist overwhelmingly of raw materials, whereas the vast bulk of the exports of the industrialised countries to the developing countries are still manufactures. In recent years, however, there has been a marked, slow but steady increase in manufactures exported from developing countries as a proportion of total world exports of manufactured goods. Recognition of this fact is a first important step towards understanding a potential change in the structure not only of world trade, but also, and more importantly, of the world economy itself. This change is especially evident in the rapid expansion of textile and garment exports from the developing countries to the industrialised countries.

International trade and world-wide industrial production, however, provide only a very superficial picture of the increasing interpenetration of national economies. World trade is increasingly becoming a flow of commodities between the plants of the same company spread throughout the world, or at least a flow between companies and their partners in subcontracting agreements. (For instance company A in Federal Germany delivers semiprocessed products for further manufacturing to a subcontractor B abroad; the finished manufactures are subsequently re-imported into Federal Germany.) In this case, foreign trade is not just simply an exchange of commodities between two national economies, but more precisely, a concrete manifestation of the international division of labour, consciously planned and utilised by individual companies.

One, albeit incomplete, expression of this international division of labour, which has been organised by private companies in pursuit of their own profit maximisation, is foreign investment. Figures for Federal German investment show that in recent years investment abroad by Federal German companies has exceeded investment by foreign companies in Federal Germany. Taken together with the fact that investment policy in Federal Germany has concentrated on rationalisation schemes for a number of years, this would suggest that Federal Germany has now apparently become less 'interesting' as a site for the expansion of industrial production. (Figures on the development of industrial assets of Federal German companies, including the re-invested profits, both at home and abroad would, in all probability, if available, demonstrate this phenomenon even more clearly.)

However, perhaps the clearest expression of the structural changes in the world economy which can be observed in the mid-1970s is the relocation of production. One form of this relocation (among other equally important ones) is the closing down of certain types of manufacturing operations in undertakings in the industrial nations and the subsequent installation of these parts of the production process in the foreign subsidiaries of the same company. The Federal German textile and garment industries represent one of the best-known examples of such relocations. Trousers for the Federal German market are no longer produced for example in Mönchengladbach, but in the Tunisian subsidiary of the same Federal German company. The process of relocation is also gaining momentum in other branches of industry. Injection pumps which were formerly made for the Federal German market by a Federal

German company in Stuttgart, are now manufactured partly to the same end by the same company at a site in India. Television sets are produced on the same basis by another company in Taiwan; car radio equipment in Malaysia, car engines in Brazil, watches in Hong Kong, electronic components in Singapore and Malaysia all fall into the same category.

The Federal German worker rendered unemployed by the relocation of production has been replaced by a newly hired worker in a foreign subsidiary of 'his' or 'her' company.

1.2 Main tendencies in the contemporary world economy

The question which we began with was the following: What has happened in the world economy to have occasioned the forecasts published by the OECD and Business International? To answer this we started with an outline of the economic situation of both the industrialised and the developing countries and we were occasionally obliged to resort to the vague term 'the rest of the world'. We have tried, however, to correct some of the misleading implications of this initial procedure by subsequent reference to some of the mutual relations and dependencies between the economies of the industrialised countries and the developing countries, which make up one world economy. We have chosen this descriptive procedure by way of introduction in order not to have to use more information, where possible, than is already available to any newspaper reader who is interested in political and economic matters.

Our next step is to undertake a *systematic presentation of essentially the same observable facts* and to show how they can only be understood as an *expression of the development of a single world economy.* (In Chapter 2 we try to explain the development of the world economy over the last five centuries showing how this development can only be understood as a necessary expression of the development of a *capitalist* world system.)

The origins of the present-day world economy are to be found in the sixteenth century. Its genesis was inextricably connected with the simultaneous emergence of a regional division of labour which affected the whole world. Different forms of the organisation of labour were used in different regions of the world (or introduced from outside the region itself) for different types of production. The following represent some characteristic examples:

From the sixteenth century to the eighteenth century

(a) Independent crafts and domestic labour (the putting-out system) formed the basis in Western Europe of manufactures such as textiles and metals, ship-building and arms production. Wage labour was also already used in individual large-scale manufacturing enterprises.

(b) Forced or slave labour formed the basis of silver mining in Peru and Mexico, and also of sugar plantations established by European colonial masters in Brazil and the West Indies. Serf labour formed the basis of grain production in Eastern Europe; the 'second serfdom', a reversal in the trend towards the disintegration of landlord/serf relations, was utilised and even intensified owing to the demand for corn from Western Europe.

Eighteenth and nineteenth centuries

(a) Wage labour supplanted other forms of labour as the basis of the industrial revolution, which spread from England where cotton manufacturing, the steam engine and railways were developed.

(b) Slave labour became the basis of raw cotton production in the West Indies and in the Southern United States; India's indigenous cotton manufacturing which had initially been stimulated by world trade was destroyed; China and Japan were 'opened up' for world trade (the Opium Wars etc.).

First half of the twentieth century

(a) Wage labour formed the basis of manufacturing in Europe, USA and Japan.

(b) A peculiar form of wage labour (which will be discussed below) formed the basis of the extraction and production of raw materials in the enclaves of Latin America, Africa and Asia (coffee in Brazil, saltpetre and copper in Chile, gold and diamonds in South Africa). These were primarily for export onto the world market. A partial industrialisation process was established in a small number of developing countries through a policy of import-substitution.

The regions of Latin America, Africa and Asia have therefore been integrated for centuries into the developing world economy chiefly as producers of agricultural and mineral raw materials, sometimes as the suppliers of a labour-force (e.g. African slaves). This integration was enforced wherever it was feasible and necessary by the military, technological and economic superiority which the West European nations and rulers developed after the sixteenth century.

Some countries of the so-called Third World have, under certain very specific conditions, experienced a weak process of industrialisation based on a policy of import-substitution: for instance, parts of Latin America during the partial disintegration of the world economy between 1930 and 1945. During this period it was possible for a modest local industry to develop in some underdeveloped countries for the purpose of supplying a very restricted domestic market. This development was possible only behind a barrier of selective import restrictions and was facilitated by the preoccupation of the most powerful industrialised nations with their 'own' problems during this period, a preoccupation which prevented them from intervening in the so-called Third World. This modest profitable local industry, however, very quickly reached the limits of local effective demand, and since it was non-competitive on the world market, receded into stagnation almost everywhere after the Second World War, and even in some cases, such as Argentina, collapsed into agony.

Our earlier descriptive sketch of some typical aspects of the contemporary world economy has already indicated that the old or 'classical' international division of labour is now open for replacement. The decisive evidence for this hypothesis is the fact that developing countries have increasingly become sites for manufacturing – producing manufactured goods which are competitive on the world market. The three case studies presented in this book provide extensive documentation of this world market oriented production of manufactures which is now being established and developed on new industrial sites, especially those in the developing countries.

This world market oriented industrialisation which is emerging today in many developing countries is not the result of positive decisions made by individual governments or companies. Industry only locates itself at those sites where production will yield a certain profit, sites which have been determined by five centuries of development of the world economy. In the 'classical' international division of labour which developed over this period, industrial sites for manufacturing basically only existed in Western Europe, and later in the USA and Japan. Since it is evident that the developing countries are now providing sites for the profitable manufacture of industrial products destined for the world market to an ever-increasing extent, we quickly come up against the question: What changes are responsible for this development?

Three preconditions taken together seem to be decisive for this new development.

Firstly, a practically inexhaustible reservoir of disposable labour has come into existence in the developing countries over the last few centuries. This labour-force is extremely cheap; it can be mobilised for production for practically the whole of the year, and all hours of the day, on shift work, night work and Sunday work; in many cases it can reach levels of labour productivity comparable with those of similar processes in the developed countries after a short period of training; companies can afford to exhaust the labour-force by overwork as it can easily be replaced, and they can also select their employees very specifically according to age, sex, skill, discipline and other relevant factors as there is an oversupply of people who are forced to take any job which is available.

Secondly, the division and subdivision of the production process is now so advanced that most of these fragmented operations can be carried out with minimal levels of skill easily learnt within a very short time.

Thirdly, the development of techniques of transport and communication has created the possibility, in many cases, of the complete or partial production of goods at any site in the world – a possibility no longer ruled out by technical, organisational and cost factors.

The coincidence of these three preconditions (which are supplemented by other, less important ones) has brought into existence a world market for labour and a real world industrial reserve army of workers, together with a world market for production sites. Workers in the already industrialised countries are now placed on a world-wide labour market and forced to compete for their jobs with their fellow workers in the developing countries. Today, with the development of a world-wide market in production sites, the traditional industrialised and the developing countries have to compete against one another to attract industry to their sites.

In other words, for the first time in the history of the 500-year-old world economy, the profitable production of manufactures for the world market has finally become possible to a significant and increasing extent, not only in the industrialised countries, but also now in the developing countries. Furthermore, commodity production is being increasingly subdivided into fragments which can be assigned to whichever part of the world can provide the most profitable combination of capital and labour.

The term which we shall use to designate this qualitatively new development in the world economy is the *new international division of labour.*

Of those countries which were able to supply vast reserve armies of potential industrial workers and to offer these workers' labour-power at a low price, the first to attract the relocation of parts of the production process were countries with close geographical and commercial links to existing industrial centres. The first shifts of US industry were to Western Europe and to countries 'south of the border'; West European companies transferred production to other regions in Europe, such as Eire, Greece, Portugal and the south of Italy; Japanese industry moved into South Korea and Taiwan. At the same time, industrial firms recruited labour from countries with high rates of unemployment and drew it in to the traditional sites of industrial production. Hence the appearance of *Gastarbeiter* in Western Europe, and Mexican and Puerto Rican immigrant workers in the USA.

Since then, sites for relocated manufacturing are not only being supplied in the border areas of Western Europe, Central America, North Africa, and South East Asia, but increasingly in Eastern Europe, South America, Central Africa and South Asia. The transfer of production to places with cheap labour not only affects the more or less labour-intensive production processes but also processes which are heavily dependent on raw materials and energy, and those which are a source of environmental pollution, given that the new sites can also offer favourable conditions as far as other factors of production are concerned. It has even affected capital-intensive production processes, contrary to the unsubstantiated prejudices of a number of international economists. Not only are investments, production capacities and output expanded and developed at these new sites, but existing facilities at the traditional sites which have become obsolete in terms of profitability are closed down.

This means that any company, almost irrespective of its size, which wishes to survive is now forced to initiate a transnational reorganisation of production to adapt to these qualitatively new conditions.

By far the most important means by which companies have secured their continued survival in the past has been through 'investment in rationalisation' – the installation of more efficient machinery and a reduction in the size and skills of the labour-force. This device alone (along with other 'classical' devices) is no longer adequate. The development of the world economy has increasingly created conditions (forcing the development of the new international division of labour) in which the survival of more and more companies can only be assured through the relocation of production to new industrial sites, where labour-power is cheap to buy, abundant and well-disciplined; in short, through the transnational reorganisation of production.

1.3 Selected case studies

Until now we have tried to locate the tendency towards a new international division of labour as an aspect of the continued development of world economy, an economy which can only be understood as a single, integrated system. In Chapter 2 we shall try to explain this growing tendency as the necessary expression of the operation of the world capitalist system – the valorisation of capital. Though this theoretical insight into the nature of the development of the world economy must be our starting point, it is not in itself sufficient to deduce in specific terms the extent to which the tendency towards a new international division of labour has already become a reality. Actual empirical research is needed to answer this question.

Three case studies were selected out of a long list of possible studies: these were based both on considerations of the availability of the relevant information, and our own research capabilities. They were:

I The structural changes in the Federal German textile and garment industries which have been determined by economic developments occurring in the world economy.

II Production and employment of foreign labour abroad (outside the EEC) by Federal German manufacturing industry, excluding the textile and garment industry.

III New industrial sites for world market oriented production in developing countries: free production zones.

The first of these three case studies was an in-depth investigation of the most important structural changes in one branch of industrial production. The second analysed the world-wide redistribution of production sites for all manufacturing industry (with the exclusion of the textile and garment industries) of one important industrialised country. The third examined the establishment of new industries in underdeveloped countries with reference to specific examples. Each case study attempted to arrive at a complete coverage of the subject under investigation, and was not merely a study of either random or specifically selected samples.

The data collected in these case studies is systematically presented and interpreted to provide information about the structure of the world labour market and the world market in production sites, the redistribution of industrial sites and the conditions and consequences associated with these phenomena. Each of these case studies in fact represents only a small part of the global process. But taken together they provide adequate information to allow an empirical assessment and elucidation of the fundamental forms in which the new international division of labour is appearing, and the determining forces which are shaping it.

Detailed evidence is provided of the new industrial sites and the number of people at work in them, along with details of wage differentials and differences, and variations in other important working conditions. The study includes the world-wide reorganisation of production illustrated by an investigation into the industrial branches of one important industrialised country, and world market oriented manufacturing in the underdeveloped countries. The closing down of production at the traditional sites and the connected relocation of production and structural changes in world trade are also examined. We discuss the relationship between rationalisation and the decision to relocate production, both of which are instruments companies employ to guarantee their competitiveness. Two examples are taken here: the textile and garment industry, and the production of electronic components.

We also attempt to provide some answers to other questions which were not the main focus of our empirical research, which means that our answers in these areas are only partial or provisional in nature. This applies, for example, to the effects of new technologies on the transnational organisation of production, effects on the size and structure of total employment in individual countries, and changes in the distribution of skills among the work-force at different industrial sites. By 'skill structure' or 'distribution of skills' we refer to the occupational skills or technical qualifications available in an economy regardless of whether the bearers of these skills are in employment or not. We use the term 'pattern of employment' to indicate the types of jobs, defined in terms of their skill requirements, which are available to the holders of different types of skill, regardless of whether these jobs are occupied or exist as unfilled vacancies. These jobs and vacancies constitute the social demand for labour-power: workers' skills and qualifications the supply. Whether the worker is able to find a buyer on the labour market is a circumstance which is dependent on the structure of available employment on the one hand, and the previous pattern of training on the other.

We can only allude to, but not elaborate on, the social and political consequences of the findings in our study. These include changes in the international structure of the dependency of national economies on one another, and the reproduction of the world-wide industrial reserve army. For these, and other topics, further empirical research is needed.

The results of our empirical studies are presented in Parts I, II and III. Some of the results are presented in summary form immediately below. If read without being placed in the context of our later more extensive presentation they may lead to distorted interpretations. The figures mentioned in this summary should therefore only be taken as approximate indications of the extent to which the new international division of labour has already developed.

Case study I is a survey of 214 textile and 185 garment companies from Federal Germany. In 1974 these companies accounted for roughly 60% of turnover and employment in the Federal German textile industry and 40% in the Federal German garment industry. In each of these samples about a hundred companies had *subsidiaries* producing abroad by 1974/75. These figures do not include production abroad by a quite significant number of nominally independent foreign producers, in particular through subcontracting and export-processing cooperation agreements with Eastern European and East Asian firms. These figures should be compared with those of other studies which identified about thirty firms from each industry in 1966, and forty firms from each in 1970 producing either in wholly or partly owned subsidiaries abroad.

A breakdown of our findings by region shows that in 1974 foreign production in the subsidiaries of the companies covered by our case study was concentrated in the industrialised countries (chiefly, the EEC countries, Austria and Switzerland) on the one hand, with a share of 50–60%, and in certain of the developing countries on the other hand (the textile industry in Africa and the Mediterranean countries, and the garment industry in the Mediterranean countries and Asia). The concentration of production in these regions is confirmed statistically regardless of whether we look at the number of foreign subsidiaries or the number of employees.

The following figures are the numbers of employees in the foreign subsidiaries of the Federal German textile and garment industries. In the textile industry, the numbers of employed increased from 8000 in 1966 to 14200 in 1970 and finally to 29500 in 1974: these are minimum estimates. In the garment industry, the equivalent figures are 15000, 24800 and 31000. The sizes of the labour-force employed in foreign subsidiaries as a proportion of these industries' domestic employment in the Federal Republic of Germany are as follows: in the textile industry, 1.5% in 1966, 2.8% in 1970 and 7.5% in 1974/75; in the garment industry, 3.7% in 1966, 6.5% in 1970 and 10.0% in 1974/75. Foreign employment in Federal German subsidiaries in the 'low wage countries' as proportion of the total foreign labour employed by Federal German subsidiaries abroad in the textile and garment industries has increased from approximately 25% in 1966 to approximately 45% by 1974/75.

A breakdown of employment abroad by sex and age group reveals that the subsidiaries of Federal German garment companies in the 'low wage countries' employ an extremely high percentage of young female workers. Roughly 43% of the employed are younger than twenty, and more than 90% are female.

If one includes *subcontracting arrangements* with foreign firms, then the Federal German textile and garment industries are employing at least 69000 workers in subsidiaries and subcontracted firms abroad, and very probably significantly more; a figure of over 80000 employees for the Federal German textile and garment industry abroad is not an improbable estimate for 1974/75.

In short, the foreign employment of the Federal German textile and garment industries has more than doubled between 1966 and 1974/75, whereas domestic employment has decreased by roughly a quarter over the same period. An estimate for 1977 would show that for every hundred workers employed by the Federal German textile and garment industries in Federal Germany itself, there are more than ten foreign workers employed abroad.

In 1974/75, some 30000 employees in the foreign production facilities of the Federal German textile and garment industry were producing either exclusively or predominantly for the Federal German market. This is an indication of the extent to which companies have relocated production for the domestic market from production sites in Federal Germany to sites abroad.

The case study analyses in some detail the following indicators of the new international division of labour in the sphere of the textile and garment industries: the drastically increased negative balance of trade in textiles and clothing of Federal Germany; the structural unemployment in the traditional industrial centres which has been caused by this development in the world economy; the export-oriented industrialisation of the developing countries; the corresponding relocations of production as industry is moved from sites in the 'centre' to the 'periphery'; and the increasing subdivision of the production process into fragmented routines which can be distributed throughout the world. The growing significance of these factors over the last ten to fifteen years in the sphere of the textile and garment industries provides incontrovertible evidence of the fact that the economic pressure of the world-wide labour market and the world market for industrial sites is forcing companies to undertake a global reorganisation of their own production processes. Rationalisation schemes, both at home and abroad, and industrial relocation abroad (especially to 'low wage countries') go hand in hand.

What this process means for those it directly affects is, first and foremost, unemployment and the devaluation of skills for workers in the traditional industrial countries, and the subjection of the populations of the developing countries to inhuman working conditions, with no hope for improvement in the foreseeable future. Furthermore, the inevitable development of this process means that in the years to come working people will be threatened even more drastically than in the past with the degradation and rigid discipline which reduces them to the status of mere appendages of the machine.

Case study II surveys 602 Federal German manufacturing companies (excluding the textile and garment industries) which have had at least one subsidiary producing abroad (outside the EEC) between 1961 and 1976. The sum total of these subsidiaries (Federal German formal share-in-capital between 25% and 100%) of these companies producing outside the EEC is 1760. Of these companies, 339 have one subsidiary abroad, 528 companies have up to four subsidiaries abroad, and twelve companies have twenty or more. These subsidiaries are located in a total of seventy-seven countries, with Brazil, Spain, the USA and Austria each accounting for more than a hundred. Of the 602 companies in our survey, 335 have 709 subsidiaries in industrialised countries, and 444 have 1051 subsidiaries in developing countries.

It was possible to collect employment figures for 1178 of the 1760 subsidiaries surveyed; in 1975 these subsidiaries employed 560788 persons. If the EEC countries and the textile and garment industries are included, our estimate of the total employment abroad by Federal German manufacturing companies amounts to 1.5 million workers. That is, the number of workers directly employed by Federal German manufacturing companies in foreign countries amounts to 20% of the total domestic labour-force in Federal German manufacturing industry. This figure, which is based on quite conservative estimates, is considerably higher than any other estimate published to date.

Foreign production is fairly well distributed over the different branches of industry. The mechanical engineering branch has the highest number of companies involved in production abroad, the chemicals industry has the most subsidiaries, and the electrical engineering industry has the most employees abroad. The data collected shows that nearly all branches of Federal German industry participate to a significant degree in production abroad and industrial relocation.

Between 1961 and 1976 the number of foreign subsidiaries belonging to the companies surveyed in this case study increased fourfold, with much of this increase first starting at the end of the 1960s. The increase in the number of employees abroad has been even more striking since many existing foreign subsidiaries have expanded their production and employment during the period of time under investigation. Complete data is available for a subsample of the companies surveyed, and reveals that the number of employees employed abroad by these companies increased fivefold between 1961 and 1974.

The above figures represent only a fraction of all foreign production by Federal German industry. This is due not so much to lack of information on the companies producing abroad but more significantly to our operational definition of what constitutes Federal German production abroad, i.e. production where the Federal German share in the subsidiaries' capital was at least 25%, which therefore excludes instances of Federal German foreign production where the direct holding is low or non-existent. However, it is possible for Federal German industry to use foreign production facilities without any direct capital participation, as evidenced by such cooperative arrangements as international subcontracting, management, supply and licence agreements. Our case study does not provide statistical data on the extent of this type of foreign production, and it is difficult to estimate how widespread it is. In some parts of the world, at least, this type of foreign production is more important than that controlled through direct capital holdings (e.g. in Eastern Europe and India).

These complexities must be taken into account in estimating the amount of industrial relocation. The procedure must start not only with individual companies and take note of all changes in industrial sites for the totality of production organised by those companies, but must add to this processes of relocation at the level of whole branches of industry which are not organised by domestic companies alone; for example, if domestic production in a given company is cut back or shut down completely because the product is now obtained from non-Federal German companies producing abroad. An assessment of the tendencies towards the relocation of industry throughout the world, and hence of the structural changes in the world economy and its subeconomies, can only be obtained by a global estimate of the redistribution of industrial sites.

The results of case study II (the study of industry in one major industrial country) testify to the changed conditions for the worldwide valorisation of capital which are forcing industrial undertakings, regardless of size and industrial branch, to reorganise their production. In an increasing number of cases, this reorganisation involves the relocation of production abroad. To conclude: the new international division of labour is manifested in the changing world distribution of, in this case, Federal German production facilities. The high level of structural unemployment in Federal Germany is an inevitable result of the transfer of industrial employment elsewhere in the world.

Case study III is based on data embracing 103 countries in Asia, Africa and Latin America. Whereas in the mid-1960s manufacturing for the markets of the industrialised countries was virtually non-existent in the underdeveloped countries, ten years later, there were literally thousands of factories in production in the underdeveloped countries producing goods almost exclusively for the markets of the industrialised countries. Such factories existed in at least thirty-nine underdeveloped countries; fifteen of these countries were in Asia, eight in Africa and sixteen in Latin America. This spread of industrial production in the so-called Third World is tied up with the creation of a new type of industrial site – the free production zone – and with the creation of a new type of factory – the world market factory.

Free production zones are industrial areas which are separated off from the rest of the country, located at places where labour is cheap and designated as sites for world market oriented industry; world market factories are factories which are built on these sites, but can also be situated elsewhere, and intended for the industrial utilisation of the available labour and the processing of goods destined essentially for the markets of the industrialised countries. In 1975, seventy-nine free production zones were in operation in twenty-five underdeveloped countries; eleven of these countries were in Asia, five in Africa and nine in Latin America.

As far as the structure of production at these sites is concerned, nearly all branches of manufacturing industry are represented. On the other hand, as far as individual zones and countries are concerned, there is a tendency for the development of industrial mono-structures. In 1975 the bulk of production was accounted for by the products of the textiles and garment industry on one hand, and those of the electrical engineering industry on the other. Production in world market factories is highly vertically integrated into the transnational operations of the individual companies and involves non-complex production operations; as regards the processing of each product or product group, the production process is largely confined to part operations: the manufacturing of parts, assembling of parts, or final assembly. Only in the case of a few product groups, and in a few countries, can one identify anything resembling complex manufacture; textiles and garments are one example.

The employment structure in free production zones and world

market factories is extremely unbalanced. Given a virtually unlimited supply of unemployed labour, world market factories at the free production zones, or other sites, select one specific type of worker, chiefly women from the younger age groups. The criteria used for the selection of workers are quite unambiguous: the labour which is employed is that which demands the least remuneration, provides the maximum amount of energy (i.e. fresh labour which can be expected to work at a high intensity) and which is predominantly unskilled or semiskilled.

The case study attempts to provide an answer to the question as to whether the aims of development policy, which are allegedly linked with world market oriented industrialisation, are being attained. These are: reduction in unemployment, training of skilled personnel, access to modern technology, and increases in the foreign currency earned by the country concerned. The historical record up to now and the foreseeable future both indicate that the answer to this question is an unequivocal 'no'.

2 ❧ The new international division of labour: a phase in the development of the world capitalist system

2.1 Forms of the valorisation of capital

The economic, social and political history of the last five centuries has been shaped by the global development of the capitalist form of society, which has essentially been determined by the movement of capital, however much the struggle of the oppressed classes may have been directed at the conscious and revolutionary transformation of society (e.g. in the Russian, Chinese and Cuban revolutions). According to Marx's analysis of capital, which we shall use in this chapter, the valorisation (*Verwertung*) and accumulation of capital together constitute the basis of the movement of capital. The sole motive of the capitalist, inasmuch as he functions as the conscious representative of this movement, is the unlimited appropriation of abstract wealth in the form of money.

It would appear, therefore, that the analysis of capitalist development has to proceed from the process of the valorisation and accumulation of capital, and its determinants, i.e. its requirements, possibilities and obstacles, and not, for example, from the development of the wage labour/capital relation, or the development of the forces of production, or, for that matter, developments in belief, value or idea systems: Weber's *Geist des Kapitalismus*. In other words: the creation of a free labour-force and the unfolding of the productive forces are only particular means, albeit decisive ones under specific conditions, which exist alongside others for ensuring the valorisation and accumulation of capital. Capital only develops the wage labour/capital relation and the productive forces (a) if the restraints (often extra-economic ones) which impede the further development of wage labour and the productive forces can be overcome, and (b) if greater profits can be made in doing so.

For example, given the conditions for the valorisation and accumulation of capital which existed during the early history of capitalism (roughly up to 1700), it was necessary to invest money in trade, luxury production or even mass production (e.g. grain, cloth, sugar) *without* resort to free wage labour to any significant degree; on the contrary, capital predominantly utilised the labour-force of small commodity producers (often in the form of the putting-out system), serfs, and even slaves. A long period of so-called primitive accumulation was required (with its social and political revolutions) before the large-scale valorisation and accumulation of capital on the basis of free wage labour became both possible and necessary.

The determining force, the prime mover, behind capitalist development is therefore the valorisation and accumulation process of capital, and not, for example, any alleged tendency towards the extension and deepening of the wage labour/capital relation or of the 'unfolding' of the productive forces.[1]

Thus, in considering the law of motion which underlies capitalist development, it is imperative that any historical analysis is aware, first of all, of the different forms which the valorisation and accumulation of capital has assumed and can assume. These forms base themselves on different modes of production, preserving them, dissolving them, adapting and combining them according to the requirements, possibilities and obstacles which apply to the valorisation of capital under given, or self-generated, circumstances.

In order to secure the unlimited appropriation of abstract wealth and the valorisation and accumulation of capital, the capitalist social formation presupposes both conscious strategies and intrinsic mechanisms through which the economic, social and political conditions of pre- and non-capitalist social formations and of the developing capitalist formation itself can be transformed and developed, so as to allow not only for the appropriation of abstract wealth at this or that particular favourable moment, but concomitantly for the

1. It is difficult to 'prove' in any straightforward sense that valorisation and accumulation (extended reproduction) constitute the absolute law of capital. For this reason, the assertions above may appear dogmatic. They can, in a sense, only be justified by their capacity to provide a more coherent interpretation of the history of capitalist development than, say, interpretations based on assumptions about the correlation of capitalism and free wage labour, or the autonomous development of the productive forces. On further analysis, it should be possible to demonstrate how the pursuance of self-interest by individual actors or simply the sheer necessity for economic survival *under specific conditions* (above all, under conditions of a politically non-unified world economy as opposed to a politically unified world empire) necessitates the permanent search for surplus profits which results in a system of the extended reproduction of capital. See Immanuel Wallerstein, 'The rise and future demise of the world capitalist system: concepts for comparative analysis', *Comparative Studies in Society and History* 16, no. 4 (1974), pp. 387–415: cf. Ernesto Laclau, 'Feudalism and capitalism in Latin America', *New Left Review* 67 (May/June 1971), pp. 19–38.

continuous and systematic reproduction of the preconditions for further capital valorisation and accumulation. Presented rather schematically, and disregarding for a while any intermediary forms, two main forms can be distinguished.

(1) Non-wage labour-relations of subsumption to capital are established and preserved, mainly by extra-economic forces exercised by slave-holders, feudal landlords, the state etc., which enable the capitalist class to appropriate part or most of the surplus produce of the direct producers on a permanent basis.

(2) The direct producers are deprived of their means of production (= primitive accumulation/original expropriation) and are then forced, seemingly through 'the dull compulsion of economic relations' alone, to sell their labour-power permanently on the labour market to the owners of the means of production in order to obtain their means of subsistence (i.e. capital accumulation proper on the basis of the specifically capitalist relation of production/exploitation of the free wage labourer).

The forms of the valorisation and accumulation of capital which belong under case (1) can be found throughout the history of capitalism, and include the use of slave labour for production for profit, forced labour (serfdom, sharecropping, indentured labour) and subcontracting outside the capitalist mode of production proper. According to an established terminology, the underlying modes of production are called 'non-capitalist'. Historical investigation has, however, revealed the strategies, forces and mechanisms through which these original modes of production are, under appropriate conditions, modified so as to contribute to the valorisation and accumulation of capital. This not only embraces the rise of capitalism from within European feudalism but more generally the subsumption (incorporation) of non-capitalist social formations by capitalism once it is established. Detailed discussions on the subject of how the preconditions for the valorisation and accumulation are reproduced can be found in the literature.[1] These investigations are 'historical'

1. Apart from the historical literature in the strict sense of the term see too for example: Stephen Hymer, 'Robinson Crusoe and the secret of primitive accumulation', *Monthly Review* 23, no. 4 (1971), pp. 11–36; Samir Amin, *Le développement inégal. Essai sur les formations sociales du capitalisme périphérique* (Paris 1973); Perry Anderson, *Lineages of the Absolutist State* (London 1974); Andre Gunder Frank, *World Accumulation 1492–1789* (New York and London 1978); Immanuel Wallerstein, *The Modern World-System* (New York and London 1974).

when seen from the standpoint of an analysis of capital understood in a narrow sense, inasmuch as the analysis of capitalism merely presupposes the actual existence of the preconditions for the valorisation and accumulation of capital at the points of transition from feudalism to capitalism, or the incorporation of prior social forms. On the other hand, the analysis of the release of certain elements and processes which bring about the integration of former social formations into the capitalist formation – be this through an intrinsic process, as in the case of West European feudalism, or through external forces such as commerce or war, as in many 'Third World' countries, or by an interaction of the two, as was probably the case in Japan – is not part of the analysis of capital *sensu stricto.*[1] Of course, it is not necessary to suppose that the agents of the process consciously aimed, or aim, at the development of capitalism *per se.*[2] The only factor of importance here is the objective function of their actions for the valorisation and accumulation of capital, and not their subjective motives.

As far as case (2) is concerned, the starting point is constituted by

'But as soon as peoples whose production still moves within the lower forms of slave labour, the *corvée*, etc. are drawn into a world market dominated by the capitalist mode of production, whereby the sale of their products for export develops into their principal interest, the civilised horrors of over-work are grafted onto the barbaric horrors of slavery, serfdom etc. Hence the Negro labour in the southern states of the American Union preserved a moderately patriarchal character as long as production was chiefly directed to the satisfaction of immediate local requirements. But in proportion as the export of cotton became of vital interest to those states, the over-working of the Negro, and sometimes the consumption of his life in seven years of labour, became a factor in a calculated and calculating system. It was no longer a question of obtaining from him a certain quantity of useful products, but rather of the production of surplus value itself. The same is true of the *corvée*, in the Danubian principalities for instance.' Karl Marx, *Capital* I (Harmondsworth 1976), p. 345, cf. pp. 412, 424–5, 645.

1. See, for example, Maurice Dobb, *Studies in the Development of Capitalism* (London 1946), and the critical discussion which it gave rise to, to which contributed Paul Sweezy, Maurice Dobb, Kohachiro Takahashi, Rodney Hilton, Christopher Hill, Georges Lefebvre, Giuliano Procacci, Eric Hobsbawm, John Merrington, reprinted in: Rodney Hilton (ed.), *The Transition from Feudalism to Capitalism* (London 1976); Eric Hobsbawm, *The Crisis of the Seventeenth Century*, republished in Trevor Aston (ed.), *Crisis in Europe 1560–1660* (London 1969); Immanuel Wallerstein, 'From feudalism to capitalism: transition or transitions', *Social Forces* 55, no. 2 (1976), pp. 273–83.
2. The analysis of capital as an independent form of social production with its own specific features, and the propaganda for it, first began in quantity around the year 1800 (Quesnay, Turgot, Smith, Ricardo, Babbage, Ure, etc.), although there were a number of predecessors in the field, such as the unknown author of *Considerations on the East India Trade* (1701), reprinted in J. R. McCulloch (ed.), *Early English Tracts on Commerce* (London 1970), pp. 541–629. Of course, this does not apply to all those businessmen and politicians who had long before this period contributed towards the development of capitalist elements within the framework of the feudal social formation in an objective sense (Fugger, Colbert etc.), or to the intellectual assistants in this task, such as Peutinger, Defoe and Mandeville.

the transitional forms in which capital is valorised and accumulated, within which industrial capital first emerges from money as it existed in the form of merchants' capital, a form which itself parasitically exploited 'non-capitalist' modes of production. It is at this point that the sphere of production is first subjected to the unrestricted movement of capital. This process of primitive accumulation/original expropriation transforms land into an alienable commodity on a massive scale,[1] produces an internal market for the workers' means of subsistence and, most important of all, creates the preconditions for further valorisation and accumulation, seemingly through the 'dull compulsion of economic relations' alonc, i.e. creates a class of 'free' wage labourers.[2] The putting-out system represents one relevant example, and the enclosure movement in Britain another. Resistance, sheer force, class conflict, cultural degradation, social insecurity, and more often than not, impoverishment, were the constant accompaniments to the process of the creation and stabilisation of these preconditions.[3]

Once a class of 'free' wage labourers has been created, the further valorisation and accumulation of capital can be enhanced by means of the prolongation of the working day, so long as capital is not restricted by legal regulations which are a result both of the strength of workers' organisations and the capitalists' realisation of diminishing returns on the excessive prolongation of the working day. Of course, this possible source of profit is limited by the maximum number of exploitable working days available under the 'given'

1. Just as the development and growth of towns and merchant capital is inherent in the development of West European feudal society, so is the transformation of land into an alienable commodity. See Margaret Fay, 'The influence of Adam Smith on Marx's theory of alienation', part II, *Science and Society* (1978).
2. According to Eric Hobsbawm's interpretation of the origin of the 'Industrial Revolution' in Britain, the stable base for a generalised industrial economy was provided by the existence of a stable domestic market principally for mass consumption goods, and the igniting spark by exports, backed up by the systematic and agressive help of the government. Eric Hobsbawm, *Industry and Empire* (Harmondsworth 1969), especially chapter 2.
3. See, for example: Josef Kulischer, *Allgemeine Wirtschaftsgeschichte des Mittelalters und der Neuzeit*, vol. II (1928–29; new edition, Darmstadt 1971), pp. 113–37, on the putting-out system; Karl Marx, *Capital* I, chapter 26 (in part 8 entitled 'So-called primitive accumulation'); Paul Mantoux, *The Industrial Revolution in the Eighteenth Century* (revised edition, London 1964); Karl Polyani, *The Great Transformation. The Political and Economic Origins of our Time* (1944; Boston, Mass. 1957); Christopher Hill, *Reformation to Industrial Revolution* (Harmondsworth 1968); Edward P. Thompson, *The Making of the English Working Class* (Harmondsworth 1968); Stephen Hymer, 'Robinson Crusoe and the secret of primitive accumulation', *Monthly Review* 23, no. 4 (1971), pp. 11–36; William Lazonick, 'Karl Marx and enclosures in England', *The Review of Radical Political Economists* 6, no. 2 (1974), pp. 1–59.

conditions. By increasing the productivity of labour and consequently the 'rate of exploitation', the limits placed on the valorisation and accumulation of capital which had their origins in prior modes of production can be largely overcome. The two most important methods for raising the productivity of labour are the division of the labour process into elements which can be assigned to the most appropriate labour-power, and the introduction of new machinery.[1]

The epoch-making function of the specifically capitalist mode of production – provided that the conditions for the valorisation and accumulation of capital facilitate it or force it to develop – consists in the following:

(a) The unprecedented speed of the development of the productive forces, which include not only the means of production but also science and technology, transportation, communication and techniques of management.

(b) The unprecedented production of material wealth even in terms of goods for mass consumption, albeit with an extremely unequal distribution both within and between nations, a process which embraces the absolute, and not merely relative, impoverishment of roughly two-thirds of the population of the 'periphery'. This is essentially because capitalist production is production for *effective* demand and not for fulfilling human *needs*.

(c) Means are created which allow the relative proportions of the active and reserve army of workers to be varied within certain limits. The aim of this is to maximise profits by, for example, checking the rise in the 'historical' or 'moral' element in the wage,[2] even though the creation of additional wage labourers

1. Apart from Adam Smith's *Wealth of Nations*, see the chapter dealing with the production of relative and absolute surplus value in Karl Marx, *Capital* I, chapter 16. See too: Charles Babbage, *On the Economy of Machinery and Manufactures* (1835; New York 1971); Andrew Ure, *The Philosophy of Manufactures. Or an Exposition of the Scientific, Moral, and Commercial Economy of the Factory System of Great Britain* (1835; London 1967); Frederick Winslow Taylor, *Scientific Management* (1903, 1911, 1912; Westport 1976); Sidney Pollard, *The Genesis of Modern Management. A Study of the Industrial Revolution in Great Britain* (London 1965); Harry Braverman, *Labor and Monopoly Capital* (New York and London 1974).

2. It is easy to fall into the trap of overestimating the historical and moral element of the wage in contemporary capitalist society. It is likely that a high percentage of the mass consumption (wage) goods is necessary (cannot be substituted for) for the reproduction of labour-power under the present given conditions. See: Utz-Peter Reich, Philipp Sonntag & Hans-Werner Holub, *Arbeit-Konsum-Rechnung. Axiomatische Kritik und Erweiterung der Volkswirtschaftlichen Gesamtrechnung. Eine problem-orientierte Einführung mit einem Kompendium wichtiger Begriffe der Arbeit-Konsum-Rechnung* (Cologne 1977).

through the process of primitive accumulation and original expropriation may have reached insurmountable demographic and social limits.

(d) Capital secures 'the monopoly of knowledge to control each step of the labour process and its mode of execution'[1] and thereby enforces the cultural degradation of the employed, where the machine employs the worker, and not the worker the machine.

The third form in which capital is valorised and accumulated is a mechanism which links (1) and (2) together. By extracting subsidies (including labour) from the 'non-capitalist', 'traditional', 'informal' or 'backward' sectors, and by combining this with overworking the human labour-power at its disposal, sometimes temporarily beyond the limits of individual physical reproduction, capital can, within certain limits, 'transform the workers' necessary fund for consumption...into a fund for the accumulation of capital'.[2] Actual material production (as opposed to the production and reproduction of labour-power and its means of subsistence) is carried out within the framework of the specifically capitalist mode of production, whereas the labour-force itself and/or a part of its means of subsistence are drawn from the 'non-capitalist' sectors, which in addition often have to provide for the care of workers too 'old' for capitalist production, once the capitalist sector has bled them dry. Hence, viewed from the capitalist sector proper, the costs of the reproduction of the work-force are to a great extent externalised. The daily wage provides only for the immediate cost of reproduction from one working day to the next, without covering the costs of raising a new generation of workers or taking care of redundant 'old' or invalided members of the work-force. These 'traditional' sectors, however, are non-capitalist only in that their material reproduction, including the production of the labour-force and a part of its means of subsistence which are for the benefit of the capitalist sector proper, is not carried out within the specifically capitalist mode of production, or is based on a low capital intensity (relative to the level of world-wide capitalist development) combined with a high physical exploitation of its work-force (long working day, high intensity of labour, child labour and generalised poverty). It is due to these circumstances that these 'traditional' sectors manage to sustain their precarious existence. And it is by virtue of their subsidising function mentioned

1. Harry Braverman, *Labor and Monopoly Capital* (New York and London 1974), p. 119.
2. Karl Marx, *Capital* I, p. 748.

above that these 'traditional' sectors are integrated into the world-wide process of the valorisation and accumulation of capital and sometimes consciously preserved for its benefit.[1] Nonetheless, despite these policies, the anarchy which characterises the valorisation and accumulation of capital is still tending to destroy these 'traditional' sectors (compare the effects of the different forms of agribusiness).

2.2 Capitalist development

Within all these possible forms of capital valorisation and accumulation, the individual capital, driven by the pursuit of abstract wealth (the constant search for surplus profits), organises the production of social wealth (the 'wealth of nations') by withholding the surplus product from the direct producers to as great an extent as possible and, provided that realisation is successfully accomplished, recapitalising it for the most part. All those forms of the redistribution of abstract wealth which has already been produced, somewhere and somehow, have to be clearly distinguished from the production of abstract wealth. Such forms of redistribution include enrichment by fraud, robbery, commercial overpricing, speculation and usury, all the redistributive measures carried out by the state, premia paid in order to guarantee the conditions for further exploitation, and all forms of monopoly rent (which accrue to capital through the holding of patents, through natural monopolies, and monopolies created through the sheer size of the capital).

World history over the last five centuries, inasmuch as it is the produce of human effort and actions, is hence the result of:

(1) the historical specificity of different social formations,
(2) the inherent logic of the valorisation and accumulation of capital, with its tendency towards the totalisation of its environment, and
(3) attempts at the conscious transformation of society.

1. See e.g. Giovanni Arrighi, 'Labour supplies in historical perspective: a study of the proletarianisation of the African peasantry in Rhodesia' in Giovanni Arrighi & John S. Saul, *Essays on the Political Economy of Africa* (1969; New York and London 1973), pp. 180–234; Harold Wolpe, 'Capitalism and cheap labour power in South Africa: from segregation to apartheid', *Economy and Society* 1, no. 4 (1972), pp. 425–56; Ruy Mauro Marini, *Dialéctica de la dependencia* (Mexico 1973); Claude Meillassoux, *Femmes, greniers et capitaux* (Paris 1975).
Domestic work and child care by women clearly represents another very important example of this type. It is, however, widely distributed also in pre- or non-capitalist social formations and cannot therefore be understood by an analysis of capital alone.

In order to be able to analyse the current state of the capitalist social formation it is also necessary to take into consideration those limitations which are externally imposed by nature, i.e. the limitation and uneven distribution of natural resources which permits oligopolistic 'abuse', and the natural limits imposed on the unrestricted development of the social forces of production which have their basis in physical and physiological factors. It is precisely because capitalism develops through the logic of competitive accumulation that it is structurally incapable of taking consistent account of such limitations.

A history of capitalist development would therefore have to analyse in detail the combination of the forms in which the valorisation and accumulation of capital is unfolding, and why, where and when this is taking place. In other words: the task not only involves a detailed description of when and where particular modes of the valorisation and accumulation of capital have flourished, but also, simultaneously, an explanation as to why this pattern and its evolution (with proper consideration of the prevailing restrictions, self-generated conditions and the class struggle) were both feasible and most profitable for individual capitals, and therefore – in accordance with our basic approach – necessary.

Of course, it is not possible to accomplish this here.[1] Rather, we merely refer to those factors which are central to the development of the capitalist social formation:

(1) The splitting up of the capitalist social formation into 'centre' and 'periphery', and also possibly 'semi-periphery', both intra- and internationally, that is, the development of an international division of labour with different forms of control over labour for different types of production in different regions of the capitalist world economy.
(2) The short-, medium-, and long-term cycles apparently inherent in the valorisation and accumulation of capital, and the associated role of crises of realisation and overaccumulation, including crises due to major technological, organisational and institutional innovations.
(3) The development of class structures, in particular the specific

1. In addition to our remarks in Chapter 1, see too the works already cited of Samir Amin (*Le développement inégal*), Perry Anderson (*Lineages of the Absolutist State*), Maurice Dobb (*Studies in the Development of Capitalism*), Andre Gunder Frank (*World Accumulation 1492–1789*), Eric Hobsbawm (*The Crisis of the Seventeenth Century*), and Immanuel Wallerstein (*The Modern World-System*).

role of wage labour in the capitalist sector proper as opposed to the labour-force drawn from the subsidising 'traditional sectors', in the economic and political stabilisation of the valorisation and accumulation of capital.

(4) The role of different types of state-forms in the creation and maintenance of the preconditions for the valorisation and accumulation of capital, culminating in the bourgeois liberal state at one extreme and the colonial administration on the other, or the social democratic interventionist state on one hand, and the authoritarian repressive state on the other, depending on the respective functions which different territories at a given stage of world capitalist development were obliged to or could fulfil within the global division of labour established by the valorisation and accumulation of capital, and also depending on the balance of power in the class struggle.

Capitalist development is therefore the unfolding of those combinations of the forms of the valorisation and accumulation of capital which, under 'given' conditions (naturally world-wide), yield the maximum profit for the respective individual capitals. This means, *inter alia* but most importantly, that the valorisation and accumulation of capital is transnational from the very outset. This is not contradicted by the fact that capital is still in the process of literally encompassing the globe, including both the real and demographic 'virgin territories'. What might appear as the national reproduction of capital turns out on closer inspection to be reproduction under conditions which make the valorisation and accumulation of capital the most profitable at one particular place and one particular time.

2.3 Present-day conditions for the valorisation of capital

There are a large number of easily observable phenomena in the capitalist world economy which strongly suggest that the present conditions for the valorisation and accumulation of capital have passed through fundamental qualitative changes. These phenomena include the far-reaching industrial relocation of manufacturing from the 'centre' towards and even within the 'periphery'; stagnating or declining investment rates and rising structural unemployment in industrial branches of the 'centre'; and increasing export-oriented manufacturing in the 'periphery' (see Chapter 1).

The following represents a set of conditions which we regard as crucial in the present-day valorisation and accumulation of capital (which is expressed in the phenomena mentioned above). We assume here that a history of capitalist development which employed the conceptual framework indicated would be able to explain these conditions as the result of previous capitalist development.

(a) *The development of a world-wide reservoir of potential labour-power.* This reservoir is practically inexhaustible in that capital can call on several hundred million potential workers, mainly in Asia, Africa, and Latin America, and even, in one particular sense, in the 'socialist' countries. Most of this labour-force consists of the latent overpopulation in rural areas which, through the employment of capital in agriculture ('Green Revolution' etc.), provides a constant flow of people into the urban areas and slums in the search for jobs and an income where they constitute a nearly inexhaustible supply of labour. Another section consists of workers who are integrated into the production process of capital by means of contract-processing in the 'socialist' countries on behalf of capitalist firms. Brought about by the development of transport and communications technology and the increasing subdivision of the labour process (see below) a world-wide industrial reserve army has come into existence, because – and inasmuch as – all these potential workers now can compete 'successfully' on the world labour market with workers from the traditional industrial countries. More specifically, this world-wide reserve army displays the following characteristics which indicate its potential use in the valorisation and accumulation process of capital.

(1) The wages which capital actually has to pay in the 'low wage countries' are approximately 10% to 20% of those in the traditional industrialised capitalist countries, taking into account social overhead costs. Due mainly to the subsidising mechanisms mentioned above, these wages have only to, and do only, cover (if at all) the cost of the immediate daily reproduction of the worker during the actual period of employment (which as a rule is very short).

(2) The working day (week or year) is, as a rule, considerably longer in 'low wage countries' than in the industrialised capitalist countries. Shift, night and Sunday work are, in comparison, much more widespread, which facilitates the 'optimal' utilisation of fixed capital through extended running times.

(3) Productivity in 'low wage countries' generally corresponds with that of the traditional capitalist industrial countries for comparable processes.
(4) The labour-force can be hired and fired virtually at the discretion of the company. This means, *inter alia*, that a higher intensity of labour can be enforced through the more rapid exhaustion of the labour-force: an exhausted labour-force can be replaced by a fresh one virtually as the company sees fit.
(5) The huge size of the available reserve army allows for an 'optimal' selection of the most suitable labour-force (for example, young women) for the specific purpose required.

So far the trade unions have more or less succeeded in preventing the large-scale penetration of these adverse conditions into the 'centre'. However, the competition on the world labour market, and the large amount of structural unemployment in the traditional industrialised capitalist countries which results from it, are increasingly undermining this not inconsiderable achievement (relative of course to the criteria for success which apply within the capitalist system).

(b) *The development and refinement of technology and job organisation makes it possible to decompose complex production processes into elementary units such that even unskilled labour can be easily trained in quite a short period of time to carry out these rudimentary operations.* In this way skilled labour receiving higher wages can be replaced by un- or semiskilled labour receiving lower wages (inasmuch as they are paid by capital). If it is impossible, for economic reasons, to use machinery in place of fragmented operations, then the access to, and use of, a very cheap, un- or semiskilled work-force provides the opportunity for an improved valorisation of capital (Babbage's principle). The fragmentation of jobs has progressed so far, especially in manufacturing, that the execution of the respective fragmented operations of even very sophisticated overall processes now often requires a training period of no more than a few weeks even for unskilled labour. In this way capital acquires a monopoly of the knowledge related to the control and execution of the labour process: this knowledge is removed from the work-force, which reduces the worker to a mere servant of the production process, which is managed exclusively by capital. The disciplining effect of the cultural degradation of the worker has been stressed by Ure and Taylor, who developed and glorified these weapons of capital against the 'moodiness' of the skilled worker. Bourgeois institutions like the traditional school system contribute to the successful implementation of discipline by instilling such capitalist virtues as subservience, obedience and punctuality.[1]

(c) *The development of a technology which renders industrial location and the management of production itself largely independent of geographical distance.* This technology includes modern transport technology, which allows the rapid and relatively cheap transport of products between sites of intermediate or final production and consumption, of both large bulk cargoes and fragile items by specialised ocean carriers; containerisation and air-freight; efficient telecommunications systems, data-processing technology and other organisational methods.

We do not attempt here to present a complete list of all the major conditions which are at present the determining forces of the valorisation and accumulation of capital. A list which tried to be fully comprehensive would have to include, just by way of example, the development of technologies for the exploitation of previously inaccessible natural resources (either for technical or economic reasons), such as the utilisation of low-grade ores, ocean-floor mining etc.[2] We focus our investigation on the analysis of the consequences of the above list in order to reveal the effects of this qualitatively new set of conditions for the valorisation and accumulation of capital.

These basic developments have given further impetus to the development of an international capital market, the function of which is the global mobilisation of capital and, more generally, the creation of an international capitalist superstructure. The role of this superstructure is to carry out, at a transnational level, functions which are indispensable for the reproduction of capital which the individual capital either cannot afford to perform, or which are better carried out by national or international public bodies in order not to introduce disequilibria into the area of competition. However much

1. The particular principles for the valorisation of capital associated with Babbage and Ure are elaborated in an appendix to this chapter.
2. Cf. Dorothea Mezger, *Konflikt und Allianz in der internationalen Rohstoffwirtschaft: das Beispiel Kupfer* (Bonn, Bremen 1977). Forthcoming English edition, Heinemann Educational, 1979.

the transnational valorisation and accumulation of capital may take advantage of national disparities (in infrastructure, corporate taxation, wage levels, labour legislation etc.), the expansion and deepening of transnational reproduction nonetheless requires certain elements of an international superstructure. These elements include, for example, the rudiments of institutionalised multilateral or bilateral cooperation in monetary and trade policies (IMF, GATT); tax agreements to avoid double taxation; treaties for investment protection; increasing the compatibility of training and education; international military cooperation; 'neutral' international organisations which pave the way for transnational capital under the guise of supplying technical and managerial expertise for 'development' (World Bank, UNIDO, FAO).[1]

Appendix: Babbage and Ure on the advantages accruing to capital from the division of labour

The division of labour, of which Adam Smith was the first great scientific advocate, has a number of decisive advantages for the capitalist. Firstly, the worker's annexation to a single operation increases the productivity of labour. Frequently these fragmented operations can be allotted to a machine, which likewise results in increased productivity. Secondly, the division of labour makes it possible for the capitalist to monopolise control over the labour-process which had formerly been a monopoly of craftsmen, and was jealously guarded by them. A third 'most important and influential cause of the advantage resulting from the division of labour' was revealed by Charles Babbage, the same Charles Babbage who also clearly saw the possibility of the division of labour in the realm of mental work, and who was the first to conceive and design a programmable calculating machine, his 'calculating engine'.[2]

1. See Erich H. Jacoby, *The Problem of Transnational Corporations within the United Nations System* (mimeo, 1976).
2. Charles Babbage, *On the Economy of Machinery and Manufactures* (1835; New York 1971), pp. 191–202. Drawing on a concrete historical example, the computation of mathematical tables, Babbage demonstrates the division of labour (= separation between conception and execution) between a few (five or six) 'eminent mathematicians', several (seven or eight) 'persons of considerable acquaintance with mathematics', and many (sixty to eighty) persons who mostly had 'no knowledge of arithmetic beyond the first two rules' (simple addition and subtraction). The members of the third section had to perform the most mechanical work, 'requiring the least knowledge and by far the greatest exertions...Such labour can always be purchased at an easy rate.' 'These persons were usually found more correct in their calculations, than those who possessed a more extensive knowledge of the

Now, although all these are important causes, and each has its influence on the result; yet it appears to me, that any explanation of the cheapness of the manufactured articles, as consequent upon the division of labour, would be incomplete if the following principle were omitted to be stated.

That the master manufacturer, by dividing the work to be executed into different processes, each requiring different degrees of skill or of force can purchase exactly that precise quantity of both which is necessary for each process; whereas, if the whole work were executed by one workman, that person must possess sufficient skill to perform the most difficult, and sufficient strength to execute the most laborious, of the operations into which the art is divided.[1]

Babbage uses the example of English pin manufacture to explain his point. He lists the elements of the production process of pins, adding the respective type of work required (by age, sex and daily wage rate):[2]

Drawing wire	Man	3s 3d
Straightening wire	Woman	1s 0d
	Girl	0s 6d
Pointing	Man	5s 3d
Twisting and cutting heads	Boy	0s 4½d
	Man	5s 4½d
Heading	Woman	1s 3d
Tinning or whitening	Man	6s 0d
	Woman	3s 0d
Papering	Woman	1s 6d

If the minimum wage of a skilled man, who could carry out all these elementary operations, were the same as the highest wage rate on the list, and if only skilled workers were employed in this process, the total wage bill would nearly quadruple for the manufacture of a given quantity of pins, even using the same division of labour and assuming that the craftsman works at the same speed as the specialised workers.

Harry Braverman, who has analysed the connection between the labour process and the valorisation process and the resulting degradation of work, drawing on Babbage, Ure, Taylor and Marx (who in *this* instance made extensive use of Babbage and Ure), concluded the following:

Babbage's principle is fundamental to the evolution of the division of labor in capitalist society. It gives expression not to a technical aspect of the division of labor, but to its social aspect. Insofar as the labor process may be dissociated, it may be separated into elements some of which are simpler than others and each of which

subject.' Babbage foresaw that these mechanical tasks could one day be performed by machines.

1. Babbage, pp. 175 f.

2. Babbage, pp. 176–86.

is simpler than the whole. Translated into market terms, this means that the labor power capable of performing the process may be purchased more cheaply as dissociated elements than as a capacity integrated in a single worker.[1]

The subdivision of the production process into elements is, therefore, a means to cheapen the manufacturing cost of commodities, as the capitalist can buy that kind of labour-power which does not need more than the minimum skill for each respective element, and which can therefore 'always be purchased at an easy rate'. In other words, it is a means of getting rid of the 'excessive' demands and 'refractory tempers' of skilled workers. The pressure of competition turns this possibility into a necessity.

There is no simple answer to the question as to why the labour-power of an unskilled worker is, as a rule, much cheaper for the capitalist than that of a skilled worker. It is not adequate to point to the more extensive and longer training of a skilled worker (which involves higher costs) in order to draw the conclusion that this is why skilled workers have to be paid a higher wage, as these costs are often frequently borne to a great extent by society, leaving no reason why the skilled worker, as an individual, should be compensated for these expenses. In addition, the somewhat higher occupational skill transmitted by the bourgeois educational system usually bears no relation to the disproportionally higher wages received by skilled workers. This is especially true if the counterweight of trade unions – who tend to push in the direction of equality – is absent. The crucial reason has been quite unmistakeably spelled out by Babbage and Ure: provided there are no effective workers' organisations, workers are forced to compete against each other on the overcrowded labour market for unskilled and semiskilled labour. This competition keeps the level of wages down. This is precisely the most powerful force behind the constant attempts by capitalists to fragment complex labour processes into a large number of uncomplex operations.

Babbage's principle of the valorisation of capital has been analysed earlier by Marx, and more recently by Braverman, as constituting the general law of the capitalist division of labour. They have focussed on its economic and social consequences in *individual* developed capitalist countries. However, now that an enormous world-wide industrial reserve army has come into existence, Babbage's principle has acquired a new relevance and actuality. The

1. Harry Braverman, *Labor and Monopoly Capital* (New York and London 1974), p. 81.

subdivision of the production process into elementary operations allows the utilisation of unskilled or semiskilled labour. Un- or semiskilled labour, however, can be bought at extremely low rates in many 'low wage countries', the vast industrial reserve army of which is either not, or only weakly organised, by effective trade unions. (In view of the enormous size of the available labour supply, capital can even select the most suitable labour-force – possibly even a relatively skilled labour-force – without being compelled to pay significantly higher wages.) If, therefore, the extra cost (higher outlays for transportation, customs' duties, more administrative effort, cost of closing down existing plant, even the capital costs of the higher risk of transfer to a 'politically unstable' region etc.) is more than compensated for by the gains accruing from the use of cheap labour, those parts of the production process will have to be shifted to those locations which offer cheap and abundant un- or semiskilled labour, i.e. the production process has to be reorganised on a *world scale*.

Babbage's principle, as we have expressed it here in an explicit world-wide context, cannot be restricted to the mere search for the cheapest production site for each elementary operation with the overall aim of reducing the cost of the complete commodity under consideration, once a particular division of labour has been attained. On the contrary, Babbage's principle has to be understood as prescribing a comparison of *all the possible* subdivisions (and if necessary the development of the required technology) which can minimise the cost of production. This is the only correct formulation of Babbage's principle in a world context. One parameter in this world-wide optimising strategy is represented by the technology utilised for each of the elementary operations. Now, given that the production process is a capitalist one, improved machinery is usually only introduced if the cost of the machinery is at least made up for by the reduction in the wage bill of the workers who are either made redundant or deskilled by the introduction of the new machinery. The existence of an abundant supply of cheap labour in the 'low wage countries' may well mean that a world-wide calculation would lead to the conclusion that the substitution of labour by new machinery is, given all the relevant factors, simply not profitable whereas a similar calculation on a *national* scale might produce exactly the opposite result. (Of course under present conditions of the valorisation and accumulation of capital such a calculation on a national basis is purely hypothetical!) As is well known, people were already quite aware during the early years of the English Industrial Revolution that too cheap a labour-force may prevent the introduction of improved machinery. The selection of a specific technology, however, is only one parameter in this world-wide optimising strategy; other important parameters include factors which vary from country to country, such as taxes, subsidies, customs, transport costs, availability of the required labour-force in terms of skill and discipline, ease of hiring and firing, 'political stability', and also the likely duration and extent of the demand for the product.

Given the new conditions of the valorisation and accumulation of capital, the sites for manufacturing industry (and not merely as formerly for mining and plantations) now have to be decided upon, from the outset, on a global basis. It is hardly surprising, therefore, if business is currently stressing the necessity of a 'renewed reliance on true entrepreneurship'. In the view of one German industrialist, 'the development of the world economy is based not only on new and diverging technologies, but also on a new science, a new logic, a new set of ideas . . . This leads back to the first phase of development [clearly capitalist development], in which innovative entrepreneurship was the foundation of industrial survival.'[1] The analogy here with Schumpeter's entrepreneur is unmistakeable.

Babbage's principle – a fundamental expression of the capitalist laws of motion – calls for the maximum replacement of skilled labour in order to attain a reduction in labour costs. It is implemented through the *world-wide* organised allocation of the elements of the production process to the cheapest or most adapted labour force which can be found.

Andrew Ure, and later Frederick Taylor, stressed in particular the second decisive advantage of the division of labour for capital, namely: control over the labour process.[2] Ure, the 'Pindar of the automatic factory' as Marx called him, differentiated between the mechanical and the moral machinery of the factory. As far as

1. Gerrit van Delden Jr in *Frankfurter Allgemeine Zeitung/Blick durch die Wirtschaft*, 3 July 1975 ('Die Textilindustrie von morgen – Zukunftsvisionen eines Unternehmens'). In future references, *Frankfurter Allgemeine Zeitung* will be abbreviated to *FAZ*. *Blick durch die Wirtschaft* is the business supplement to the *FAZ*.
2. Andrew Ure, *The Philosophy of Manufactures. Or an Exposition of the Scientific, Moral, and Commercial Economy of the Factory System of Great Britain* (1835; London 1967); Frederick Winslow Taylor, *Scientific Management* (1903, 1911, 1912; Westport 1976). Babbage's principle can be found in substance in Ure and Taylor but not expressed with same exemplary clarity with which Babbage expressed it.

the mechanical machinery is concerned, the decisive step forward had already been taken by Richard Arkwright's 'noble achievement'. According to Ure the main difficulty had consisted

in training human beings to renounce their desultory habits of work, and to identify themselves with the unvarying regularity of the complex automaton. To devise and administer a successful code of factory discipline, suited to the necessities of factory diligence, was the Herculean enterprise, the noble achievement of Arkwright. Even at the present day, when the system is perfectly organised, and its labour lightened to the utmost, it is found nearly impossible to convert persons past the age of puberty, whether drawn from rural or from handicraft occupations, into useful factory hands.[1]

Arkwright was the designer of a number of types of spinning machines: his 'noble achievement' had enabled the factory masters to substitute the unskilled and semiskilled labour of primarily women for the craft skills and physical strength of artisans, thus taming the 'rebellious' craftsmen.

According to Ure, however, this does not mean that the task is complete. It is not sufficient to transform the workers into degraded appendages of machinery. In order to become really useful limbs of the machine system, the workers have to voluntarily accept their subjection, and internalise its dictates. In other words, the moral machinery of the factory must also be put in proper order.

Manufactures naturally condense a vast population within a narrow circuit; they afford every facility of secret cabal and cooperative union among the work-people; they communicate intelligence and energy to the vulgar mind... Persons not trained up in moral and religious nurture, necessarily become, from the evil bent of human nature, the slaves of prejudice and vice; they can see objects only on one side, that which a sinister selfishness presents to their view; they are readily moved to outrage by crafty demagogues, and they are apt to regard their best benefactor, the enterprising and frugal capitalist who employs them, with a jealous and hostile eye.[2]

For Ure the conclusion to be drawn from this is quite evident.

It is, therefore, excessively the interest of every mill-owner to organise his moral machinery on equally sound principles with his mechanical, for otherwise he will never command the steady hands, watchful eyes, and prompt cooperation, essential to excellence of product.[3]

And how can the moral machinery of the factory be improved? By suitable schools:

In such seminaries they are sure that the children learn to be obedient and orderly, and to restrain their passions... One hundred and fifty children, from three to nine years of age, have had for many years the benefits of education, with the happiest

1. Ure, p. 15. 2. Ure, p. 407. 3. Ure, p. 417.

consequences. The mule-spinners, even the most rude and uneducated, and who do not make very nice distinctions, always prefer children who have been educated at an infant school, as they are most obedient and docile... It is a most unequivocal proof of their [the school's] usefulness, equally pleasing to the parents and the patrons.[1]

The factory workers' life may not be the most pleasant, notwithstanding the advantages praised by Ure, but:

The first and great lesson – one inculcated equally by philosophy and religion – is that man must expect his chief happiness, not in the present, but in a future state of existence.[2]

For Ure then, an adequate mechanical and moral machinery (machines and division of labour, schools) would finally bring about what an anonymous English author had promised would follow the full development of capitalism, in a text written in 1701.

The *East-India* Trade is no unlikely way to introduce more Artists, more Order and Regularity into our *English* Manufactures, it must put an end to such of them as are most useless and unprofitable; the People imploy'd in these will betake themselves to others, to others the most plain and easie, or to the single Parts of other Manufactures of most variety; for plain and easie work is soonest learn'd, and Men are more perfect and expeditious in it; And thus the *East-India* Trade may be the cause of applying proper Parts of Works of great variety to single and proper Artists, of not leaving too much to be perform'd by the skill of single Persons; and this is what is meant by introducing greater Order and Regularity into our *English* Manufactures.[3]

Cheapening labour-power and control over the work-force: this is, according to Babbage and Ure, the principle of the division of labour in the capitalist process of production and valorisation, and the function of the education of children (the future workers) in schools which properly perform the task of the reproduction of a suitable and adapted labour-force.[4]

1. Ure, p. 423. 2. Ure, p. 423.

3. *Considerations on the East India trade* (1701) in J. R. McCulloch (ed.), *Early English Tracts on Commerce* (London 1970), pp. 590 ff. The author of this remarkable tract is arguing here in favour of free world trade. As our quotation shows, the unknown author was fully conscious of the international division of labour's effects on the skill structure of the work-force.

4. In addition to Harry Braverman, *Labor and Monopoly Capital* (New York and London 1974), see too: Samuel Bowles & Herbert Gintis, *Schooling in Capitalist America. Educational Reform and the Contradictions of Economic Life* (New York 1976); William Lazonick, 'The appropriation and reproduction of labour', *Socialist Revolution* 33, vol. VII, no. 3 (1977), pp. 109–27; Edward P. Thompson, 'Time, work-discipline and industrial capitalism', *Past and Present* 38 (1967), pp. 56–97: Michel Foucault, *Surveiller et punir. Naissance de la Prison* (Paris 1975).

In the case studies in this book we have not systematically investigated in which ways the educational and professional training systems of contemporary developing countries

Working people are not only degraded to the position of mere appendages of machinery, but are even pressed to give this degradation their free assent.

2.4 The tendency towards a new international division of labour

It was predominantly capital itself which *produced* the above-mentioned set of conditions for its valorisation and accumulation in the course of its centuries-long historical movement; the chief of these conditions are the existence of a world-wide industrial reserve army, the possibility of far-reaching subdivision of the production process into fragments, and an efficient transport and communications technology. Single *elements* of this set have been gradually developing for a long time, but as long as the *full* set was not effectively developed, the reproduction of capital on a world scale merely generated the 'classical' international division of labour: a few industrial countries producing capital-goods and consumer goods on one hand, confronting the vast majority of underdeveloped countries which were integrated into the world economy as producers of raw materials. That is, given the 'classical' conditions of a couple of hundred years, capital, spreading out from Europe and later from North America and Japan, was only able to valorise itself in Asia, Africa and Latin America through the production of mineral and agricultural raw materials, but not to any significant degree through the production of manufactured goods, despite the fact that capital was operating on a world scale from its origins.

Our main thesis is that this new set of conditions for the valorisation and accumulation of capital first began to be really operative in the 1960s. It has generated a world market for production sites and for labour which embraces both the traditional industrialised and the underdeveloped countries. Individual capital which *encounters* this set of conditions is able to secure surplus profits by correspondingly reorganising its production, i.e. by utilising the *world-wide* industrial reserve army by means of the appropriate subdivision of the production process and by employing advanced transport and communications technology. The overriding pressure of competition turns this possibility into a necessity for the survival of any individual capital. This means, in many cases, that for the first

creates such favourable preconditions for the moral machinery of factories; chance observations strongly confirm influences to this effect however.

time in the history of capitalism industrial sites in developing countries are now profitable for partial or even complete manufacture in manufacturing industry, and can produce competitively for the world market. As a consequence, these new sites have to be utilised for production for existing markets, and given the very restricted *effective* demand in developing countries (a result of the development of the capitalist world system), production at these new sites is predominantly for foreign markets.

We use the term 'the new international division of labour' to designate that tendency which:

(a) undermines the traditional bisection of the world into a few industrialised countries on one hand, and a great majority of developing countries integrated into the world economy solely as raw material producers on the other, and

(b) compels the increasing subdivision of manufacturing processes into a number of partial operations at different industrial sites throughout the world,

where the division of labour should be understood as an on-going process, and not as a final result.

It may be helpful to illustrate this tendency by reference to a process which is well known from the history of capitalism, and which is analogous in certain respects. The rigidity of guild organisations in the towns on the one hand, and of feudal society (in its narrow sense) in the country on the other, had proved a major obstacle in the transformation of merchant capital into industrial capital during the period we can characterise as Early Modern Europe, and had prevented merchant capital from exercising a direct influence on the production process – the *formal* but not *real* subsumption of labour to capital. However, inasmuch as the crisis of feudal society unleashed new possibilities, merchant capital was able to use cheap labour in the country as compensation, labour which had been set free by the erosion of feudal society. Rural industry came into existence, mostly in the form of the putting-out system, for instance in the 'New Draperies' which did not require too many highly skilled workers.[1] This rural labour-force was relatively cheap, for which two reasons can be adduced. Firstly, rural industry was

1. See, for example, Hans Medick, 'The proto-industrial family economy: the structural function of household and family during the transition from peasant society to industrial capitalism', *Social History* III (1976), pp. 291–315; Peter Kriedte, Hans Medick & Jürgen Schlumbohm, *Industrialisierung vor der Industrialisierung* (Göttingen 1977).

frequently carried out as a supplementary activity, and was hence based on the partial self-sufficiency of the labour-force. Secondly, the rural dispersal of the labour-force was an obstacle to any effective organisation by workers against the, in contrast, monolithic merchant capital. However, whereas at that time merchant capital was only able to exercise the formal subsumption of the production process to capital – technology and the organisation of the labour process were simply taken over as they existed – today the subsumption of the production process in the developing manufacturing industries of the underdeveloped countries is real from the outset: that is, the technology of production and organisation of the labour process are subject to the exigencies of the specifically capitalist mode of production from the very beginning, despite the existence of 'subsidies' in the form of labour and the means of subsistence obtained from 'non-capitalist' sectors.[1]

We therefore interpret the currently observable relocation of production in industry (both within the traditional 'centre' and towards the 'periphery'), and in addition the increasing world-wide subdivision of the production process into separate partial processes as being the result of a qualitative change in the conditions for the valorisation and accumulation of capital, which is forcing the development of a new international division of labour. This new international division of labour is an 'institutional' innovation of capital itself, necessitated by changed conditions, and not the result of changed development strategies by individual countries or options freely decided upon by so-called multinational companies. It is a consequence and not a cause of these new conditions that various countries and companies have to tailor their policies and profit-maximising strategies to these new conditions (that is, to the requirements of the world market for industrial sites).

From the standpoint which is adopted in our analysis it would be quite inappropriate to attribute this new international division of labour to a fall in the rate of profit in the traditional industrial countries, which is forcing capital to relocate production to new sites.

1. The role of the erosion of feudal society in the countryside and of the genesis of rural industry in the 'crisis of the seventeenth century' is well known. It mediated between the flourishing merchant capital within the old European feudal society (fifteenth and sixteenth centuries) and the so-called Industrial Revolution (eighteenth and nineteenth centuries). The stated analogy between the genesis of rural industry in the West European seventeenth century on the one hand, and the present export-oriented industrialisation of developing countries on the other is, of course, not meant to imply a future 'Industrial Revolution' in the 'Third World' in line with the pattern which prevailed in Western Europe.

Our aim here is not to dispute the possible existence of such a fall in the rate of profit, but rather principally to answer the question – which is in reality answered by the world-wide migration of capital – simply as to whether production at the new sites or production at the traditional sites provides for an improved valorisation and accumulation of capital, which means in practice any valorisation at all, under the 'given' conditions.[1]

The phenomena of crisis which are at present observable in the 'centre' (rising unemployment; growing number of bankruptcies and mergers, even of major firms; stagnating or declining investment; fiscal problems for the state etc.) and which are often described as the expression of a world-wide cyclical recession, should, according to our approach, be explained as fundamentally the manifestation of the trend towards a new international division of labour. The pace at which this trend proceeds is, however, limited by a number of obstacles: for example, it is often necessary to use existing facilities as long as is economically feasible, concessions granted by the state and by the unions in the 'centre' to deter capital from leaving may have some effect, 'political instability' in the 'periphery' may deter firms, and, in some cases, companies may have the possibility of obtaining the same profits by rationalisation in the 'centre' rather than relocation (which results in more 'technological unemployment').[2]

The crisis of the 'centre' does not, however, mean the same thing as an equally serious crisis for capital as it operates on a world scale. Of course, an institutional innovation in the valorisation and

Of course this has to be taken *cum grano salis.* Even if it is accepted that the greed for maximum rather than 'normal' or 'legitimate' etc. rates of profit is the law imposed by competitive capital valorisation and accumulation, national protective measures (and the threat thereof) nonetheless may force capital to establish less profitable production sites in order to secure prospective markets.

2. So-called technological unemployment as well as the devaluation of existing skills of the ex-employees who have been set free because of rationalisation schemes may be, therefore, the immediate consequences of the pressures deriving from the trend towards a new international division of labour, even if this trend should not yet be unambiguously visible for the superficial observer through massive industrial relocation within the industrial branch or sub-branch concerned.

The empirical surveys of the present book focus on the increasing subdivision of the labour process as well as on the world-wide redistribution of manufacturing sites (industrial relocations). Case studies (a) on the interconnection between rationalisation schemes, de-skilling, unemployment, and industrial relocation (necessitated by the substitution of electronic for electro-mechanical components) and (b) on the structure and development of the world-wide industrial reserve army are being prepared by Anne-Marie Münster and Barbara Stuckey at the Max Planck Institute, Starnberg, Federal Germany.

accumulation of capital on the scale of a new international division of labour will occasion the collapse of a great many individual capitals and far-reaching adjustments by those capitals which survive. A comparison with the 'crisis of the seventeenth century' is not inappropriate: on closer examination this crisis sealed the downfall of Central and Southern Europe as centres of the valorisation of capital, while at the same time establishing the rise of the Netherlands and, above all, England as new capitalist centres. It is fairly safe to assume that the present clear indications of a new international division of labour could well open a new phase of stagnating capital valorisation in the 'centre' and a both relative and absolute growth in parts of the 'periphery'. In other words, this shift of the centre of gravity of valorisation from the traditional centres to the 'periphery' does not necessarily imply a mortal crisis of world capital. On the contrary, it is exactly that capital which operates on a world scale which is adjusting to the changed conditions in the valorisation and accumulation of capital. This by no means excludes, and in fact necessarily embraces, the fact that individual capitals – and hence figuratively, individual countries – will face stagnation and decay in this process of 'creative destruction', a process in which the needs of those people affected by it will inevitably be utterly disregarded.

Part 1

The development of the Federal German textile and garment industry as an example of the new international division of labour

Preliminary note

The aim of this case study is to provide evidence of the tendency towards a new international division of labour, taking the development of the Federal German textile and garment industry in the period 1960–75 as an example.

This tendency is the necessary outcome of the development of the world economy. It poses the rearrangement of the traditional partition of the world as it has developed under the dominance of the capitalist mode of production, with – essentially – a small number of industrial countries on the one hand, and a large number of developing countries producing raw materials on the other.

Some indicators of this new international division of labour (understood as an ongoing process and not a final result), in the sphere of the textile and garment industry, are: the drastically increased negative trade balance of Federal Germany and other traditional industrialised countries; the structural unemployment in the traditional industrial centres which is caused by factors connected with external trade; the export-oriented industrialisation of many developing countries and the corresponding shifts in production from 'centre' to 'periphery' (both intra- and international); and the increasing decomposition of the production process into a number of partial processes at different locations throughout the world. The development of these indicators over the period 1960–75 is an unmistakable pointer to the strength of economic forces on the world market for labour-power and for production sites, which is why it is at the heart of the analyses in this case study.

In addition, this case study will give at least some indication of what the present stage of this new international division of labour has already meant for those sections of the population it has affected in terms of their material welfare, working conditions, political discipline etc. – in short, their general conditions of life – and what this development might imply for the future.

However, it is not the intention of this case study to provide a comprehensive analysis of the Federal German textile and garment industry, or of all the main aspects of structural change within it, or to make recommendations for or against a particular policy on foreign trade, development and economic structure for Federal Germany or the EEC which would affect the textile and garment industry.

The present study also largely dispenses with a particular analysis of foreign trade policy, development policy and structural policy (sectoral, regional and qualificational), especially as far as the traditional industrial nations are concerned. The aim of these policies is to channel the consequences of the tendency towards a new international division of labour in such a way to ensure that the capitalist world economy and its nationally delimited subeconomies function as free from crises as possible, within the overall framework and limits which are already in existence.

Finally, this study completely dispenses with any discussion of developments or strategies which constitute an alternative to the new international division of labour – that is, alternatives to the capitalist world economy. This is not merely a consequence of the necessary constraints imposed on a case study by the particular demands of research, but also of the conviction that an analysis and evaluation of these complex questions would inevitably be inadequate unless preceded by a thorough investigation into the conditions, stage of development, and effects of the new international division of labour.

(Those readers who are eager to obtain a cursory overview of the case study are recommended to read Chapters 6.3 to 6.5, 7 and 9.)

3 World production and employment in the textile and garment industry, and world trade in textiles and clothing

3.1 World production and employment in the textile and garment industry: 1960–75

In 1970 the share of the textile and garment industry (including leather and footwear) in total world industrial production was approximately 8.3 %. In the same year as many as 20.5 % of all those employed in industry throughout the world were employed in the textile and garment industry (including leather and footwear).[1]

The corresponding values for the various groups of countries (traditional industrial, developing, centrally planned economies) differ considerably from these world average values; however, this does not have a substantial impact on the generally relatively high weight which the textile and garment industry (including leather and footwear) possesses in relation to total industrial production and employment.[2]

In 1970 the developing countries' share of world production in textiles and clothing (including leather and footwear) was estimated at 16 %, with the share of the East European centrally planned economies (including Yugoslavia) standing at 22 %.[3]

1. See Table I-1(c) (world excluding East Asian centrally planned economies). In this, and in a number of other instances, the only available statistics are for the garment industry including leather and footwear, and not for the garment industry alone. For practical reasons, the classification and ordering of the sources employed are also used in this study. One example is the demarcation between the three major groups of countries: traditional industrial countries, developing countries, centrally planned economies (= countries with a state monopoly of foreign trade), and the assignment of individual countries to these groups. Of course, we have attempted to make those assertions which are central to the argument invariant as far as the specific choice of which country belongs in which group, which is sometimes a problematic question (for example, the allocation of countries such as South Africa, Israel, Yugoslavia or Turkey to one of the groups).
2. See Table I-1(c).
3. Authors' own calculation, on the basis of statistics in UN, *Statistical Yearbook 1976* (New York 1977), Tables 3, 4, 9.

Table I-1

(a) Population, industrial production and employment, and exports of selected country groupings as percentages of world totals: 1970

Country grouping	Population[a]	Production (ISIC)[b]				Employment (ISIC)[c]				Exports (SITC)[d]			
		2–4	3	321	322–324	2–4	3	321	322–324	0–9	5–8	65	84
World	100	100	100	100	100	100	100	100	100	100	100	100	100
IC	26	68	69	61	65	41	42	23	39	72	84	78	65
LDC	61	9	8	19	11	35	35	59	41	18	6	15	21
CPE	13	22	23	20	24	24	23	17	22	11	10	7	14

(b) Average annual percentage of growth rates of population, industrial production and employment, and exports of selected country groupings: 1960–75

Country grouping	Population[e]	Production (ISIC)[f]				Employment (ISIC)[g]				Exports (SITC)[h]			
		2–4	3	321	322–324	2–4	3	321	322–324	0–9	5–8	65	84
World	2.0	6.1	6.1	3.7	3.6	2.5	2.7	1.2	3.3	7.1	n.a.	n.a.	n.a.
IC	1.0	4.6	4.6	2.8	1.9	0.8	1.0	−1.1	1.0	7.5	8.6	n.a.	n.a.
LDC	2.6	7.1	6.7	3.8	6.1	4.4	4.6	2.7	6.5	5.7	10.7	n.a.	n.a.
CPE	1.0	9.0	9.2	5.4	6.3	2.9	3.2	1.3	2.6	n.a.	n.a.	n.a.	n.a.

(c) Industrial production and employment of manufacturing, textile and garment (including leather and footwear) industries as percentages of total industrial production and employment; exports of manufactured goods, textiles and clothing as percentages of total exports: selected country groupings 1970

Country grouping	Production (ISIC)[i]				Employment (ISIC)[j]				Exports (SITC)[k]			
	2–4	3	321	322–324	2–4	3	321	322–324	0–9	5–8	65	84
World	100	86.8	4.5	3.8	100	92.2	11.8	8.7	100	64.8	4.0	2.0
IC	100	88.0	4.0	3.5	100	93.4	7.6	7.5	100	75.4	4.3	1.8
LDC	100	71.1	8.8	4.3	100	91.8	22.3	10.8	100	23.7	3.5	2.4
CPE	100	89.2	4.1	4.0	100	90.0	8.2	9.0	100	60.8	2.5	2.8

(d) Regional structure of world trade (SITC 0–9) between selected country groupings: 1963, 1970, 1976

Area of origin	Share of world exports			Share of area of destination (total exports of area of origin = 100)								
				IC			LDC			CPE		
	1963	1970	1976	1963	1970	1976	1963	1970	1976	1963	1970	1976
World[l]	100	100	100	67	71	68	21	18	21	12	10	10
IC	67	72	65	74	77	71	22	18	22	4	4	6
LDC	21	18	25	72	74	73	21	20	22	5	6	4
CPE[l]	12	11	10	19	23	29	13	13	13	66	61	55

Sources: UN, *Statistical Yearbook, 1976* (New York 1977) (= A); UN, *Monthly Bulletin of Statistics* XXX, 8 (1976), XXXI, 6 (1977), XXXII, 2 (1978) (= B; C; D); UNCTAD, *Handbook of International Trade and Development Statistics, 1976* (New York 1976) (= E); GATT, *International Trade 1976/77* (Geneva 1977) (= F); own calculations

ISIC: International Standard Industrial Classification of All Economic Activities, Rev. 2 (1968 edition)

ISIC 2–4: Mining, manufacturing, electricity, gas and water; ISIC 3: Manufacturing; ISIC 321: Textiles; ISIC 322–324: Wearing apparel, leather and footwear

SITC: Standard International Trade Classification, Rev. 1 (1961 edition)

SITC 0–9: All commodities; SITC 5–8: Manufactured goods; SITC 65: Textiles; SITC 84: Clothing

IC (industrial countries): North America (Canada and United States), Europe (other than Eastern Europe), Australia, Israel, Japan, New Zealand and South Africa

LDC (less developed countries, developing countries): Caribbean, Central and South America, Africa (other than South Africa), Asian Middle East, and East and South-East Asia (other than Israel and Japan)

CPE (centrally planned economies): Bulgaria, Czechoslovakia, German Democratic Republic, Hungary, Poland, Romania, USSR

World: the above mentioned countries

Growth rates and weight of industrial production are, in most cases, calculated on the basis of value-added in constant US dollars (generally at factor cost). Growth rates of exports refer to volume of exports ('quantum index')

a: From A, Tables 2, 18 b: From A, Tables 3, 4, 9 c: From A. Table 10 and E, Table 6.8 d: From B, Special Table C (excluding the intra-trade of centrally planned economies of Asia, trade between Federal Republic of Germany (FRG) and German Democratic Republic (GDR) and the trade of Southern Rhodesia) e: From A, Tables 2, 18 f: From D, Special Table 1 g: From A, Table 10 (1960–74) h: From C, Special Tables E, F (generally excluding the trade of centrally planned economies) i: From D, Special Table A j: From A, Table 10 k: From B, Special Table C (excluding the intra-trade of centrally planned economies of Asia, trade between FRG and GDR and the trade of Southern Rhodesia) l: including Albania

Table I-2. *Industrial employment in thousands in manufacturing, textile and garment (including leather and footwear) industries of selected country groupings: 1970*

	Manufacturing total	Textile	Garment (including leather and footwear)
World	183036	22520	19131
IC	76550	5281	7397
LDC	64270	13294	7753
CPE	42714	3734	4276

Source: UNCTAD, *Handbook of International Trade and Development Statistics, 1976* (New York 1976), p. 386
For the definition of the country groupings, see the notes to table I-1

Table I-2 gives the figures for employment in world manufacturing industry in 1970. According to these statistics the share of the developing countries in total world employment in the textile and garment industry (including leather and footwear) was 51% in 1970, with the East European centrally planned economies accounting for 19%.

The divergent rates of growth for each group of countries for industrial employment are especially noticeable. As Table I-1(b) shows, between 1960 and 1975 the importance of the textile industry in the traditional industrial countries declined relative to industry as a whole, both in output and employment; in addition employment has actually fallen in absolute terms. Essentially the same applies to the garment industry (including leather and footwear), although in this case the volume of employment has increased slightly in absolute terms. For the developing countries over the same period the size of the textile industry relative to industry as a whole has also declined, both in output and employment: but in absolute terms employment has increased. The relative weight of the garment industry (including leather and footwear) has fallen slightly in terms of production but clearly increased as far as employment is concerned. Employment has increased considerably in absolute terms. The centrally planned economies occupy an intermediary position in all these areas. This process of structural differentiation in industrial production between the industrial and developing countries gained tremendous momentum towards the end of the period under consideration (see Table I-3).

Table I-3. *Average annual percentage, growth rates of industrial production for selected branches of industry and selected country groupings: 1960–76; 1960–68, 1968–73, 1973–76*

ISIC	2–4	2	21	22	23	3	LM	HM	31	321	322–324	33	34	35	36	37	38	4
World																		
1960–76	6.2	4.4	0.5	6.6	3.5	6.2	4.6	7.1	4.3	3.9	3.9	4.9	4.4	8.3	5.6	5.0	7.5	7.6
1960–68	6.9	5.3	0.8	7.8	5.1	6.9	5.1	8.2	4.2	4.0	4.0	5.5	5.7	9.7	5.7	6.0	8.4	8.4
1968–73	6.5	4.6	−0.6	7.2	2.9	6.7	5.1	7.3	5.0	4.7	3.5	6.0	4.7	8.4	6.7	5.8	7.6	8.4
1973–76	3.7	1.7	1.4	2.1	0.3	3.7	2.7	4.1	3.6	2.5	4.2	1.6	0.6	4.2	3.4	1.1	4.8	4.1
Industrial countries																		
1960–76	4.9	1.9	−1.9	3.7	1.4	4.9	3.8	5.4	3.7	3.2	2.3	4.0	3.8	7.5	4.2	3.7	3.0	6.8
1960–68	6.0	2.5	−1.2	4.4	2.6	6.2	4.5	7.0	4.0	3.8	2.8	4.7	5.1	9.2	5.1	5.2	6.9	7.5
1968–73	5.5	2.0	−3.7	4.5	1.5	5.3	4.3	5.9	4.2	4.3	1.9	5.7	4.2	8.0	5.5	5.4	5.6	8.3
1973–76	0.8	0.0	−0.4	0.9	−1.7	0.8	1.1	0.5	2.0	0.0	1.5	−0.5	−0.3	2.3	−0.3	−2.6	0.8	2.6
Developing countries																		
1960–76	7.1	6.7	3.7	8.0	3.0	6.8	5.1	8.8	5.3	4.0	6.5	5.8	6.4	7.6	7.8	8.2	10.7	11.0
1960–68	7.0	8.3	4.2	10.1	3.8	6.1	4.4	8.6	4.5	3.4	5.9	7.3	6.9	8.0	7.1	8.6	9.8	11.3
1968–73	8.3	7.7	1.6	9.5	2.4	8.2	6.6	10.2	6.5	5.1	5.2	4.9	11.5	8.7	8.9	7.2	13.1	11.4
1973–76	5.2	1.1	6.0	0.5	2.2	6.1	4.6	7.3	5.6	3.8	10.6	3.3	−2.7	4.7	8.1	8.7	9.3	9.5
Centrally planned economies																		
1960–76	8.8	6.3	2.8	8.4	7.6	9.1	6.4	10.5	5.2	5.4	6.3	6.3	7.3	10.7	7.8	7.1	11.3	9.1
1960–68	9.2	7.2	2.9	10.0	10.7	9.4	6.4	11.0	5.1	5.0	5.9	6.0	7.7	11.6	8.0	7.7	11.5	10.4
1968–73	8.5	5.3	3.0	6.8	6.5	9.0	6.6	9.9	5.6	5.9	6.5	7.1	7.2	10.0	8.2	6.0	11.2	8.3
1973–76	8.4	5.4	2.4	6.9	1.4	8.6	5.8	10.0	5.1	5.8	6.8	6.0	6.4	9.6	6.5	7.1	10.9	7.2

Sources: UN, *Monthly Bulletin of Statistics* XXXII, 2 (1978), Special Table A; own calculations

ISIC 2: Mining; 21: Coal; 22: Crude petroleum and natural gas; 23: Metal

ISIC 3: Manufacturing: LM (light manufacturing): 31–33, 342, 355–356, 39; HM (heavy manufacturing): 341, 351–354, 36–38; 31: Food, beverages, tobacco; 321: Textiles; 322–324: Wearing apparel, leather and footwear; 33: Wood products, furniture; 34: Paper, printing and publishing; 35: Chemicals, coal and rubber products; 36: Non-metallic mineral products; 37: Basic metals; 38: Metal products

ISIC 4: Electricity, gas and water

For the definition of the country groupings, see the notes to table I-1

3.2 World trade in textiles and clothing: 1960–75

In 1970 world exports of textiles and clothing amounted to 6.0% of total world exports.

The corresponding share of the export of textiles and clothing as a proportion of total exports deviates only very slightly from this world average for each group of countries.[1]

In 1970 the developing countries' share of total world exports of textiles and clothing was 17.9%, with the centrally planned economies (excluding Yugoslavia) accounting for 9.0%.[2]

Compared with the corresponding shares of the other major product groups in manufacturing industry (excluding non-ferrous metals), the share of exports of textiles and clothing which originates from the developing countries in total world exports is exceptionally high: in addition, this share is growing strongly. Whereas 15.2% of total world exports of textiles and clothing originated in the developing countries in 1963, this figure had risen to 23.2% by 1975. The corresponding share of the centrally planned economies (excluding Yugoslavia) was approximately 9.5% over this period.[3]

The real tendency behind these figures becomes even more evident if one takes the share of textile and clothing exports from the developing and centrally planned economies to the traditional industrial countries (as a proportion of world exports in textiles and clothing to the traditional industrial countries), excludes trade within the EEC, and includes non-EEC countries in Southern Europe within the developing countries' group. The share of this group (as defined above) rose from 34.7% in 1970 to 48.9% by 1974.[4]

1. See Table I-1 (c).
2. See Table I-4. Federal Germany's share of total world exports and imports of textiles stood at approximately 12% in the first half of the 1970s; its share of world imports of clothing was almost 20% (and increasing), with its share of world exports stagnating at around 7%. In 1976 Federal Germany was the world's largest importer and exporter of textiles, and the largest importer of clothing. The world's largest exporter of clothing in 1976 was Hong Kong. See GATT, *International Trade 1976/77* (Geneva 1977).
3. See Table I-4.
4. For textiles (SITC 65) from 27.2% to 36.8%; for clothing (SITC 84) from 46.6% to 65.2%. Calculated from GATT, *Recent Trends in Production and Trade in Textiles and Clothing* (Geneva 1975), Table 3.

Table I-4. *Exports of selected country groupings as percentages of world exports by commodity classes: 1963, 1966, 1970, 1972, 1974, 1975*

		1963	1966	1970	1972	1974	1975
Total exports[a]	IC	67.4	69.9	71.7	71.9	64.7	66.2
	LDC	20.5	18.7	17.8	17.8	26.8	24.1
	CPE	12.2	11.5	10.5	10.3	8.5	9.7
Total primary products	IC	48.1	48.8	50.0	49.7	38.1	39.7
	LDC	40.8	39.8	39.9	40.9	54.5	51.1
	CPE	11.1	11.4	10.1	9.4	7.4	9.1
Food	IC	55.1	57.6	59.3	62.7	62.2	63.3
	LDC	35.4	32.4	31.5	29.0	29.5	28.7
	CPE	9.5	10.0	9.2	8.4	8.2	8.0
Raw materials	IC	56.0	55.4	58.9	60.3	61.2	61.5
	LDC	32.7	31.3	29.6	28.4	27.8	25.9
	CPE	11.3	13.3	11.5	11.2	11.0	12.6
Ores and minerals	IC	54.0	55.2	58.2	54.3	55.8	53.9
	LDC	32.7	33.2	31.2	33.6	34.2	33.3
	CPE	13.3	11.3	10.6	12.1	10.1	12.9
Fuels	IC	26.4	24.1	26.6	24.2	15.4	17.4
	LDC	60.4	63.6	63.0	66.5	78.9	73.9
	CPE	13.2	12.3	10.4	9.2	5.7	8.7
Total manufactures	IC	81.4	83.4	83.6	83.5	83.8	83.8
	LDC	5.6	5.7	6.5	6.5	7.8	6.8
	CPE	13.0	10.9	9.9	10.0	8.4	9.4
Non-ferrous metals	IC	62.6	62.2	63.4	64.9	64.5	67.9
	LDC	29.9	30.8	29.2	24.4	27.2	22.0
	CPE	7.5	7.0	7.5	10.7	8.3	10.1
Iron and steel	IC	79.6	80.8	82.6	83.1	88.3	86.5
	LDC	1.9	2.0	3.3	3.5	3.4	2.7
	CPE	18.5	16.1	14.1	13.4	8.3	10.8
Chemicals	IC	86.4	88.5	88.7	87.7	88.4	87.3
	LDC	4.1	3.6	4.3	4.8	5.6	5.4
	CPE	9.3	7.8	7.1	7.5	6.0	7.3
Machinery and transport equipment	IC	85.6	86.8	87.6	87.0	87.2	87.1
	LDC	0.8	0.9	1.6	2.3	3.2	2.8
	CPE	13.6	12.3	10.8	10.8	9.6	10.1
Textiles	IC	n.a.	77.5	77.8	76.3	74.6	74.4
	LDC	n.a.	15.0	15.5	16.5	18.6	17.8
	CPE	n.a.	7.6	6.7	7.3	6.8	7.8
Clothing	IC	n.a.	71.0	65.2	59.3	54.6	54.5
	LDC	n.a.	14.5	21.3	26.6	31.8	32.0
	CPE	n.a.	14.4	13.6	14.0	13.6	13.5
Other manufactures	IC	n.a.	85.2	83.1	84.2	83.4	82.8
	LDC	n.a.	5.7	8.1	7.6	9.2	9.3
	CPE	n.a.	9.5	8.8	8.2	7.4	7.9

Table I-4. (*cont.*)

Commodity class	World export value (1975) (US $ million fob)	Percentage of total world exports
Total exports: SITC 0–9	872580	100.0
Total primary products: SITC 0–4	339521	38.9
Food: SITC 0, 1, 4, 22	115573	13.2
Raw materials: SITC 2 excluding 22, 27, 28	34283	3.9
Ores and minerals: SITC 27, 28	21103	2.4
Fuels: SITC 3	168562	19.3
Total manufactures: SITC 5–8	518193	59.4
Non-ferrous metals: SITC 68	18243	2.1
Iron and steel: SITC 67	45831	5.3
Chemicals: SITC 5	60957	7.0
Machinery and transport equipment: SITC 7	244152	28.0
Textiles: SITC 65	26557	3.0
Clothing: SITC 84	16737	1.9
Other manufactures: SITC 6, 8 excluding 65, 67, 68, 84	105716	12.1

Sources: UN, *Monthly Bulletin of Statistics* xxiii, 3 (1969), xxvi, 7 (1972); UN, *Yearbook of International Trade Statistics 1975, 1976* (New York 1976, 1977); GATT, *International Trade 1970* (Geneva 1971); own calculations

The data cover world trade with the exception of the inter-trade of the centrally planned economies of Asia, trade between Federal Republic of Germany and German Democratic Republic and exports of Southern Rhodesia. For the definition of the country groupings IC, LDC and CPE, see the notes to table I-1

a: 1976 figures: IC = 65.0%, LDC = 25.4%, CPE = 9.5%

3.3 World economic interdependence in the textile and garment industry: 1960–75

The average annual rate of growth of the volume of world exports amounted to 7.2% between 1960 and 1975: of this, agricultural products grew at 3.4%, minerals, oil and non-ferrous metals at 4.7%, and the products of manufacturing industry at 8.9%. By comparison the average annual rates of growth of the production of these commodities was as follows: all commodities 4.9%, agricultural products 2.4%, mining 4.4%, and manufacturing 6.0%.[1]

These figures show that without exception the rate of growth of foreign trade has been higher than the rate of growth of output for the major product groups. In other words: global economic interdependence, inasmuch as it can be expressed as the proportion of foreign trade to output, has grown strongly between 1960 and 1975 for each of the major product groups.

Precisely corresponding statistics for the textiles and clothing sector are not available. However, since the traditional industrial

1. Calculated from GATT, *International Trade 1976/77*, Table 1.

countries play such a quantitatively dominant role in total world production and trade (cf. Table I-1), a study of the development of their import and export ratios provides an adequate substitute.[1]

Between 1960 and 1975 the import and export ratios in textiles and clothing of the traditional industrial countries have all, apart from minor exceptions, shown a clear increase. Within this group Federal Germany has relatively high ratios and the USA and Japan have relatively low ratios. In general, the ratios are higher for the smaller industrial countries.[2]

At the beginning of the 1970s, Federal Germany's import ratio stood at approximately 30% for textiles and 20% for clothing. The export ratio was approximately 25% for textiles and 10% for clothing. Whereas the export ratio increased more or less in parallel with the import ratio for textiles between 1960 and 1975, it remained a long way behind for clothing.[3]

Inasmuch as the development of import and export ratios can be taken as an indicator, world economic interdependence has also clearly grown in the field of textiles and clothing. For the Federal Republic of Germany in particular, it can be seen that the growing share of imports in the internal market is not matched by a corresponding increase in the export of clothing.

3.4 The decline in employment in the textile and garment industry in the European Community and Federal Germany: 1960–75

Table I-1(b) shows the decline in total employment in the textile industry for the traditional industrial countries between 1960 and 1975.

In the European Community (EC: the 'Six' plus the United Kingdom), the volume of employment in the textile and garment industry fell by 762 000 between 1965 and 1974, a fall of around 18% (from 4 215 000 to 3 453 000).[4]

1. Import ratio: ratio of imports to domestic production plus imports minus exports. Export ratio: ratio of exports to domestic production (all amounts expressed in value terms).
2. Cf. Ifo-Institut für Wirtschaftsforschung, *Verhältnis der Einfuhren an Textilien und Bekleidung zur entsprechenden Inlandsproduktion und zum Inlandsverbrauch in der EG und den wichtigsten Industrieländern* (Munich 1974). Classification: textiles = SITC 65+841.4; clothing = SITC 84 (excluding 841.4).
3. See Table I-5.
4. See Comité international de la rayonne et des fibres synthétiques (CIRFS), *The Future of the Man-Made Fibres Industry in Western Europe* (Paris 1976). Cf. also *Textil-Wirtschaft* 52

Table I-5. *Domestic production, domestic market and external trade of Federal German textile (T) and garment (G) industry: 1960, 1965–75*

		1960	1965	1966	1967	1968	1969	1970	1971	1972	1973	1974	1975
							(1000 million DM)						
Turnover from	T	17.51	22.06	22.14	20.75	23.59	25.87	26.65	28.69	28.81	30.02	31.05	29.22
domestic production	G	9.50	14.61	15.10	14.05	14.31	15.49	16.79	18.04	20.09	19.79	19.82	20.13
Imports	T	2.96	5.05	5.13	4.23	5.24	6.33	6.87	8.13	9.32	9.80	10.28	10.90
	G	0.38	1.22	1.46	1.24	1.54	2.18	2.57	3.24	4.27	4.79	5.88	6.61
Exports	T	1.68	2.71	2.89	3.08	3.50	4.21	5.22	6.04	6.47	7.77	8.84	7.95
	G	0.31	0.66	0.81	0.78	0.94	1.11	1.11	1.32	1.64	1.96	2.16	2.38
Trade balance	T	−1.28	−2.34	−2.24	−1.15	−1.74	−2.12	−1.65	−2.09	−2.85	−2.03	−1.44	−2.95
	G	−0.07	−0.56	−0.65	−0.46	−0.60	−1.07	−1.46	−1.92	−2.63	−2.83	−3.72	−4.23
DAP	T	18.79	24.40	24.38	21.90	25.33	27.99	28.30	30.78	31.66	32.05	32.49	32.17
	G	9.57	15.17	15.75	14.51	14.91	16.56	18.25	19.96	22.72	22.62	23.54	24.36
							(Percentages)						
Import ratio	T	15.8	20.7	21.0	19.3	20.7	22.6	24.3	26.4	29.4	30.6	31.6	33.9
	G	4.0	8.0	9.3	8.5	10.3	13.2	14.1	16.2	18.8	21.2	25.0	27.1
Export ratio	T	9.6	12.3	13.1	14.8	14.8	16.3	19.6	21.1	22.5	25.9	28.5	27.2
	G	3.3	4.5	5.4	5.6	6.6	7.2	6.6	7.3	8.2	9.9	10.9	11.8
Turnover/DAP	T	93.2	90.4	90.8	94.7	93.1	92.4	94.2	93.2	91.0	93.7	95.6	90.8
	G	99.3	96.3	95.8	96.8	96.0	93.5	92.0	90.4	88.4	87.5	84.2	82.6

Sources: *Textil-Wirtschaft* 24, 26 (1976) (according to data from the Statistisches Bundesamt); own calculations

Commodity classification according to 'Warenverzeichnis für die Industriestatistik'

Trade balance = exports minus imports

DAP (domestically available product) = turnover from domestic production plus imports minus exports

Import ratio = imports as a percentage of domestically available product

Export ratio = exports as a percentage of turnover from domestic production

Turnover/DAP = turnover from domestic production as a percentage of domestically available product

Table I-6. *Employment and labour market of Federal German textile (T) and garment (G) industry and trades: 1960–77 (thousands/percentages)*

	Employees (*Gewerbe*)		Employees (*Industrie*)			Annual average percentage growth rate of employment			Employees (*Hand-werk*)	Employed home-workers		Short-time workers (*Gewerbe*)		T plus G jobs	
	T	G	Total	T	G	Total	T	G	G	T	G	T	G	jobless	vacan-cies
1960	672	536	8081	620	356	4.1	3.1	4.4	n.a.	42	43	1	0	10	32
1961	666	n.a.	8316	612	370	2.9	−1.2	4.1	n.a.	44	46	1	1	7	35
1962	644	n.a.	8339	590	384	0.3	−3.7	3.8	n.a.	44	45	1	0	6	38
1963	629	n.a.	8264	573	388	−0.9	−2.9	1.0	n.a.	48	44	1	1	6	37
1964	611	n.a.	8301	556	388	0.4	−3.0	−0.1	n.a.	44	38	0	0	6	38
1965	602	548	8460	547	398	1.9	−1.6	2.7	n.a.	44	42	0	0	5	43
1966	591	547	8385	538	406	−0.9	−1.6	2.1	n.a.	44	41	2	4	5	38
1967	538	504	7843	490	371	−6.5	−9.0	−8.8	n.a.	38	30	18	18	21	17
1968	537	492	7899	489	367	0.7	−0.2	−1.1	n.a.	38	30	1	1	10	31
1969	558	502	8308	508	382	5.2	3.9	4.3	n.a.	42	31	0	0	5	43
1970	547	487	8603	501	379	3.6	−1.3	−0.8	70	42	28	1	1	6	36
1971	524	469	8538	481	372	−0.8	−4.0	−2.0	60	38	26	3	2	9	28
1972	497	459	8340	458	372	−2.3	−4.9	0.1	53	36	25	5	1	9	25
1973	472	439	8368	434	360	0.3	−5.3	−3.3	46	31	24	5	17	13	22
1974	430	380	8144	394	310	−2.7	−9.3	−13.8	42	26	19	20	13	31	9
1975	390	351	7616	357	288	−6.5	−9.4	−7.1	37	23	17	39	15	38	8
1976	n.a.	n.a.	7428	342	277	−2.5	−4.3	−4.1	34	21	16	11	10	32	9
1977	n.a.	n.a.	n.a.	n.a.	n.a.	0.2	−3.0	−2.9	n.a.	20	17	15	8	29	8

Sources: Statistics from Statistisches Bundesamt and Bundesanstalt für Arbeit

In general, annual averages; home-workers: end of September (1960–63) or end of June (1964–77)

Federal German statistics for branches of production are broken down, for historical reasons, into *Gewerbe* and *Industrie*. *Gewerbe* covers all establishments in a branch, and hence comprises large establishments, establishments with nine or fewer employees, and the so-called handicraft (*Handwerk*) sector together with home-workers. *Industrie* comprises industrial establishments with more than ten employees

Employment in the textile and garment industry in Federal Germany fell by 357 000 between 1960 and 1976, a drop of 37% (from 976 000 to 619 000).[1] Compared with the relative changes in employment in other sectors which are significant in terms of numbers employed in Federal Germany (engineering, electrical engineering, chemicals, vehicle building, food industry) over the same period, the percentage for textiles and clothing is way out of proportion.[2]

Table I-6 gives a detailed picture of the labour market and employment in the field of textiles and clothing in Federal Germany between 1960 and 1976.[3] Whereas employment in the textile industry accounted for 7.7% of total industrial employment in 1960, it had fallen to only 4.6% by 1976. The corresponding figures for the garment industry were 4.4% (1960) and 3.7% (1976). Whereas the average annual change in the volume of industrial employment was −0.5% between 1960 and 1976, the figure for textiles was −3.6%, and for the garment industry −1.6%.[4]

The fall in employment in textiles had already begun by the beginning of the 1960s, and accelerated after 1971. For industry as a whole, including the garment industry, this fall did not start until the beginning of the 1970s. The fall in industrial employment which took place in the recession of 1967 was more than made up in the subsequent three years; however, no such evening-up occurred in the textile and garment industry ('the economic cycle as the executor of structural change').

(1976), p. 22. Employment figures for the textile and garment industries in the EC taken from various sources – e.g. UN, Co-ordination Committee for the Textile Industry in the EC (Comitextil), the Association européenne des industries de l'habillement (AEIH), CIRFS and OECD – all exhibit astounding divergences from one another. This can normally be explained by differences in the classification of those employed. However, the trends indicated here, and elsewhere in this work, are invariant as regards such divergences and differences between sources.

1. See Table I-6.
2. See Statistisches Bundesamt, *Lange Reihen zur Wirtschaftsentwicklung 1976* (Stuttgart–Mainz 1976), Table 5.2.2.
3. Federal German statistics for branches of production are broken down, for historical reasons, into *Gewerbe* and *Industrie*. *Gewerbe* covers all establishments in a branch, and hence comprises large establishments, establishments with nine or fewer employees and the so-called handicraft (*Handwerk*) sector together with home-workers. *Industrie* comprises industrial establishments with more than ten employees.
4. For the period of the last economic cycle (1967–75) the corresponding figures are: industry as a whole, −0.4%; textile industry, −3.9%; garment industry, −3.1%.

3.5 Case study I: principal areas covered

The preceding survey has shown the significance of the textile and garment industry in total world industrial production and employment, and in world trade. It goes without saying that certain types of structural developments within such an important sector must have a profound effect on the regional distribution of industrial production and employment throughout the world. One such structural development is constituted by the relocation of production[1] which has been observable for a number of years in the textile and garment industry. The introductory survey above has already shown that these shifts in production, inasmuch as they are out of the traditional industrial countries and into the developing or centrally planned economies, are currently expressed in the differential rates of growth of industrial production and employment in different groups of countries, and in a change in the structure of world trade in textiles and clothing.

These indications, together with the reflections on the development of the current capitalist world economy sketched out in the Introduction, lead us to the thesis that the present-day development of the Federal German textile and garment industry is an example of the effects of the structural tendency towards a new international division of labour.

In order to prove this thesis we shall first of all document the stage which the new international division of labour has currently attained, using the Federal German textile and garment industry as an example. Three indicators will be used:

(a) Structural unemployment in the Federal German textile and garment industry with external economic factors as its cause.

(b) Export-oriented industrialisation of developing countries in the field of textiles and clothing.

(c) Relocation of production by Federal German textile and garment companies to other countries, especially the so-called low wage countries.

Secondly, we shall analyse those conditions which determine the new international division of labour:

1. In this study the expression 'shift in production' or 'relocation' means the abandonment of production at one site *and* its commencement at another. Unless the expression is so qualified, it is irrelevant whether the abandonment of production *and* its commencement elsewhere are undertaken by *one and the same company*.

(a) The determinants of the development of the world market in production sites, especially in the developing countries.
(b) Direction of the new international division of labour by the political institutions of primarily the traditional industrial countries, or the reaction of these institutions to the development of these conditions.

A more detailed investigation into the bases of the international division of labour as exemplified in the textile and garment industry will also serve to provide some indications as to whether, and under what conditions and for which other industrial sectors or sub-manufacturing processes within sectors, analogous developments can be expected.

However, we do not attempt to provide a quantitative estimation of the influences which the new international division of labour can be expected to have on total employment in Federal Germany in the foreseeable future, let alone a more comprehensive prognosis of the Federal German labour market as it may be affected by other relevant determining factors, such as changes in retirement age, to name but one example.

4 ❧ Unemployment in the Federal German textile and garment industry as determined by developments in the world economy

4.1 The decline in employment in the Federal German textile and garment industry: the joint effect of domestic consumption, balance of foreign trade and turnover per employee: 1967–75

Table I-6 shows the development of employment and the labour market in the textile and garment industry in Federal Germany between 1967 and 1975. Table I-5 provides a quantitative picture of the development of domestic turnover, foreign trade interdependence and the domestically available product (= turnover plus imports minus exports = (basically) domestic consumption) for the Federal German textile and garment industry over the same period. (Cf. also Diagrams 1 and 2.) These figures, together with the given relationship between the volume of employment, domestically available product, trade deficit and turnover per employee, enable us to draw the following conclusions:

(1) The drastic decline in the volume of employment in the Federal German garment industry between 1967 and 1975 is, alongside increased productivity (turnover per employee), also attributable to a great extent to the rapid growth in the Federal German import surplus for clothing: this applies to the industry as a whole, although not necessarily to every individual part of it. The effects of these two factors have not been compensated for by a growth in the domestic consumption of clothing large enough to have a balancing impact on the volume of employment.

(2) The drastic decline in the volume of employment in the Federal German textile industry between 1967 and 1975 is – again taking the industry as a whole – primarily attributable to the increase in productivity (measured as turnover per employee), and additionally, though to a lesser extent, to the increase in the

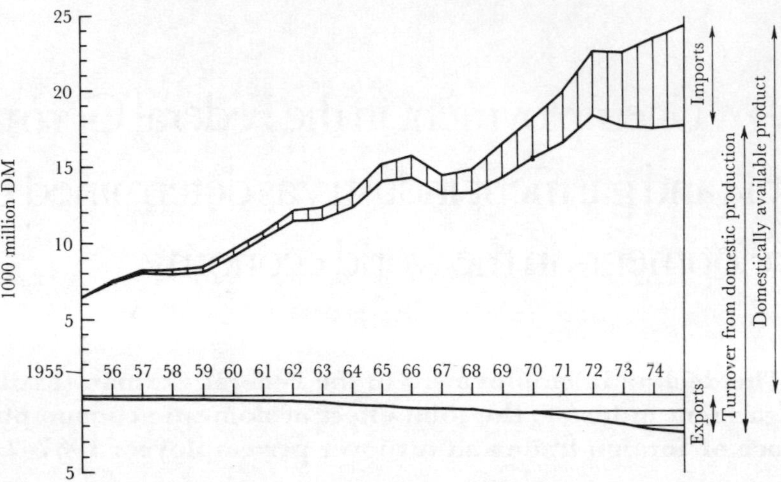

Diagram 1. Federal German garment sales and foreign trade: 1955–75. Source: *Textil-Wirtschaft* 24 (1976)

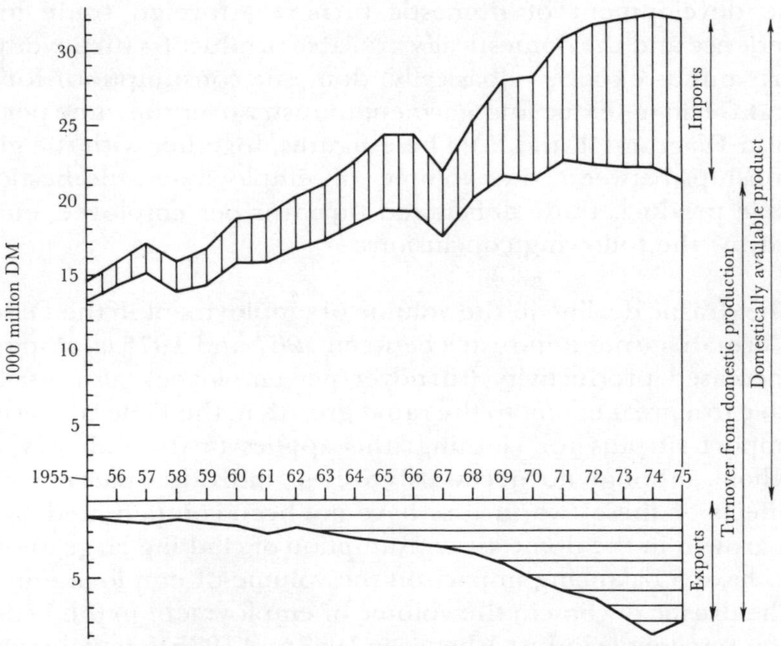

Diagram 2. Federal German textile sales and foreign trade: 1955–75. Source: *Textil-Wirtschaft* 24 (1976)

Federal German trade deficit on textiles. The effects of these two factors have not been compensated for by a growth in the domestic consumption of textiles large enough to have a balancing impact on the volume of employment.

On point 1

Between 1960 and 1975, the Federal German trade deficit on clothing rose from almost nothing to DM 0.46 billion (thousand million) by 1967, and further to DM 4.23 billion by 1975: hence by the end of the period under consideration it was no longer negligible in comparison to domestic turnover. Employment in the domestic garment industry was therefore curtailed not only by the effect of higher productivity, but also significantly by the increased trade deficit. Real annual growth of domestic consumption of clothing at, on average, 3% between 1967 and 1975 was too small to compensate for this negative influence on employment.[1] An approximate quantitative estimation of the fall in employment which can be attributed directly to the increased import surplus can, for example, be made by dividing the relative fall in employment into the sum of three factors which approximately give the contribution of the changes in domestic consumption, import surplus (both as proportions of domestic turnover) and the relative change in the turnover per employee during the period under consideration.[2] We can estimate from this that, of the total fall in employment in the Federal German garment industry between 1967 and 1975 of 153 000, approximately a half (*circa* 78 000) is directly attributable to increased import surpluses. In order to appreciate the significance of these figures, one only has to look at the volume of employment

1. Of course, this observation should not be simply recast as saying that a higher real annual rate of growth in the domestic consumption of clothing is desirable because of the supposed 'positive employment effect' which this would be expected to have on the Federal German garment industry.
2. If E is the volume of employment in a sector, T its turnover from domestic production, A the amount of goods available domestically from this sector and $M-X$ the corresponding import surplus (imports minus exports), then it follows (with all values applying to one year) that by definition: $E = (A-[M-X])/(T/E)$. One then forms the logarithmic derivation of this equation ($d \log E =$ etc.), substitutes the differentials thus obtained by approximation by the corresponding differences for the time period under consideration and, instead of using the remaining undifferentiated values which relate to one particular year, one uses as an approximation the arithmetic mean for the time period under study. (The period 1967–75 was chosen as it covered the last complete economic cycle.) An estimate in the magazine *Textil-Wirtschaft* 26 (1976) carried out using slightly different assumptions comes to roughly comparable results.

in the Federal German garment industry in 1967: a total of approximately 504 000.

On point 2

The Federal German import surplus for textiles between 1960 and 1975 was kept within relatively modest dimensions, in comparison to domestic turnover. Consequently, the drastic fall in employment in the textile industry is predominantly attributable to increases in productivity. The real annual growth in the domestic consumption of textiles between 1967 and 1975 was, at on average 2 %, insufficient to compensate for this negative influence on employment. An approximate estimation, analogous to that in the previous section, allows us to state that out of a fall of employment of 148 000 in the Federal German textile industry between 1967 and 1975 only a quarter (*circa* 35 000) can be directly attributed to increased trade deficits.[1] Again, these figures should be seen in relation to total employment in textiles in Federal Germany: approximately 538 000 in 1967.

Since our main concern is to give some quantitative idea of the processes at work here, we have not refined these estimates by a systematic consideration of the input-output structure of the Federal German economy.[2] However, even without this, the observations we have just made can be qualitatively refined in two ways.

1. As a glance at Table I-5 shows, out of all possible longer time periods between 1960 and 1975, the period chosen (1967–75) is that in which Federal Germany's import surpluses for textiles are most significant in estimating the contribution of increased import surpluses to the observed drop in employment. For all other longer time periods between 1960 and 1975 the proportion of the fall in employment in the Federal German textile industry which can be directly attributed to increased import surpluses is still less than a quarter.
2. Cf. Dieter Schumacher, 'Verstärkter Handel mit der Dritten Welt: Eher Umsetzung als Freisetzung deutscher Arbeitskräfte', *DIW Wochenbericht* 5 (1977); Dieter Schumacher, 'Beschäftigungswirkungen von Importen aus Entwicklungsländern nicht dramatisieren', *DIW Wochenbericht* 1 (1978). Based on certain assumptions DIW use a statistical model to compute the direct and indirect employment effects of increased imports from the developing countries on the basis of the 1972 DIW input–output table, assuming that these increased imports will be balanced by equally increasing exports from Federal Germany to the developing countries. Given this assumption (which is extremely questionable for the coming period!) it is shown that there is only a minor overall employment effect on the Federal German economy as a whole. By contrast, there will be a problem for the workers affected as the workers who lose their jobs do not possess the appropriate skills or qualifications for the newly created jobs. It is surprising that these studies would have us believe that these 'frictions' should not be 'dramatised' – surprising since a significant portion of the present high unemployment is to be attributed to these 'frictions' in the structure of skills and qualifications.

Table I-7

(a) Turnover derived from domestic production in Federal German textile and garment industry; Federal German domestic market for textiles and clothing (both at constant prices of 1970): 1960, 1965–75 (1000 million DM)

		1960	1965	1966	1967	1968	1969	1970	1971	1972	1973	1974	1975
Turnover from	T	18.41	22.13	22.12	21.24	23.92	25.79	26.65	28.49	27.62	25.31	24.03	23.43
domestic production	G	11.54	15.86	15.96	14.82	15.16	16.17	16.79	17.23	18.49	17.17	16.11	15.75
Domestically	T	19.53	24.24	24.06	22.15	25.51	27.74	28.30	30.57	30.15	27.07	25.42	25.99
available product	G	11.61	16.48	16.51	15.23	15.67	17.14	18.25	19.06	20.88	19.55	18.96	18.94

Source: see Table I-5

(b) Potential net volume of production at full capacity utilisation of Federal German manufacturing, textile and garment industries: 1960, 1965, 1970, 1975

	Million DM at constant prices of 1970				Index (1960 = 100)	Average annual percentage growth rates						
	1960	1965	1970	1975	1975	1960–65	1965–70	1971	1972	1973	1974	1975
Manufacturing industry	185251	254974	314748	372060	201	6.6	4.3	5.1	4.1	3.2	2.6	2.0
Textile industry	9848	12262	14132	14873	151	4.5	2.9	2.6	1.8	1.2	0.2	−0.6
Garment industry	6386	7700	7892	7117	111	3.8	0.5	−0.1	−1.1	−1.9	−3.1	−4.0

Source: Deutsches Institut für Wirtschaftsforschung, *DIW Wochenbericht* 18 (1976)
Data for 1975 provisional

For the textile industry we should note that its biggest customer, the domestic garment industry, has been restricted in the internal expansion of its production by increased import surpluses of clothing combined with only moderate expansion in the domestic consumption of clothing: the consequence has been a barely increased turnover in domestic production in the garment industry (see Table I-7(a)), which has indirectly restricted the textile trade.[1] As Table I-7(b) shows, the potential net total output at full capacity of the Federal German garment industry has contracted even more strongly since 1970 (only domestic plants): the same applies, with a slight time-lag, to the textile industry.[2] The domestic market for textiles has been indirectly curtailed in this way by factors operating on the world economy. On the other hand, the exports of the Federal German textile industry will gain to a far from negligible extent by the growing foreign output of the Federal German garment industry, or more generally, from the growing output of the garment industries of other countries.[3]

Secondly, we should note that the accelerated pace of rationalisation[4] in the Federal German textile industry is itself a means of remaining competitive on the world market. To this extent the figures for those employees made redundant from the Federal German textile (and garment) industry nominally because of increases in productivity also contain a share of workers who have in fact been made redundant because of factors originating on the world market.

However, the foregoing considerations should not be misunder-

1. The same applies one stage 'higher' in the relation between the textile and synthetic fibres industry. Cf. CIRFS, *The Future of the Man-Made Fibres Industry in Western Europe* (Paris 1976).
2. Cf. *VWD-Textil*, 18 September 1976: 'In July 1976 the German textile industry showed an increase in orders of 12% over the same month in 1975, with orders from abroad and home behaving very differently. As the Federation of the German Textile Industry announced on 18 September, domestic orders were up only by 5%, whereas foreign orders were up by 50%... Orders in the garment industry, the textile industry's biggest customer, were good over the first seven months of 1976 (up by 23%), although according to the figures, these orders did not lead to increased output. This fell by 1% over the first seven months. And since no corresponding orders arose in the textile industry the most obvious suggestion, according to the Textile Federation, is that "clothing orders were transferred to production facilities abroad".'
3. See subsequent notes on subcontracting.
4. Between 1970 and 1976 the average annual rate of growth of labour productivity (output per employee) in the Federal German textile industry was an above average 7.8% (cf. manufacturing industry as a whole, 4.2%; garment industry, 4.0%). Calculated from Statistisches Bundesamt, *Statistisches Jahrbuch für die Bundesrepublik Deutschland 1977* (Stuttgart–Mainz 1977), p. 178.

stood as having given an 'explanation' of that unemployment in the Federal German textile and garment industry which is directly or indirectly caused by factors operating on the world market (and which can hence be designated 'structural'). A meaningful explanation has to demonstrate why, to what extent, and for which commodities or subprocesses the production of textiles and clothing ceased to be profitable in Federal Germany under the conditions which prevailed on the world market for production sites after 1960.

4.2 Federal Germany's foreign trade in textiles and clothing broken down by national groupings (1962–76) and commodity groups (1968–76)

Table I-8 provides an overview of the long-term development of the shares of various groups of countries in the import and export of textiles in and out of the Federal Republic of Germany. From this data we can see that the EEC's (the 'Nine's') share of imports of textiles and clothing into Federal Germany clearly fell between 1962 and 1976, whereas the share coming from the developing and centrally planned economies increased over the same period, for textiles from 15% to 32% and for clothing from 24% to 65%. Clothing imports originated primarily in the Mediterranean countries and from South East and East Asia.

With the exception of the EEC countries, Federal Germany's most important trading partners in 1976 were (by value, in descending order with a lowest limit of DM 100 million):

Export of textiles: Austria, Switzerland, Yugoslavia, Sweden, Greece, Hungary, East Germany, Poland, USA, USSR, Iran, South Africa

Export of clothing: Switzerland, Austria, Greece

Import of textiles: Greece, Iran, East Germany, Switzerland, Hong Kong, Austria, Yugoslavia, Turkey, USA, South Korea, Taiwan, India, Brazil, Pakistan, Romania, Spain

Import of clothing: Hong Kong, Greece, Yugoslavia, South Korea, East Germany, Hungary, Taiwan, Poland, India, Austria, Turkey, Spain, Brazil, Romania

Particularly noteworthy are the high rates of growth of clothing imports into Federal Germany from Greece and South Korea, and also (with a relatively low absolute volume of imports)

Table I-8. *Percentage share of selected country groupings in Federal German textile and clothing exports and imports: 1962, 1965, 1970–76*

(a) Exports

	Textiles									Clothing								
	1962	1965	1970	1971	1972	1973	1974	1975	1976	1962	1965	1970	1971	1972	1973	1974	1975	1976
World	100	100	100	100	100	100	100	100	100	100	100	100	100	100	100	100	100	100
Industrial countries	86.4	85.8	81.3	80.2	77.8	76.9	73.7	74.9	76.2	92.5	90.7	84.9	84.0	82.7	82.5	82.0	81.3	82.0
EEC (the 'Nine')	45.0	50.3	53.6	53.4	53.4	52.5	51.4	53.8	54.2	43.6	53.5	57.0	59.7	58.1	56.6	56.1	57.5	58.0
EFTA[a]	31.7	26.4	17.7	16.4	16.5	15.7	15.6	16.3	17.3	38.0	31.3	22.8	20.4	21.2	22.5	22.4	21.3	21.4
Other[b]	9.7	9.1	10.1	10.4	7.9	8.7	6.7	4.8	4.7	10.9	5.9	5.1	3.9	3.4	3.4	3.5	2.6	2.6
Developing countries	11.4	10.3	8.7	7.4	7.8	9.7	10.5	10.0	10.9	6.7	5.2	7.7	9.7	10.5	10.6	11.8	12.1	13.2
Mediterranean[c]	3.7	3.8	3.5	3.5	3.7	5.3	5.5	5.3	5.9	2.2	2.7	5.5	7.5	9.0	9.2	10.1	10.6	11.5
Central and South America	1.6	1.4	0.9	0.8	1.0	0.9	1.2	0.6	0.6	1.4	0.6	0.8	0.7	0.4	0.4	0.3	0.2	0.1
Africa[d]	3.1	2.7	1.6	1.4	1.4	1.3	1.6	1.8	1.5	1.1	0.8	0.5	0.5	0.4	0.3	0.3	0.3	0.2
South West Asia[e]	1.8	1.3	0.9	0.6	0.8	1.4	1.3	1.5	2.2	1.4	0.8	0.7	0.8	0.6	0.6	0.8	0.9	1.1
South, South East and East Asia	1.2	1.2	1.7	1.1	0.8	0.8	0.8	0.7	0.7	0.6	0.3	0.2	0.2	0.2	0.3	0.3	0.2	0.3
Centrally planned economies	2.2	3.8	10.0	12.4	14.4	13.4	15.8	15.1	12.9	0.8	4.1	7.5	6.3	6.9	6.9	6.6	6.6	4.7
German Democratic Republic	1.5	1.3	2.6	2.5	3.5	1.9	1.7	1.8	1.6	0.6	2.1	1.6	1.1	2.1	2.3	2.3	2.2	1.0
Eastern Europe[f]	0.7	2.5	7.3	9.8	10.9	11.5	13.8	13.3	11.3	0.3	2.0	5.8	5.2	4.8	4.6	4.3	4.4	3.7
South East and East Asia	0.0	0.0	0.1	0.0	0.0	0.0	0.0	0.0	0.0	0.0	0.0	0.0	0.0	0.0	0.0	0.0	0.0	0.0

(b) Imports

	Textiles									Clothing								
	1962	1965	1970	1971	1972	1973	1974	1975	1976	1962	1965	1970	1971	1972	1973	1974	1975	1976
World	100	100	100	100	100	100	100	100	100	100	100	100	100	100	100	100	100	100
Industrial countries	84.7	82.3	78.6	76.8	75.6	74.0	73.4	71.8	67.6	75.9	70.2	60.3	56.5	52.8	48.4	42.4	39.1	35.7
EEC (the 'Nine')	68.0	68.2	69.2	68.4	67.4	65.6	64.0	62.6	57.7	47.6	49.0	48.4	47.4	45.7	42.0	37.1	33.9	29.5
EFTA[a]	11.1	8.6	5.1	4.7	4.6	4.6	5.0	5.4	6.4	17.0	11.9	5.9	4.8	3.6	3.2	3.0	2.9	3.5
Other[b]	5.6	5.5	4.2	3.7	3.7	3.7	4.4	3.8	3.5	11.3	9.3	5.9	4.4	3.4	3.1	2.3	2.3	2.7
Developing countries	11.8	13.2	14.4	15.2	15.6	17.3	17.8	19.7	23.2	16.2	17.2	20.5	21.3	24.9	30.1	36.2	39.6	44.5
Mediterranean[c]	1.4	2.0	3.4	3.9	4.6	5.4	6.2	6.4	8.1	3.2	4.1	6.2	6.7	8.0	9.7	11.8	12.6	13.5
Central and South America	1.6	1.2	0.5	0.6	1.0	1.3	1.7	1.9	2.1	0.2	0.3	0.8	1.0	1.4	2.0	2.1	2.8	3.1
Africa[d]	0.7	0.6	0.2	0.2	0.2	0.1	0.2	0.2	0.2	0.0	0.0	0.0	0.0	0.0	0.0	0.0	0.1	0.2
South West Asia[e]	4.0	4.1	4.4	5.2	5.0	5.2	3.3	3.6	3.5	0.0	0.0	0.1	0.1	0.1	0.1	0.0	0.0	0.0
South, South East and East Asia	4.1	5.3	5.8	5.4	4.9	5.4	6.4	7.5	9.3	12.8	12.8	13.4	13.6	15.5	18.3	22.3	24.2	27.7
Centrally planned economies	3.5	4.4	7.0	7.9	8.7	8.6	8.9	8.6	9.2	7.9	12.6	19.3	22.0	22.3	21.6	21.3	21.2	20.0
German Democratic Republic	2.3	2.6	2.9	3.2	2.9	2.8	3.2	3.2	3.3	3.9	7.2	6.3	6.3	5.2	4.1	4.5	4.9	4.3
Eastern Europe[f]	1.0	1.5	3.7	4.4	5.5	5.5	5.3	5.0	5.3	3.9	5.1	12.6	15.4	16.8	17.1	16.3	15.7	14.9
South East and East Asia	0.2	0.3	0.4	0.3	0.3	0.4	0.4	0.4	0.6	0.2	0.3	0.3	0.3	0.3	0.4	0.6	0.7	0.8

Sources: Statistisches Bundesamt, Fachserie G (Außenhandel), Reihe 7, Sonderbeiträge: *Außenhandel nach Ländern und Warengruppen und -zweigen des Warenverzeichnisses für die Industriestatistik* (Stuttgart–Mainz); Statistisches Bundesamt, Fachserie F (Groß- und Einzelhandel, Gastgewerbe, Reiseverkehr), Reihe 6: *Warenverkehr mit der Deutschen Demokratischen Republik und Berlin (Ost)* (Stuttgart–Mainz): own calculations

Commodity classification according to 'Warenverzeichnis für die Industriestatistik' (WI): WI 63 = textiles; WI 64 = clothing

a: Post 1973, excluding Portugal b: Australia, Canada, Israel, Japan, New Zealand, South Africa, USA c: Algeria, Andorra, Cyprus, Egypt, Gibraltar, Greece, Lebanon, Libya, Malta, Morocco, Portugal, Spain, Syria, Tunisia, Turkey, Vatican City d: Excluding Mediterranean countries and South Africa e: Excluding Israel f: Including Yugoslavia

Table I-9. *Federal German external trade in textiles and clothing by commodity groups: 1968–77 (international subcontracting indicated separately) (million DM/percentages)*

	Textile fibres (not manufactured)			Textile yarn and thread			Textile fabrics (woven, knitted or crocheted)			Clothing		
	Total	IS	Share IS (%)	Total	IS	Share IS (%)	Total	IS	Share IS (%)	Total	IS	Share IS (%)
Exports												
1968	841	10	1.2	1347	38	2.8	2242	188	8.4	1529	57	3.7
1969	927	6	0.6	1748	25	1.4	2700	164	6.1	1858	61	3.3
1970	836	2	0.2	2109	27	1.3	2882	193	6.7	1964	59	3.0
1971	822	2	0.3	2397	19	0.8	3433	329	9.6	2287	111	4.9
1972	945	2	0.2	2276	21	0.9	3639	409	11.2	2601	158	6.1
1973	1265	4	0.3	3087	26	0.8	4342	462	10.6	2949	193	6.5
1974	1399	5	0.4	3526	29	0.8	4998	611	12.2	3245	199	6.1
1975	1058	1	0.1	2725	27	1.0	4583	638	13.9	3387	193	5.7
1976	1298	3	0.3	3333	33	1.0	5511	658	11.9	4295	185	4.3
1977	n.a.	n.a.	n.a.	2963	n.a.	n.a.	5601	n.a.	n.a.	4789	n.a.	n.a.
Imports												
1968	1818	3	0.2	1392	31	2.2	2694	79	2.9	2319	256	11.0
1969	1924	0	0.0	1648	17	1.0	3075	41	1.3	3362	270	8.0
1970	1699	0	0.0	1613	14	0.9	3229	34	1.1	3897	332	8.5
1971	1685	0	0.0	1903	7	0.4	3845	32	0.8	4858	534	11.0
1972	1889	1	0.1	1889	7	0.4	4368	28	0.6	6162	792	12.9
1973	2145	0	0.0	2016	11	0.5	4609	33	0.7	6642	924	13.9
1974	2133	0	0.0	2019	9	0.4	4839	50	1.0	7652	1118	14.6
1975	1824	0	0.0	2037	6	0.3	5067	39	0.8	8622	1239	14.4
1976	2463	1	0.1	2420	7	0.3	5617	63	1.1	10156	1288	12.7
1977	n.a.	n.a.	n.a.	2535	n.a.	n.a.	6136	n.a.	n.a	10768	n.a.	n.a.

Sources: Statistisches Bundesamt, Fachserie G (Außenhandel), Reihe 1: *Zusammenfassende Übersichten* (Stuttgart–Mainz); own calculations

Excluding trade with the German Democratic Republic

IS (international subcontracting): Export *to* passive improvement, or import *after* passive improvement

Commodity classification according to 'Warengruppen und -untergruppen der Ernährungswirtschaft und der gewerblichen Wirtschaft': II A 1–6 = textile fibres (not manufactured); II B 1–6 = textile yarn and thread; II Ca 1–5 = textile fabrics (woven, knitted or crocheted); II Cb 1–9 = clothing

Table I-10. *Domestic production, domestically available product and foreign trade for selected sub-branches of Federal German textile and garment industry: 1976 (million DM/percentages)*

	Domestic production	Imports		Exports		DAP	Import ratio (%)	Export ratio (%)	Imports after IS as percentage of	
		Total	IS	Total	IS				Total imp.	Dom. prod.
Cotton yarn and thread	1343	633	0	116	1	1860	34.0	8.6	0.0	0.0
Yarn of wool	789	267	2	125	3	931	28.6	15.9	0.9	0.3
Yarn and thread of synthetic fibres	1273	337	2	1022	3	589	57.2	80.2	0.5	0.1
Textile fabrics, woven	3324	1569	17	1688	353	3205	49.0	50.8	1.1	0.5
Floor coverings on textile basis	2089	1724	2	524	3	3289	52.4	25.1	0.1	0.1
Knitted or crocheted fabrics	1017	395	21	854	133	558	70.8	84.0	5.2	2.0
Outer garments, knitted or crocheted	2388	2619	162	748	6	4259	61.5	31.3	6.2	6.8
Ladies' fashion hose	525	236	108	137	69	624	37.9	26.1	45.8	20.6
Men's outer garments, woven	3394	1497	262	607	14	4284	34.9	17.9	17.5	7.7
Women's outer garments, woven	6670	1823	366	966	9	7528	24.2	14.5	20.0	5.5
Men's shirts, woven	510	673	104	142	0	1040	64.7	27.8	15.5	20.5
Brassieres, corsets etc.	395	176	38	88	20	482	36.4	22.4	21.7	9.6
Bed linen	653	149		50		752	19.8	7.6	0.0	0.0

Sources: Statistisches Bundesamt, Fachserie 4 (Produzierendes Gewerbe), Reihe 3: *Produktion im Produzierenden Gewerbe 1976*; Statistisches Bundesamt, Fachserie 6 (Handel, Gastgewerbe, Reiseverkehr), Reihe 6: *Warenverkehr mit der Deutschen Demokratischen Republik und Berlin (Ost) 1976*; Statistisches Bundesamt, Fachserie G (Außenhandel), Reihe 2: *Spezialhandel nach Waren und Ländern, Dezember und Jahr 1976*; Statistisches Bundesamt, Systematische Verzeichnisse: *Gegenüberstellung des Warenverzeichnisses für die Industriestatistik (WI) mit dem Warenverzeichnis für die Außenhandelsstatistik (WA), Stand 1976*; own calculations

Note: Owing to the use of two not completely corresponding commodity classifications, some entries of the table may involve slight margins of error

International subcontracting: Exports *to* improvement or imports *after* improvement from Malta and Tunisia. The seven more important developing countries (including Yugoslavia) as sources of Federal German imports in 1975 accounted for 70% of the textile imports and almost 85% of the clothing imports from developing countries.[1]

Table I-9 gives a breakdown of Federal Germany's foreign trade in textiles and clothing by broad commodity groups between 1968 and 1977.

Table I-10 summarises the principal data on shares of domestic industrial production, foreign trade and domestically available product, import and export ratios and the share of subcontracting trade[2] for selected products and product groups for 1976. In view of the fact that the various sub-branches of the Federal German textile and garment industry exhibit quite markedly diverging import ratios, degrees of subcontracting etc. (as shown in the table), it is clear that any investigation into which types of production are more 'susceptible' to being relocated has to be undertaken and structured in an adequately detailed breakdown. It is insufficient to regard the textile and garment industry as an undifferentiated whole.

4.3 The structure of employment and of the decline in employment in the Federal German textile and garment industry: 1960–75

According to the evidence of the censuses of work-places carried out in 1961 and 1970, the number of work-places and the number of employed clearly fell between these two dates for almost all the sub-branches of the textile and garment industry in Federal Germany, and particularly drastically in the bespoke tailoring business. The figures rose in only a few instances, such as fur and hides processing and manufacturing, and in the mass production of women's clothing.[3] The fact that the decline of employment in

1. Calculation and order according to figures published by the Statistisches Bundesamt.
2. See Chapter 6.2 on subcontracting. Figures showing the share of Federal German domestic textile and garment industries' own imports in total textile and clothing *imports* (above and beyond subcontracting) are almost impossible to come by. Estimates from various sources vary between 15% for textiles and 60% for textiles and clothing. A spokesman for the trading concerns estimated that the 1977 share for textile and clothing imports into the Federal Republic accounted for by the industry itself would be around 50% in value terms (*Textil-Wirtschaft* 47 (1977)). According to estimates from the Haka-Verband (quoted in the *Süddeutsche Zeitung*, 3 March 1977), 10%–15% of all current Federal German *production* of men's clothing comes from subcontracting work abroad.
3. Statistisches Bundesamt, Fachserie C (Unternehmen und Arbeitsstätten), *Arbeitsstättenzählung vom 27. Mai 1970, Heft 3, Heft 9* (Stuttgart–Mainz 1972/73).

industry, craft and home-work (out-work) has accelerated since 1970 has already been adequately proven in Table I-6.

In 1975 the proportion of foreign workers in the total work-force was approximately 10% for the whole of the Federal German economy, 15% for manufacturing industry (excluding construction), 21% for textiles and 12% for garments.

In 1975 the proportion of female workers in the total work-force was 38% for the Federal German economy as a whole, 29% for manufacturing industry (excluding construction), 53% for textiles and 81% for garments.[1]

Given this (traditional) high proportion of cheap labour-power (foreign workers and women) it is not surprising that total wages and salaries per employee in the Federal German textile and garment industry only amounted to 77% and 63% respectively of the average figure for industry as a whole in 1975.[2]

Within the context of the growing relocation of production abroad by companies from the Federal German textile and garment industry, primarily but not exclusively to the low wage countries, which will be dealt with in more detail in Chapter 6, it is mainly those processes with relatively low skill requirements which are shifted. For this *specific* reason, and not an *unspecific* or general one, such as the tendency towards an increase in levels of skill falsely attributed to technical progress, it ought to have been expected that those sectors of the economy particularly affected by relocation, such as the Federal German garment industry, would exhibit a tendency towards an increase in the share of jobs with higher skill requirements.[3]

The available relevant statistical material for Federal Germany originates principally from the Wages and Salaries Surveys of 1951,

1. According to figures published by the Bundesanstalt für Arbeit.
2. Calculated from Statistisches Bundesamt, *Statistisches Jahrbuch 1976* (Stuttgart–Mainz 1976), pp. 236, 244. Compared with the industrial average the share of low-rated activities is especially high in the textile and garment industry: that means that the supply of potential labour-power for these activities is also especially high. This fact, together with the further reduced bargaining power of the union concerned in the face of threatened shifts in production, probably constitute the main reasons why wages and salaries per employee are far below the average in the textile and garment industry.
3. The connection between the development of technology and work organisation on the one hand, and the skill requirements placed on the work-force on the other, and their change over time, have been the subjects of numerous studies of national economies looked at in isolation. The nature of this connection has been fundamentally modified by the coming into being of a world market for labour-power and production sites. See the Introduction on 'Babbage's principle'.

1957, 1962, 1966 and 1972, and from ongoing earnings' surveys. These statistics do not supply information appertaining to the skills and qualifications of employees (understood as those acquired, taught, professionally obtained or otherwise learned abilities embodied in the person of the worker which can be set to work in the labour process); they are rather statistics which correspond to the skill requirements asked of the work-force. The grading of employees is based on their activity, and not on their skills. A fully trained craftsman might, for example, be occupying the post of an unskilled worker, and would then count for statistical purposes as an unskilled worker.

The most important propositions about the occupational structure as it is of concern in this context can be summarised as follows:[1]

In *productive industry* as a whole, a relative decline in the more highly rated activities can be discerned between 1960 and 1976, especially amongst male workers. In round figures the structure at the end of the period under consideration was (highest rated on the left) 45–35–20, with the structure for male employees as 60–30–10 and for female employees 5–45–50.

In the *textile industry* over the same period, there was a slight decline in the more highly rated activities. In round figures the occupational structure at the end of the period under consideration was 25–55–20, with the structure for male workers as 45–45–10 and for female employees 10–65–25.

In the *garment industry*, a slight polarisation can be observed. Both the highest and lowest groups gained in importance between 1960 and 1976 in comparison to the middle-rated occupations. By the end of the period under consideration, the structure was in round figures 20–65–15, with the structure for male employees as 55–30–15 and for female employees 15–70–15.

All the economic sectors studied exhibited a clear trend towards more highly-rated activities in the white-collar category. In addition, the proportion of white-collar workers grew in relation to total employment.[2]

Among the points which emerge from this are: Firstly, the share

1. The grading structure is as follows: grade 1 = skilled workers; grade 2 = semiskilled workers; grade 3 = unskilled workers. The occupational structure is defined by the percentage share of each of these three groups and set out in the form (G1–G2–G3).
2. Statistisches Bundesamt, *Statistik der Bundesrepublik Deutschland*, Bände 90, 91, 246; Statistisches Bundesamt, Fachserie M (Preise, Löhne, Wirtschaftsrechnungen), Reihe 15,

of skilled worker activities in the Federal German textile and garment industry is far below the average and the share of semiskilled far above the average when compared with industry as a whole – a result of the 'successful rationalisation' of the textile and garment industry. Secondly, unskilled and semiskilled jobs are overproportionally occupied by women.[1] We can only draw attention to those facts here, but not deal with them in any detail.

Using the material as presented, the fall in employment in the Federal German garment industry 1973–75 can be broken down according to the occupational status and wage grade of its employees. The number of unskilled employees contracted the most (by around 24%), whereas the number of proprietors and white-collar workers fell the least (by 14%).[2] An alternative breakdown reveals that the relative fall in the number of proprietors, white-collar workers and skilled workers was, at 18%, less pronounced than the relative fall in unskilled and semiskilled workers (21%). Complementary to this is the fact that semiskilled and unskilled activities clearly predominate in the foreign plants of the Federal German garment industry, far more than for corresponding activities in domestically located plants.[3]

The increase in the proportion of proprietors, white-collar workers and skilled workers, which can also be observed in other branches of Federal German industry for reasons which cannot be gone into here, may well, therefore, be caused by the relocation of production abroad, or contributed to by this process.[4] What appears

Arbeitnehmerverdienste in Industrie und Handel: I. Arbeiterverdienste, II. Angestelltenverdienste, various years; Statistisches Bundesamt, Fachserie M (Preise, Löhne, Wirtschaftsrechungen), Reihe 17, *Gehalts- und Lohnstrukturerhebungen: I. Gewerbliche Wirtschaft und Dienstleistungsbereich: Arbeiterverdienste, II. Gewerbliche Wirtschaft und Dienstleistungsbereich: Angestelltenverdienste,* various years; Statistisches Bundesamt, *Wirtschaft und Statistik* 7 (1953), 6 (1959), 7 (1959), 5 (1965), 3 (1969), 6 (1969), 11 (1975).

1. The same applies for foreign workers. In April 1972 the occupational structure for foreign workers in the Federal German textile industry was: male workers, 14–56–30; female workers, 5–65–30. For the garment industry: female workers, 13–63–24. See Bundesanstalt für Arbeit, *Beschäftigung ausländischer Arbeitnehmer – Repräsentativuntersuchung '72* (Nuremberg 1974), pp. 81 f.
2. In view of the absolute fall in employment which has also taken place amongst the skilled trades in the textile and garment industry, it is not surprising that the proportion of apprentices receiving training in the textile and clothing trades should have fallen in relation to total employment, from 3.0% in 1969 to 2.4% in 1975 (calculated from Bundesministerium für Bildung und Wissenschaft/Statistisches Bundesamt, *Berufliche Aus- und Fortbildung,* various years).
3. See Chapter 6.
4. Cf. *Textil-Wirtschaft* 38 (1975), p. 20. 'Between 1972 and 1975 the proportion of white-collar workers in total employment in the Federal German textile and garment industry increased from 18.9% to 21.9%. This was not merely an expression of increased automation (more

to be a tendency towards an increase in the level of occupational skill in those jobs which remain in Federal Germany (skill as defined by the Federal Statistical Office) should not make us forget of course that in recent years there has been a drastic fall in the numbers employed in all categories in the Federal German garment industry.

It is not possible in this study to go into the relevance of these individual, branch-specific findings for other sectors of the Federal German economy. Nevertheless, it should have become clear that the development of the aggregate volume of employment and the occupational structure of the Federal German economy, and how and to what extent these variables change, are determined by the fact that this economy is merely one element in a capitalist world economy, and can only be isolated from this economy at the risk of abandoning any explanatory power.

supervisors), but also of the fact that although the relocation of production means that actual processing and finishing is carried out abroad, planning, distribution and similar functions continue to be carried out in the Federal Republic, by white-collar employees.'

5 ❧ The export-oriented industrialisation of the developing and centrally planned economies in the field of textiles and clothing

5.1 Development of textile and clothing exports and production and employment in the textile and garment industries of selected countries: 1960–75

In Chapter 4.2 we showed that in recent years the import of textiles and clothing into Federal Germany from countries outside the EEC has come predominantly, and to an increasing extent, from developing countries in the Mediterranean region, South East Asia and East Asia, and the East European centrally planned economies. A number of countries have been selected on account of their close trade links with Federal Germany as examples of each group: they are Hungary, Yugoslavia, Greece, Malta, Hong Kong and South Korea.[1] The aim of the study is to investigate whether and in what sense one can speak of a process of export-oriented industrialisation generated *inter alia* by the development of the textile and garment industry in these countries over the period under consideration.

Table I-11 shows the export figures of these countries for textiles and clothing for the period 1968–76. Table I-12 relates these export figures to the total exports for the respective countries and with world exports of textiles and clothing. One fact which these tables reveal is that in 1976 between one-third and one-half of the total exports of South Korea, Hong Kong and Malta were in textiles and clothing, with clothing taking the greater share: the corresponding figures for Hungary, Yugoslavia and Greece were between 7.5% and 17.3%. (In comparison, the figures for Federal Germany, Japan and the USA range from 2.2% to 5.5%.) Hong Kong and South Korea stand out

1. Whereas the remaining countries have been chosen because of their quantitative importance in foreign trade in textiles and clothing, Malta was included because of its high rates of growth which are related to the settlement of relocated Federal German textile and garment establishments.

Table I-11. *Textile (T) and clothing (G) exports of selected countries, Federal German textile and clothing imports from these countries: 1968–76 (million US $)*

		Total exports								Federal German imports[a]						
		1968	1970	1971	1972	1973	1974	1975	1976	1970	1971	1972	1973	1974	1975	1976
Hungary[b]	T	84.0	85.0	91.1	119.7	147.4	169.9	193.0	200[c]	2.7	3.3	6.0	8.8	10.0	10.4	11.7
	G	92.2	99.6	118.3	152.7	204.9	226.7	270.7	270[c]	8.6	19.3	38.1	58.1	76.0	85.6	104.7
Yugoslavia[d]	T	55.8	79.6	80.6	103.7	138.2	151.9	177.9	227.5	15.1	16.2	21.4	24.3	14.1	7.5	19.8
	G	70.4	85.0	99.4	135.8	145.2	149.3	203.7	234.5	59.8	93.5	152.6	213.2	251.3	284.1	274.8
Greece[e]	T	15.4	36.9	47.4	78.7	132.5	185.0	173.7	241.9	17.9	27.7	45.8	70.4	81.6	79.8	97.9
	G	5.9	9.9	11.4	21.4	53.6	88.3	123.9	199.6	18.8	27.0	50.9	96.1	152.0	232.1	307.4
Malta	T	4.8	4.6	4.6	7.1	10.6	11.7	9.4	11.3	0.5	0.6	1.0	1.0	1.1	0.3	0.7
	G	5.5	8.9	13.5	20.8	35.8	50.0	72.3	95.3	1.1	2.1	5.0	5.1	7.1	21.5	38.5
Hong Kong	T	171.2	275.0	308.0	383.7	667.4	721.7	592.7	822.6	3.9	4.5	8.3	10.1	7.3	9.4	11.3
	G	483.5	698.9	895.3	1078.7	1423.6	1688.9	2032.9	2906.5	117.1	150.4	218.3	306.0	387.3	487.7	608.6
South Korea	T	61.2	84.9	137.8	176.6	435.2	492.6	648.9	954.5	2.1	5.0	5.5	8.6	16.7	21.9	27.4
	G	112.2	213.6	304.3	442.2	749.9	957.0	1148.2	1845.5	6.1	8.8	19.4	46.4	100.7	162.1	194.8

Sources: UN, *Yearbook of International Trade Statistics* (New York); OECD, *Statistics of Foreign Trade, Series B: Trade by Commodities, Country Summaries* (Paris); Statistisches Bundesamt, Fachserie G (Außenhandel), Reihe 5, *Special Trade according to the Classification for Statistics and Tariffs (CST)* (Stuttgart–Mainz); GATT, *International Trade 1976/77* (Geneva 1977)

Commodity classification according to SITC, Rev. 1

(a) Trade with the German Democratic Republic is excluded from the import figures. Imports after improvement and repair (international subcontracting) are included at full transaction values

b: Improvement and repair trade (international subcontracting) is included at value-added only in the Hungarian export figures

c: Data for 1976 provisional

d: Active and passive improvement and repair trade (international subcontracting) is excluded from the Yugoslavian export figures

e: Exports from the free areas of Piraeus and Salonika and passive improvement and repair trade (international subcontracting) are excluded from the Greek export figures

Table I-12. *Textile and clothing exports of selected countries as percentage of total exports of the countries, and as percentage of world textile and clothing exports: 1968–76*

		Share of national textile/clothing exports in total national exports								Share of national textile/clothing exports in world exports of textiles/clothing						
		1968	1970	1971	1972	1973	1974	1975	1976	1970	1971	1972	1973	1974	1975	1976
Hungary[a]	T	4.7	3.7	3.6	3.6	3.3	3.3	3.2	3.2	0.7	0.6	0.7	0.6	0.6	0.7	0.7
	G	5.2	4.3	4.7	4.6	4.6	4.4	4.4	4.3	1.6	1.6	1.6	1.6	1.5	1.6	1.4
Yugoslavia[b]	T	4.4	4.8	4.4	4.6	4.6	4.0	4.4	4.6	0.6	0.6	0.6	0.6	0.6	0.7	0.8
	G	5.6	5.1	5.4	6.1	4.8	3.9	5.0	4.8	1.4	1.3	1.4	1.1	1.1	1.2	1.2
Greece[c]	T	3.3	5.7	7.2	9.0	9.1	9.1	7.6	9.5	0.3	0.3	0.5	0.6	0.7	0.7	0.8
	G	1.3	1.5	1.7	2.5	3.7	4.4	5.4	7.8	0.2	0.2	0.2	0.4	0.6	0.7	1.0
Malta	T	19.4	15.6	12.6	12.6	12.4	10.6	7.1	6.0	0.0	0.0	0.0	0.0	0.0	0.0	0.0
	G	22.6	30.4	37.2	36.9	41.7	45.3	55.0	50.7	0.1	0.2	0.2	0.3	0.3	0.4	0.5
Hong Kong	T	12.3	10.9	10.7	11.0	13.2	12.2	9.8	9.7	2.2	2.2	2.3	2.9	2.6	2.2	2.8
	G	34.8	27.8	31.2	31.0	28.2	28.6	33.8	34.1	11.2	11.9	11.1	11.3	11.3	12.2	14.8
South Korea	T	13.4	10.2	12.9	10.9	13.5	11.0	12.8	12.4	0.7	1.0	1.0	1.9	1.8	2.4	3.2
	G	24.6	25.6	28.5	27.2	23.3	21.5	22.6	23.9	3.4	4.0	4.6	5.9	6.4	6.9	9.4
Federal	T	4.0	4.4	4.7	4.4	4.5	4.1	3.6	3.8	12.0	12.8	11.8	13.2	13.1	12.3	12.9
Germany	G	1.3	1.3	1.4	1.4	1.3	1.1	1.3	1.4	6.7	7.0	6.8	7.2	6.5	6.8	7.3
Japan	T	11.1	9.0	8.6	7.6	6.6	5.5	5.2	4.9	14.1	14.4	12.8	10.6	11.1	11.0	11.1
	G	3.0	2.4	1.9	1.5	1.0	0.6	0.6	0.6	7.4	6.2	4.4	2.9	2.2	2.0	2.1
United	T	1.5	1.4	1.5	1.6	1.7	1.8	1.5	1.7	4.9	4.5	4.6	5.4	6.6	6.2	6.6
States	G	0.6	0.5	0.5	0.5	0.4	0.4	0.4	0.5	3.6	2.9	2.6	2.3	2.8	2.6	2.9

Sources: see table I-11; own calculations

a: Improvement and repair trade (international subcontracting) is included at value-added only in the Hungarian export figures

b: Active and passive improvement and repair trade (international subcontracting) is excluded from the Yugoslavian export figures

c: Exports from the free areas of Piracus and Salonika, and passive improvement and repair trade (international subcontracting) is excluded from the Greek export figures with their relatively high share of total world exports of clothing (1976: 14.8% and 9.4% respectively). Greece, Malta and South Korea are characterised by their especially high rates of growth of textiles and especially clothing exports. (It should be noted that the export figures for Yugoslavia and Hungary do not include, or in the case of Hungary only partially include, the quantitatively significant subcontracting trade. If this trade were to be included then these countries do not turn out to be substantially different, as far as their growth rates are concerned for textile and clothing exports, from the other countries selected.)

Federal Germany's imports from these countries are overwhelmingly concentrated in finished products (clothing, including knitted goods): the only country which supplies a significant amount of yarn and fabrics in addition is Greece. In contrast, Federal Germany mainly exports textile raw materials (synthetic fibres), semifinished goods (threads and yarn) and pre-products for finished goods (woven and knitted fabrics).

Table I-13 provides a picture of the development of industrial production and employment in the textile and garment industries of the selected countries. Apart from a few small exceptions (chiefly Hungary), the *rates of growth* of each of the variables in the selected countries are either above, or far above, the world average. The *proportion* of total value-added of manufacturing industry accounted for by the textile and garment industries of these countries ranged, in 1970, from around 10% (Hungary) to more than 45% (Hong Kong), and was therefore usually far above the corresponding figure for the traditional industrial countries. The same applies for the share of industrial employment accounted for by the textile and garment industries, which stood at just short of 15% in Hungary and at least 45% in Hong Kong.

In addition, industrial employment in the garment industries of the selected countries and in the textile industry in Greece grew faster than total employment in manufacturing industry in these countries. The share of clothing exports in the total exports of these countries is far higher than the share taken by the garment industry of total value-added in industry. The same cannot be said, however, of the textile industry, which is an indication of the fact that these countries' textile industries function primarily as suppliers to their respective (export-oriented) garment industries.

The facts established above justify the assertion that the indust-

Table I-13. *Weight of textile and garment industry in manufacturing industry of selected countries: 1970;* and *average annual growth rates of production and employment of manufacturing, textile and garment industries of selected countries: 1967–75 (both in percentages)*

	Weight 1970 (manufacturing (ISIC 3) = 100)				Average annual growth rates 1967–75					
	Production		Employment		Production			Employment		
	321	322	321	322	3	321	322	3	321	322
Hungary	6.9	2.8	9.4	5.4	6.0	0.2	2.5[a]	0.8[b]	−1.3[b]	1.3[b]
Yugoslavia	9.6	2.8	14.1	3.9	8.6	5.9	7.8[a]	3.7	2.7	9.1
Greece	14.5	2.2	17.8	4.2	8.9	10.9	10.6[a]	3.2	7.1[c]	13.0[c]
Malta	15.0	5.5	14.9	8.5	9.8[a]	10.8[a]	31.7[a]	8.3[d]	20.1[d]	
Hong Kong	27.3[e]	20.0[e]	20.5[e]	25.8[e]	n.a.	n.a.	n.a.	3.9	0.8	10.4
South Korea	13.9	2.8	24.2	6.1	22.8	25.0	36.4[a, f]	12.1	8.5[g]	23.5[g]
Federal Germany	4.2	3.9[h]	6.1	4.6	3.9	2.9	0.8[a]	−0.2	−3.9	−3.1
Japan	6.4	1.2	11.5	3.1	6.8	2.2	2.9[a]	0.9	−4.4	3.5
United States	3.8	3.3	6.1	6.4	1.9	1.1	0.8[a]	−0.7	−1.0	−1.9
World[i]	5.1	4.4[h]	12.8	9.4[h]	5.3	3.7	3.4[a, h]	2.4[a]	1.5[a]	3.3[a, h]

Source: UN, *Yearbook of Industrial Statistics, 1975* (New York 1977); UN, *Statistical Yearbook 1976* (New York 1977); ILO, *Year Book of Labour Statistics 1976* (Geneva 1976); Statistisches Bundesamt, *Lange Reihen zur Wirtschaftsentwicklung 1976* (Stuttgart–Mainz 1976); own calculations
a: 1967–74 b: 1968–75 c: 1970–73 d: 1967–73 e: 1973 f: ISIC 322, 324 g: 1970–74 h: ISIC 322–24 i: Excluding Albania, China, Mongolia, North Korea and North Vietnam
Weight and rates of growth of production calculated on the basis of the value-added at constant prices

rialisation of these countries is an *export-oriented* industrialisation, inasmuch as the textile and garment industry has been of particular significance within it. This means that by international standards of comparison industrial production is either directly (garment industry) or indirectly (textile industry) directed to an above average extent, and an increasing extent, towards exports, and to a less than average extent towards the internal market.[1]

One other form of export-oriented industrialisation should be distinguished from that presented above: it manifests itself as initial steps towards the same basic phenomenon, but does not necessarily

1. This also applies to the economies as a whole of these countries. The share of exports of goods and services in the total gross domestic products of the countries selected has in almost all cases noticeably increased over the period 1960–75 (particularly drastically in the case of South Korea), actually gained further in the first half of the 1970s, and was disproportionally high by international standards. Only Federal Germany of the larger industrial and socialist countries has a comparably high share of GDP going to exports. Cf. UN, *Yearbook of National Accounts Statistics 1975, Volume III: International Tables* (New York 1976).

have to express itself in disproportionally high growth rates for industrial production and employment in the textile and garment industries, or a disproportionally high share of total value-added in industry taken by these industries in the countries concerned. An example of such a new form of export-oriented industrialisation in the textile and garment field are the new world market factories in countries where industrial production and employment in such establishments are not (yet) of great quantitative significance in comparison to other branches of the economy and their employment. One particular example would be the world market textile and garment factories in Egypt's free production zones (see Part III).

5.2 Export-oriented industrialisation in the textile and garment industry: prelude to a complex industrialisation of the developing countries?

Can the export-oriented industrialisation of developing countries, as can be observed in many instances at the present time, lead to the development of a complex industrial structure in those countries? A number of indications suggest that this question has to be answered in the negative.

One of these indications is the fact of the growing dependency of a large number of developing countries on the import of capital-goods from the traditional industrial countries. The import of textile machinery is of particular interest in the present context. Since Federal Germany is by far the most important exporter of textile machinery,[1] it is sufficient here to take Federal Germany's trade in this area as an example. In 1975 half of Federal German exports of textile machinery (in value terms) went to the developing and centrally planned economies (with a clear tendency for this share to rise). The following countries imported more than US $ 25 million worth of textile machinery from Federal Germany in 1975: Spain (US $ 45 million), Yugoslavia (59), Greece (40), Turkey (64), East Germany (*circa* 36), USSR (36), Poland (34), Bulgaria (31), Mexico (28), Brazil (77), Iran (91).[2]

1. In 1974 Federal Germany's share of world exports of textile machinery (SITC 717) stood at 31.5% for free market economies. See UN, *Yearbook of International Trade Statistics 1975* (New York 1976).
2. See Statistisches Bundesamt, Fachserie G (Außenhandel), Reihe 5, *Special Trade according to the Classification for Statistics and Tariffs* (*CST*), *4th Quarter and Year 1975* (Stuttgart–Mainz 1976).

Set against Federal Germany's 1975 trade deficit of US $ 2900 million for textiles and clothing was a trade surplus of US $ 1500 million for textile machinery alone in the same year. The corresponding figures for Federal Germany's foreign trade with the developing countries are US $ 1500 million and US $ 700 million respectively.[1]

A further factor is the large, and in all probability growing, significance of international subcontracting, where the production of a good is split up into numerous suboperations which are undertaken in different countries with the aim of securing the lowest production cost for the final product. For example, fabrics are manufactured and cut in Federal Germany, then sent for further work to be done on them (such as sewing) to a low wage country, before finally being re-imported into Federal Germany for eventual sale. (See Chapter 6.) It is clear that the increasing significance of such separated processes makes it all the more difficult for a country to achieve complex industrialisation as the country concerned merely functions as an extended work-bench, which, depending on the fluctuating possibilities for capital valorisation offered by one individual low wage country in competition with other similar countries, may or *may not* be used.[2]

However, we cannot necessarily deduce from these and other similar factors that there is no likelihood of a gradual future broadening and deepening of the industrial bases of individual low wage countries should this process of the increasing atomisation of industrial manufacture also open up new possibilities for valorisation through diversification, which, in accordance with the logic of the valorisation of capital, would *have* to be exploited. There already seem to be some initial steps towards a complex industrialisation of

1. It is useful to have such figures in mind when spokesmen for the Federal German textile and garment industry insist on an approximate equilibrium in the balance of trade between Federal Germany and individual East European countries in textiles and clothing. When one considers the high export surpluses of Federal Germany (for example in textile machinery), and the fact that around two-thirds of the foreign trade of Federal Germany in woven and knitted fabrics and clothing with East European countries (excluding the GDR and including Yugoslavia) is via subcontracting arranged and transacted directly from Germany, such demands are quite astonishing.
2. One can compare here the buffer role played by rural out-workers in the history of capitalism (for example, the English hand-loom weavers in the first half of the nineteenth century). In the present case study we cannot go into the much discussed question as to whether multinational firms deliberately thwart the development of a complex process of industrialisation in the developing countries in order to prevent these countries from removing themselves from the capitalist world system.

individual low wage countries of this kind in the sphere of the textile and garment industry. Two examples are briefly discussed below.

The developing countries' share of the world production of synthetic fibres, one of the most important basic materials for the textile and garment industry, rose from 7.9% in 1970 to 13.8% in 1975.[1] In addition, the list of projects initiated by engineering firms involved in the construction of synthetic fibre plant reveals the enormous extent to which new production facilities for synthetic fibres are to be set up in the developing and centrally planned economies in the next few years, rather than in the traditional industrial countries.[2] It is evidently profitable to produce synthetic fibres at the newly developed sites for the production of textiles and clothing, rather than ship them half-way around the world from the traditional industrial centres to sites for export-oriented production.

This tendency of supplier industries, either in the short or long term, to follow the production which was originally relocated to the new sites (e.g. on grounds of wage or transport costs) is not confined to a few individual examples (see Part II). The textile and garment industry is notable for the number of instances in which Federal German textile companies have started up production in countries where the manufacture of clothing for the world market already plays an important role, or now may be beginning to do so.[3]

We should also mention in this context the large number of 'integrated' textile plants which have recently been commissioned or are planned in a large number of countries, in particular in Africa. Such plants, some under Federal German participation, are partially conceived initially for the internal market, and also partly from the outset for the world market.[4]

1. Cf. *Textil-Wirtschaft* 18 (1976), p. 19.
2. Cf. the survey 'Projekte der Ingenieurfirmen im Chemiefaser-Anlagenbau', *chemiefasern-textil-industrie* 6 (1975), pp. 482, 484.

   'In 1971 capacity for 680000 tonnes of synthetics per year was installed in West Germany. By the end of 1976 this had increased by 260000 – to 940000. In South Korea and Taiwan the increase in capacity for the same period was from 140000 to 790000 – up by 650000 tonnes.' *Textil-Wirtschaft* 6 (1977), p. 21.

   The Synthetic Fibres' Confederation stated that in Europe in the latter part of the 1970s the supply of synthetic fibres would be greater than the demand and that an adjustment of European capacity to the possibilities of finding outlets was imperative: see *Süddeutsche Zeitung*, 24 May 1976. According to the Confederation's figures the import surplus of semi-, and finished products from non-European countries resulted in an annual sales' loss of around 120000 tonnes for Federal German synthetic fibre manufacturers: see *Textil-Wirtschaft* 19 (1976).
3. See the reports on the Delden and Nino companies in Chapter 6.4.
4. Two examples. 'The firm of Cotonnière Ivoirienne (COTIVO) and the Société des Impressions sur Tissus (ICODI) have established an integrated textile project which

Nevertheless, such indicators are not really sufficient to allow the firm conclusion that an economically complex process of industrialisation is beginning to emerge in a large number of developing countries.

Firstly, in most cases industrial expansion is merely focussed on one branch, which does not in itself mean that the complex industrialisation of the entire economy has begun. The equipping of the industry with textile machinery keeps and leaves the developing countries dependent on imports from the traditional industrial countries (or possibly in the future on imports from world market factories in particular developing countries which are under the control of companies from the traditional industrial countries). The traditional dependency of the developing countries, the outcome of centuries of uneven development within the world capitalist system, is not merely confined to the furnishing of the developing countries with capital-goods from the traditional industrial countries. It implies much more: the almost total dependency of the developing countries' economies as regards technology, work organisation, product structure, management, marketing and finance on decisions taken in the head offices of companies from the traditional industrial countries, even given the imaginary supposition of a relatively technically complex industrial structure in individual developing countries. Secondly, and this is the more general and decisive argument, the general tendency of the present-day capitalist world economy, namely that of splitting industrial production into subprocesses which are then allocated on a global basis according to the dictates of optimal profitability to the most suitable sites for the purpose, contradicts the development of underdeveloped economies towards a complex industrialisation which might release these countries from their dependency on the industrial structure of the rest of the world at certain key points in their industrial structure: in fact this contradiction is all the more pronounced when one

extends from processing local cotton to the part-finishing of the manufactured material into jeans and working clothes. 70% of the end product of COTIVO's production is to be exported. Around 1400 jobs will be created once full production has been reached. Former imports of raw materials will be replaced by local production.' DEG, *Geschäftsbericht 1974*, pp. 24 ff.

The enterprise Industrie Dahoméenne des Textiles (IDATEX), in which the Federal German Arbatex company has a stake, is setting up an industrial complex ranging from weaving to making-up. 94% of output will be exported, chiefly to Federal Germany (e.g. industrial clothing, towelling material, underwear). 2340 workers will be employed (700 according to another source). See *L'industrie africaine en 1975*, special issue of *L'Afrique noire*, p. 11 of the section on Dahomey.

considers that this general tendency is even leading to the partial de-industrialisation and growing world-wide economic dependency of the traditional industrial countries with their, in comparison, still relatively complex industrial structure.[1]

5.3 Advanced export-oriented industrialisation under the conditions of *laissez-faire* capitalism: Hong Kong

From its very inception, the export-oriented industrialisation of Hong Kong has developed under the conditions of unrestricted free trade and an explicit policy of *laissez-faire*. As history shows, such a system has a particularly blatant tendency to regard the worker merely as an appendage of the machine, as a mere factor of production whose existence is only acknowledged as a necessary requirement for the making of profits.

Investors in Hong Kong expect to recoup two or three times the value of their investment within five years. The big commercial banks in Hong Kong, who finance the bulk of these investments, want their loans repaid within this time. Manufacturing processes which are easy to get into operation are quite simply abandoned if better possibilities for profit arise elsewhere at a later date. Hong Kong is utterly permeated by the mentality of the 'fast buck'. Or, as Hong Kong's Chinese business community prefers to express it with a little more grace: 'pluck the flower while it blooms'.[2]

The export-oriented production of clothing (including knitwear) has been the main pillar of the economy of Hong Kong for two decades. Its position is currently threatened from two main areas: firstly, the import restrictions imposed by the traditional industrial countries; secondly, countries such as Taiwan, South Korea, the Philippines, Malaysia, Singapore and others, whose labour is between two and four times cheaper.[3]

Reaction to the first threat has taken the form of industrial diversification into such products as electronics, toys, watches, leather goods, office machinery, household goods. Attempts have been made to open up new markets for clothing outside the

1. See Parts II and III below for a discussion of the question of the complex industrialisation of developing countries in the process of the new international division of labour.
2. Joe England & John Rear, *Chinese Labour under British Rule. A Critical Study of Labour Relations and Law in Hong Kong* (Hong Kong 1975), pp. 34, 60.
3. *Textil-Wirtschaft* 38 (1976), p. 18 'Hong Kong – Letzter Freihandelsplatz der Welt', interview with T. K. Ann and Len Dunning, President and General-Director of the Hong Kong Trade Development Council.

traditional industrial countries. But the main policy has been to opt for higher quality (at higher prices) in order to retain the ability to expand in traditional markets for clothing which are only protected by volume-based orderly marketing agreements.[1]

In fact the restrictions imposed on Hong Kong under Article 4 of the Multi-Fibre Arrangement have led to problems in the apportionment and supervision of the quotas. Listed manufacturing companies are allocated quotas which are determined by the firm's exports over the preceding reference period. Incomplete use of the quota results in a reduced new allocation.[2] New applicants for quotas, who initially are given quotas below that requested, can buy quotas from firms who do not use up their own full allocation.[3] The 'going rate' on this quota market is even reported in the relevant business press in Europe.[4] Some modifications have now been undertaken to the system for the distribution of quotas in order to eliminate the 'quota farmers', 'quota parasites' and 'quota vampires' who have by and large confined themselves to trading in quota allocations, without seriously seeking to produce for export.[5]

Hong Kong has done fairly well out of the orderly marketing agreements in comparison to its competitors as these agreements have fixed the level of exports at that previously attained, which in the case of Hong Kong is a relatively high level, with a low annual growth rate in volume terms of 6%.

The import restrictions imposed by the traditional industrial countries have consequently not yet seriously affected Hong Kong's clothing exports. The question remains as to why the manufacture of clothing has been able to continue in the face of competition from countries which offer substantially cheaper labour on the world market. In other words: what is the basis for the confidence that 'textiles will continue to play a dominant role because Hong Kong can make garments more competitively than any other place in the world'?[6]

1. *Textil-Wirtschaft* 38 (1976), p. 18.
2. Commerce and Industry Department, Hong Kong, *Textiles Export Control System*, 5 November 1975.
3. Cf. *Textil-Wirtschaft* 12 (1976), p. 24; *Nachrichten für Außenhandel* (BfA/NfA), 30 April 1976; *Financial Times*, 17 May 1976; *Far Eastern Economic Review*, 24 September 1976, p. 60.
4. Cf. 'Quotenpreise drücken Jeansproduktion', *Textil-Wirtschaft* 29 (1976), p. 20; 'Die Quotas für Strickwaren werden mit etwa 45 Hongkong-Dollar per Dutzend gehandelt gegenüber 55 Dollar vor einigenWochen', *Textil-Wirtschaft* 33 (1976), p. 18.
5. See *Textil-Wirtschaft* 42 (1976), p. 28; *Der Spiegel* 44 (1976), pp. 177–9.
6. *Asia Research Bulletin*, 31 May 1976, p. 204. Quote from Len Dunning.

One possible answer to this question might be that the productivity of labour in factories in Hong Kong is comparatively high.

> Industrialists complain that Hong Kong's transformation into an industrial city state from an entrepot is threatened by cheaper manufactures from Singapore, South Korea and Taiwan. In their moments of truth though, these industrialists confess that they can survive, since labour in Hong Kong has greater productivity than that of less costly workers elsewhere.
>
> An Indian businessman says he gets 3000 shirts a day from his 40 machines in Hong Kong: with the same number of machines his Bombay factory produces only 1000 a day. Another manufacturer claims that his Singapore plant is barely half as productive as his Hong Kong operation although its machines are more modern and its running more rationalised.[1]

The oft-expressed assertion that in production for the world market the 'advantage' of lower wages is negated by the disadvantage of corresponding low productivity is quite clearly false. We can see (cf. Chapters 7.2 and 16.3) that productivity in manufacturing establishments oriented towards the world market in the low wage countries is certainly comparable with that of equivalent processes in the traditional industrial countries. Within this overall framework there is, of course, always plenty of room for specific differences in productivity, and in particular for variations in the low wages paid. Admittedly, the wage differences between the garment industry in Hong Kong, on the one hand, and a country such as South Korea, on the other, are too large and the productivity differences between garment manufacturing establishments in each country too small to explain why the garment industry in Hong Kong has, up to now, been able to fend off competition from countries such as South Korea with a considerable measure of success.

It is clear therefore that it is Hong Kong's comparatively large quota, based on orderly marketing agreements, and the relatively small quotas of its competitors which guarantee the continuing 'competitiveness' of the production of clothing in Hong Kong.

Of course, this has no direct bearing on the comparatively high productivity of labour in the garment industry in Hong Kong. If one refuses to be satisfied by such ideologically laden statements as 'the Hong Kong worker is dexterous, painstaking and flexible', then one is still confronted by the question as to the real conditions which determine the comparatively high level of productivity in Hong Kong, and similar countries. To assist in answering this question the following provides data on working hours, economic activity and age

1. *The Times*, 8 May 1973.

structure of the working population, child labour, general working conditions and the role of trade unions in Hong Kong.

According to the official *Hong Kong Population and Housing Census 1971* of the persons aged ten years or over who had worked at least 15 hours in productive employment in the week preceding the census, more than half had worked more than 54 hours per week. In manufacturing industry the average working week stood at 56.1 hours per week. Of the total work-force, 23% worked between 55 and 64 hours, 13.5% between 65 and 67 hours, 7.7% from 75 to 84 hours and 3.3% for 85 or more hours per week.[1] Expressed in absolute figures, 174439 workers worked for at least 75 hours per week, and 13792 for at least 105 hours per week.[2]

The great majority of activities (80%) are categorised as 'unskilled' or 'semiskilled'. The opportunities for promotion are very restricted. Workers start off in the work-room and stay there. In 1971 one-third of all full-time employees were under twenty-five years old. Their physical capacity to work is consequently very high.[3]

According to official statistics, in 1971, 35925 children aged between ten and fourteen were 'economically active'. Of these, 24545 (18411 of them girls) were in full-time employment. In all, 12449 of these children worked in the textile and garment industry (the majority of them girls). All these figures are for legal child labour: the illegal employment of children may well be much more widespread. The penalties imposed upon employers who are discovered illegally employing children are extraordinarily mild.[4]

Until 1973 wages rose faster than the prices of consumption goods. One reason why prices did not rise excessively rapidly was that the People's Republic of China supplied water, foodstuffs and other basic articles at lower prices than suppliers in Hong Kong itself in order to obtain foreign currency.[5] This changed after 1972: since that time China has charged the prevailing world market prices. Together with the drastic increase in the price of oil this led to a steep rise in prices in Hong Kong and real wages have fallen noticeably since 1973. Despite the increase in real wages prior to 1973, the share of overall

1. England & Rear, *Chinese Labour under British Rule. Financial Times,* 4 February 1974.
2. Robin Porter, 'Child labour in Hong Kong and related problems: a brief review', *International Labour Review,* Vol. 111, 5 (1975), p. 436.
3. England & Rear, *Chinese Labour under British Rule,* pp. 62 f.
4. England & Rear, pp. 63, 139–45; Porter, 'Child labour in Hong Kong'.
5. In 1971 just under 50% of all imports of foodstuffs came from the People's Republic of China.

value-added which actually accrued to the work-force fell during this period relatively to the share accruing to the owners of capital, who were therefore the main beneficiaries of that period of economic growth.[1] Since 1975 real wages seem to have risen slightly again, but by March 1976 had still not reached their previous highest level of March 1973.[2] According to a survey carried out by the International Labour Office (ILO) in October 1975, the hourly rates for adults in the textile and garment industry stood, on average (excluding overtime), between HK $ 3.28 for a seamstress and HK $ 3.90 for a weaver.[3]

There are other advantages in what is a permissive society for employers. The Hong Kong worker has a higher tolerance of substandard working conditions and neglect of industrial safety. Employers have fewer welfare services to support either directly or through taxes – or even provident funds.

Only 619684 of the total labour force of 1500000 work in the 21386 industrial units registered with the Government – those with more than 20 employees. A total of 136300 are selfemployed; the rest run small-scale family enterprises or work in small units, usually in a single room in a high rise slum. These are fire hazards; they are the main source of the seven fires a day that occur in Hong Kong...The nightmare of labour officials is the apathy and indifference of many employers to industrial safety. A typical reaction of which they complain is that of the employer who argues that 'safety means additional costs of production. No factory owner in Hong Kong likes to see his profits sliced'. With only five inspectors, breaches of regulations are hard to detect.[4]

Given such conditions, which cannot be described in more detail here,[5] it is difficult to imagine that workers in Hong Kong are 'largely contented', or even 'affluent'.[6] The following seems to be a more credible indication of the appalling living conditions which prevail there.

1. England & Rear, *Chinese Labour under British Rule*, pp. 35, 41 f.
2. *Far Eastern Economic Review*, 17 September 1976, p. 97.
3. ILO, *Bulletin of Labour Statistics, 2nd Quarter 1976*, p. 119. HK $ 9.45 = £1. Inflation allowances and bonuses are included in the figures. In the literature it is pointed out that in Hong Kong the total amount of a working-class family's income is the independent variable which determines the amount of overtime worked, and the number of members of the family who go out to work (including children). See *Far Eastern Economic Review*, 17 September 1976, p. 97; Porter, 'Child labour in Hong Kong'. The situation is very reminiscent of the early stages of the so-called Industrial Revolution in Western Europe when one of the main problems in the development of the capitalist mode of production was to force workers to work as regularly and as long as possible.
4. 'Worker lives only for today', *The Times*, 8 May 1973.
5. See England & Rear, *Chinese Labour under British Rule; Far Eastern Economic Review*, 18 March 1977, pp. 33–80. In 1971 more than 90000 dwellings in Hong Kong contained more than 5 people to a room. (Porter, 'Child labour in Hong Kong', p. 436.)
6. *The Times*, 8 May 1973.

In Western countries the early stages of industrialisation have been characterised by a widespread resort to alcohol as a means of escape from current realities. The equivalent forms of escapism in Hong Kong are addiction to gambling and narcotics. The Colony has the highest rate of narcotic addiction in the world with some 100000 addicts or one in every ten male employees...at least 70000 are believed to be heroin addicts. Whisson's study of drug addiction in Hong Kong led him to suggest that it is directly related to those features of working class life described above: the breakdown of families in the flight from China and the subsequent loss of traditional social controls; the problems of adapting to factory discipline; the lack of promotion prospects at work or of security in old age; and gross overcrowding. Heroin moreover gives to casual workers 'the additional energy at those periods when they most need it to sustain a long effort, and provides them with a relaxing and initially inexpensive habit when they are not actually working'. 'The poorer workers have no future – and few have much faith in an existence after the present one. For such men, heroin, if available, provides a fairly cheap way of enjoying the present and forgetting the future. It can be seen as a rational response to an accurate appraisal of their lives and future.'[1]

Trade unions do not play a significant role in Hong Kong. In March 1971, 101390 workers were employed in the garment industry in Hong Kong: in the same month the three clothing trade unions had a membership of 1965.[2] One of the reasons for the low level of trade union organisation appears to be the small average number of workers per establishment (around 25), which tends to lead to paternalistic and dependent relationships at the work-place.[3] On the other hand, the innumerable small rival trade unions in Hong Kong seem to be incapable, under the present circumstances, of effectively representing workers' interests.[4]

These references should suffice to indicate the kinds of conditions under which Hong Kong has been able to attain its relatively high levels of labour productivity. And should the conditions for valorisation ever deteriorate in particular branches of Hong Kong's garment industry (for example, for standard items), probably due to a change in the structure of individual traditional industrial countries' import restrictions,[5] then Hong Kong's indigenous and foreign capital has long been ready with the answer: production will be shifted to other low wage countries.[6] And this is the correct and

1. England & Rear, *Chinese Labour under British Rule*, p. 67.
2. England & Rear, p. 89.
3. *The Times*, 8 May 1973.
4. England & Rear, *Chinese Labour under British Rule*, passim.
5. One conceivable example would be the introduction of global import quotas by the traditional industrial countries instead of the present orderly marketing agreements bilaterally negotiated between individual developing countries and individual industrial countries or the EEC, based on previous exports.
6. TAL (Textile Alliance Ltd) has, for example, plants in Malaysia, Indonesia, Singapore, Taiwan, Thailand, Mauritius, Nigeria; out of a total employment of 40000, more than 20000

rational treatment following an accurate diagnosis – rational, that is, from the point of view of capital, but not from that of the worker.

There is no doubt that Hong Kong is currently the most extreme example of advanced export-oriented industrialisation, and of its economic and social effects. The question then arises as to how representative an example this is – representative, that is, of other developing countries which are being increasingly drawn into the international division of labour. Our thesis is that the world market for labour and for production sites, in which the developing countries are forced to engage in mutual competition, will bring about comparable social and economic effects in all those countries who manage to compete 'successfully'. The model instances of such an inclusion of developing countries into the world market are the free production zones and other forms of world market factories, whose economic and social effects will be dealt with in Part III, inasmuch as these effects are already perceivable. The effects of this particular form of export-oriented industrialisation show clearly that Hong Kong is not a special case but simply a particularly advanced example of a development which will embrace more and more sections of the populations of the developing countries in the foreseeable future.

5.4 World market production in a centrally planned economy: the case of Hungary

In Chapter 3.1 we showed that tendencies towards an export-oriented industrialisation based, among others, on the development of a textile and garment industry exist in a number of developing and centrally planned economies. Given the present conditions of the capitalist world system, such a form of development is the only possible form of (further) industrialisation in those countries which have a very restricted domestic market owing to the fact that the effective demand of the mass of the population for wage-goods is too small to guarantee a sufficiently large market for local industrial production. However, this restricted internal market for wage-goods is precisely the characteristic outcome of the, in some cases, centuries of integration of the developing countries into the

are employed outside of the Crown Colony. Via Mauritius (garments, 600 sewing machines) and Nigeria (spinning and weaving mill), TAL has access to the markets of the EEC without tariff, customs and import restrictions. See *Textil-Wirtschaft* 8 (1975), p. 20.

capitalist world system, which has meant the impoverishment of the mass of the population. The markets for the industry of such countries have to be sought abroad, and this means essentially in the traditional industrial countries. Only a fraction of the production of luxury goods can be sold to that small minority of the population who have the necessary means to pay (e.g. motor cars in Brazil). In view of the low incomes of the mass of the population in most developing countries we may assume that a large portion of the output of the textile and garment industries of these countries can be counted as belonging to that category of goods which can only be disposed of through the medium of export and/or the relatively few local recipients of high incomes.

Where this form of export-oriented industrialisation receives the active support of governments – and this is the case in nearly all the capitalist developing countries – it implies the complete fulfilment of the requirements for as profitable a production site as possible for the world market. This support is usually officially based on or legitimated by reference to the following aims and expectations: the creation of more industrial jobs; the improvement in the social conditions of the working population; achievement of equilibrium in the balance of payments; and the acquisition of technology and know-how. The fact that these and other expectations, assuming they are honest ones, have usually been spectacularly disappointed up to now, and the further fact that this will not change in the medium term because of the competition between the capitalist developing countries on the world market for production sites, is a crucial finding which is elaborated in Part III of this work (see also Chapter 5.3).

We now propose to investigate whether the determining influence of the world market for commodities and production sites also asserts itself in the centrally planned economies (the 'socialist' countries) when they pursue a strategy of export-oriented industrialisation. In planning their external economic relations such countries have to take into account the criteria for success on the world market. We cannot investigate in depth here why a considerable number of socialist countries have gone over to a strategy of export-oriented industrialisation, which in effect means an increased integration into the international division of labour within the capitalist world system. The most commonly heard argument in official reports is that further industrialisation is dependent on the import of capital-goods, technology, know-how and management expertise etc. from the traditional industrial capitalist countries: the acquisition of these conditions is supposed to be facilitated by the export earnings of their export-oriented industries. (Behind this conception lurks the myth that technology, as such, is both a central and a neutral tool which can be used to bring about the sought-for transition to a communist society.)

The case of Hungary will show in greater detail precisely how a strategy of export-oriented industrialisation also imposes the imperatives of the (capitalist) world market on a centrally planned economy. For the sake of clarity we summarise the results of the investigation beforehand.

Given the conditions of the present-day capitalist world economy, export-oriented industrialisation has the following implications for a centrally planned economy:

(1) Industrial production must be rearranged, in terms of product, quality and price-structure, to manufacture those commodities which can compete on the world market. In other words, the choice of export-oriented production adopted must fit the pre-existing niches in the capitalist world market – must, in fact, insert itself into the international division of labour. To complement this, the production of unprofitable commodities must be restricted, or completely shut down. Manufacturing enterprises must be economically motivated on the basis of their own individual plant performance, i.e. individual plant profitability.

(2) In order to attain this, a disproportionate amount of investment has to be made in the export-oriented industries, compared with the economy as a whole. This can mean that domestic consumption grows less fast than national income.

(3) In order to obtain the required technology, market analysis and understanding, and marketing channels (because of the quotas imposed by the traditional industrial countries), cooperation has to be established with firms from the capitalist countries. Domestic establishments who are involved in cooperation with foreign undertakings have to be given preferential treatment in the issue of credit etc. The foreign company has to be kept interested in such cooperation by means of economic incentives such as: relatively cheap, adequately qualified and disciplined labour; adherence to certain standards of quality and delivery

dates; willingness to supply particular types of goods on demand; ease of access to East European markets.

(4) Foreign trade policy must be amended so as to remove the import restrictions of the most important trading parties by offering substantial reciprocal concessions (importance of membership of GATT).

(5) As a rule, labour-intensive manufacture is favoured (e.g. mechanical engineering, garment industry) as the prospects for profit are especially favourable given the local 'factor endowment'.[1]

The foregoing points are the result of an examination of almost exclusively official Hungarian sources; as a rule the documents which are available are intended to capture the attention and interest of firms from the capitalist countries and direct them towards the possible advantages of cooperation with Hungarian enterprises. The following extracts are from such documents and substantiate the points already listed above.

On point 1

The economic targets contained in the Five Year Plan which commenced on 1 January 1976 are also of interest to Hungary's foreign trade partners as they envisage a growing participation in the international division of labour. The prime task of economic policy at the present time consists in the implementation of measures to increase the competitiveness and the promotion of exports...The utilisation of capacities in our enterprises, and hence the possibility of their development, is coming to depend increasingly on the pace at which they can increase their supply of competitive products to the markets of countries with convertible currencies... Planning in a balanced process of development necessitates the extension of the product-mix in accordance with the requirements of the market, the development of particular branches of industry at a faster or slower rate, and the closing down of the production of unprofitable products.[2]

...in the final analysis the motivations of the managers of enterprises are, in fact, firmly rooted in the system of central planning. In practice, Hungarian enterprises are, nonetheless, equally motivated on a plant basis, with due consideration to general political and economic policy aims. Individual enterprises also enjoy the corresponding power to take decisions.[3]

1. The overlap between this list and the one drawn up for the capitalist developing countries is quite evident: see, for example, Chapter 7.4 or Part III below.
2. Gerd Biró (General Director of the Hungarian Chamber of Commerce), 'Stellung auf dem Weltmarkt wird stärker ausgebaut', *Handelsblatt*, 23 March 1976, p. 21.
3. Károly Ravasz (Marketing Director of Intercooperation Handelsförderung AG, Budapest), *Cooperation* 3 (1974), p. 32.

Since the end of the Second World War the Hungarian economy has been characterised by an increasing participation in international trade. The turnover in foreign trade increased faster than total national product during the Five Year Plan which ended in 1975. The main conception of the 1976–80 Five Year Plan has shifted its emphasis towards achieving equilibrium in the balance of trade, alongside other aims... In addition to the growth in the volume of the supply of goods for export to achieve equilibrium, great attention is also being devoted to development and structural change which should increase the international competitiveness of Hungarian products. Development and utilisation of the productive bases already available in order to adjust to the demands of the world market are the main guidelines towards which policy in the field of the domestic pricing system, exchange rate policy, taxation and systems of central and enterprise management will be oriented. Fundamentally, our economic policy is one of increasing our orientation to exports. The interconnection between production and consumption, as well as the more complex system of interests, are to be aligned towards the expansion of exports to the non-socialist countries... In view of the insufficient amount of labour available it is necessary to cut back the production of goods in the mechanical engineering sector which yield a lower profit margin. The shortfall in these products can be made good by imports... Decisions as to which agricultural products to produce will be made in the light of extensive consideration of demand on the world market.[1]

On point 2

Under due consideration of this aim [balance of payments equilibrium] the Plan envisages a restructuring of the proportions of primarily domestic consumption. In the coming Five Year Plan domestic consumption is envisaged as rising by 23%–25%, as against an increase in national income of between 30% and 32%. 'Restraint' will be chiefly concentrated in the field of investment; however, a deceleration in the pace of personal consumption can also be awaited.[2]

With an increase of industrial production of 33%–35%, domestic sales will only rise by 25%–27%, whereas exports (in roubles) will rise by 44%–48%, and to countries with convertible currencies by 65%–70%.[3]

On point 3

Enterprises will be granted credits for developments with a five year pay-back period in foreign currencies which lead to profitable export business.[4]

...one of the most fundamental advantages as far as Federal Germany is concerned is that exports made in the context of cooperation do not fall under the scope of the import quota system... Businessmen in Federal Germany should be aware that

1. Hungaropress, 'Voraussichtliche Tendenzen im ungarischen Außenhandel im V. Fünfjahrplan 1976 bis 1980', *Cooperation* 2 (1976), Ungarische Sonderbeilage, pp. vii f.
2. Hungaropress, 'Voraussichtliche Tendenzen'.
3. Biró, 'Stellung auf dem Weltmarkt', p. 21.
4. Biró, p. 21.

the Hungarian financial authorities have built in a significant area of credit for financing those investments to be realised in the Five Year Plan...Clearly, if the applicant intends to set up a cooperation arrangement with a reliable and recognised partner from the West, most consideration will be given to the idea. In Hungary we believe that technical development is better secured through the cooperation of a foreign partner than through business which is regarded as being finally concluded with the sale of equipment to the Hungarian partner. Consequently the Hungarian partner has a greater chance of obtaining the sums required for development if the application is made within the context of cooperation. This is an additional reason for the Hungarian partner to give preference to a Western undertaking which is willing to cooperate.[1]

Cooperation agreements have made a substantial contribution to raising the technical level of Hungarian industry, and hence to increasing Hungarian exports. Seen from the other side, they have increased the competitiveness of Federal German firms and often helped them to find outlets on the markets of the socialist countries.[2]

Firms from West Berlin are induced to enter into cooperation arrangements with establishments from East and South East Europe for a number of concrete reasons: making up for the shortage of labour which plays such a role in the economy of West Berlin, deliveries at favourable costs because of lower wage levels, stable prices through long-term agreements, larger turnover through the utilisation of the spare capacities in the socialist countries, and a high quality of work after the initial setting up period. In addition, companies from West Berlin often wish to consolidate and expand their own position in the COMECON countries, as well as to seek to set up close cooperation as regards joint distribution in third markets.[3]

On point 4

We are fully aware of the fact that our most important task consists in raising the exportability of Hungarian goods...It should not be forgotten, however, that increasing Hungarian exports is still limited by considerable trade restrictions, and in a great number of instances by discriminatory measures. Despite our membership of GATT the number of Hungarian export articles which are subject to physical import controls adds up to 500, around 20% of our total exports. In 1975 it was impossible to increase those exports subject to quantitative restrictions: they are expected to rise by around 6% in 1976...The bulk of the products concerned are subject to EEC regulation, which cannot be fully predicted beforehand, and which is hence a constant source of problems to our exporters.[4]

1. Iván Toldy-Ösz (Director of Intercooperation AG für Handelsförderung, Budapest), 'Wachsender Export durch Kooperation', *Handelsblatt*, 23 March 1976, p. 22.
2. Hungaropress, 'Entwicklung der Wirtschaftsbeziehungen zwischen der Ungarischen Volksrepublik und der Bundesrepublik Deutschland', *Cooperation* 2 (1976), Ungarische Sonderbeilage, p. vi.
3. L. Großkopf, 'Berlin als Partner in der Ost-West-Kooperation', *Cooperation* 3 (1974), p. 34.
4. László P. Tóth (Trade Section of the Hungarian Consulate in Federal Germany), 'Gewichte im Handel müssen gleichmäßiger verteilt werden', *Handelsblatt*, 23 March 1976, p. 24.

Hungary has been a full member of GATT since September 1973. This allows us to participate in multilateral negotiations with the other parties to the GATT agreement, including the EEC and its member states. These negotiations cover all the basic questions of trade. Amongst other things, they could mean the progressive dismantling of discriminatory quotas.[1]

On point 5

An expansion in exports from the mechanical engineering industry has been alloted a fundamental and structurally significant role in the Plan. This follows, in the first instance, from the fact that mechanical engineering is responsible for a large share of industry as a whole: but, in addition, it can be explained by the fact that this branch assembles the most labour-intensive products, i.e. manufactures, and which therefore require a relatively high utilisation of Hungarian labour. Such manufactures can as a result make a significant contribution to the shaping of an economically effective export structure with a positive effect on the balance of trade.[2]

Extracts from the Fifth Five Year Plan of the Hungarian People's Republic prove quite conclusively that these reports were not simply written to impress potential Western partners.

Raising the exportability of our products... Intensification of our participation in the international division of labour...consolidation of the autonomy and responsibility of individual units of production...domestic consumption to rise at a lower rate than national income...the profitability of production is to be increased...a rapid increase in the production of those goods which can be economically manufactured and compete on the world market.

In the context of investment in the productive sectors, the share assigned to the energy industries should be increased, especially those which are seeking to boost their exports.

More encouragement for the rapid development of those sides of manufacturing industry which can increase their market-share in various markets and bring profitable exports...The development of the garment industry should both cover requirements and allow for an increase in exports. The progress of reconstruction should allow for an increase in the manufacture of goods for which there is a domestic market and which are competitive in foreign markets...We are seeking to deepen economic relations with the developed capitalist states on the basic principle of respect for the respective mutual advantages and interests. In addition to the necessary trade in goods, it is proposed that cooperation, and all types of relation which facilitate the acquisition of know-how, should be strengthened...

An interest in exporting...an increase in efficiency and a more rapid restructuring of exports must lead to the steady but vigorous increase in exports and their profitability...Instruments of economic regulation should be developed so that long-term exchange relations on the world market are more faithfully reflected in

1. Bundesstelle für Außenhandelsinformation, Ungarische Handelskammer, Institut für Konjunktur- und Marktforschung (Cologne–Budapest), *Handbuch der Kooperation zwischen Unternehmen in der Bundesrepublik Deutschland und in der Volksrepublik Ungarn* (Cologne–Budapest 1975), pp. 22 f.
2. Hungaropress, 'Voraussichtliche Tendenzen'.

prices, so that differences in efficiency are more reliably reflected in profitability, and so that the accumulation and use of funds becomes more flexible at the level of the individual enterprise... The price system is to be developed so that prices (1) constitute a basis for efficient economic management, (2) are more in line with prevailing world market prices, and (3) reveal the extent and magnitude of social subsidies existing in Hungary itself. In addition, the modifications to selling prices carried out by the authorities should lead to a situation in which enterprises will be better able to take into account long-term price trends on foreign markets in their economic decision making. Budgetary measures should encourage the establishment of a profitable structure of production and the curbing or holding back of unprofitable areas...in particular, the level of compensation for losses should be reduced, and subsidies for the development of profitable production increased ... Credit policy should encourage profitable sales and development projects... developments credits...especially with an eye to the expansion of capacities for export production... The income of the enterprise, together with the regulation of production and retail prices, should be so arranged so as to improve budgeting in the enterprise and more clearly express the perceivable differences in the efficiency of operation in the form of profits. The enterprise will be given the free choice of either using profits to increase personal incomes or for development purposes...

Productive establishments are to develop an interest in profitable exports and the fulfilment of intergovernmental obligations... The autonomy of the enterprise is to be safeguarded and the responsibility of economic units for the efficiency of their operations and decisions is to be increased ... [Parliament] requests the trade unions, and all other social organisations, to give their support to the implementation of this legislation and the realisation of the aims embodied in the Plan by mobilising all those involved in productive activities.[1]

It is not our intention to deal here with those aspects of the Five Year Plan which are concerned with the material welfare of the Hungarian population. Our prime concern in this context is to provide sufficient proof of the extent to which a strategy of export-oriented industrialisation also imposes the imperatives of the (capitalist) world market on a centrally planned economy.

The Western business world pays great attention to the incentives granted by the Hungarian government to Hungarian enterprises when they conclude cooperation agreements with Western partners as 'these incentives indirectly benefit the Western partner as well.'[2] A form of exchange or market has developed on which Hungarian enterprises make their offers for cooperation. Some of the more recent offers on this exchange read as follows:

1. From: 'Der Fünfte Fünfjahrplan der Ungarischen Volkswirtschaft (1976–1980)'. Complete text in Hungaropress, *Wirtschaftsinformationen – Informationsdienst der Ungarischen Handelskammer* (1976), nos. 1–2.
2. Business International, Eastern Europe Report, 'Hungary offers incentives for cooperation ventures', *Business Eastern Europe – A Weekly Report to Managers of East European Operations*, 4 June 1976.

The cooperation partner is asked to supply all equipment necessary for the new factory specialising in flat knitwear as well as technological know-how; moreover the cooperation partner will ensure the production organisation and take a fixed quantity – about 50% – of the production.

It will be the duty of the Hungarian cooperation partner to erect the buildings, to buy all the equipment and to provide the employees.[1]

Cooperation for the production of socks and hosiery. A Hungarian enterprise of the textile industry is looking for a cooperation partner for the production of ladies', gentlemen's and children's hosiery. The Hungarian partner could perform the processing of about 2 to 2.5 million pairs of semimanufactured (knitted) products, according to the demand of the partner.

The foreign partner is supposed to ensure the confectioning-, processing and packing equipment, furthermore the auxiliary materials for the production. The products manufactured would be put at the disposal of the foreign partner.[2]

Clothing industry. The Hungarian ready-made clothes industry with the main lines of women's, men's and children's clothes would be interested in a cooperation, in the frame of which, through taking over machines, an increase in capacity and productivity of labour could be achieved.

In addition to special machines, the Hungarian enterprises would take over from the foreign partner know-how for the manufacture-technology and organisation. Cooperation in this field would be fruitful for a foreign partner which would make use part or full of the capacity thus expanded for a period of 3–5 years.[3]

Production cooperation of embroidered children's and ladies' garments and ladies' blouses. We are looking for a partner to cooperate with us in producing hand- or machine-embroidered children's and ladies' garments. The Hungarian partner offers an up-to-date confectioning capacity as well as skilled manpower. The foreign partner is expected to deliver basic material, machinery and models. Articles produced in cooperation would be taken over by him.[4]

On the subject of incentives for Western partners and Hungarian enterprises, the Deputy Director of Intercooperation AG (Hungarian state coordinating bureau for cooperation) presented the following statement:

Dr Toldy-Ösz, taking examples of cooperation with Western partners, showed that the Western partner supplied capital-goods and technical knowledge to Hungary at the beginning of the cooperation, and replacement parts in the first years of the course of the agreement, whilst the Hungarian partner increasingly took over the manufacture of these parts and in individual cases even the complete manufacture of various types of production programme. *The incentive for the Western partner consists in lower production costs, utilisation of the Hungarian establishment as an extended work-bench and marketing advantages. The Hungarian partner obtains a faster pace of*

1. *Cooperation* 2 (1974), p. 67.
2. *New Hungarian Exporter*, vol. 25, 6 (June 1975), p. 21.
3. *New Hungarian Exporter*, vol. 25, 9 (September 1975), p. 10.
4. *New Hungarian Exporter*, vol. 25, 9 (September 1975), p. 10.

technical development, improvement in the possibilities for foreign trade and the utilisation of spare capacity. At the present time between 400 and 700 cooperation agreements have been concluded by Hungarian enterprises, depending on whether subcontracting without cooperation strings is included or not. 40% of these contracts are with firms from Federal Germany.[1]

It is almost superfluous to point out that the Hungarian textile and garment industry has been reorganised in accordance with this perspective.

We intend to increase the volume of the exports of light industry to the socialist countries by 34%, and to other countries by 100%...Reorganisation in the structure both of production and products [in the garment industry] will be directed towards boosting the production of goods with a high going value, which can be profitably sold in all markets and profitably manufactured. Reconstruction will pay special attention to the deployment of unutilised labour which is available in any given area into productive employment.[2]

These extracts are sufficient to show the extent to which a strategy of export-oriented (further) industrialisation will increasingly bring about the replacement of planning in a country like Hungary, where the state has a monopoly of foreign trade, by market mechanisms.

One hopes that the Hungarian workers do not become transformed into 'frantic senseless machines' in their 'deployment' into 'productive employment', as one piece-worker experienced in a Hungarian factory when he expressed that: 'Piece-work is not a fundamental institution of socialism. In fact it is incompatible with socialism.'[3]

1. *Cooperation* 6 (1975), p. 58 (emphasis added). The Hungarian garment industry has recently concluded cooperation agreements with more than thirty Federal German companies. See *New Hungarian Exporter* (1977), Special Issue, p. 5.
2. Mrs J. Keserü (Minister for Light Industry) at a press conference, July 1976. Source: Hungaropress, *Wirtschaftsinformationen* (1976), nos. 15–16, p. 3.
3. Miklós Haraszti, *A Worker in a Worker's State* (Harmondsworth 1977), p. 162.

Additional material on East–West cooperation (in particular between Federal Germany and Hungary) can be found in the following publications: Klaus Bolz & Peter Plötz, *Erfahrungen aus der Ost–West-Kooperation* (Hamburg 1974); Bundesstelle für Außenhandelsinformation, *Einfache und erweiterte Ost–West-Kooperation* (Cologne 1973); *Handbuch der Kooperation* (see above). See too the following periodicals and journals: *The Hungarian Economy – A Quarterly Economic and Business Review; Ungarischer Außenhandel; New Hungarian Exporter – Periodical of the Hungarian Chamber of Commerce;* Hungaropress, *Wirtschaftsinformationen – Informationsdienst der Ungarischen Handelskammer; Marketing in Ungarn – Vierteljahrzeitschrift der Ungarischen Handelskammer; Business Eastern Europe – A Weekly Report to Managers of East European Operations.*

6 ❧ The relocation of production of companies from the Federal German textile and garment industry to sites abroad

6.1 Methodology, sources, criteria for selection, representativeness, presentation of the material

No accessible official list of Federal German textile and garment companies with production abroad, in one form or another, is available in Federal Germany.[1] It is therefore necessary to use a wide variety of non-specific sources to obtain information about the foreign production of the Federal German textile and garment industry. Two especially helpful starting points are provided by two lists drawn up by the magazine *Textil-Wirtschaft* in 1966 and 1970.[2] In addition, use was made of the economic sections of a number of daily newspapers over a period of two to three years: they included *Süddeutsche Zeitung, Frankfurter Allgemeine Zeitung* (*FAZ*) and its economic supplement *Blick durch die Wirtschaft, Handelsblatt*, the information service *VWD-Textil* and a number of specialist papers such as *Textil-Wirtschaft*. The commercial guides *Hoppenstedt'sches Handbuch der Großunternehmen* and to a lesser extent the *ABC der deutschen Wirtschaft* were also drawn on. Annual company reports played only a minor role as sources as a large number of the firms which are of relevance in this context are not obliged to make their reports public. In certain instances foreign chambers of commerce supplied information.

1. In contrast the US official publication, United States Tariff Commission, *Economic Factors Affecting the Use of Items 807.00 and 806.30 of the Tariff Schedules of the United States*, TC publication 339 (Washington 1970), gives aggregated employment figures for particular types of foreign manufacturing by US firms. The new Federal German notification provision set out in §56a of the Außenwirtschaftsverordnung on the size and structure of Federal German assets abroad states that the supplying of employment data for foreign affiliates is desirable but not obligatory. It remains to be seen whether adequately detailed regional and sectoral breakdowns of aggregate employment figures may one far-off day be made available to the public.
2. 'Deutsche Produktion im Ausland', *Textil-Wirtschaft* 41 (1966); 'Sollen wir im Ausland produzieren', *Textil-Wirtschaft* 42 (1970).

However, these plus a number of other less important sources were not sufficient to provide an even tolerably adequate survey of the foreign production of the Federal German textile and garment industry. As a result, around 330 undertakings were requested (some several times) to supply information about their production abroad, if any such existed, on a data sheet which was provided. In order not to reduce the chances of obtaining a large number of replies from the outset, the number of questions was deliberately kept to a minimum.[1]

The spectrum and the number of companies selected was determined by two considerations. *Firstly,* we wished to include *all* the larger companies, which between them accounted for 50% of the total turnover of the Federal German textile and garment industry. *Secondly,* we approached the firms for which the information from the above sources made us suspect they were undertaking some production abroad. The general reason why firms from the textile and garment *industry,* as opposed to the *trade* (e.g. wholesale distributors etc.) were included is twofold. Firstly, some limitation was necessary on the simple grounds of the capacity to deal with and process all the information; secondly – given that such a limitation was necessary – our preference was to find out in what ways the world market for production sites occasioned or compelled domestic producers to reorganise their production on a world-wide basis.

Using the material which was collected – and reserving later additional specifications – it was possible to show that 45% of all firms in the textile survey and 70% of all firms in the garment industry survey maintained some form of production abroad. Unfortunately, we cannot offer a reliable estimate of the extent to which the procedure employed covered the foreign production of *all* undertakings in the Federal German textile and garment industry. Occasional indirect controls indicated that, measured by the number of foreign establishments, around 50% to 75% of the foreign

1. At this point we would like to thank all the firms which participated in the questionnaire (about 200 out of 330 asked). Apart from a few individual cases, no doubts can be placed on the reliability of their answers. Naturally, in a large number of cases the reply consisted of a nil return, meaning that the company had no production abroad. We had the impression that firms without production abroad participated to an above average extent in the questionnaire. In a few cases we were requested to deal with the data confidentially. For those companies who did not reply, or who did not enter into the investigation until after the survey (late summer 1975) – around 70 firms in all – other sources were used, the reliability of which cannot be established in strictly comparable ways for each individual case.

production of the Federal German textile and garment industry could have been covered for the years 1974/75 (excluding subcontracting to socialist countries and nominally independent foreign concerns).

Each firm about which information was held, together with the source of this information, was allocated a data sheet on which the information was stored. A list was drawn up from this data, which provided an overview in table form of the most important variables on the foreign production for the firms under investigation: this constituted the 'List of Firms'.[1] However, because of its size, and because in some instances confidentiality was requested, it is not possible to reproduce the data sheets or list here. Instead, the original material is presented in the form of aggregated tables and summaries of the foreign operations of individual companies.

6.2 Subcontracting

A significant and very probably rapidly growing portion of the external trade between countries is trade within companies who maintain production facilities in various countries, or trade between undertakings which are formally independent. (An example would be the domestic company A and its foreign contract company B.) In such an instance, foreign trade, seen in concrete terms, is nothing more than an expression of the conscious organisation or exploitation of the international division of labour by a single concern. For example, a large proportion of the export of hosiery from Federal Germany to Yugoslavia and Greece, and an equally large proportion of the import of hosiery from Yugoslavia and Greece into Federal Germany comes about through the fact that Federal German companies A1, A2,... supply hose in the form of unfinished stocking to the Yugoslavian or Greek firms B1, B2,... (it is immaterial here whether B is a subsidiary of A or not), and that B1, B2,... make up the raw stocking and supply it, in finished form, back to A1, A2,... in Federal Germany.

Examples of this kind show quite clearly that a knowledge of the dealings, conduct and strategies of individual companies is indispensable in reaching an understanding of the structure and devel-

1. The list is set out similarly to the lists in *Textil-Wirtschaft.* Where known, the following data is given: Federal German company: turnover and domestic work-force; production facilities abroad: name, place, country, size of capital holding, markets; where relevant, any existing subcontracting with Federal German firms (all data 1974/75).

opment of world trade. Of course, these actions and strategies themselves can only be explained by the constantly changing imperatives which the development of the world economy imposes on the individual undertaking, on pain of extinction.

The trade in subcontracting, to the extent that it is recorded in Federal German foreign trade statistics, offers the opportunity of obtaining a quantitative picture of at least one small part of this transnational division of labour within and between undertakings.[1] Subcontracting (which is recorded in official German statistics under the heading *passiver Veredelungsverkehr*: passive improvement trade) basically involves Federal German external trade in those commodities and with those countries

(1) for which the EEC imposes tariffs,
(2) where it is worthwhile for the company concerned to export raw materials and pre-products (e.g. fabrics) to one of those countries in order for processing to take place and finally re-import into the EEC at preferential tariffs,
(3) where there are no quantitative import restrictions in the way (or if such do exist that they do not apply to so-called cooperation trade).

In toto these conditions only apply to a very small segment of Federal Germany's foreign trade; in 1975 the proportion of imports of all commodities accounted for by subcontracting was a mere 1.3%. However, in the case of clothing this share was as high as 14%.

Broken down by country, 69% of all subcontracting imports into Federal Germany in 1975 came from the centrally planned economies and the developing countries of the Mediterranean area and East Asia, with Yugoslavia alone accounting for 28%. Broken down by commodity, 52% of all subcontracting imports in 1975 were accounted for by clothing, with the next largest item being electrical goods, with a share of 16%. Consequently, textiles and clothing on the one hand, and the socialist countries of Eastern Europe (excluding East Germany, USSR and Albania), the developing countries of the Mediterranean area (including Yugoslavia) and East Asia on the other, accounted for by far the greater part of Federal Germany's trade in subcontracting.[2]

1. See Chapter 7.1 on the economic rationality of international contract processing (subcontracting).
2. The statistics in the previous two paragraphs were taken from Statistisches Bundesamt, Fachserie G (Außenhandel), Reihe 1, *Zusammenfassende Übersichten 1975* (Stuttgart–Mainz 1976).

Table I-9 shows that in 1975 (with a rising tendency since 1969) almost 14% of all fabric exports and 6% of all clothing exports from Federal Germany were for the purpose of subcontracting; at the same time a good 14% of all clothing imports into Federal Germany were the result of subcontracting. These figures indicate the minimum extent to which the production of textiles and clothing for the Federal German market is divided into manufacture of pre-products in the EEC area, and finishing in the countries listed (which are predominantly low wage countries). Because of the regulations governing the granting of import licences for imports from subcontracting in the East European centrally planned economies, we can add that, as far as the trade with these countries is concerned at least, the subcontracting imports of textiles and clothing were effected by Federal German industry (in a division of labour with establishments from these countries). These few countries alone (Poland, Czechoslovakia, Hungary, Romania, Bulgaria and Yugoslavia) were responsible for more than 85% of all the clothing imports from subcontracting into Federal Germany in 1974.

In 1974 the share of these countries (*excluding* Yugoslavia) in the subcontracting imports of clothing into Federal Germany was over 30%. Two-thirds of the exports of woven and knitted fabrics, and one-third of Federal Germany's exports of clothing to these countries, and in addition two-thirds of the imports of clothing from these countries into Federal Germany was transacted via subcontracting. Yugoslavia is by far Federal Germany's most important partner in subcontracting. In 1974 Federal Germany exported DM 250 million worth of fabrics and DM 130 million of clothing to Yugoslavia, and imported DM 561 million of clothing via subcontracting trade. Approximately 70% of the exports of fabrics and 85% of the exports of clothing from Federal Germany to Yugoslavia, and 90% of Federal Germany's imports of clothing from Yugoslavia were made in the context of subcontracting.[1]

1. Own calculations using information from Statistisches Bundesamt. It should be stressed again that the contribution of the so-called economic contract-processing to the transnational division of labour, both within and between companies, apart from individual cases cannot be disclosed by the Statistisches Bundesamt 'on personnel grounds' and must therefore remain hidden from public view.

6.3 Foreign production by companies from the Federal German textile and garment industry: summary 1974/75

Our investigation covered 214 undertakings (or groups) in the textile industry and 185 undertakings (or groups) in the garment industry.[1] In order to achieve a better degree fo comparability with the two lists published in *Textil-Wirtschaft* in 1966 and 1970, the Deutsche Entwicklungsgesellschaft (DEG: German Development Company) and, to a very insignificant extent, a number of trading concerns were included in the companies under investigation.

These companies accounted for at least 60% of the total turnover of the Federal German textile industry, and 45% of the turnover of the garment industry in 1974. In terms of employment they accounted for 60% and 40% of their respective totals.

Of the firms investigated it was possible to show that in 1974/75 around 100 firms in the textile industry (around 45%) and 125 (around 70%) of the garment industry were engaged in production abroad.[2] This should be understood as meaning both production in wholly or partly owned subsidiaries, as well as in the form of cooperation with nominally independent foreign undertakings (primarily, subcontracting with East European countries).

A comparison with both of the *Textil-Wirtschaft* lists shows that the number of Federal German companies proved to be involved in production abroad demonstrably increased between 1966 and 1974/75, both in absolute terms, and even more in relative terms because of the falling number of domestic concerns. The figure rose from thirty firms each in the textile and garment industry in 1966, to around forty in 1970, and by 1974/75 had reached a hundred (excluding subcontracting throughout).

Table I-14(a) supplements the results of the 1966 and 1970 lists from *Textil-Wirtschaft* with the results of the 1974/75 study. We have dispensed with a computation of the turnover of foreign establish-

1. In the period since carrying out the survey a number of additional examples of foreign manufacturing by companies from the Federal German textile and garment industry have come to light: however, the subsequent statistical remarks are based on the survey of the original 399 companies selected.
2. Cf. *Ifo-Schnelldienst* 7 (1975), according to which 58% of firms in the Federal German garment industry which were surveyed maintained production facilities abroad, as against an average of 29% for manufacturing industry. See too Axel J. Halbach 'Produktionsverlagerungen in Entwicklungsländer. Zum Ergebnis einer Ifo-Umfrage', *Ifo-Schnelldienst* 35 (1976). Where the two studies overlap, this study comes to quite similar conclusions to the Ifo study.

ments of the Federal German textile and garment industry in view of the number of uncertainties involved. The 1974/75 study only deals with those foreign establishments which have at least a 25% Federal German share in capital, and therefore excludes, for example, Eastern European subcontracting partner enterprises. A figure of 20% was added to the recorded employment figure to take account of non-recordable cases, or cases where no employment figures were supplied to match the procedure adopted by *Textil-Wirtschaft*.[1] For 1974/75 this additional sum was certainly a conservative one.

As table I-14(a) shows, the volume of employment which can be proved to exist (as shown above) in Federal German productive establishments abroad has increased both absolutely and relatively. This substantial growth over the eight years has led to a situation where, in 1974, out of every hundred employees in the textile industry eight were foreign employees working abroad, and in the garment industry, ten: this only takes into account employment where the Federal German capital share is at least 25%.

As Table I-14(b) shows, approximately 20% of the foreign production of Federal German textile and garment companies is accounted for by the EEC countries, with a further 30%–40% in the other traditional industrial countries (measured by the number of holdings and subsidiaries abroad and the volume of employment). The bulk of the remainder is divided between the developing countries of the Mediterranean area,[2] the developing countries of Africa (textile industry) and the developing countries of Asia (garment industry). The numbers employed in Federal German establishments in the low wage countries as a proportion of the total foreign employment of the Federal German textile and garment industry rose from around 25% in 1966 to 45% by 1974/75, with a more or less equal rise for each industry.[3]

The breakdown by turnover (Table I-14(c)) shows, on the one hand, that the largest Federal German companies in the textile and garment industry contribute relatively more to employment abroad

1. In some instances employment figures for years other than 1974 were taken from the period 1970–75 if the 1974 figures were not available, and if there were no grounds to suppose that major changes had taken place between the two years.
2. Counted by the number of subsidiaries, Tunisia (around thirty), Greece (more than twenty) and Malta (eight) are particularly significant.
3. Computed from the list of firms in *Textil-Wirtschaft* 41 (1966) and the list used in this study (not reproduced here).

Table I-14

(a) Employment in foreign subsidiaries of Federal German textile and garment industry: 1966, 1970, 1974

	Textile industry			Garment industry		
	1966	1970	1974	1966	1970	1974
Domestic employment	538 500	501 500	393 700	406 400	379 100	310 400
Employment in foreign subsidiaries (estimates)[a]	8 000	14 200	29 500	15 000	24 800	31 000
Employment in foreign subsidiaries as percentage of domestic employment (estimates)	1.5%	2.8%	7.5%	3.7%	6.5%	10.0%

Sources: *Textil-Wirtschaft*, 41 (1966), 42 (1970); Statistisches Bundesamt, *Statistisches Jahrbuch für die Bundesrepublik Deutschland*; own survey of 399 companies

a: Estimates based on a survey of Federal German production facilities abroad. In order to account for cases not surveyed or cases without known employment figures, 20% was added to the recorded employment figures. A few foreign subsidiaries of non-industrial Federal German companies (e.g. DEG) are included. 1974: Only foreign subsidiaries with at least 25% Federal German holding

(b) Regional distribution of foreign subsidiaries of Federal German textile and garment industry: 1974 (percentages)

		EEC	Austria Switzerland Sweden	Other industrial countries	Mediterranean countries	Latin America	Africa	Asia
Regional distribution according to the number of foreign subsidiaries	T	26	28	13	12	4	13	5
	G	19	27	3	35	3	3	11
Regional distribution according to the number of foreign employees abroad	T	21	26	7	11	1	28	5
	G	21	33	4	23	9	1	10

Source: own survey of 399 companies with about 300 foreign subsidiaries (about 150 each in the textile and garment industry)

Only foreign subsidiaries with at least 25% Federal German holding

In some cases the regional allocation of the companies' foreign employment abroad is based on estimates

(c) Distribution of foreign employment of Federal German textile and garment industry by turnover of the surveyed companies: 1974 (percentages)

		Companies with turnover of (million DM)				
		above 250	100–250	50–100	20–50	below 20
Percentage share of domestic employment	T	39	27	17	15	2
	G	20	10	34	30	6
Percentage share of foreign employment	T	48	16	11	11	14
	G	56	3	20	16	5

Source: own survey of about 390 companies (excluding DEG and other companies without domestic production)

Only foreign subsidiaries with at least 25% Federal German holding

Owing to the selection criteria for the companies surveyed, the table entries are not representative for the Federal German textile and garment industry as a whole

Table I-14. (*cont.*)

(d) Distribution of foreign employment of Federal German textile and garment industry by sex and age: 1974

	Employees covered	Male (%)	Female (%)	Employees covered	Age (%) below 20	20–40	40–60	above 60
Textile industry	5826	30	70	1972	25	60	14	1
Industrial, socialist countries	2901	36	64	1665	26	59	14	1
Developing countries	2925	23	77	317	22	68	10	0
For comparison:								
Federal Germany (1970)	—	46	54	—	8	47	39	6
Garment industry	4311	12	88	3367	31	53	14	2
Industrial, socialist countries	3081	14	86	2133	25	53	20	2
Developing countries	1230	8	92	1234	43	52	4	1
For comparison:								
Federal Germany (1970)	—	13	87	—	18	42	33	7

Sources: own survey (replies by about 40 companies); Statistisches Bundesamt, Fachserie A (Bevölkerung und Kultur), *Volkszählung vom 27. Mai 1970, Heft 20: Erwerbstätige nach Beruf und Alter*; own calculations
Industrial, socialist countries: EEC, Austria, United States, Canada, Japan, Hungary
Developing countries: Yugoslavia, Greece, Portugal, Spain, Malta, Tunisia, Israel, Iran, Malaysia

than corresponds with their share of domestic employment.[1] On the other hand, it should not be overlooked that the smaller companies in terms of turnover also make a considerable contribution to the volume of employment abroad. This in itself is a proof of the thesis that – contrary to what a great deal of discussion obsessed with multinationals is willing to admit – the stage which the world capitalist system has now reached contains a tendency which is forcing companies, regardless of their size, to undertake a global reorganisation of their manufacturing processes on pain of extinction: this means, in numerous instances, the relocation of production within the traditional industrial countries and to the developing and centrally planned economies. Admittedly, the larger undertakings have more possibilities of tackling this problem because of their sheer size, i.e. the resources at their disposal, and their often pre-existing international links.

One particular fact which emerges from the breakdown of employment in Federal German establishments abroad into sex and age groups (Table I-14(d)) is the extraordinarily high percentage of

1. The far above average share of firms with a large turnover from the garment industry in manufacture abroad can be attributed to the exceptionally high foreign employment of Triumph International.

young female workers in the garment industries of the low wage countries: around 43% of employees are younger than twenty years old, and over 90% are women or girls.

As the information supplied by numerous firms almost without exception states, employment abroad is practically solely that of unskilled labour which is trained by the firms themselves.

Hence, the typical employee of a Federal German garment firm in a low wage country is a young woman (between fifteen and twenty-five) who has been trained by the firm and works as a seamstress, probably at a simple sewing machine which may have been already scrapped in the firm's German plant, and then shipped to the low wage country.[1]

This section has so far dealt with employment abroad in establishments with at least a 25% Federal German share in capital. In addition, a count of the available data on subcontracting reveals that in foreign establishments producing on this basis without any formal capital links, at least 2650 employees were producing for the textile industry and 4250 for the garment industry. If we add 20% for non-recordable cases or where no employment figures were available we obtain a figure of 3200 for subcontracting employment in textiles and 5100 for garments for the Federal German industry, in the sense defined above. In this context, 20% is a particularly low figure.[2]

These two large groups, employment in foreign establishments with at least 25% Federal German holding, and employment in nominally independent subcontracting partners, admittedly cover only two, if two of the most important, categories in an estimate of the numbers employed in the foreign production of the Federal German textile and garment industry. Cooperation with East European establishments (unless included under subcontracting), so-called economic contract-processing, and other imports transacted by the Federal German industry itself, would also have to be

1. 'The Tunisian women manage best with the simplest sewing machines', states one report. What such reports do not state is that the 'combination' of unskilled Tunisian seamstresses with machines which have become worthless in Federal Germany itself is extremely profitable.
2. Federal Germany's balance of trade in international subcontracting in textiles and clothing (chiefly with East European socialist countries, including Yugoslavia) amounted to a deficit of DM 400 million in 1974. If one assumes an annual average payment of DM 25000 for processing per employee in East European subcontracting establishments, this yields a figure of 16000 employees as the extent of Federal German textile and garment industry's production in East Europe. (More likely, the average of DM 25000 is far too high an estimate here, which is confirmed by individual company statistics on turnover and employment. The figure of 16000 should therefore be regarded as the lower limit.)

taken into consideration, but cannot be included here due to a lack of adequate material.

In summary, our investigation revealed that in 1974/75 the Federal German textile and garment industry probably employed at least 69 000 workers in its own establishments abroad and via international subcontracting, and very likely significantly more: a figure of 80 000 workers is not improbable. However, we shall keep to the precise figure of just over 57 000 employees for the textile and garment industry which could actually be obtained from reliable sources of employment data rather than the larger estimate.

Taking this figure as a basis, the proven foreign employment of the Federal German textile and garment industry has more than doubled in the period 1966–75, whereas over the same period the domestic employment in this industry has fallen by around a quarter. By the beginning of 1977 there were clearly more than ten people employed abroad by the Federal German textile and garment industry for every hundred employed in Germany itself.

A further result of the survey for this case study is that finally, in 1974/75, just over half the foreign production facilities of the Federal German textile industry, with around 11 000 employees, and over two-thirds of the foreign production facilities of the Federal German garment industry, with around 18 500 employees, were producing overwhelmingly or exclusively for the Federal German market. These (minimum) figures provide an approximate picture of the extent to which Federal German firms in the textile and garment industry have shifted production for the Federal German market from Germany to sites abroad.[1]

6.4. Selected data on the foreign manufacturing operations of a sample of Federal German textile and garment companies

In 1974 the *Delden* Group of Gronau/Westphalia, one of the largest and most expansionist groups in the European textile industry, had a turnover of DM 643 million and employed 6295 employees in

1. It should be stressed that this section only considers those relocations of production undertaken by the Federal German textile and garment industry itself. Consequently only a part of the shift of production out of Germany is covered. Those relocations of production which have been carried out by companies not from the Federal German industry itself, but which – as an analysis of the differential international rates of growth of industrial production and manufacture in the textile and garment sphere plus trade in textiles and garments would show – are not insignificant in dimensions, cannot however be dealt with here.

Federal Germany. It owns three foreign plants, in Austria, Brazil and the USA, which with 514 employees in 1974 had a turnover of DM 41 million, although the plants in Brazil and the USA have only just started production. The company expounded the basic principles of its strategy for the next twenty-five years in a multi-page insert in a business journal on the occasion of the hundredth anniversary of the group's foundation.

The Delden Group operates according to the principle of decentralisation. This means: the head office sets out general business policy – forward planning, coordination, control and the exercise of collective functions. The divisions operate as extensively autonomous profit-centres. The Delden concept is based on seven basic principles:

(1) Delden manufacture is concentrated on large-scale industrial mass production.
(2) The Delden Group retains its orientation towards synthetic fibres.
(3) The Delden Group's production programme is directed towards a small number of, but widely usable products in the middle price range. Each product must attain a position of market leadership in its field.
(4) ...
(5) ...
(6) The Delden Group operates internationally.
(7) The Delden Group regards the textile industry as a growth industry of the first order. It will therefore direct its operations towards the textile sector. Diversification into other areas is not envisaged...

Parallel to this, new establishments will be set up in those parts of the world which hold promise for the future... Internationalisation is one of the most important tasks for the next twenty-five years. Why is it necessary to operate on a world-wide basis?

All current prognoses indicate that we are entering a period which will be dominated by large economic blocs. To be able to compete in the future companies will have to be able to produce and sell inside these blocs. An additional factor has to be taken into account: economic growth is slowing down in the highly developed industrial countries. In contrast, an unparalleled expansion is awaited in the new industrial nations. One consequence of this will be a more than proportional growth in the demand for textiles. The Delden Group must adjust itself to these new developments if it wishes to remain competitive.

The impression has gained ground amongst the public at large that the German textile industry is moving out into the world because of lower wage costs. This is absolutely false. No one can doubt, of course, that a substantial wage difference does exist at the present time. However, this only applies to today. Over the next twenty-five years wage costs in the old and new industrial countries will extensively converge. Any company which sets up a new establishment has to be prepared for such an equalisation in wage costs. For this reason, the relatively short-term differences are of no significance in the context of a long-term programme of internationalisation.

Other factors are of key importance for long-term development. The most important are freight costs, distribution costs and tariffs. They are now such a burden that it is impossible to supply the world from Europe. Minimising risks is also a factor to be taken into account. Internationalisation will greatly ease the spreading of risks inside the Delden Group. It will now be possible to balance out slumps in one part of the world. This signifies more security for the concern as a whole. Finally, internationalisation will facilitate a more intensive use of know-how.

The Delden Group has completed its conception of a programme of internationalisation. In the future we shall think in terms of continental, not national, operational areas. The current areas of operation are Europe, North America and South America. We are in the process of investigating the possibilities of setting up additional areas of operation...South America: Curitiba, where operations to literally carve Cicade Industrial out of the bush, started at the beginning of 1973. Cicade Industrial, a new type of industrial city, is fifteen kilometres long, two to three kilometres across, and has an area of forty-three square kilometres. It has been planned to incorporate all the most modern ideas, and was constructed direct from the drawing board. So far, forty-five companies from all over the world have made the decision to produce there. The Delden Group was one of the first companies to decide to set up in Cicade Industrial. Gronau SA Industrias Texteis was completed in the record time of twelve months...After completion of the first stages of expansion it will employ 1000 workers and have a turnover of DM 120 million.

The employees are almost exclusively Brazilians. Of the present work-force, 20% have received a specialist training in the German works of the Delden Group. This training programme was the largest ever carried out in Europe for Brazilians.

Delden's plans by no means end with the commissioning and operation of Gronau SA. The group is currently working on plans to attract an internationally competitive making-up and finishing industry to Cicade Industrial. Thousands of jobs could be created when this project is brought to fruition.[1]

This is the language of a transnational company: both in what it says and what it omits to say.

The future development of the world economy and the structural changes which are now apparent require 'a return to a renewed reliance on true entrepreneurship'...Gerrit van Delden Jr:

Let's start with the clothing field: the various stages are the manufacture of yarn, the production of the fabrics, making-up and distribution. New techniques are beginning to emerge in the manufacture of yarn and fabrics. Open-end spinning, water-jet looms and similar techniques which will facilitate further technical development and hence cost reduction are just two examples. But what about making-up? This stage has a current wage share of turnover of between 30% and 50%. So far no development has emerged which, from the technical point of view, could enable a fundamental modernisation and reduction in costs to take place. This implies that even the most modern and well-managed undertaking involved in the manufacture of yarns and fabrics cannot exist if its market – making-up – is no longer on hand...

Our view is that making-up will operate on an increasingly international level. But we also believe that it is possible, taking advantage of constantly improving transportation, to move the high quality goods made in the highly industrial countries to the developing countries. However, this only applies to certain restricted types of textiles. We consider that all those textiles which are made from cotton will be increasingly manufactured directly in those countries where the crop

1. *Textil-Wirtschaft* 26 (1975).

is cultivated: Egypt, Turkey and Greece come to mind here. This means that a larger section of the present textile industry will have to cope more and more with this severe competition.

The opportunity for the textile industry in the highly developed countries is clearly – and, we would add, almost exclusively – in the application of synthetic fibres.

The following points stand out as far as the garment industry is concerned: (1) extremely strong tendencies towards internationalisation, (2) increasing production of cotton textiles in countries of cultivation, and (3) increasingly strong tendency towards application of synthetic fibres in the highly industrialised countries.

For the home textile industry: (1) with the exception of the carpet branch, the home textile sector will be a branch for special products, (2) because of the necessary high level of know-how carpets will still be able to be manufactured in the highly industrialised countries in the future, (3) large undertakings will have a hard task coping with this sector as the philosophy involved is different to that of simple mass production, (4) the largest sector in the field of home textiles, the carpet branch, still has great opportunities for the future, not least because of the rapid strides forward which can be made through technology.

For industrial textiles: the extremely high requirements for technical know-how will guarantee the future development of this branch in the highly industrialised countries.[1]

The van Delden Group is involved in a great deal of activity abroad... Business in the USA has shown excellent developments... As a consequence the production of Delden Fabrics Inc. is to be shifted to the new works in Lindhurst/New Jersey. Production at Lindhurst is to be doubled to 70000 metres of fabric daily. A US turnover of DM 42 million is planned for 1976. Expansion will also take place in Brazil.[2]

After the initial running-in phase is completed, it is intended to expand production at Gronau SA Industrias Texteis in Curitiba. Production capacity is to be increased by 25%. Measures to expand capacity have already been got under way. In addition to the main product, fabrics for women's day wear, the company would like to establish a second centre for the manufacture of shirt and trouser materials. All in all, better sales prospects are awaited. Delden wishes in particular to increase its cooperation with the Brazilian making-up industry. Gronau SA is planned to have a turnover of DM 33 million by 1976.[3]

Gerrit van Delden noted that the development of the present-day world economy 'is not only based on new and diverging technologies, but also on a new science, a new logic, a new set of ideas... This leads back to the first phase of development in which innovative entrepreneurship was the foundation of industrial survival.'[4]

Looked at as a whole, these very specific extracts are a striking

1. *FAZ/Blick durch die Wirtschaft*, 3 July 1975, 'Die Textilindustrie von morgen – Zukunftsvisionen eines Unternehmens'. Cf. *Textil-Wirtschaft* 34 (1976), p. 24.
2. *Süddeutsche Zeitung*, 19 May 1976, 'Delden hat im Ausland viel vor'.
3. *VWD-Textil*, 17 May 1976, 'Umsatz der Delden-Gruppe zieht spürbar an'.
4. *FAZ/Blick durch die Wirtschaft*, 3 July 1975.

confirmation of the degree of awareness with which the qualitative changes occurring in the capitalist world system are perceived by corporations and integrated into a global reorganisation of industrial production in the cause of higher profits. The interests of the population (which will not share in Delden's social fund) are, nonetheless, passed over without comment in the effusive prognostication of the dawning of new age, with its analogies with the early period of capitalism.

Important details which should be borne in mind are: the varying estimates of the possibilities of wage cost reductions via new technology (essentially positive in the textiles sphere, and negative in the garment industry); the supposition that it will be profitable for the traditional industrial countries to produce special products in the future, especially in the textile industry; the view that the growing application of synthetic fibres will also allow profitable mass production in the traditional industrial countries in the future – in contrast to the use of cotton.

The latter view calls somewhat critically to mind what was said on the development of the synthetic fibres industry in the developing countries in Chapter 5.2. Do fabrics made out of synthetic fibres constitute an exception to the claim made previously that freight costs make it impossible to 'supply the world from Europe'?

The claim that wage differences play no role in the relocation of Federal German textile production to sites abroad is likewise scarcely credible. It is first of all quite clearly false for important branches of the Federal German and international textile industry (not only knitwear), as a whole series of concrete examples cited in this study prove. Secondly, this assertion contradicts numerous statements made by the German employers' federation (Gesamttextil), who never tire of referring to the deleterious effects of the relatively high wage costs which burden the international competitiveness of the Federal German textile industry. Or should such statements simply be regarded as a tactical feint on the part of Gesamttextil for use in wage negotiations?

In 1974/75 the textile operations of the *Greiling* Group of Mannheim ('Felina') had a turnover of approximately DM 97 million and employed 1500 employees. It also had its own works, or contract partners, in Austria, Greece, Yugoslavia, Poland, Czechoslovakia and Hungary; in addition there are plans for manufacturing in other parts of the world. One undertaking in the group expressed itself as being very satisfied with the quality and punctuality of subcontracted production (supervised by German technicians); in addition, production costs are about 40% less than in Germany.

After the closure of the second plant in Steinau (Pompadour) and Worms (Felina) the number of employees will probably fall to 1000.

Two new plants have recently been set in operation in Yugoslavia and Greece: they will finish underwear and bathing fashion, partly for sale in Federal Germany. The rates of growth which can be observed in the Near East and Africa should lead to additional production facilities there which will supply these new markets.[1]

...a profit has been achieved for the first time in two years. This is principally attributable to rationalisation measures, such as reducing personnel in non-productive areas and shifting production to contract suppliers abroad. Outside Germany, the company produces at various locations in the Eastern Bloc and in its own subsidiary plant in Austria. The reduction in personnel from 1150 to 1000 has now finally been achieved.[2]

Felina's current aim is to maintain the present level of output in its German plants and secure increases in output by the use of contract plants abroad. The sole reason for this is the wage difference between the company's own plants in Germany, and the finishing carried out under contract in Yugoslavia, Hungary, Czechoslovakia and Italy, which produce up to a third more cheaply for Felina. At the present time 55% of the pieces are still produced in Federal German plants, with 45% coming from the Felina works in Austria and from subcontracting. Subcontracting abroad is constantly being expanded...The groups general profit situation has improved following the extensive cost-cutting measures of recent years which have stabilised the work-force at 1000 at home and 300 abroad.[3]

There has recently been an increase in the number of instances in which undertakings in the textile industry have started manufacturing in those countries where the production of clothing for the world market already plays an important role. The *Nino AG* company of Nordhorn is one recent example of this development.

Nino AG/Nordhorn, one of the largest European textile concerns, is now following the trend towards the foreign manufacture of the making-up stage. The internationalisation which already characterises the distribution sphere – with 50% of its turnover going to exports Nino is represented in almost one hundred countries – will now be joined by internationalisation in the sphere of production. Dr Günther Mordhorst, Chairman of the Board of Management, currently outlines the company's plans with the formula of 'grasping' the opportunity for production facilities abroad.

One particular model which has been thought up would be cooperation with an already resident partner, with finance taking place by means of an exchange of

1. *FAZ*, 9 May 1975.
2. *FAZ*, 23 October 1975.
3. *FAZ*, 18 November 1976.

equity...The package which Nino wishes to bring into such cooperation arrangements embraces, alongside Nino's distribution potential and brand-name, creativity in fashion and technical know-how. As a first step towards production overseas Nino has established Nino Far East, with its head office in Hong Kong: Nino has an 85% stake in Nino Far East through its administrative subsidiary Schweizerische Nino Verwaltungs AG, with the remaining 15% being held by local distribution partners. The first step in Hong Kong is intended to be the manufacture of wadding and lining, given that the world manufacture of shirts and blouses is centred on the Far East: almost two-thirds of all German imports of shirts come from this region...Fundamentally our overseas plans do not mean that the Nordhorn site in Germany is to be 'starved out', but rather made secure. The process of saving on personnel will indeed continue, but not as drastically as formerly. By the end of the current financial year (1975/76) Nino will have cut back the work-force in the group by 25%, or 1600 employees, from the highest level of 1972.

However, the necessary improvement in the profits' position will not be created solely through more internal cost reduction measures...This in turn goes to show just how important overseas planning is for the future of the company. It represents by far the most important, and at the same time most profitable, of the tasks which face the company in the future.[1]

In a 'Letter from Ireland' written on the occasion of the laying of the foundation stone for Nino's new spinning-mill in Wexford (Eire) the following report was made under the heading 'Competition for Industrial Settlers'.

...confirms the exceptionally good climate in this country, at least as far as the foreign investor is concerned...This climate cannot be reduced to a mere list of key 'incentives' – incentives used to create new industrial jobs – but is more characterised by the psychological support which a project like the Nino spinning-mill enjoys from the Industrial Development Authority. For example, after speeches from the Minister and the Town Mayor, the Chairman of the IDA, Mr Swann, addressed the gathering of distinguished guests from the area – town councils, officials, economic representatives, churchmen and headteachers: 'You have heard', he said, 'that this German company wishes to extend its operations here in Wexford from an initial stage employing 120 people through various phases to a weaving-mill employing 550. However, the plans for this expansion do not only depend on the state of the economy, but also on how much you people here in Wexford are willing to cooperate with this undertaking. You should regard yourselves as being fortunate in having a company like this here – not least because of its envisaged training programme, the most intensive supplied by any foreign investor. In addition to that, you should also bear in mind that we are competing with many other countries in the world to obtain new industries, and that there are development corporations everywhere. We therefore have to convince the investor that he is going to find himself in surroundings which will let him succeed...'

The Republic of Ireland, with only three million inhabitants and a labour-force of potentially 1.2 million, still has 9% unemployment: the country is mid-way through a process of restructuring from an agricultural country to a land which is also industrial. Mr Swann's appeal does not therefore fall on deaf ears. His

1. *VWD-Textil*, 16 October 1975, 'Nino will "Zugriff" auf Produktion in Übersee'.

authority, the IDA, has therefore had no difficulty in convincing the influential Church that Nino ought to work twenty-four hours a day, seven days a week: this means a four-shift operation, with a total of 168 hours per week (the plant will employ almost exclusively men because of the shift work). By contrast, the plant could only be worked with three shifts in Nordhorn, giving 120 hours a week, or 126 at most with overtime.

One particularly powerful argument which the IDA can bring to bear in attracting foreign investors, in addition to investment grants which are either measured according to the number of jobs created or the amount of capital invested (which in the case of Nino may not be less than if the company had built in a German development area with state support), is tax exemption for export profits – which applies for fifteen years. If one also adds the stable political framework in Eire, and in addition takes into consideration the plentiful assistance of the IDA which clears the way of all red-tape, then it is easy to understand why Eire has been successful in its policy of industrial settlement...

It should be noted that Ireland will not be used to conquer new markets – at least not initially – but is intended to supply weaving plant in Nordhorn and neighbouring Holland. This example already clearly illustrates the unequal competition between local development areas in their attempts to recruit new factories and branches of industry, and locations on the 'Emerald Isle'.[1]

Apart from the prototypical nature of the description of competition between countries on the world market for production sites, what is especially interesting in this report is the reference to the fact that countries such as Ireland are particularly advantageous for capital-intensive production because of the possibilities of keeping the plant and equipment permanently in operation, unlike in Federal Germany. It is important to stress this point to counter the thesis that low wage countries are only 'interesting', basically, for labour-intensive processes.

By far the most important foreign manufacturing operations undertaken by a Federal German textile firm are those of the *Triumph International* Group, Munich. They own or have a controlling interest in production facilities in more than twenty countries.

After years of stagnation – foundation garments have become too burdensome for young women – Triumph International AG, Munich, has been able to increase its world turnover by a healthy 10% to DM 750 million. Profits (previous year DM 15 million) may have risen by more than 10%. Rationalisation and the relocation of production abroad, with its lower wage costs, are paying off. By contrast, small plants are still being shut down at home: factories in Kötzting and Wegscheid are to be closed down in the next few months. Quite a number of these factories were constructed with state aid.

An agreement with a successor company has already been made for the

1. *FAZ/Blick durch die Wirtschaft*, 6 March 1975.

Wegscheid works, which, with its 133 employees, is to be abandoned at the end of March. The situation looks less favourable in Kötzting (75 employees) where no one has yet been found to take over the plant. In 1975, as Board members G. Spiesshofer and Dr L. Sickinger announced to the press, Triumph closed down a large number of mostly small plants in Germany. For example, the lingerie works in Ulm was shut down without an interested party having been found to take over the plant. By contrast, the works in Tittling (95 employees) and Landau (64 employees) continued in production, mostly of jeans and shirts. Five small establishments each with between 36 and 66 employees in the Heubach area were closed down, including the Heubach works itself which employed 200. The Donauwörth works, with 100 employees, was transferred to Monheim, where 200 people are now employed.

A breakdown of the turnover shows that production abroad is pushing ahead (in Japan, Hong Kong and Brazil), whilst production at home is stagnating. Thus in 1975 DM 330 million (329 previous year) out of total company turnover, were accounted for by domestic operations, DM 258 million (239) by European operations, and DM 160 million (109) by overseas operations. The estimate for 1976 is that turnover will reach DM 800 million, with a contraction of between 2%–4% at home, a growth of 8% in Europe, and an increase of between 20% and 30% overseas. Out of the 17900 employees in 1975, 5200 were in Federal Germany (compared to 6000 in the previous year), 5900 were in Europe (compared with 6300) and 6800 were overseas (compared with 5300 the previous year).

In fact, Triumph has not only transferred production abroad, but was also able to build up new markets...Japan and Brazil are the most interesting in this connection. In Europe the largest production facilities are in Austria, followed by France, Greece, England, Italy and Spain. In this connection, wages in Federal Germany are twice as high as in Austria (wages in Germany have increased 153% in the last ten years). As a consequence, the share of imports within the company is growing.

To summarise: a comparison between the miserable performance of the last few years with the 1975 results can lead to only one conclusion. Something has triumphed at Triumph![1]

After the foundation garment giant kept to its hard path of consolidation in the current year, investment in the group will not exceed depreciation (1974 DM 5.8 million). 'At home the movement of investment is even slightly downwards.'

Foreign production facilities, including subcontracting in the Eastern Bloc, contribute around 20% to 25% to German sales of foundation garments. The share of goods from the Far East is relatively slight. The share of imports from the company's own production – principally here in fact from contract-processing – may be higher in the case of underclothing than for foundation garments. Triumph does not wish to extend its capacity to any noticeable extent in the current year, including abroad.[2]

The relocation of production abroad is not only a product of the higher wage levels in the Federal Republic: it is also a function of the need to open up new markets...

The development of employment at Triumph inside Federal Germany reveals

1. *Süddeutsche Zeitung*, 17 February 1976. 2. *Handelsblatt*, 17 February 1976.

the entire structural crisis of the German textile industry; in 1970 employment was still 11400, distributed over a variety of plants; since then their number has been reduced by several hundred each year, so that by the end of 1975 there were only 5200 on Triumph's wage bill. And this development has still not ceased. More small plants will be closed with, in each instance, an attempt being made to find a successor employer who can continue to employ the work-force. If this meets with no success then in each case Triumph must draw up a redundancy scheme: expenditure per employee has established itself at up to DM 6000. However, Spiesshofer calculates that 'this sum will be recouped within a year by the transfer of production abroad'. For the German workers affected the redundancy payments which they get through the scheme are small consolation. A number of Triumph plants are in regions of high unemployment such as the Bavarian Forest region, or Upper Palatinate, where jobs are very hard to come by for women. Triumph did not receive government assistance for setting up in these areas for nothing.

The Triumph management defends the plant closures and dismissals on grounds of economic necessity: since 1970 wage levels in Federal Germany have risen by 153%. However, the reduction in personnel can mostly be explained by rationalisation and changes in production. In 1970 twenty-four minutes were allowed for sewing together a brassiere: today only ten minutes are needed. However, these changes and the increase in turnover per employee over the period from 30500 to 41700 DM are still not enough to make up for the advantages of producing abroad.

Finally, the annual surplus, which was DM 15 million for the group in 1974, is being very cautiously expressed as being 'no worse' for 1975, with an eye to current wage negotiations. Nonetheless, as management admits, the surplus has increased more strongly than turnover, and foreign operations contributed a great deal to this.[1]

More than two-thirds of this year's investment of DM 14.2 million will be in the overseas sphere, predominantly in the new plants in Manila and Bangkok and the Brazilian plant which currently employs 2200 workers. Whereas the number of foreign manufacturing sites (with 60% of total capacity) has increased to thirty-two, the company is attempting to reduce the number of plants in Germany from twenty-five (twenty-eight at the end of 1974) to twenty-one.

Hausner cites structural change as the reason behind the process of the shifting of capacity abroad which has been going on for a number of years. In his view, a number of processes can be simplified. Manufacture is not as labour-intensive as formerly. The average sewing time for parts of foundation garments has fallen by a half over the last ten years to the current figure of 10.4 minutes. On the other hand, the average earnings of a seamstress have risen from DM 3.60 in 1966 to DM 7.74. Hausner regards wage costs as being an important reason behind the expansion of production abroad: 'We are just at the beginning.'[2]

On the occasion of the tenth anniversary of their first agreement the Hungarian Foreign Trade Association, Hungarocoop, and Triumph International Holdinggesellschaft/Munich, agreed in Budapest in September to a renewal of cooperation for a further five years. According to the new agreement the Hungarian cooperation partners will manufacture Triumph models to an annual value of DM 5 million for the period 1976–80 of which 50% will go to cooperation agreements

1. *FAZ*, 17 February 1976.

2. *Süddeutsche Zeitung*, 23/24 August 1975.

and 50% to subcontracting. The small cooperatives in the west region of Hungary which have been involved in such work for years will sew ladies' lingerie, brassieres, bathing fashion, foundation garments, towelling articles and bath robes with equipment and technology supplied by the German partner. Over 100 out of the total of 200 of Triumph's range of articles are made in Hungary. The basic machinery customary in the making-up stage will be purchased by the Hungarian cooperatives, and the specialised machines for particular Triumph articles will be supplied to Hungary by the Munich company under customs' bond and lent to the cooperatives for three years. The Triumph company supplies the market with three million brassieres annually. Of these 450000 will be manufactured in Hungary.[1]

Knowledge has been transformed into strategy: one foreign production facility has been started up after another, first in Europe, then overseas. Since the actual methods of production are not difficult to learn, but in fact easy, and since no large infrastructure for the setting up of sewing machines and similar simple machines is required, the figures have risen. Between 1965 and 1975 domestic turnover fell, with some fluctuations, from DM 375 million to DM 334 million: it may well have fallen further over the last year. At the same time foreign turnover has increased from DM 116 million to DM 424 million. Foreign turnover is therefore not only higher than domestic turnover but is also responsible for the fact that the entire undertaking is once more growing in a contracting branch of industry. The development of employment runs parallel to these shifts in production. In 1965, 13200 employees were employed in Germany; by 1976 this figure had fallen to a mere 4400. By contrast, the number of workers employed abroad rose from 4800 to 13500, so that the total number of employees remained almost constant. This tendency will continue: new jobs are being created abroad because of wage costs at home.[2]

What still has to be added to these press reports (information could not be obtained directly from the firm) is that the DEG is involved in Triumph plants in Israel, Thailand and the Philippines in accordance with the recommendation which the DEG makes on the subject of 'profitable business activity': namely, 'capital-intensive investments in the field of rationalisation should be made at home, and labour-intensive investment to complement it should be re-located to the developing countries.'[3]

Tono *Volmary*, Münster, known as an importer and producer of shirts and aprons in the lower price range (annual turnover DM 53 million) has filed a petition for bankruptcy. Volmary, originally deeply involved in business with the East, no longer numbers among the dealers. He has his own plant in Malta and a co-holding in a shirt factory in Malaysia...Recently large delays in shipments of shirts have been the subject of criticism. Volmary commented on this: 'Unfortunately we have to concede that you are right: our capacity in Malaysia has not grown sufficiently in

1. Hungaropress, *Wirtschaftsinformationen – Informationsdienst der Ungarischen Handelskammer* 18 (1975), p. 6.
2. *Die Zeit*, 25 February 1977, 'Wandern die Arbeitsplätze aus?'.
3. DEG, *Geschäftsbericht 1973*, p. 10.

step. In addition we had to put up with strikes. Ships carrying cloth were held up in harbour for up to a fortnight and more.'[1]

...bankruptcy proceedings have been opened. Nothing concrete can be said as yet as to exactly when the schedule will be submitted as there are large loan claims on the company in Malaysia and Malta. Dobrick (the official liquidator) regards the chances of realising these claims as being very slim... Whereas the round hundred employees in Zierenberg and the sixty employees in administration, despatch and central stores will lose their jobs, the eighty employees at the second works will be employed by a new employer. The company in Malaysia is as yet unaffected by the bankruptcy.[2]

This is not the first time that a Federal German clothing company has gone bankrupt in Germany following a build-up of production abroad. Of course to the outsider the question may well arise as to why there are large claims on the company in Malaysia, yet it is precisely this company which is not affected by the bankruptcy proceedings.

Wiedekind/Sprendlingen is one of the few firms who have recently taken the path back from production abroad to production in Germany. Friedrich Wiedekind gives the following explanation as to why production was shifted back from the Far East: 'We kept encountering delays in supplies; now we can fill in the gaps and additional deliveries and a more rapid entry into current fashion trends is more feasible. In addition, goods kept on getting dearer because of constantly rising air-freight costs, as fashion articles can no longer be transported by sea these days. If one calculates that the freight cost share is more than DM 2.00 for a pair of trousers, and then adds handling charges, a pair of jeans from Asia costs DM 25–38.' Moving production back requires only a price increase of 5%–10% for the same goods.

The new jeans factory was equipped with the latest machines, and was completely reorganised. The seamstresses were retrained to work an 'assembly system' – it is necessary to think in industrial terms here. 'The production of jeans can be much more automated than the production of trousers which yields a substantial cost advantage'... However, Wiedekind have remained faithful to overseas manufacture in one area: extravagant items such as braided belts, which can only be made by hand. The share of foreign manufacture has also increased for normal trousers. However, the company is staying here in Europe.

Commercial criteria such as costs and speed are not the only factors which led to the decision to bring back the production of jeans. Friedrich Wiedekind also sees the political aspect. 'One has to show a preparedness to invest here if we want to preserve what we have achieved.'[3]

As this example shows, production sites which have for the time being become obsolete can become profitable again in the course of development, given that certain conditions come about (new tech-

1. *Textil-Wirtschaft* 42 (1975).
2. *VWD-Textil*, 13 November 1975.
3. *Textil-Wirtschaft* 52 (1975).

nology, changed freight costs, extra profit on fashion articles etc.). Once this has happened it is – literally – possible to afford to take into account the possible explosive political consequences of too rapid a massive shift of production out of the mass markets *alongside* economic calculations. All in all, this constitutes a classic example of the planned world-wide exploitation of the opportunities which the new international division of labour offers. We shall deal later with the question as to whether new technologies in the manufacture of clothing could one day make Federal Germany an 'interesting' site, once more, for a wide range of production. (See Chapters 7.5 and 7.6.)

6.5 Federal German foreign production in a low wage country: details of operations of a textile manufacturer and a garment manufacturer

The following section presents information on the foreign manufacturing operations of two Federal German companies, one from the textile sphere and one from the garment sphere. These reports are based on factory visits and conversations between the authors and managers of the foreign establishments carried out in 1974.[1]

The first of these foreign plants was set up by a Federal German textile company whose European customers had increasingly turned to importing cheap goods from South East Asian suppliers, after the German company was no longer able to offer its German-made goods at competitive prices on the German market: in order not to lose the market completely, and to try to regain its former market share, the company decided to shift production to a non-European low wage country. Several sites originally considered in Europe and overseas were dropped (danger of strikes in one country, language difficulties in another). The site which was eventually chosen recommended itself to the German company, amongst other things, because of its supply of good and cheap labour, and its extensive infrastructure (in particular as far as energy was concerned). Production started within ten months of the beginning of construction. The new plant had approximately the same legal status as a plant in a free production zone: a customs fence surrounded the factory. Knitted goods were produced by a work-force of *c.* 300 employees. Only

1. Since the following information originates from sources which are not available to the public or from written replies from the companies concerned, the name of the firm and the country are not given here.

sections of the various areas of production were shifted from Europe: the manufacture of exclusive high quality goods from individual areas was left behind. The final stage of the plan envisaged the employment of several thousand workers in a total of four plants.

The majority of the employees were young women; men were employed for particularly heavy work and for attending to the complex machinery. Technically trained labour was required for the latter (mechanics, aircraft mechanics etc.).[1] Twenty skilled German workers were employed in the setting up, fitting and adjustment of machines and in training the local work-force.

For the simple machines the training period lasted approximately three months; on the more complex machines up to a year was needed before the productivity of a semiskilled worker in Germany was attained. For female workers the training costs (according to the manager) amounted to 10% of the equivalent costs in Federal Germany. Three months output was sufficient to demonstrate that quality production was possible.

Untrained local workers received DM 4 per day on starting (DM 5–6 per hour in Federal Germany). The firm paid above average wages for the low wage country concerned, with the deliberate intention of creating a good working atmosphere. In addition, as management stated, DM 3 per day was simply not enough. The male fitters who were needed to attend to the complex automatic machinery could not be hired for less than DM 400 per month.

As compared with other plants in the country concerned, the working conditions seemed to be well above average. On the other hand the high intensity of work was evident during the course of the factory visit.

The majority of the machines arrived from the German plants of the company as already used machines. After an initial phase they operated remarkably reliably; the workshops were air-conditioned to prevent the rapid rusting of the machinery.

To begin with, raw materials came from Federal Germany. Subsequently they were obtained from neighbouring countries: for the same quality they could be obtained more cheaply, with freight costs playing a role here. Perhaps in the future raw materials could even be obtained from within the country itself.

1. It should be noted that the types of occupation in which skilled workers are available in these countries are in areas of work which are important for the needs of the local upper class, not those of the mass of the population.

This plant represented a unit which was capable of undertaking independent production. In the long term the fitting, setting, adjusting and maintenance of the machinery would have to be carried out by local workers without assistance from abroad. By contrast, at that time no local skilled workers had been trained up to technical management or production planning. The German parent company was clearly satisfied with the new plant: although this was not said, it appeared as if the company could bank on having long-term high profits.

The second of the two plants was set up by a Federal German garment company as the East European contract-processor with which it was previously cooperating could only manage unpunctual deliveries, and in addition because the wages in the low wage country selected were very 'attractive'. Furthermore, the company had a chance to take over a firm in the low wage country which had run into difficulties.

About 500 employees (95% women) produced shirts on two shifts, the output of which was partly supplied to the customer by direct container service, e.g. sent to a Federal German mail order firm under an imaginary brand-name. Freight costs per shirt by sea-borne container (21 days) amounted to DM 0.60: air-freight for items needing swift delivery were around DM 1. If need be, production capacity could be increased sufficiently to take the entire production both of shirts and other garments from the German parent company.

The company tried to obtain all the raw materials for shirt manufacture from local sources, as in this case the Federal German import duty of 17% on shirts no longer applied. This may not have been significant in view of the 'attractive' wages, but was nonetheless exploited.

The technology employed was in principle the same as that employed in Federal Germany. 'The training period soon makes it clear whether the worker is any good, or whether it will be necessary to "lose" them.'

The management had switched from time to piece rates in order to reach an output corresponding to that level of productivity prevailing in Germany. It was said that one section of the women had already registered a success: they had increased their performance very rapidly. Another section of women had clearly not grasped, however, that working harder was worthwhile: that instead of earning DM 3 per day, with piece rates they could make DM 3.20, 3.30 or even DM 3.50–4.00 per day. The norms for piece rates were based on the Federal German norms, slightly reduced during the initial phase. It was admitted that although the pace of work was pretty lively, it had to become even quicker still. Some of the shops were air-conditioned, as this held out the prospect of a higher pace of work.

Plant management was autonomous as far as local decisions were concerned. Basic decisions (production programme, design, market and sales) were made in the head office in Federal Germany.

If, as is expected perhaps in ten years, labour becomes short as a result of advancing industrialisation, it may no longer be possible to produce textiles by labour-intensive methods at the plant's present location. Then, we were told, the company would simply pack its bags and go to another country where labour could be hired for lower wages.

7 Determinants of the development of the world market for production sites

7.1 Babbage's principle: examples of its effects in the textile and garment industry

In the course of his glorification of the division of labour in the *Wealth of Nations* Adam Smith observed that the increase in productivity achieved through the progressive division of labour was the central means by which capital expanded its value. According to Smith an upper limit was placed on the division of labour by the size of the available markets on which the product can be sold.

A more specific, and in fact more important, aspect of the division of labour as a means towards the valorisation of capital was formulated by Charles Babbage. Increased division of labour would allow the substitution of skilled labour-power by less skilled labour-power. Moreover, a large number of the individual operations which arise out of the progressive division of labour could then be economically performed by machines.

The replacement of skilled labour-power by less skilled is economically advantageous in many instances, and therefore becomes a necessity: the basic reason is that less skilled labour-power can often be purchased at a significantly lower price on the labour market than more highly skilled labour-power. Why? The fact that there are potentially many more workers who possess labour-power with lower levels of skill means that the competition between these workers to sell their labour-power on the labour market is greater and tends to force down wages. Hence, according to Babbage, the size of the available *labour market* also determines the extent of the division of labour.

During the phase of the 'classical' international division of labour, the organisations of the working populations of the traditional industrial countries by and large succeeded, at least for a while, in obstructing the tendency of competition between less skilled workers to drive wages down. What is especially novel about the new international division of labour is the enormous expansion of the labour market for less skilled workers. This expansion will result in the competition between less skilled workers, which had been more or less prevented by the trade unions in the traditional industrial countries, regaining its economic impact. According to Babbage this will mean a new and powerful impulse for the spread of the division of labour, which at the moment is taking, *inter alia*, the form of a new international division of labour.

In other words, the present-day conditions for the world-wide valorisation of capital mean that capitals must completely recalculate the allocation of the elements of the manufacturing process to the most advantageous combination of 'factors of production' as regards the cost of the final product *on a global basis* – taking into account the enormous reserve army of less skilled workers which has recently come into existence. In many instances, the end-result of this calculation (which includes as its variables changed production technology with changed requirements as far as the number and skills of the workers needed) will be the relocation of industrial production (and subassembly) to new sites, chiefly in the developing countries with their practically inexhaustible reservoir of unskilled and extremely cheap labour-power.

This expression of Babbage's principle under the current conditions for the valorisation of capital will now be demonstrated by reference to a number of examples taken from the textile and garment industry.

Today large sections of the production process of clothing (from the preparation of the thread to the packing of the finished article) are already extensively mechanised or automated. The result is that the few jobs which remain are not of great significance in terms of wage costs, even if they require high levels of skill.[1] A higher share of wage costs occurs in the process of making-up (in the narrow sense), in particular at the sewing stage and similar operations.

1. Even then additional 'rationalisation' is undertaken with the aim of reducing the number of unduly 'demanding' skilled workers who are still necessary. Thus Süddeutsche Baumwoll-Industrie AG, Kuchen/Württ state in one of their publicity inserts 'Thoughts on today...and beyond', 'the textile industry has already rationalised its manufacturing capacity so much that the pressures placed on the labour market potential of specialist workers, can be kept very low.' This is supposed to help counter the 'excessive expectations' of the 'unindustrious' (!) skilled workers. See *Textil-Wirtschaft* 41 (1976), p. 19.

Working on a sewing machine does not require a particularly high level of skill and can be learnt in a short period of time: 'After elementary instruction in the handling of a sewing machine – and it requires very little time – the rest of the learning process consists of a progressive and relatively rapid acquisition of maximum operating speed.'[1]

At the present time there is a superabundant potential of labour-power for such easily learnt operations distributed throughout the world, but particularly in the low wage countries. The consequence is that sewing especially, and similar work, is being increasingly shifted from the traditional industrial countries to the low wage countries. It is quite clear that company calculations persistently yield the result that this available labour-power is too cheap for it to be *economically* feasible to undertake such part-operations using mechanisation or automation at the traditional sites in the industrial countries. (In contrast, the corresponding *technical* problems appear, in principle, to be capable of solution: cf. Chapter 7.5.)

A few examples: trouser material is cut in Federal Germany, sent to Tunisia for sewing into trousers, and finally shipped back, in made-up form, to the home market in Germany. A high proportion of the international subcontracting trade between Federal Germany and East European countries takes place in the form of the material being manufactured and cut in Federal Germany (EEC) and temporarily exported for contract-processing. In the knitted goods industry, as in the manufacture of fashion hosiery, the capital-intensive parts of the production process (e.g. with circular knitting machines) are undertaken in Federal Germany, whilst outfitting, making-up, packing etc. takes place in low wage countries (for example, Hudson in Greece, Schulte & Dieckhoff in Yugoslavia): the finally packed goods are then, for the most part, re-exported to the Federal Republic of Germany.

Although these examples deal with the relocation of semi-manufacturing processes, other examples show that complete processes (in particular, but not exclusively, of 'standard articles') are, and must be, transferred to sites with relatively less skilled and extremely cheap labour. For example, Egeria manufactures standard towelling articles in Mauritius; Schiesser obtains standard articles from its Irish subsidiary. The subsidiary of a Federal German knitted goods

1. *NACLA's Latin American & Empire Report*, vol. XI, no. 3 (March 1977), p. 8.

undertaking produces the full range of products of the parent company in a low wage country, with the exception of high quality articles (Chapter 6.5).

Those parts of the manufacturing process which still require relatively high levels of skill (design, styling etc.) predominantly remain in the traditional industrial countries, although a trend towards their relocation is also becoming evident (as in Hong Kong, Chapter 5.3). Tendencies towards mechanisation and automation are especially intensive in this sphere. Unlike the previous example, in this case there is no *pre-existing* world-wide reservoir of low skilled and extremely cheap labour which can be *utilised* in the form of the new international division of labour: companies rather attempt to lower the requirements, in terms of numbers and skill, of the labour-force through mechanisation and automation. In other words, they seek to *create* the *possibility of access* to the economic advantages conferred on capital by the large market for less skilled labour through technical and operational changes (or to reduce the number of skilled workers; cf. Chapter 7.5).

The training period for the relatively less skilled workers is usually short; in the order of a few weeks (Chapter 7.2). Under the pressure of competition on the world market for production sites several countries are already trying to meet the companies half-way by providing individual training for the specific operational needs of private companies in government training establishments (for example, Tunisia, Chapter 8.4).

7.2 Working hours, productivity and intensity of work in the textile and garment industries of selected countries

Detailed reports on the working hours, wages and labour productivity in the export-oriented industries of a large number of developing countries are provided elsewhere in this work, and it is therefore sufficient here simply to enumerate the relevant figures for the textile and garment industries of a number of selected countries, and compare them with the figures for the traditional industrial countries.

Table I-15 gives the average working hours and wages in the textile and garment industries of a number of countries according to data from the International Labour Office. By and large the length of the working weeks in the centrally planned economies mentioned,

Table I-15. *Average hours of work and earnings in the textile and garment industry of selected countries: 1975*

	Average hours of work (hours per week)		Average hourly earnings (US $ per hour)	
	ISIC 321	ISIC 322	ISIC 321	ISIC 322
Hungary	36.5	36.9	A 1.80	1.60
			B 0.75	0.67
Yugoslavia	41.3	41.5	0.77	0.74
Greece	43.6	41.6	1.12	0.97
Malta (1972)	41.1	41.7	0.68	0.40
Hong Kong	48.0	n.a.	0.72	0.66
South Korea	51.1	52.9	0.31	0.23
Federal Germany	39.7	38.8	3.34	3.00
Japan	39.8	40.0	2.22	1.87
United States	39.2	35.1	3.40	3.19

Sources: ILO, *Yearbook of Labour Statistics 1976* (Geneva 1976); ILO, *Bulletin of Labour Statistics, 1976, 2nd Quarter*; UN, *Monthly Bulletin of Statistics*, xxx; own calculations

Exchange rates for conversion from national currencies into US $ taken from ILO *Yearbook* and (Hungary) UN *Monthly Bulletin* (A = fixed rate, B = non-commercial rate applying to tourism and to remittances from countries outside the rouble area)

Hours of work on monthly basis converted into weekly hours of work by division with 13/3

Hungary: State industry; hours actually worked; earnings include the value of payments in kind

Yugoslavia: Socialised sector; includes salaried employees; hours paid for

Greece: Hours paid for

Malta: Hours paid for; includes salaried employees; earnings for adult males (ISIC 321) and adult females (ISIC 322)

Hong Kong: Normal hours of work for females in textile mills; earnings for male spinners and female sewing machine operators (October 1975)

South Korea: Hours actually worked; includes salaried employees; earnings include family allowances; hours of work for ISIC 321 and ISIC 322, 324

Federal Germany: Hours paid for; earnings include family allowances paid directly by the employers

Japan: Hours actually worked; includes salaried employees; earnings include family allowances, mid- and end-of-year bonuses

United States: Hours paid for

and in Malta and Greece are comparable with those in the traditional industrial countries: in South Korea and Hong Kong they are much longer.[1] The differences as far as wages are concerned are incomparably greater (sometimes with differences of more than 1000%). A statement by the DEG gave the following as the hourly rates for seamstresses including indirect wage costs for mid-1975.[2]

Federal Germany DM 10; USA DM 9; France DM 8.20; Switzerland DM 5.80; Italy DM 5.70; England DM 5.00; Austria DM 4.75;

1. See Chapter 5.3 on Hong Kong. What is important here is that restrictions on shift, night, and holiday working do not, by and large, apply in the majority of low wage countries, which specifically favours the shifting of capital-intensive production to these locations. The effective running times of expensive machinery are much greater in such countries than in Federal Germany – with great advantages as far as the plant's profitability is concerned.
2. *FAZ*, 10 June 1976.

Japan DM 4.60; Greece DM 3.25; Portugal DM 3.20; Iran DM 2.10; Tunisia DM 1.80; Brazil DM 1.15; Malaysia DM 1.00; Taiwan DM 1.00; South Korea DM 0.90.

The sensitivity of the Federal German garment (and to some extent textile) industry to variations in wage differences between countries has already been shown in previous examples.[1] Since 1960 the average foreign textile wage costs, weighted by their share of Federal German foreign trade, have grown proportionally to average Federal German wage costs; since 1965 these average foreign textile wage costs have amounted to approximately 75% of the domestic costs (see Table I-16(a)).[2] In view of the rising wage costs in textiles in Federal Germany, this means that the absolute wage cost differences between domestic and foreign production has grown. If Federal Germany's imports of textiles, in particular those from low wage countries, have not increased more strongly despite this, it is undoubtedly principally attributable to Federal German (EEC) import restrictions on textiles and clothing.

The variations in wage rates just mentioned reflect wage costs as they figure in the calculations of *companies* when they make international comparisons of so-called labour costs. However, what do these wages mean for the material standard of living of the workers in the respective countries? As a rough indicator, we can take the purchasing power of the respective gross hourly wage rates for a number of selected basic subsistence goods (bread, rice, fish, milk, butter, beans, sugar and the like). With small deviations in individual instances the result emerges that the purchasing power of wages in the textile and garment industries in the respective countries by and large corresponds to the wage rates as expressed in Deutschmarks. This means, as far as purchasing power is concerned, that wages in South Korea are at the bottom end of the scale, followed by Hong Kong, then with a gap, Greece, Yugoslavia and Hungary: at the

1. Cf. Chapters 6.4 and 6.5. One example: 'Consideration is already being given to new shifts of production to Tunisia or the Far East now that wage costs have risen by around 25% in Yugoslavia' (Lodenfrey). At the other end of the spectrum the USA has recently started to become 'interesting' again from the perspective of wage costs, productivity and length of the working year – an example of the retroactive effect of the new industrial sites on working conditions in the traditional industrial countries. Higher unemployment and the threat of further shifts of production mean that US workers will have to be prepared to make further concessions. See too 'Capital's flight. The apparel industry moves south', *NACLA's Latin American & Empire Report* (March 1977).
2. Table I-16(b) demonstrates just how enormous the wage cost differences behind these averages are.

Table I-16

(a) Textile labour costs in Federal Germany and abroad since 1955

	Federal Germany (DM/h)	Other countries[a] DM/h	Other countries[a] FRG = 100	Difference (DM/h)
October 1955	1.87	1.97	105	+0.10
October 1960	3.13	2.49	80	−0.64
October 1965	4.79	3.61	75	−1.18
October 1970	7.40	5.22	71	−2·18
October 1975	12.30	9.61	78	−2.69
October 1976 (p)	13.28	10.08	76	−3.20
July 1977 (p)	14.23	10.69	75	−3.54

(b) Textile labour costs of selected countries: 1974–77

		DM/h				FRG = 100			
	Weight[b]	Oct. 1974	Oct. 1975	Oct.[c] 1976	Mid[d] 1977	Oct. 1974	Oct. 1975	Oct. 1976	Mid 1977
Sweden	0.9	12.84	16.27	18.04	18.05	113	132	136	127
Netherlands	15.5	12.70	14.44	15.60	16.63	112	117	117	117
Norway	0.4	11.68	14.61	15.88	16.47	103	119	120	116
Belgium	9.7	11.56	13.65	14.88	15.81	102	111	112	111
Denmark	1.0	12.21	13.15	14.84	15.48	108	107	112	109
Federal Germany		11.34	12.30	13.28	14.23	100	100	100	100
Switzerland	3.7	10.07	11.48	12.53	12.58	89	93	94	88
United States	1.5	11.03	11.29	12.37	11.86	97	92	93	83
Italy	15.1	8.26	10.57	10.72	11.22	73	86	81	79
France	12.3	8.28	9.58	9.42	9.72	73	78	71	68
Austria	4.3	6.43	7.29	8.01	8.24	57	59	60	58
Japan	0.9	6.43	6.47	7.22	7.98	57	53	54	56
Great Britain	2.8	5.98	6.82	5.83	6.11	53	55	44	43
Hong Kong	4.6	1.72	1.85	n.a.	n.a.	15	15	n.a.	n.a.
German Democr. Rep.	3.8	4.52	4.75	4.99	n.a.	40	39	38	n.a.
Romania	0.8	4.33	4.61	4.91	n.a.	38	37	37	n.a.
Czechoslovakia	1.0	4.68	4.88	4.81	n.a.	41	40	36	n.a.
USSR	0.5	2.67	2.79	2.92	n.a.	24	23	22	n.a.
Poland	1.4	2.11	2.34	2.48	n.a.	19	19	19	n.a.
Bulgaria	0.4	2.21	2.24	2.12	n.a.	19	18	16	n.a.
Hungary	1.6	0.87	0.92	1.07	n.a.	8	7	8	n.a.
Yugoslavia	4.7	2.88	2.97	3.05	n.a.	25	24	23	n.a.
Total[a]	86.9	8.33	9.61	10.08	(10.69)	73	78	76	(75)

Source: Arbeitgeberkreis Gesamttextil, *Löhne und Arbeitskosten der Textilindustrie – Internationaler Vergleich – 1977* (Frankfurt)

Labour costs include all individual contributions for industrial employees (wages and salaries per man/hour actually worked, bonuses and gratuities, remuneration for time not worked, social insurance paid by employer, social benefits). Overall contributions (social services, training centres etc.) are excluded.

a: Average calculated on the basis of weighted foreign trade shares

b: Percentage share in Federal German textile foreign trade (exports plus imports) 1975

c: Partly provisional data (especially Eastern European countries)

d: Calculated on the basis of collective agreement rates of wage increases

upper end of the scale we find Japan, and also after a gap, the USA and Federal Germany.[1]

The question then arises as to how the reproduction of labour-power can be ensured, given the low level of wages. The answer, to put it quite bluntly, is that in countries such as South Korea wages are only sufficient for the immediate, day to day reproduction of labour-power, but not for either the raising of a new generation of workers nor for an adequate provision for old age, sickness or invalidity. These additional costs have to be borne by a sector which is not capitalist, strictly defined, but which is characterised by an even higher burden of physical exertion imposed on its members: its features are extremely long working hours, high intensity of work, child labour, and extreme poverty. This sector, which is not directly integrated into the specifically capitalist mode of production of the 'modern sector', is also often however linked to the production process of the capitalist sector, in its narrow sense, in another form: namely through the medium of out-work (home-work).[2]

As far as the productivity of labour is concerned, we shall basically gather together certain items of data which can also be found distributed throughout the study, with the principal aim of eradi-

1. Figures are basically derived from the ILO annual survey of hourly rates and retail prices for selected consumer goods: ILO, *Bulletin of Labour Statistics, 2nd Quarter 1975, 1976*; supplemented by individual data from ILO, *Yearbook of Labour Statistics 1976* (Geneva 1976), and Statistisches Bundesamt, *Allgemeine Statistik des Auslandes, Länderberichte: Süd Korea 1975* (Stuttgart–Mainz 1976). A general picture of the material living conditions of the peoples of the developing countries can be found in Folker Fröbel, Jürgen Heinrichs & Otto Kreye (eds.), *Die Armut des Volkes. Verelendung in den unterentwickelten Ländern. Auszüge aus Dokumenten der Vereinten Nationen* (Reinbek 1974). See Chapter 5.3 for reference to living conditions in Hong Kong.
2. Out-work undertaken for the capitalist sector (*in sensu stricto*) is not only distributed throughout the numerous towns and cities of the 'Third World' but sometimes still plays a surprisingly large role in the traditional industrial countries. The secret of the imports of cheap knitted goods from Italy, which caused a good deal of complaint in Germany in 1976, consisted to a great extent in the amount of home-work carried out for the Italian textile industry, work which means low wages for the workers and low personnel costs for the employers, as it has always done. See 'Die Masche der kleinen Strumpfhersteller – Heimarbeit verbilligt in Italien die Produktion – "Kein Dumping"', *Süddeutsche Zeitung*, 9 September 1976. See too *Financial Times*, 22 September 1976: 'Under this system (outworking or 'family working') companies put out parts of the manufacturing process to workers at home, causing allegations of unfair competition to be levelled by other textile producers in Europe who claim Italian companies can in this way reduce costs by avoiding social and other charges acompanying full time employment'. Cf. on this subject *Handelsblatt*, 9 November 1976, and *Textil-Wirtschaft* 42 (1976), p. 27.

   In 1973 it was estimated that in addition to the 910000 workers in the textile and garment industry (including small businesses and the craft sector) a further 330000 out-workers were employed. L. Frey, 'Family work in the textile and clothing sector', in CIRFS, *The Future of the Man-made Fibres industry in Western Europe* (Paris 1976).

cating the widespread myth that the advantages of low wages for capital are, in many countries, offset by the fact that labour productivity is usually also low.

The data from the two examples of foreign manufacturing by Federal German companies presented in Chapter 6.5 clearly shows that after a certain period of training the productivity of labour in foreign plants is not noticeably below that of German plants engaged in comparable operations. The same also seems to apply to the 'Chinese girls on the production line' (sic!), who are praised for their 'personal and vocational skills' which are 'in no respect' inferior to their 'European colleagues'.[1] The DEG writes on the subject of Tunisia: 'Dutch and German firms, for example, have reached *c.* 75%–80% of their European norms within six to nine months of starting operations.'[2] In another DEG brochure: 'Tunisian workers can attain performance levels which are in line with European norms, if management, plant organisation, and working conditions correspond to European standards.'[3] The Federal German Bureau for Foreign Trade Information reports: 'Malta's level of wages and salaries for a comparable productivity is far below that of Western and most of Southern Europe . . . Labour is hired after a selection test: in general trainees can be set to work quite well after six weeks. Demanding tasks can be reckoned to require six months of training, after which the results correspond to the norms for the industrialised European countries.'[4]

Such examples could easily be multiplied:[5] they show that principally for semiskilled tasks (but not only for these) the productivity of labour in plants relocated to low wage countries is hardly below that of Federal German plants, operating with comparable processes. This result was, of course, predictable: the massive shift of production by the Federal German textile and garment industry to low wage countries can hardly be explained

1. Willy Kisselmann, *Errichtung von Fertigungsstätten in Niedriglohnländern – Unter besonderer Berücksichtigung der feinwerktechnischen Industrie* (Cologne 1975).
2. DEG, *Tunesien – Herstellung von Bekleidung* (*1/1976*), p. 2.
3. DEG, *Produzieren in Tunesien* (*Oktober 1973*), p. 7.
4. BfA, *Mitteilungen der Bundesstelle für Außenhandelsinformation*, vol. 25, no. 87 (May 1975), 'Merkblatt für Kapitalanlagen im Ausland – Malta', pp. 10 f.
5. Cf. for example CIRFS, *The Future of the Man-made Fibres Industry*. Taking productivity in Federal Germany as 100, productivity in the garment industry in Hong Kong, South Korea and Taiwan is between 60–80, Portugal is 70, Tunisia between 50–80 (the latter in Federal German owned plants), Brazil 40–80, Yugoslavia 60–80, Hungary 50–70 and Poland 70–90, not considering differences in quality.

solely by the extremely low wages in these countries (and other related locational advantages) if the benefits of low wages were fully outweighed by a low productivity of labour.

So far in this case study 'productivity' has been tacitly understood to mean the number of units of output per employee/hour, or something similar. It would be interesting to go beyond this and distinguish between productivity of labour as determined by mechanical equipment and organisation of the labour process on the one hand, and that determined by the intensity of labour, with a given level of equipment and organisation, on the other; that is, the speed of work and the breadth of activity of the worker, such as the number of machines simultaneously minded by one worker. Unfortunately the amount of available material on this theme is very sparse. However, occasional references do seem to indicate that the relatively high productivity of labour (units per employee/hour) in relocated manufacturing is at least in part attributable to an above average intensity of labour and less than average to capital equipment of a higher technical specification. One such indication could be that in relocated plants used – and that means under certain circumstances no longer up to the most modern technical standard – sewing machines are installed, whilst at the same time companies report levels of labour productivity comparable with those of European industrial countries (units of output per employee/hour). In addition, factory visits often convey the impression of a particularly high pace of work: the higher than average proportion of young, as yet still fresh, workers also points in this direction.

7.3 Transport

Improved techniques and connections in transport and communications are one of the factors which has made the current large extent of relocation of textile and garment manufacture from the traditional – and consumer – countries, to other sites, in particular the low wage countries, possible. Fast and efficient transport systems, such as air container transportation, are a typical example.

A glance at the share of the various branches of transportation in the import of clothing shows that since 1968 (the first year in which appropriate statistics were available)[1] the share in both volume and value terms carried by rail has fallen steeply (in value terms 1976:

1. Statistisches Bundesamt, *Wirtschaft und Statistik*, various years. See *WiSta* 7 (1977), p. 455*.

16.9 %). By contrast, the proportion of road transportation in value terms has increased over the same period (1976: 53.0 %). Both of these methods of transportation are primarily of importance for clothing imports into Federal Germany from countries in West and South (East) Europe. To give just one example, there is a regular lorry service for clothing from Greece to the Federal Republic of Germany.

Naturally, the strong growth in the import of clothing from overseas in recent years corresponds to a growth in the proportion moved by sea and air transport. Thus, in value terms in 1976, 21.4 % of Federal German clothing imports came by sea and 8.0 % by air. Whereas the cheaper and slower sea transport is mostly used for standard goods, air transport is used for fashionable, more rapidly 'perishable' goods. Even though sea and air transport experience delays from time to time,[1] this and other difficulties have not really hindered the expansion of overseas clothing imports into Federal Germany. Thus – to give another example – there has been a regular freight flight using Jumbo jets (Boeing 747) from Hong Kong to Federal Germany carrying clothing for some time.

In 1976 (1970) almost 18 000 tonnes (5000 tonnes) of clothing reached Federal Germany by air: this is no less than 10.4 % (5.4 %) of the total freight landings of commercial flights from abroad.[2] For the commodity group 96 (textile and leather goods) Federal Germany obtained 32 000 tonnes in all by air in 1976: 50 tonnes originated from Malta, 2030 tonnes from Greece, 1200 tonnes from Turkey, 385 tonnes from Tunisia, 75 tonnes from Mauritius, 1670 tonnes from the USA, 1220 tonnes from Brazil, 1550 tonnes from Iran, 1420 tonnes from Pakistan, 6260 tonnes from India, 340 tonnes from Thailand, 2700 tonnes from Hong Kong, 375 tonnes from Taiwan and 345 tonnes from South Korea.[3]

An idea of the level of freight rates can be obtained from a look

1. Cf. BfA, *Nachrichten für Außenhandel*, 16 June 1976, 'Luftfrachtprobleme im Indien-Geschäft'; *Handelsblatt*, 9 June 1976, 'Luftfracht-Run für Textilien aus Indien', according to which more than 1000 tonnes of clothing were helt up at Delhi and Bombay airports at the beginning of May 1976. One of the main sources of the problem was insufficient air-freight capacity: there was a lack of a balancing freight return from Europe, and to fly empty aircraft from Europe to India is not profitable at the special rates charged for textile exports. Such difficulties show why sites in Europe are chosen for 'hot fashion' items; higher production costs are more than made up for by the prices which can be charged for 'today's' fashion items. Naturally, it cannot be assumed that such difficulties will persist.
2. High shares were also accounted for by cut flowers, fruit, vegetables, and engineering parts and machinery.
3. Statistisches Bundesamt, Fachserie 8 (Verkehr), Reihe 6, *Luftverkehr 1976* (Stuttgart–Mainz 1977).

at two concrete examples: the rates of the IATA and shipping companies are difficult to disentangle because they are based on weight and because of the large number of individual rates. In 1974 one company calculated that freight costs from South East Asia to Federal Germany amounted to DM 1.00 per shirt by air-freight and DM 0.60 per shirt by sea-borne container: another company calculated air-freight costs for a pair of trousers from South East Asia to Federal Germany at over DM 2.00.[1] Despite periodic complaints about rising freight costs, in most cases the costs advantages of production even in a 'no-longer-a-complete-low-wage-country', such as Hong Kong, still outweigh any other disadvantages, especially in the production of clothing. After Japan, Hong Kong wage rates are the highest in the large Asian textile producing countries (Japan's are 30% higher than Hong Kong's). These relatively high wages are beginning to have an effect in some spheres. Hong Kong's garment manufacturers no longer produce to their own designs but to orders from US department stores: within two months of placing an order the goods are in the shops in the East Coast states of the US, which is quicker and cheaper than US producers can manage to supply. This is only possible because of the existence of air-freight, and Hong Kong's wages are still low enough to make this worthwhile.[2]

Developing countries pay great attention to pointing out the advantages of their transport facilities when presenting themselves on the world market for production sites: a link to an existing or specially newly created sea or air route is essential (cf. Part III). This point is illustrated in a DEG report.

Door to door transportation of larger loads (above 40 cubic metres per shipment) has proved economical by road haulage and ferry links (Genoa or Marseilles–Tunis). The journey time of a vehicle on a round trip Germany–Tunis–Germany (supplying raw materials and transporting finished articles) amounts to between ten and fourteen days, going by the experiences of German manufacturers operating in Tunisia. Costs for a round trip, door to door, including indirect costs for a lorry and trailer (83 cubic metres: 20–25 tonnes) is DM 15000–17000. Air freight can

1. See Chapters 6.4 and 6.5.
2. *Financial Times*, 17 May 1976. (The comparison between wage costs in Japan and Hong Kong is dubious; cf. Tables I-15 and I-16(b).) Nonetheless, transport costs do play a role in the competition between low wage countries with roughly comparable unit costs; countries with clearly lower unit costs can cope with higher freight rates (Hong Kong in competition with Brazil and India in woven cotton garments for the European market, or Hong Kong in competition with Portugal and Italy in lower quality knitted goods, also for the European market). Cf. *Asia Research Bulletin*, 31 July 1976, pp. 224 f. Transport costs similarly hinder or prevent the supplying of distant markets for the products of industrial branches with world overcapacity (e.g. synthetic fibres) and corresponding intensive (price suppressing) competition. Cf. CIRFS, *The Future of the Man-made Fibres Industry.*

also be carried by Lufthansa and Tunis Air scheduled passenger flights. Lufthansa have recently begun to operate a weekly service for freight only on the run Frankfurt–Tunis.[1]

To summarise these points, it is not going too far to say that, apart from possible 'fashion high flyers', the transport of clothing (and to some extent textiles) half-way around the world does not represent a serious technical, organisational and financial problem. From the transportation point of view the preconditions for a new international division of labour are fulfilled.

7.4 Criteria for the selection of sites abroad. An example of management consultancy for firms in the Federal German garment industry

Three determinants of the development of the world market for production sites have been stressed in the preceding sections: the division of the production process into elements and the global allocation of these rudimentary elements to various labour-powers according to the criterion of valorisation; the development of efficient transport systems; the existence of a world-wide reserve army of workers. These three determinants are central in the trend towards a new international division of labour. Of course for individual firms a number of additional factors enter into the decision to relocate production, some of which can be illustrated here by reference to an actual example.

In a practically oriented analysis of the opportunities, possibilities and limits which applied to foreign manufacture by Federal German firms in the garment industry the following were listed as factors in addition to 'wage pressure' and 'obtaining raw materials': 'Securing markets, tax incentives, lower social overhead costs (e.g. on training), less extensive co-determination by workers, shifts in exchange rates etc. In the clothing industry the dominant factor was clearly the question of wages (since low raw material costs no longer subsidise a high level of wages – DM 11.30 in 1974 including employers' contributions).'[2]

1. DEG, *Tunesien – Herstellung von Bekleidung* (*1/1976*), p. 3. If it is assumed that two articles of clothing weigh one kilogram, then the transport costs for one article of clothing from Tunisia to Federal Germany are less than DM 0.50 per piece.
2. E. A. Häussermann, 'Auslandsinvestitionen der deutschen Bekleidungsindustrie – Chancen, Möglichkeiten und Grenzen', *DOB+haka praxis* 7 (1975), 8 (1975). We are grateful to Herr Ackert of the Federation of the Bavarian Garment Industry for drawing our attention to this article.

The advantages and disadvantages of the various forms of foreign operation are weighed up against each other: production under licence, contract-processing, cooperation agreements and establishing subsidiaries are all subjected to a process of evaluation from the perspective of yielding the greatest benefit for the Federal German garment industry, in this context. International contract-processing emerges as the 'least risky and most capital-saving option for foreign operations'. Before any decision is taken for any particular involvement abroad the following tests are recommended to companies:

(A) Carry out a site analysis using Business Europe's check list (see below). Information, if available, should be quantified and graded as good, satisfactory or poor and *compared with alternative sites* (e.g. *Greece* compared with *Tunisia*).
(B) ...contractual issues.
(C) The following three strategic planning concepts should be applied:

(1) Timely *pre-planning* of foreign involvements *with actual* (subcontract, own investment) and *potential alternatives* (possible bottlenecks, problems). Don't relocate entire production (!) – fashion trends should be pursued from home.
(2) Using *models* compute and compare
(a) investment promotion (e.g. development aid tax laws) and legal obligations, costs, tax, tariff and investment assistance,
(b) investment costs, supply of materials,
(c) supply of labour, including training,
(d) organisation and deadlines,
(e) technical repair and maintenance, replacements,
(f) transport and transport costs etc.
(3) Cooperation with other Federal German companies is recommended. A subsidiary in a country where West German clothing firms are already operating can be advantageous, as firms are normally in a stronger position when acting together (this ranges from pooled services, to obtaining a maintenance service from a sewing machine maker, to having a stronger presence with the authorities).[1]

Guidelines for investment
Checklist for the choice of site abroad

I. ECONOMY

- resistance to recession
- relative dependence on imports/exports
- foreign exchange reserves
- balance of payments, stability/convertibility of currency
- remittance and repatriation guarantees
- relative importance of agriculture, industry and trade
- size of market for the company's products; growth outlook

1. Emphases added. The points mentioned in C3, the assessment of the general 'investment climate' of individual countries and other geographical factors (e.g. proximity of the Mediterranean countries to the Central European market) taken together go a long way towards explaining the observable geographical concentration of the foreign production of the Federal German garment industry in a small number of countries.

- population size, growth rate
- per capita income, growth
- income distribution
- benefits from any preference tariff schemes
- price level, stability

II. POLITICAL SITUATION

- form, stability of government
- degree of class antagonism
- special ethnic, religious, social problems
- government attitude toward private/foreign investment
- nationalisation threat
- importance of state industries
- preferential treatment of state industries
- soundness of fiscal and monetary policy
- freedom from red tape
- freedom from corruption
- degree of antiforeign discrimination
- fairness of the courts
- clear and modern investment law
- price controls
- restrictive provisions on foreign-owned property

III. GEOGRAPHIC FACTORS

- ease of access
- existence of free ports, free zones, bonded warehouses
- proximity to export markets
- proximity to suppliers, customers
- access to raw materials
- existing supplier industries
- availability of local raw materials
- reliability of local services
- ready passage of imports/exports
- availability of sites
- costs of suitable land

IV. TAX FACTORS

- tax rates on personal incomes and profits
- general tax morality
- fairness of officers, corruptibility
- long-term tax trends
- taxation of income earned abroad on exports
- tax holidays, incentives for new investments
- depreciation rates
- carry forward/carry back losses
- tax treaties with home country of company
- duty and tax drawbacks on imported goods when re-exported
- tariff protection

V. SOURCES OF CAPITAL

- availability, cost and conditions on local finance
- availability of foreign currencies locally
- modern banking system
- government credit aids to new investments
- availability of, cost of export finance insurance/guarantees

VI. BUSINESS CLIMATE

- availability of investment insurance from country of origin
- general business morality
- simplicity, effectiveness of administrative procedures
- usual profit margins in the firm's own industry
- competitive situation in the firm's industry (cartels)
- existence of anti-monopoly laws

VII. LABOUR FACTORS

- availability of managerial, technical, office staff who are proficient in necessary languages
- availability of skilled labour
- availability of semi- and unskilled labour
- degree of productivity
- training facilities
- outlook for increase in labour supply
- level of morale and ability at all levels
- absence/presence of militant or communist influenced trade unions
- level of worker's voice in management: co-determination
- freedom to hire and fire
- customary and contractual fringe benefits
- social security contributions
- customary or contractual profit sharing

It is well worth studying the accompanying check list for foreign investors abroad to appreciate the variety and number of factors which companies and their advisers regard as being of importance in the world-wide reorganisation of production. Such a list on its own is sufficient to reveal the economistic limitations which characterise the dominant school of development economics (which simply takes into account the so-called factor endowment with its three 'factors of production') and to expose its irredeemable alienation from the real world, an alienation which constitutes a misty world of ideological unreality in which its practitioners simply cynically shrug aside or dismiss such real considerations in the new international division of labour as: stability of the government; class antagonisms; special ethnic, religious or social problems; nationalisation threat; freedom from corruption; clear and modern investment laws; fairness of the tax authorities; level of morale and satisfaction of the working population; absence/presence of militant or communist influenced trade unions; level of worker's voice in management; freedom to hire and fire.[1]

1. Two examples: 'In addition to these natural advantages, the enormous supply of workers who are prepared to work for comparatively low wages seems to predestine the developing countries for the manufacture of labour-intensive products' – this sentence appears on the first page of an article in the reputable journal of a reputable German economic research institute: G. Fels & E.-J. Horn, 'Der Wandel der Industriestruktur im Zuge der weltwirtschaftlichen Integration der Entwicklungsländer', *Die Weltwirtschaft* 1 (1972), p. 107. Workers who are *prepared* to work for comparatively low wages! The reasons why these human beings are *forced* to work for starvation wages is simply not part of the subject matter of this species of science. In a contribution to the weekly report of another reputable German institute we can find the following: 'A change in the commodity structure of aggregate final demand can lead to an increase in employment, both in line with the aim of as high a domestic product as possible, and also in opposition to it. However, as far as domestic final demand is concerned such variations are usually subject to relatively narrow limits.' Dieter Schumacher, 'Entwicklungsländer: Beschäftigungsorientierte Wachstums- und Außenhandelspolitik erforderlich' in DIW, *Wochenbericht* 20 (1976), p. 198. This is clearly a reference

The second section of the study of Federal German garment companies then turns to the concrete conditions for a 'foreign involvement' in a number of selected countries, in particular Tunisia:

...Morocco, which is favoured along with Tunisia by the DEG, is not completely and unshakeably stable: and how long will Bourguiba continue in Tunisia? A successive increase in wages, i.e. a sign of economic prosperity, should indeed not be deplored (cf. Hong Kong). Nonetheless, one thing holds good: if the Federal German garment industry wishes to continue to exist at all, it must seek a comprehensive and unconditional, but by no means total, involvement abroad. (One variation assumes that during the 1980s over 50% of clothing will be made abroad. One firm gave an even more liberal figure.) However, high unemployment at home and more co-determination may well lead to constraints being placed on foreign involvements, as has happened in Sweden.

We should stress at this point that manufacturers' operations abroad also promote the stability of the garment industry which remains behind (in relation to imports). (Optimal mix – the firm's facilities for marketing, technology and organisation remain, as well as the fashion oriented and perhaps in a few years also extensively automated production.)

'Optimal mix' is simply another designation of Babbage's principle (which part of manufacturing can be performed most cheaply, where ?). Other reasons are introduced to explain why the relocation of actual manufacturing (as opposed to administration, marketing etc.) should not be total: for example, the possible extra profits to be made from fashionable 'rush jobs', the possible profitable installation of further automated manufacturing processes in the traditional industrial centres, the benefical effects of higher unemployment on the valorisation of capital, and protectionist policies by the traditional industrial countries.

to the relation between luxury and mass consumption in the developing countries. The increase in mass consumption (= raising mass incomes) is subject to 'relatively narrow limits'. The fact that centuries of capitalist development have systematically distributed the material wealth of the world at two poles, and that the development of the capitalist world system continues to do this both nationally and internationally and that this constitutes an inherent reason for the restricted 'domestic final demand' (i.e. *effective* demand, backed by money) and for why this process is constantly renewed is not considered worthy of mention or even note. Such considerations are systematically excluded from economics and at best shunted into other specialised sciences which are themselves characterised by their narrow outlook and remoteness from reality.

Because of their *economic* interests businessman have a much more realistic idea of what determines the object of economics: 'The interest of German manufacturers in having their own production facilities abroad is growing from month to month, with a preference for low wage countries where a real law and order attitude prevails, such as Spain, South Africa and Brazil. The main reasons for this development are low wages, right of control over property and no problem of workers' participation. This information was made public by the Manager of Mietfinanz GmbH Mülheim/Ruhr, Gerd Koenig, after a survey by his company.' *Süddeutsche Zeitung*, 3 April 1974.

Having provided a survey of sources of information on manufacturing in Tunisia for foreign companies, the survey goes on to list a number of concrete circumstances which should be taken into account in an investigation into a possible relocation of production to Tunisia: the population is Germanophile; climatic and religious reasons mean that business trips are not recommended for three months in the year; 'economically liberal to the outside world – stable and orderly at home, though not of course without enemies: a few months ago 175 people were sentenced for being in a left-wing plot'; high unemployment, particularly in the south of the country; forty-eight hour week; holiday entitlement – one day for each month of work in the first five years of employment; maternity leave – four weeks (may be extended to twelve on medical recommendation); trade unions play a 'not unimportant part' in the working atmosphere; if no gross offence has been committed dismissal requires a redundancy payment of one day's wages per month worked; 'strikes happen as good as never'; including statutory employers' contributions, wages in the making-up stage are around DM 1.50 per hour; management positions should be at least in part occupied by Federal German personnel; basic textiles must be partly imported; transportation to the Federal Republic is not yet completely without its difficulties (daily flights planned, ferry connections exist); encouragement of export industry is 'extraordinarily comprehensive'; import of means of production for export production is free of import duties; unrestricted transfer of funds in the sphere of export production; ten year tax holiday followed by a reduction of tax to 10%; land varies in cost, free in some regions; customs enclaves can be set up anywhere in the country (sealed containers).

The establishment of a special investment promotion authority...the investment promotion agreement with the Federal Republic...considerable assistance for export oriented industry...a low level of wages, the granting of loans at favourable terms, stable political conditions at home, a language barrier which is not insuperable, proximity to Europe and finally a friendly attitude towards the Federal Republic have resulted in the fact that a series of medium-sized and larger manufacturers have set up shop in Tunisia. Additional new investments, so it seems today, would be worthwhile. A degree of involvement which goes too far can never be sensible on grounds of the risk involved and the flexibility which is necessary for fashionable short-term trends on the home market.[1]

1. See *Handelsblatt*, 20 May 1974, for an article on Tunisia as an 'interesting' supplier of production sites and labour on the world market: 'Tunesien bietet Reserven an – Lohnniveau und Disziplin der Arbeitskräfte als Investitionsgründe'. Cf. also Chapter 8.4.

Finally, a short list is given of the information offices, sources of information, government and particular features of a number of countries which are of concern and interest to the Federal German garment industry as possible areas of foreign operations. Wages figure as the prime economic feature.

USA: hourly wage rates DM 10.00 (1974) as against DM 11.30 in Federal Germany, often up to a third less in the Southern states. Large but difficult market.
Ireland: considerable allowances as far as site purchase, tax concessions are concerned. The Industrial Development Authority mentions, in the first place, fifteen years tax exemption for export profits, assumption of training costs for employees, investment aid for job creation.
France: wage costs in the textile industry DM 7.43 per hour (1974); some knowledge of German in Alsace and Lothringen; interesting market.
Portugal: favoured by foreign investors in the garment industry – wage increases far above the normal development, politically unstable (hardly recommended at the present time!).
Greece: similar to Portugal – short-term large wage increases. Probably more politically stable than Portugal, relatively favourable transport links. Long-term relationship with the Federal German garment industry.
Yugoslavia: relatively liberal Eastern Bloc country. (Problem: what happens after Tito's death?) Good relations to Federal German garment industry, in particular, gentlemen's and children's articles, underwear, subcontracting, and cooperation. To some extent greater flexibility than in other Eastern Bloc countries.
Hungary: opened up for cooperation, and subcontracting.

The list is not complete, and one could mention in addition: Iran, Israel, Turkey, Malta, Morocco, Hong Kong, Brazil, Spain, Malaysia, Thailand, Philippines, Singapore – and the catalogue would still not be complete. Who could say that Egypt couldn't become extremely interesting for investment 'tomorrow'? The fact that the USA (Puerto Rico, eventually too a Southern state) is mentioned alongside Tunisia testifies to the fact that questions of market outlet can *also* [emphasis added] play a role in the choice of foreign operation (besides that, textile wage rates in the USA – depending on the level of trade union organisation – are between DM 1–4 less than those in Federal Germany).

7.5 Criteria for the choice of site at home and abroad

A report of a speech by the Chairman of the Management Board of Enka Glanzstoff, Mr H. G. Zempelin, given on the occasion of the Second Future Symposium of the Confederation of the Westphalian Textile Industry, held on 30 September 1976 in Münster, gave the following account of the proceedings, which contained a number of key points on the question of the choice of site.

The foreign producer may have lower wage costs, but also has to accept certain disadvantages. Or: whereas one was once only too pleased to have a factory with a stable work-force and low labour turnover, today it is particularly difficult to effect reductions in employment in such a plant. Another question is the extent to which one's own plant, or customers' market, is being threatened by imports. For example, the synthetic fibres industry can compete on equal terms with imports at its particular stage of production. But this is of little comfort if semifinished and finished goods are being increasingly imported, or if manufacturing industry shifts its production abroad with the result that they soon start to obtain their threads and fabrics locally there. One point is often neglected in this discussion: as far as the level of automation is concerned, if the capital costs are more important than wage costs the scales are by no means automatically tipped in favour of production in an industrial country. One could even say, that the more capital-intensive the process is, the more interesting it can be to produce in other countries, because of the great difficulty in finding people to carry out shift work in Germany, and work on Sundays is subject to such stringent regulation. For example, Enka Glanzstoff worked out the production costs for the manufacture of a standard article, a shirt in this case, per kilo in Germany and Nigeria and came to the following conclusion: with the same number of shifts the results for a plant with several stages of production gave a cost advantage to Nigeria of DM 5.20 per kilo and up to making-up of DM 29.60 per kilo. With an additional shift being worked in Nigeria the cost advantage of the developing country rises to DM 8.20 per kilo in the textile stage, up to DM 40.60 at making-up.[1]

We reproduce this cost comparison here in diagrammatic form (see diagrams 3 and 4). It allows a comparison of the cost elements of a typical example of manufacturing in the textile and garment industry (including inputs) under realistic conditions and in particular provides a quantitative picture of the effects of different wage costs and different equipment running times. Even if the transport costs from Nigeria are included (calculation is on a fob basis: some idea of relative freight costs can be found in Chapter 7.3), it is clear that the manufacture on this basis in a low wage country exhibits cost advantages, at least on standard articles, even when the same number of shifts are worked.

In the meantime, voices have been raised in Federal Germany demanding the increased utilisation of capital-intensive installations. On the occasion of the Thirtieth Annual Meeting of German Managers in Berlin, the textile proprietor, Hendrik E. van Delden, 'made a strong attack on the DGB's [German TUC] ideas of a slowing down of the pace of investment in rationalisation. In fact one should be considering going over to four-shift operation to obtain a better utilisation of machines which are constantly increasing in price.'[2] Another author offered the following contribution:

1. *Textil-Wirtschaft* 41 (1976), p. 17.
2. *Handelsblatt*, 19 January 1976.

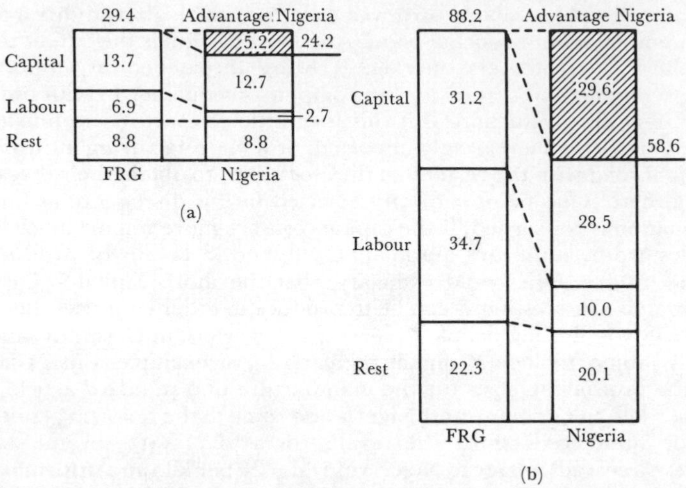

Diagram 3. Cost comparison of shirt production (hfl./kg: fob) in Federal Germany and Nigeria, same number of shifts: (a) yarns and fabrics (cumulative from yarn to finishing; 3 shifts); (b) clothing (cumulative from yarn to clothing; 1 shift)

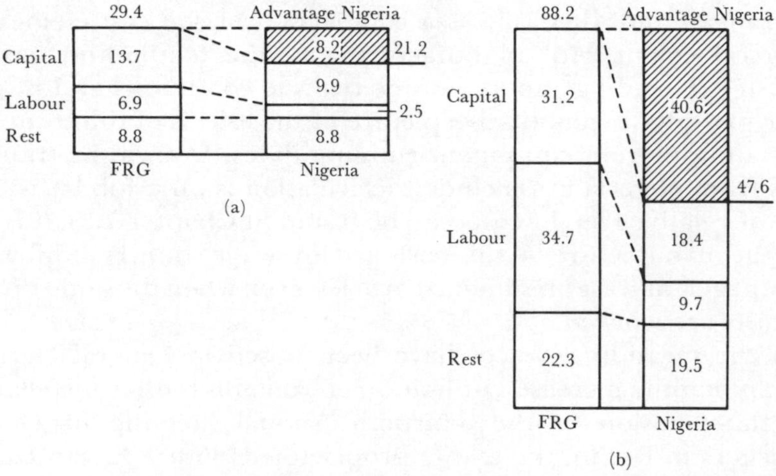

Diagram 4. Cost comparison of shirt production (hfl./kg; fob) in Federal Germany and Nigeria, additional shift in Nigeria: (a) yarns and fabrics (cumulative from yarn to finishing; Germany 3 shifts, Nigeria 4 shifts); (b) clothing (cumulative from yarn to clothing; Germany 1 shift, Nigeria 2 shifts)

Modern technology is not only expensive but automated plant must be used for more hours than previously precisely because it is so expensive – when feasible with three-shift operation. Machine running times of 6000 to 7000 hours a year, as in the USA or Hong Kong, are restricted here by the ban on night work for women, and the quite clear and insuperable rejection of even unemployed German workers of night work on a machine. As far as we are concerned here, a third shift can practically only be worked with immigrant labour.[1]

Mr H. Rösner (Lauffenmühle company) was quoted as making the following demand: 'Aim for a four-shift operation at home. Its refusal leads to long periods of idleness for increasingly expensive machinery. The key factor is the highest possible utilisation.'[2]

These are ideas and conceptions which in fact stem from the 'early' phases of capital's development and are in the process of being revived in the context of the new international division of labour in 1976 – at a time when certain academics and analysts would have us believe that we are in fact living in 'late' capitalism, or even 'post industrial' society!

The cost comparisons illustrated above clearly show that even if the number of shifts worked were to be increased in Federal Germany it could not make up for the wage cost 'advantages' of the low wage countries. As a result technical development is being concentrated on those types of installations which require no operators.

Efforts to increase productivity must be primarily directed at the labour-intensive stage of making-up, as 70%–80% of the total wage costs for the manufacture of an item of clothing occur at this stage. Opportunities exist in the making-up stage in contrast to the low wage countries in two areas: (1) manufacture of fashion items with a swift reaction to market needs and high quality goods; (2) increased mechanisation and automation. As a consequence, efforts to cut costs are being focussed on the optimal use of materials by employing computerised designs; mechanisation and automation of certain part-operations; automatic, computer controlled cutting out; reduction of sewing times by using plastic contouring. On the other hand, the drive to more automation can only be seen as a real solution if our companies have the capital to invest, and if these machines can be used for more hours than they have been up to now. In relation to current running times, our equipment is standing idle for 30% of the time available. It is therefore the task of research and development to create processes which require less attendance, so that equipment can operate for longer periods practically without attendance ...These are not dreams for the future, but are schemes actually being worked on now.[3]

The question as to what is supposed to happen to the workers who are displaced inside Federal Germany by such attempts at ration-

1. *Textil-Wirtschaft* 42 (1976), p. 4. Would the author of this article be prepared to work nights on a machine, year in, year out?
2. *Textil-Wirtschaft* 49 (1976), p. 22.
3. *Textil-Wirtschaft* 41 (1976): report by G. Egbers, Director of the Institut für Textiltechnik, Reutlingen, presented at the Second Future Symposium. Cf. CIRFS, *The Future of the Man-made Fibres Industry*, where a comparison is made between the production costs for the manufacture of selected textiles using different technologies, broken down by costs of raw materials, depreciation, overheads, energy and labour.

alisation is not considered in such reflections on those technical developments which are being made necessary by the trend towards a new international division of labour. It is evidently scepticism about the future competitiveness of a manufacture confined to Federal Germany at the scale which has been common hitherto which underlies the statements being made by the representatives of industry.

World-wide corporate strategy does not mean that the hour for a greater degree of internationalisation has now struck for all companies. For many it will be the correct answer to the challenges of the coming years. Other companies will have to tread other paths, from cooperation on the home market to specialisation and the defence of a specialist market. What all considerations have in common is the fact that no company will be able to find the correct strategy if it remains imprisoned within the confines of national or even provincial thinking when trying to set out its strategy. The basis of information for decision making must extend far beyond national borders. The change in international rates of exchange, the flow of capital across national borders, relative wage differences, the development of import and export prices must all be taken into account in the future in the corporate strategy of companies which might have usually based their sales and output targets on a small amount of information derived from the domestic economy. What a global strategy primarily means is global thinking – whether world-wide action has to follow is a question which each individual company has to decide for itself.[1]

Textiles from low price countries will achieve a greater penetration into the markets of the industrialised countries. However, the utilisation of their technical and aesthetic advantages will mean that the producers in the industrial countries will possess the capacity to prevent themselves from being priced out of the market. The production of textiles in Central Europe will become so capital-intensive by the year 2000 that wage costs will no longer play a key role. The successful company in the year 2000 will not necessarily produce all its own supply to the market, but will select the optimal mix of cost and management advantages at home and abroad.[2]

7.6 Principal determinants of the relocation of textile and garment production from Federal Germany

The previous sections have shown the complexity and the degree of interaction between the large number of factors which lie behind the relocation of manufacturing industry, in which the Federal German textile and garment industry served as an example. We shall now summarise the most important points.

1. *Textil-Wirtschaft* 41 (1976), p. 17. Statement by H. G. Zempelin at the Second Future Symposium.
2. *Neue Zürcher Zeitung*, 11 June 1976: 'Die Zukunftschancen der Textilindustrie', report from President of Gesamttextil, W. Hardt.

In the garment industry technical factors obstruct (but do not prevent) a greater degree of automation of the production process: these are primarily the nature of the materials which have to be worked on (pliable), combined with the necessity to match the product to the relatively complex contours of the human body. However, one particular economic fact is of key importance: the manufacture of clothing is characterised by the proverbial multiplicity of rapidly changing products – 'fashion' – and apart from a few areas (such as the manufacture of jeans), this does not allow for the mass production of exactly the same products over a long period of time. As a result there is a not inconsiderable risk involved in further automation with large outlays on fixed capital. Because of this, gross capital per employee is comparatively low in the garment industry (around DM 13 000 in Federal Germany as against DM 47 000 for the average in manufacturing industry).[1]

On the other hand the subdivision of the labour process (cutting, sewing, pressing, packing etc.) has made it possible to extensively reduce the skill requirements of the labour-force. Attempts at automation are therefore particularly concentrated in those areas in which relatively high levels of skill are still required (e.g. cutting, grading). In view of the general relatively low skill requirement, the garment industry has an almost inexhaustible supply of cheap labour at its disposal throughout the world.

The conclusion is obvious:

> Despite significant advances, the technology of apparel production is still relatively simple and investment in fixed capital is low compared to most other industries. Lightweight and small, even 500 sewing machines can be transported more easily than a steel furnace or an auto-assembly line. An apparel plant can be dismantled and reassembled elsewhere in a very short time, leaving virtually no fixed capital behind...The shift to predominantly unskilled workers has ended the industry's dependence on a dwindling supply of skilled labour in the Northeast...The functional separation of production from entrepreneurial tasks allows for the geographic separation as well. Certain functions performed by the jobber require skilled labour (designers, pattern makers, cutters etc.) and proximity to markets. Meanwhile the sewing and finishing stages of production, involving 95% of the total work-force, can be located in far-flung regions or countries.[2]

The consequence of this extreme geographical mobility in the garment industry is that potential production sites must outbid each

1. See Ifo-Institut für Wirtschaftsforschung, *Strukturdaten für die Industrie: 4. Folge 1960–1973* (Munich 1975).
2. *NACLA's Latin America & Empire Report*, vol. XI, no. 3 (March 1977), p. 9.

other in guaranteeing the optimal conditions for the valorisation of capital. Complementary to this, capital is on a permanent migration around the world, seeking new surplus profits through the exploitation of new, more profitable, production sites.[1]

In the textile industry extensive automation has been both technically and economically feasible in many areas. Where it has not been possible (such as in parts of the knitted goods industry) basically the same conclusions apply as for the garment industry. In the relatively capital-intensive branches of the textile industry, in which long machine running times are economically necessary, there is likewise a tendency towards the relocation of production away from Federal Germany – based on the differences which exist in the prevailing labour legislation in different countries. In addition, the increasing relocation of the textile industry's most important customer, the garment industry, will force the textile industry to move to new sites.

1. This world-wide migration of capital could be shown many times over in the case of the textile and garment industry (cf. Chapters 5.3, 6.4, and 6.5). 'It is necessary for companies to become more mobile in their investment and production planning policies. This not only applies to the Federal Republic, but also abroad where companies should be prepared to switch sites quickly should the need arise in order to use the lowest wages and optimal conditions.' Statement by H. Blettenberg, Unternehmensberatung Kurt Salmon Associates (management consultants), quoted in *FAZ/Blick durch die Wirtschaft*, 28 April 1976.

8 ❧ The new international division of labour: direction by and response of institutions from the traditional industrial countries

The foregoing chapters have essentially investigated the influence of the world market for labour and production sites on the global reorganisation of the textile and garment industry.

The aim of this chapter is to provide a number of examples of how institutions in the traditional industrial countries (in particular in Federal Germany) are reacting to the tendency towards a new international division of labour, be this response in the form of seeking to influence events or in the form of adjustment.

8.1 National and supranational foreign trade policy: legislation, import restrictions, the Multi-Fibres Agreement (MFA)

Despite the basic freedom of Federal Germany's external trade the restrictive provisions of the German Foreign Trade Act (*Außenwirtschaftsgesetz*) and similar legislation offer both national and supranational bodies (EEC) a rich arsenal of relatively strong means for intervention within a broad area of discretion.

In the sphere of trade in the products of manufacturing industry these possibilities of intervention are implemented to their greatest extent in relation to the importation of textiles and clothing.

Against the background of the possibility of a return to unilateral trade restrictions (as set out in Article 3 of the MFA), the EEC can, in most instances, create a situation in which low wage countries with high or rapidly growing exports of textiles or clothing to the EEC 'voluntarily' agree to conclude 'orderly marketing agreements' which are essentially intended to prevent too rapid a growth in these imports: this applies especially to the most important country in this connection, Hong Kong. Although import restrictions are in theory perfectly drafted, in practice constant and often successful attempts are made to get around them.

Without wishing to go into the details of all these import restrictions we simply stress here the complexity of the procedure for the importation of many goods which fall under the scope of textiles and clothing, and the enormous effort and expenditure in administration and control of the numerous regulations and restrictions required. This expenditure is justified by reference to the fact that without it, that is, with an extensive liberalisation of imports in this sphere, employment in the Federal German textile and garment industry would be decimated within a very short time. The high outlays on administration and higher consumer prices for textiles and clothing are part of the price which has to be paid to secure the deceleration of the process of contraction and adjustment within the Federal German textile and garment industry.

8.2 The reaction of employers' and employees' organisations

The changes in the structure of the textile and garment industry which have been occasioned by changes in the world market, namely the trend towards a new international division of labour, have been the source of political controversy in the traditional industrial countries for a number of years. In Federal Germany this is reflected in the differing positions adopted by the employers' trade federations (in particular those representing the import trade and large retailers), employers' industrial federations and the trade unions.

Whereas the trade federations naturally urge the government to allow freedom of trade, the federations representing the textile and garment industry are demanding a slowing down of the rise in textile and clothing imports, especially from low wage countries; furthermore, the industry is demanding the establishment of reliable and predictable governmental frameworks within which companies can bring about the global reorganisation of their production at the appropriate time for their requirements, using means such as the relocation of production, subcontracting and similar arrangements.

The representation of the interests of the great majority of those affected by the new international division of labour in the sphere of the textile and garment industry takes the following form, in the analysis put forward by the international umbrella organisation the International Textile, Garment and Leather Workers' Federation (which according to the evidence of our own study must be designated as realistic).

It is obvious that a transfer of our industries from developed to developing countries would create even greater excess capacity in the latter, would intensify their mono-industrialisation, make competition among them extremely intense and would make them extremely sensitive to the numerous temporary and deep cyclical fluctuations in the industry. Eventually, this would promote the continuation of exploitation of workers as a condition for remaining competitive...

From a trade union point of view, all activities in favour of the less developed countries must aim at, and achieve, a real and constant improvement in the standard of living of the populations concerned. A too limited and narrow industrialisation of these countries is likely to secure only a very low standard of living, constitutes exploitation, and is in no way allied to real economic and social development. Industrialists who transfer their production from developed to developing countries cannot avoid the criticism that the operation is aimed only at maximum profits...

In many developing countries, the textile, garment and leather industry is dominated by multinational enterprises. There are states which have a technically highly-developed textile, garment and leather industry but where the working people never get their fair share of the growing resources. The profits go to those who represent capital. Workers only see that the profits on the goods they produce are sent out of the country. This is an injustice we cannot accept...

The wide disparities in labour costs and working conditions among nations suggests that countries engaging in world trade should be required to observe minimum terms of employment. We strongly urge the promulgation of an international code of minimum fair labour standards related to the economic capacity of the countries concerned, the desire for rising living standards and the needs of fair international competition. Such a code could be appropriately introduced into the GATT and the Arrangement Regarding International Trade in Textiles.[1]

The social clause which is being proposed for adoption by GATT consists of the following: employment guarantee, income guarantee, fair labour standards, public control of social and economic re-adaptation, anticipatory structural adjustment measures, accident prevention, health and environment protection, creation of an International Commission on Trade and Employment. In contrast to the analysis of the current situation which was quoted above, the points suggested for adoption by GATT are kept very vague.[2] Merely the demand for an income guarantee, which as things stand is meant to relate to textile, garment and leather workers in the traditional

1. International Textile, Garment and Leather Workers' Federation, *Declaration on International Trade*, mimeo (1976).
2. For example: 'Employment guarantee...To raise and guarantee employment...contracting parties shall pursue active manpower, regional and industrial policies and coordinate them internationally.'

industrial countries, contains an unmistakeable formula – it specifies, one suspects, the conditions under which the trade unions in the traditional industrial countries are prepared to accept the new international division of labour: 'The contracting parties shall be required to maintain full income and social benefits for all displaced workers through adequate national measures'.

The Chairman of IG Textil-Bekleidung, the German trade union for the industry, stated:

To the extent that living standards rise in the developing countries, the consumption of textiles and clothing also rises. At the same time production and employment also rise. Our demand for improved working conditions in the developing countries therefore has the simultaneous aim of increasing demand, employment and production in the developing countries, and eventually overcoming unemployment there.

As long as this process of adaptation takes place in the prescribed form (Multi-Fibres Arrangement) one has no need to fear the future.

As far as the developing countries are concerned any extension of industrialisation must be linked to a real and steady improvement in the living standards of the populations concerned. A too one-sided and narrow industrialisation of these countries which either does not raise standards or does so only insubstantially, has nothing to do with real social and development assistance, and leads to exploitation through the pursuit of maximum profits.

A general improvement in living standards connected with an increase in purchasing power would also create a receptive domestic market in the developing countries, would reduce their susceptibility to changes occurring in markets abroad, and at the same time unburden industries in the industrial countries.

As trade unionists we are called upon to advance social progress in the developing countries and bring it to realisation: most of the problems which we have in the textile, garment and leather industry today would then solve themselves.[1]

What is interesting here is that a similar argument can be found in a 'solemn warning' collectively published by the Coordination Committee of the EEC Textile Industries (Comitextil), AEIH (the European Federation of Garment Industries) and the European Trade Union Committee for Textiles, Clothing and Leather, on 25 May 1976.

The social partners in the European textile and garment industries...reassert absolutely that any economic activity must lead to some kind of social end as much in the industrialised countries as in the developing countries.

Furthermore, they have always felt that the economic development of the Third

1. Karl Buschmann, 'Die gegenwärtige Lage der Textil-, Bekleidungs- und Lederindustrien und ihre Zukunft in Industrie- und Entwicklungsländern', report presented at the Congress of International Textile, Garment and Leather Workers in Dublin, March 1976.

World need not necessarily be based on a copy of our own patterns, but should be thought out again and adapted to the actual needs of those countries.

This development cannot come about as the result of a policy of voluntary and artificial transfer of certain sectors of the industrialised countries, in the cause of international division of work.

The application of this theory has led to a textile mono-industrialisation in countries of the Third World, without bringing about a sound industrial development. Mono-industrialisation is particularly vulnerable to fluctuations in business and trade trends, and aggravates conditions of competition. The result has been a source of serious problems, as much for the genuinely developing countries as for the industrialised countries...

The top priority for the developing countries is undoubtedly the problem of hunger. The solution calls for an increase in agricultural production by means of urgent and adequate measures.

The second priority is the setting up of an economic and social infrastructure (ports, roads, dams, dykes, health services...) capable of contributing to the development of those countries.

All this should be done in conjunction with a special effort in the field of training, not only as regards an intellectual elite, but also skilled workers and efficient management personnel. With this in view increased aid by the industrialised countries is vital.

When these conditions have been fulfilled, a genuine industrialisation will have every chance of being brought about and of developing. (Such industrialisation should not, as is so often the case, lead, systematically, to the disappearance of traditional production, such as handicrafts. This type of production is, in fact, capable of absorbing a proportion of the unemployment, endemic in these countries. Handicraft products are usually much appreciated in the West, where tariff and other advantages have been granted.)

This industrialisation must be felt by and thought out by these countries themselves, and for the benefit of their peoples. The choice must result from a certain number of factors characteristic to the countries concerned and not from trying only to satisfy the needs of the industrialised countries.

Following a listing of the problems which would result from a new international division of labour constituted in accordance with the theory of comparative costs (such as structural unemployment in the industrial countries, the necessity for the maintenance of low wages in the developing countries, and high costs of imports of raw materials and technology), the declaration continues under the heading 'The sacrifices made by European industries and workers must benefit the genuinely developing countries':

The use in those countries [Hong Kong, South Korea, Taiwan] of very modern machinery, coupled with the exploiting of underpaid labour, has attracted a great deal of capital in search of maximum profit.

These East Asian countries, along with the Eastern European centrally planned economies, are held to possess an almost total monopoly of the Western European market for clothing imports:

In the end, the genuinely developing countries have not been able to benefit from the opening up of the markets of the industrialised countries. Their share of total exports by the so-called developing countries as a whole has remained very small; furthermore, due to the competition they have met, prices received have been unremunerative and, in fact, have contributed to a further impoverishment of their economy.

The basic requirements of a development policy:

(1) its essential objective must be the improvement of the well-being of populations in all parts of the world,
(2) it must meet the real needs of those populations,
(3) it must not lead to fresh economic and social disequilibrium,
(4) it must not lead to the benefits of development being chanelled to the few,
(5) it must not lead to excessive interdependence between states,
(6) it must ensure the fair sharing of sacrifices entailed.

A number of concrete proposals are appended to this: tariff preferences should only be given to the 'genuinely' developing countries; export subsidies and dumping should be banned as they lead to the impoverishment of the exporting countries; trade agreements should always include a social clause which should provide for the application of ILO norms (employment guarantee, income guarantee, fair working conditions, safety, hygiene and health etc.).[1]

A number of questions can be addressed to the signatories of this apparently very progressive 'solemn warning' (which in fact contains a number of very accurate observations, the rigorous analysis of which would categorise one as a 'radical' in the Federal Republic of Germany at the present time, and for which one is threatened with the *Berufsverbot* – a ban from working in the state's employ). These questions are:

(a) Who exploits the underpaid workers in the search for maximum profits? Can this criticism only be levelled at a few countries, and a few, profit-hungry, capitalists? Doesn't this list also include companies from the West European textile and garment industry with production facilities in low wage countries?
(b) Who will prevent the proposed tariff and trade preferences for the 'genuinely' developing countries leading to precisely the exploitation of underpaid workers – in the search for maximum profits – in view of the fact that there are around a hundred

1. Comitextil, AEIH & European Trade Union Committee for Textiles, Clothing and Leather, *The European Textile and Clothing Industries and the International Division of Labour*, mimeo (1976).

'genuinely' developing countries competing on the world market for production sites and labour-power (in which, as all experience has shown, there are any number of ways of getting around the ILO norms), and in view of the compulsion to find the production site with the lowest costs which is imposed on every capital in the world capitalist system?

(c) Which interest groups prevent even the more modest of the 'solemn warning's' proposals being implemented?

(d) Aren't the developments which are being complained about an expression of the operation of the capitalist world economy over the last five centuries?

(e) In which countries in the present-day world have those populations in need of development *not* shaped their economic development in accordance with our model, but have rather adopted a policy of their own in the interests of the mass of their hard-pressed populations, as advocated in the 'solemn warning'? In the People's Republic of China? In Cuba, Vietnam, Chile, Tanzania, Ethiopia...? Are the signatories prepared to support such developments, or at least refrain from defaming or sabotaging them? Why do nearly all the influential pressure groups keep silent on the systematic encouragement or at least tacit toleration of repressive regimes in the 'Third World' by governments and interests in the traditional industrial countries – in the interests of a favourable 'climate of investment'?

For the sake of the consistency of their arguments the signatories to the 'solemn warning' should not simply pass over the answers to such crucial questions. Their credibility will necessarily be measured by their response to these and similar questions.

8.3 The regional, structural and foreign development policy of Federal Germany in the context of the textile and garment industry

The following text appears under the revealing heading 'Structural Adjustment' in the 'Federal Republic's Conception of Development Policy'.

The Federal government is of the opinion that structural change is an indispensable precondition for the growth of the economy as a whole and for an improved international division of labour. Structural changes which are brought into play by the increased integration of the developing countries into the international division of labour should not be impeded: in fact, where necessary, they should be encouraged by appropriate measures in the field of structural policy. In particular the departure of labour and capital from those branches of the economy in which adjustments to changed market conditions are necessary should not be obstructed by means of supportive subsidies. Rather, the social hardships which follow in the wake of such processes of adaptation should be promptly alleviated. The *relocation of production* by means of the establishment and expansion of companies or the purchase of holdings or whole companies in developing countries will continue to be financially and fiscally *supported*, alongside the government's assumption of the function of guarantor as security against political risks; *in this connection serious disturbances to production and employment are to be avoided.* Within the overall framework of its growth-oriented policy, the Federal government encourages the adjustment of production to structural changes and the retraining of those workers affected into fields of employment which offer better opportunities – at the same time taking into account the legitimate needs of the developing countries.[1]

This conception was stressed by Federal Chancellor Schmidt in an interview with the *Süddeutsche Zeitung* when he stated that for the 'horizon of the year 2000', the Federal Republic would 'essentially be exporting patents, process technology and blue-prints'.[2]

Federal Germany's textile and garment industry constitutes a classic example of such a structural change:

The textile and garment industry is the most strongly protected sphere of industry against imports from third countries. Within the framework of the Multi-Fibres Arrangement, and through the imposition of quotas, the Federal Republic has reduced imports in volume terms in the areas of sensitive products. This *policy* is directed towards *keeping the extent of that structural change in the textile and garment industry which has been occasioned by changes on the world market within certain limits. It is a long-term policy. Short-term import restrictions would have a disadvantageous impact on our economy because of possible retaliatory measures by other countries. Because of its high export intensity, Federal Germany is necessarily interested in the greatest degree of free movement for goods possible.*[3]

These extracts are sufficient to indicate the nature of Federal German government policy in the fields of structure and develop-

1. *Entwicklungspolitische Konzeption der Bundesrepublik Deutschland* (*Fassung 1975*), Bundestagsdrucksache 7/4293 (report on Federal German development policy), pp. 53 f. (emphases added). See Chapters 8.4 and 13.2 on the financial and fiscal assistance given by the Federal German government for relocations of production.
2. *Süddeutsche Zeitung*, 24 June 1975: 'Die alte "National"-Ökonomie hilft nicht mehr weiter'. See too the interpretation which is almost identical in content given by Parliamentary Secretary Grüner of the Federal Economics Ministry in the German parliament on 18 September 1975: Deutscher Bundestag, *Stenografischer Bericht, 7. Wahlperiode, 185. Sitzung* (*18 September 1975*), p. 13079*.
3. Deutscher Bundestag, *Stenografischer Bericht, 7. Wahlperiode, 206. Sitzung* (*4 December 1975*), p. 14249* (emphasis added).

ment, both at home and abroad. The government's idea of encouraging structural change and hence the new international division of labour, without unleashing serious unemployment at home, has clearly failed in the case of the Federal German textile and garment industry. Attempts have been made to prevent catastrophic incursions into employment in the Federal German textile and garment industry in a period of sustained general high unemployment by the use of short-term ad-hoc measures such as the introduction of special permits for East German imports, import supervision and bills of entry for imports of ladies' hosiery from Italy, price checking procedures, etc. These ad-hoc measures are in addition to the 'normal' protectionist measures taken by Federal Germany in the field of textiles and clothing (see Chapter 8.1). At the moment it appears as if the full array of these protectionist measures may have managed to slow down the galloping drop in employment in the Federal German textile and garment industry, at least temporarily. Admittedly one of the prime factors in this has been the contribution of the impact of the recession on the labour market towards the improvement in the conditions for the valorisation of capital.

From one perspective it is therefore quite understandable when an economist working for the textile and garment workers' trade union writes:

> Our persistence and the logic of our constant efforts have led to success. The liberalisation fanatics in politics and the import business have been compelled to take a step backwards. The kinds of insults which have been directed at us by those 'injured parties', such as 'protectionists', 'economic ignoramuses', 'narrow-minded lobbyists', 'power-crazed bureaucrats', have been regarded with disdain and equanimity by our union. Since the beginning of the 1970s, and especially over the last few years, we have had an increasingly understanding reception from the politicians who count. We can say, with satisfaction, that the employment policies advocated by the employees in the textile and garment industry in relation to the threat to them from excessive imports have never received such attention or been so well represented by those politicians responsible for policy at the present time – disregarding a small number of regrettable and irritating 'backsliders'.[1]

However, from the other perspective it should not be forgotten that the volume of employment in the Federal German textile and garment industry has fallen by no less than 20% between 1973 and

1. E. Ringelstein, 'Wir haben eine Menge erreicht', *Textil-Bekleidung* 10 (October 1976), p. 3.

1974/75 – and in the process has made a not inconsiderable contribution to the almost stagnant high level of total unemployment in Federal Germany.

No influential political interest group can offer a strategy which will reduce this high level of unemployment. Constant references to the 'self-healing powers of the economy', to so-called 'growth sectors' whose (state assisted) development, in the view of the government, 'will on balance result in no loss of jobs'[1] and to retraining assistance for labour which is 'released' or which 'migrates' from weak sectors are all merely incantations of a blind policy of economic growth. No one has yet been able to plausibly identify these 'growth sectors' and show that they will have the desired characteristics: the creation of a sufficient number of new jobs and in particular a pattern of potential employment which is adapted to the skills of the economically active population of Federal Germany.[2]

In view of the high degree of involvement of Federal Germany in world trade (which cannot be altered in the short and medium term) no conceivable government in Federal Germany will be able to do anything but support further measures for the liberalisation of international trade. This means: the opportunity for developing countries to avoid the *volume-based* import restrictions imposed by Federal Germany (EEC) by means of orderly marketing agreements through the policy of increasing the *value* of their imports into Germany;[3] German industry's own interest in subcontracting business; constant announcements of new plans[4] to transfer the textile and garment industry from Federal Germany to more profitable sites; granting of EEC associate member status to the Mediterranean countries and the ACP countries (Africa–Caribbean–Pacific), which will induce further relocation. These are all unambiguous signs of the fact that the world-wide reorganisation of the Federal German

1. Deutscher Bundestag, *Stenografischer Bericht, 7. Wahlperiode, 185. Sitzung (18 September 1975)*, p. 13079*.
2. Cf. *FAZ*, 6 November 1975: 'Wo sitzen die mit permanentem Wachstum geplagten Branchen?', in which G. Mordhorst and H.-J. Unland are cited as asking the question: 'Where in Federal Germany are those branches which are "plagued" by growth and which are in a position to create new jobs for the "victims" of structural change, especially in those development areas or regions where the local textile plant is the sole employer?'
3. Amazingly, the government does not take this possibility of evasion into account in its statement. Cf. Deutscher Bundestag, *Stenografischer Bericht, 7. Wahlperiode, 201. Sitzung (7 November 1975)*, pp. 13911*f.; *204. Sitzung (28 November 1975)*, pp. 14188*f.
4. Plans which the 100% state-owned DEG helps bring to fruition through 'project promotion', loans and share-holdings etc. See Chapter 8.4.

textile and garment industry will continue – with assistance given to companies to adapt to these new circumstances and consolation for the employed and 'redeployed' affected by the process. In view of the quite unmistakeable tendency towards relocations of production in many other branches of Federal German industry (see Part II) and the high proportion of investment aimed at rationalisation it is difficult to see how the structural and development policies of the Federal German government – promotion of structural change without permanent unemployment – can be successfully implemented.[1]

This policy is caught in a dilemma which is determined by the conditions of the world market for labour and production sites. It is, quite simply: either lower real wages and social benefits, low enough to make Federal Germany an attractive site for the valorisation of capital once again, or continuing high unemployment.[2]

Whether this dilemma can be resolved within the confines of the present system through shortening the working week, even with a loss of income, or through a centrally planned world economic policy is extremely doubtful as not even the most elementary precondition for such a policy exists: namely a social grouping which has a fair degree of international influence and which has set itself the goal of bringing about such a resolution within the system as it currently exists.

8.4 The Deutsche Entwicklungsgesellschaft as promoter of the new international division of labour

The manner in which the Federal German government actually implements its development policy can be illustrated by the case of Federal Germany's financial institution for the promotion of investments by, predominantly Federal German, companies in the developing countries: the Deutsche Entwicklungsgesellschaft, which will be referred to, as previously, by the initials DEG.

The DEG was established by the Federal German government in

1. The powerlessness of the present Federal German government (and any other conceivable German government) in the face of the structural changes set in motion by the tendency towards a new international division of labour is betrayed by the expression which constantly finds its way into all government statements on the subject – 'adaptation'.
2. Naturally a chronically high level of unemployment would contribute to a situation in which real wages, social benefits etc. would be cut back and working conditions made worse (overtime, night work, shift work, faster pace of work).

1962 with the aim of providing assistance for the realisation of private company plans in the developing countries, for example through direct participation and equity loans. The DEG has never made a secret of the fact that it regards private profitability as the sole criterion for the granting of its 'development aid'. Furthermore, after more than ten years of very successful activity following this policy – so far as one can tell from their annual reports – they have never once made the attempt to evaluate the success of their 'development aid' from any other criterion: one might have expected, for example, that they could have measured the effectiveness of their 'aid' by whether it had demonstrably increased the material welfare of the mass of the populations in the developing countries, or at least unambiguously contributed to this process. If the DEG had seriously adopted this latter criterion the bankruptcy of its policy would have become evident[1] insofar as it would reveal that the DEG's strategy has simply created a situation in which a small privileged stratum in the developing countries, together with a number of companies from the traditional industrial countries have profited and that, in addition, the sole tangible result of the DEG's policy has been the further penetration of the capitalist mode of production into the developing countries in the form of the spread of the new international division of labour.

Right from the outset, in fact in its first annual report, the DEG set out its aims with exemplary clarity:

> The DEG wishes to contribute primarily to the development of the economies of the developing countries. At the same time the establishment of private businesses is in the interests of the industrial countries: in the long term the future of our industry cannot lie in the field of labour-intensive production, but rather in those fields where a high injection of capital and skilled labour create products which cannot be produced elsewhere, or at least not as well. The stability and growth of the German economy in the future will be determined by how well and swiftly a restructuring of those branches which cannot remain competitive in the long term can be achieved. In this sense assistance for the industrialisation of the developing countries can simultaneously lead to an improvement in the world division of labour. This in turn signifies an intensification in the exchange of goods with the developing countries – that is, growing imports from these countries and growing exports to them...
>
> What is crucial is that the utmost is undertaken in the developing countries themselves to create a favourable climate for investment – the preconditions for which are internal political stability, reasonable economic policy, legal security and

1. Cf. various statements by Robert McNamara, President of the World Bank, or Folker Fröbel, Jürgen Heinrichs & Otto Kreye (eds.), *Die Armut des Volkes. Verelendung in den unterentwickelten Ländern. Auszüge aus Dokumenten der Vereinten Nationen* (Reinbek 1974).

the protection of private property...A form of commercial charter has been carefully selected which allows the DEG to operate according to private economic criteria free from excessively stringent financial constraints. The policy of the DEG moves within the broad framework of the Federal Government's basic guidelines for development policy...

The DEG provides initial assistance for the establishment of companies through the provision of risk-capital. It will sell its holding – principally to the partner – as soon as the period of collaboration has led to *success, namely the profitable operation of the partner establishment.*[1]

From this we can see that the DEG had clearly recognised the tendency towards a new international division of labour as early as 1963, and had immediately developed a strategy which would allow Federal German companies to draw private benefit from it by means of relocation of production to the developing countries. The subsequent years have produced no change in this policy, as can be seen from a number of extracts from DEG annual reports:

...Question...what motive underlies investment which is actually carried out...The most important incentive to investment is clearly the expectation of gain. Despite all the problems which an investor sees himself as confronted by in a developing country, the prospects for return on capital are often better than in the domestic market: the shortage of goods facilitates a satisfactory pricing policy, protectionist measures and tax concessions likewise contribute to the expected good results...

An additional reason for investment is the choice of a site which is both geographically favourable and cost advantageous in a developing country from which to export to a third country. This applies in particular to countries which are party to regional economic agreements...It can be currently observed that firms who are experiencing difficulties on the German market are attempting to open up foreign markets by the relocation of their plants. Other companies are using the low costs of the developing countries to remain competitive in the German or neighbouring markets.

Finally, we should mention those instances in which the establishment of a factory by a final producer in a developing country has brought about corresponding investment from their suppliers...In many cases in which economic factors allow a choice between two or more countries for the establishment of a production facility, and hence where there is real competition between those countries who are looking for capital, the general climate of investment often turns out to be the deciding factor...[2]

The possibility of seizing such opportunities for investment and putting them at the disposal of the German economy can only be grasped by private oriented development aid. We regard the particular task of our agency as being this form of active, formative development policy.[3]

1. DEG, *Geschäftsbericht 1962*, pp. 1 ff. (emphasis added).
2. DEG, *Geschäftsbericht 1965*, pp. 7 f.
3. DEG, *Geschäftsbericht 1966*, p. 7.

...searching the world for sites...The setting up of subsidiaries in the phase of protective tariffs and subsidies with high price and low wage levels facilitates the steady accumulation of risk capital by the new company, and the early undertaking of further expansionary investment...

Direct investments contribute, in the long term, to the realisation of an equitable world division of labour. However, there can be no doubt that not all direct investments bring only benefits to the recipient developing country. Not every corporate profit is a general economic gain...

In our view the cost advantageous relocation of labour-intensive branches with the aim of re-import to Federal Germany is gaining ground as the motive for investment abroad...

The tracking down of investment opportunities and projects for potential German partners. In this way the DEG tries to carry out the role of place holder and to procure investment-, sectoral- and institutional know-how, primarily in those developing countries which have hitherto remained unobserved by German companies or which were not easily accessible to them...

Information-gathering visits have been organised to Tunisia and Malta for companies planning an overseas operation. Tunisia in particular was pointed to as being a new site for labour-intensive branches of industry...

Up to the end of the financial year sixteen German firms had obtained investment agreements in Tunisia as a result of our promotional activities. According to their production plans, this should create around two thousand jobs in the running-up phase to full production alone.[1]

Under the title 'Investments need a climate of trust', the DEG summarises its policy in the 1975 edition of its annual report in the following somewhat ominous terms, which even go as far as demanding good behaviour by the developing countries (on pain of the imposition of various sanctions).

Faced with their oppressive situation many of these countries imagine that they have found the magic formula by which they can improve their position in the world economy and raise their living standards in the, in part, utopian demand for a 'New World Economic Order'.

However, these countries will only expand their share of international trade if – in addition to improvements in agriculture – they undertake a single-minded policy of industrialisation in trust and cooperation with the industrial nations.

Trust is necessary

The establishment of productive industry in the poorer countries requires a flow of capital lasting for several years, technology, and entrepreneurial know-how from the industrial nations. The developing countries have to contribute to this by creating a favourable climate for investment, a climate of trust. Consequently, nothing could be less designed to further the aim of the increased integration of the developing countries into the world economic division of labour than the repeated mention by some of these countries of the possibility of the expropriation of foreign companies in discussions on the subject of the 'New World Economic

1. DEG, *Geschäftsbericht 1973*, pp. 9 ff.

Order', or when countries demand a raw materials policy along the lines adopted by the OPEC countries.

Uncertainty is fatal
In the long term such demands must be prejudicial to the international movement of capital. They constitute a permanent threat of expropriation to the foreign investor. Despite the concessions which many developing countries grant to foreign companies, such demands create an atmosphere of uncertainty as regards the underlying attitude of the developing countries towards direct investment in general. And uncertainty is fatal for the investment climate.

Daily woes
Amongst the bureaucratic obstacles which stand in the way of foreign companies are such things as attempts to make subsequent changes to concessions which have already been granted, the dilatory treatment of the necessary import licences for raw materials, the sudden insistence on cash deposits, restrictions on the free movement of goods and capital, arbitrary increase in personnel costs, and provisions on local proportions of manufacturing which are difficult to fulfil, the restriction of local possibilities for financing, discrimination by national development banks and many more.

Scope for entrepreneurial initiative
Despite all these obstacles there nevertheless remains a good deal of scope for business initiative in the Third World. The majority of developing countries have long ago given a positive response to the question as to whether foreign companies should play a role in the development of their economies.

As long as the foreign companies observe the conditions imposed by the host country, a broad field exists for successful investment in many developing countries. This is confirmed by more than a decade and a half of activity by the DEG.

International cooperation
The recession in the world economy has clearly shown that the industrial and the developing countries are so closely intertwined through the international flows of trade and capital that a dismantling of this mutual dependence, as would necessarily occur under the 'New World Economic Order', would inevitably result in great damage, especially to the developing countries. If space is to be created for the developing countries to have a larger share of world prosperity and economic progress in the future, the world division of labour must be extended. This aim will not be attainable without a free market world economy.

Freedom for goods and capital
This demand should be especially easy to fulfil as an ideal starting point exists between the industrial and the developing countries: one needs private capital and modern technology for development, the other good production sites and raw materials and both are looking for outlets for their products.

We therefore call upon the developing countries to grant as much freedom as possible to the international movement of capital. In turn, the industrial nations must open up their markets to products from the Third World to a greater extent than previously.

Increasing the DEG's authorised capital
The German economy must utilise the locational advantages and market opportunities in the Third World in the future to a similar extent to other industrial countries. In order to make this step easier, a step which is not without its risks, the Federal Republic has decided, amongst other measures, to increase the authorised capital of the DEG in 1976 to DM 600 million. This places an able partner with a growing financial potential alongside the German company, whose experience embraces the financing of more than 170 undertakings in fifty-three developing countries.[1]

An example of the extent of the detail which the DEG supplies to potential investors about the conditions prevailing at industrial locations can be seen in the following extracts from the brochure *Producing in Tunisia*, published in October 1973.

The Tunisian government is looking for foreign companies involved in labour-intensive manufacture for export to produce in Tunisia. Factors which favour settling in Tunisia are:
— proximity to Europe
— attractive labour market
— ten year tax holiday
— capital protection agreement with Federal Germany
— guaranteed repatriation of profits
— simple customs procedure
— EEC associate status.

These advantages make Tunisia especially attractive for the following branches:
— textile and garment industry
— leather working and processing
— footwear industry
— plastics industry
— precision engineering and optics
— ferrous metals, steel plate and other metal fabrication
— electronics and electrical goods industry
— furniture industry
— industrial processing of agricultural products.

The current and expected future dimensions of the labour market are also indicated, the system of vocational training is described, productivity is estimated as being comparable with European norms (after intensive training) and working hours, wages and holidays are specified.

White-collar employees require one month's notice for dismissal, manual workers a week. Dismissal for reasons of unsuitability or in the case of serious offences can be made without notice if the opinion of the 'Commission for Labour Affairs' is obtained beforehand. Mass redundancies require that notice be given to the labour authorities...

1. DEG, *Geschäftsbericht 1975*, pp. 11–13.

Youths under fifteen years may not be employed in industrial establishments. Women and youths under eighteen are not permitted to work at night.

The package of Tunisian promotional measures (tax and tariff concessions) are described ('transfer of capital and profits is guaranteed') and Tunisian sources of finance are indicated (the company can be up to 100% foreign owned). Particular attention is paid to transport to the EEC (air-freight, road, sea) and freight rates are given. Questions of the purchase of land, construction costs and energy are dealt with. Telephone and telex links to the EEC are held to be well developed. German promotional measures (guarantees, European Recovery Programme loans at favourable rates of interest, Development Aid Tax Law, training assistance) are also mentioned.[1]

With a substantial involvement by the Federal German textile and garment industry existing for some time in Tunisia, the DEG is now turning to the encouragement of higher levels of investment by other branches of industry.

The DEG, the Federal German financial institution responsible for the promotion of German private investment in developing countries, wishes to become 'strongly involved in co-financing' the settlement of Federal German firms in Tunisia in the overall context of its promotional activities and to open up new branches...The main focus of previous German investment in Tunisia lay in the garment sector, which operates for export taking advantage of the low wage costs. Although fifty-eight investment licences have been granted by Tunisia, the DEG has only co-financed one project. Lohmann underlined the favourable climate for investment in Tunisia and the consultative activity which took place through the API (Agence de Promotion des Investissement), which is a model example of a central investment information agency. API President Chelly is now discussing the possibility with German companies of establishing undertakings from technical branches – in particular, chemicals, petrochemicals, steel and wagon construction, toolmaking machinery and plant for the manufacture of precision engineering and electro-

1. Four years later we read: 'Because of the development of German wage costs, more and more firms are looking for sites abroad which offer cost-advantages. Tunisia is one of the favourite locations for consumer goods. At the present time, wages for unskilled workers are around DM 1.10 per hour, and for skilled workers DM 2.50, plus around an additional 35% for social costs. Furthermore, tax concessions are a further incentive for the sixty German companies who have set up production there – with the main areas being crochet work, ladies' day wear, underclothing, anoraks and shoes. The DEG is organising an informational visit between 18 and 21 April to enable sites to be assessed on the spot. The programme includes visits to German plants, with an exchange of information with their managers, and a seminar.' (*Textil-Wirtschaft* 8 (1977), p. 18.) At the beginning of 1977 fifty-four German clothing manufacturers were producing in Tunisia exclusively for the German market, employing in all more than 4000 workers. Six firms in addition had been granted a licence for the construction of plants; two firms made the decision to set up in Tunisia in the course of the trip mentioned above. *Textil-Wirtschaft* 17 (1977), p. 20; *Textil-Wirtschaft* 21 (1977), p. 18, and *Süddeutsche Zeitung*, 1 June 1977: 'Tunesien wird zur Investitions-Oase'.

technical products. According to Chelly his country is primarily interested in partners who can bring know-how to projects and provide assistance in the opening up of export markets. Participation in projects and financing could be made available. Projects with a good level of profitability can be financed through Arab banks. Tunisia has already been promised money for projects from the UAE and Kuwait. As Lohmann added, this could be the pattern in which trilateral cooperation might function – money from the oil producers, know-how from the industrial countries for projects in Third World countries. The DEG has organised an informational visit to Tunisia in the autumn for representatives from those branches mentioned...the President of the API referred to the government's measures designed to encourage foreign investment – amongst others, freedom from taxation, or tax concessions, simplified customs formalities, the significance of the supply of labour in Tunisia, favourable transport links to Europe and low wage costs. The Tunisian government is careful to keep the rate of inflation low and controls wages to remain competitive in the international arena. Tunisia has to create 60000 jobs a year. 100% of boys and about 70% of girls receive a school education. Basic training for technical workers takes place in 182 state training institutions. Specific training for particular industrial requirements at these centres is possible. Tunisian products can be imported free of tariffs into the EEC, and according to Chelly, this Maghreb country is also a good location for supplying the Arab markets.[1]

In view of this undisguised aim of doing its utmost to promote capital investment for private profit in the developing countries, and in view of the lack of any kind of analysis of the use to which the investments which have been supported by the DEG have been put as far as the bulk of the populations of the developing countries is concerned, one is stunned to read that the DEG (a 100% state-owned body) 'has set itself the task of supporting economic and *social* progress in the Third World'.[2] The DEG probably bases this unexpected assertion on the fact that approximately 47000 jobs have been directly created and 'far more' indirectly through the investments which they have promoted.[3] What we do not discover from the DEG's annual reports (which are aimed at the general public) is whether these new jobs have been created at the expense of the destruction of already existing jobs, under what conditions the people will have to work and for what wages, whether there is child labour or night work, on hiring and firing etc. (although the DEG makes such details available if they are of importance to potential investors in the form of special pamphlets). Without even attempting

1. *VWD-Textil*, 24 June 1976. See too BfA, *Nachrichten für Außenhandel*, 25 June 1976: 'The labour market in particular offers favourable preconditions with a large supply of industrious and easily trained workers at considerably lower wage levels than in Federal Germany.'
2. DEG, *Geschäftsbericht 1974*, p. 15 (emphasis added).
3. DEG, *Geschäftsbericht 1975*, pp. 15 f.

a justification for its position the DEG quite naturally proceeds under the assumption that (only) a further extension of the international division of labour within the context of the capitalist world economy will facilitate economic progress in the developing countries and growing welfare for their populations. The fact that the preceding centuries of integration of the current so-called developing countries into the capitalist world system utterly contradicts this assertion and the fact that it was their partial extrication and dis-integration out of the international division of labour in the capitalist world system which allowed certain countries at least to alleviate the direct material suffering of their populations and develop, to some extent, an independent complex economic and industrial structure is simply passed over without mention. One wishes that the DEG would occasionally take its own view seriously, namely that 'not every corporate profit is a general economic gain'.[1]

Of course, the DEG does not regard its own very successful efforts as alone creating the basis for the profitable penetration of capital into the developing countries. On the other hand, the fact these efforts are by no means a negligible factor is shown by a number of facts contained in the DEG's annual report. In 1976 the DEG's authorised capital amounted to DM 600 million. Since its establishment in 1962 the DEG has been involved in co-financing the foundation or extension of 172 companies in fifty-three developing countries. By the end of 1975 the total volume of investment in projects in which the DEG has been involved in the financing amounted to DM 2200 million. In individual cases DEG financial contributions vary from DM 80000 to DM 16 million. One of the main areas of its involvement has been in the textile and garment business.

As far as the description of its operations and strategy is concerned the DEG can scarcely be distinguished from a profit oriented commercial business (compare, for example, the extracts from the DEG's report and the report of the Triumph company, with which the DEG has close connections).

It is quite clear, and must be stated, that the DEG is no more than a publicly financed agency for the promotion of profitable private investments in the developing countries. The term 'development' and 'cooperation' in its name means simply the further penetration of the capitalist division of labour into the developing countries.

1. DEG, *Geschäftsbericht 1973*, p. 14.

9 Conclusion to Part I

The case study in this part has shown the manner and the extent to which the Federal German textile and garment industry has become integrated into the process of the new international division of labour. This process, which displays many features of 'early' capitalist unruliness, has forced a large number of German firms to relocate their production in order to remain competitive. Once a sufficiently large portion of production has been shifted to new initially profitable sites, the further competitiveness of a company can very soon only be secured by the application of the 'classical' methods – that is, essentially raising productivity – unless it succeeds in discovering new sites at which surplus profits can be made again for a while, until the competition catches up.

Out of the multitude of reasons for the global reorganisation of industrial production which have been discussed in the context of the textile and garment industry, three should be stressed as being of special importance.

(1) The Babbage principle: the production process of a good should be broken down into elements such that the world-wide allocation of these elements to the particular combinations of 'factors of production' (in particular to adequately skilled, but maximally cheap labour) will yield the optimal valorisation of capital.

The relatively low proportion of skilled workers in the textile and garment industry (compared with the industrial average), the above average drop in the share of unskilled and semiskilled activities in the Federal German garment industry, and the correspondingly high proportion of unskilled and semiskilled jobs in the foreign plants of the Federal German garment industry, and the large and probably growing significance of subcontracting for many sections of the Federal German textile, and especially, garment industry all constitute forms in which the Babbage principle appeared in this case study.

(2) The massive difference in wage levels and working conditions between the traditional industrial countries and the developing countries, especially as far as the length of the working year is concerned. It is these enormous disparities, and not as is constantly claimed government subsidies (export subsidies, cheap inputs etc.) or the financing of fixed capital by the prices obtained on the local market in the socialist or developing country concerned – although important in individual instances – which are the prime reason for the so-called dumping prices of imports of textiles and clothing from these countries into the traditional industrial countries.

Wages in manufacturing industry in the low wage countries are often only enough to cover the immediate daily costs of the reproduction of labour-power, but insufficient for the 'raising' of a new generation of new workers or for the care of sick or older workers who can no longer be used in the direct production process. These costs have to be borne by sectors of the economies of these countries which are not directly integrated into the specifically capitalist mode of production of the 'modern' export-oriented sector, but which rather subsidise this sector from the 'outside'. The continued existence of this sector and its subsidising function is bound up with the increased physical exploitation of those who live in it: extremely long working hours, high intensity of labour and enormous poverty. Apart from its basic role of subsidising the production and reproduction of labour-power in the capitalist sector (as understood in its narrow sense), these sectors are often directly integrated into the production process of the 'modern' sector in the form of out-work.

The length of the working year – that is, the number of hours worked annually – in which the existing productive equipment can be actually used for production is especially important in capital-intensive processes. Despite currently widespread opinions, the present case study has proved that not only labour-intensive but also extremely capital-intensive manufacture is 'relocatable'. This is for one simple reason: in order to pay off the high capital costs as quickly as possible locations are preferred which – given that the other necessary preconditions are present – allow the longest possible working year: this means sites with no, or comparatively minimal, limits of night work, shift work, and holiday work, and with a large reserve army of workers who are forced to work at any time dictated by the company. These conditions are being fulfilled to a growing extent in the low wage countries.

(3) The development of efficient systems of transport and communication which make the choice of site for production or submanufacture increasingly independent of geographical distance. Whereas capitalist development previously implied or required the introduction of ocean-going sailing ships, steam ships, canals and railways, the development of the capitalist system now means the introduction of bulk carriers and container ships, roll-on/roll-off ferry links and containerised air cargo. The same applies to the introduction of improved means of communication.

In Adam Smith's time it was clearly the markets for industrial products which were extended by the development of means of transport, and which as a consequence also expanded the economically feasible scope of the division of labour. Today, by contrast, it is principally the markets for low skilled and extremely cheap labour-power which are being extended by the development of the means of transport and which hence expand the economically feasible (and necessary as transmitted through the mechanism of competition) scope for the division of labour – the new international division of labour.

The most significant effect of the new international division of labour within the Federal German textile and garment industry is the sharp drop in the volume of domestic employment. Set against this fall at home is a strong increase in the volume of employment abroad, especially in the low wage countries and in the foreign plants of the Federal German industry. At the present time, including subcontracting, it can be safely said that for every hundred workers employed in Germany in the textile and garment industry over ten are employed in foreign production facilities of the Federal German textile and garment industry (disregarding here other forms of foreign operation, e.g. imports by trading concerns). The bulk of the production undertaken by these workers, especially in the garment industry, is destined for the Federal German market ('pure' relocation of production).

For the workers affected by this process it means first and foremost unemployment and the devaluation of their existing skills and qualifications in the traditional industrial countries, and miserable working conditions, with no hope for improvement in the foreseeable future, in the developing countries.

Is it possible that future technological developments might bring the process of the new international division of labour to a halt? Two possibilities emerge which are not alternatives but complementary directions in which development may proceed. Firstly, the (technically possible) introduction of capital-intensive technologies may enable production sites in the traditional industrial countries to remain profitable. For the workers there this would admittedly mean 'technological' unemployment and the devaluation of individual skills, with the effect as far as the labour is concerned of pushing down wages and worsening working conditions. Secondly, the future will see an increase in both the relatively labour-intensive forms of production with extremely cheap labour, and also relatively capital-intensive forms of production with a long operating year which will settle in profitable locations in the low wage countries.

As far as the textile and garment industry is concerned the foreseeable future will be characterised by the following trends:

In the garment industry there will be a continuation of the relocation of production in many spheres with the aim of partially or completely supplying the markets of the traditional industrial countries, in particular the Federal Republic of Germany.

In the textile industry there will be relocations of production on the same basis as the garment industry in certain spheres (e.g. knitwear).

Those processes which remain in Federal Germany will be subjected to intense 'rationalisation'.

Some particularly capital-intensive processes will be relocated in order to exploit the long working year.

Other processes in the textile industry (suppliers) will follow in the wake of the relocated production of clothing.

By all accounts, the result will be further redundancies in the Federal German textile, garment and synthetic fibres industry, even if the reasons which stand in the foreground vary from case to case.

Is it possible that the domestic textile and garment industry will be able to retain its position – and hence by and large its levels of employment – in Federal Germany by means of 'creativity', 'speed and punctuality of delivery', 'fashionable flexibility', 'high quality of manufacture' etc.? In fact, hardly at all for two main reasons. Firstly, the market for such manufactures is restricted – and is certainly considerably smaller than the market which takes up current domestic production. Secondly, there is no reason why these attributes are only attainable in the long term *inside* Federal Germany or other traditional industrial countries. Production in the low wage countries is already and increasingly characterised by these attributes – often precisely because of the involvement of firms from the Federal German textile and garment industry.

Can the process of the relocation of production be limited by state intervention? Again, hardly. The apparent scope for freedom of action which the state seems to possess in the sphere of foreign trade is extensively circumscribed by the imperatives of the valorisation of the respective national capital. A country which is as deeply involved in the capitalist world economy as Federal Germany cannot contemplate a relatively effective protectionist policy even in selected areas because of the threat of retaliation by other countries.

Is the process of the new international division of labour a first step in the overcoming of the underdevelopment and the improvement of the appalling material conditions of the bulk of the populations of the underdeveloped countries? This case study has shown that industrialisation through the textile and garment industry has taken place in a number of developing countries. (See Parts II and III for developments in other industrial branches.) However, for the most part this has involved a very local, export-oriented, fragmented mono-industrialisation, which exposes the economy of the respective developing country to the exploitative competition of the world market for production sites, and its population to the world market for labour without any real opportunity for the developing country to insulate itself from the worst effects of this competition, the benefits of which mostly accrue to the companies of the traditional industrial countries, not the populations of the industrial or developing countries, and especially not the latter.

The new international division of labour is determined by the logic of the valorisation of capital and not the interests of those who work in the production processes, either in the industrial or the developing countries. If this process spreads beyond the textile and garment industry into other forms of manufacture and production one can be certain that it will have a crucial effect on the economic, social and political development of not only Federal Germany in the next few years.

Part II

The advance of the new international division of labour: employment abroad by Federal German industrial companies

Introduction

The tendency towards a new international division of labour is concretely manifested in the world-wide redistribution of production sites for industrial production. The progress of this tendency will be examined in this part by reference to the case of production and employment by Federal German industrial companies abroad. Since no statistics on the extent and distribution of foreign production and employment are available, the first task of research in this area is to establish and verify the actual existence of production sites abroad for each individual company in turn. We attempted in particular to ascertain the numbers employed at each site for the following reasons:

(a) The progress of the tendency towards a new international division of labour can be read off from changes in the distribution of industrial labour.

(b) The most important social and political aspects of the redistribution of production sites are those involving the use of industrial labour at new sites and the impact of this on workers at the traditional sites of industrial production.

(c) Data on investment does not provide an adequate measure of the extent of production abroad for reasons which are given below.

The total amount of production abroad has been included in the study where possible in order to make it possible to identify characteristic changes in the distribution of production sites (the period covered by the study is 1961–76) and to estimate to what extent production at the present time is already determined by the tendency towards a new international division of labour. Since the relocation of Federal German industry to other EEC countries could not be designated as a main indicator of this trend it was decided not to deal with this phenomenon specifically.

The changed conditions for the valorisation of capital are forcing industrial companies, regardless of their size or branch, to reorganise production, which in many cases implies taking into account the possibility of producing abroad. As a consequence strong evidence for the advance of the new international division of labour would be established if it could be shown that:

(a) production abroad is not merely confined to a few branches which are 'ripe' for relocation but can also be found in industries which play a central role in domestic production,
(b) companies of all sizes are setting up production abroad.

The available results of the study on the development of the foreign production of Federal German companies between 1961 and 1976 can only be used to deduce the general reasons for relocation and not the specific reasons which apply in each instance, or the changes in these specific reasons over time. However, a basis for a thorough and detailed analysis is provided by an empirically based survey of the involvement of companies of various sizes, the various sectors involved in production abroad, and the development over time and geographical distribution of these companies and branches. Using this as a starting point we examine the determining factors behind production abroad in different regions and branches of industry. These indications cannot, however, serve as a substitute for a systematic treatment of all the relevant aspects, an example of which was provided by the study of the textile and garment industry in Part I. Part III should also be referred to here as it contains a description and analysis of the conditions of production and working conditions at the new sites for industrial production.

10 • The new international division of labour and employment abroad by Federal German industrial companies

10.1 Design of the empirical investigation and a summary of its results

The foreign production and employment of Federal German companies have not previously been subjected to a systematic statistical analysis. The available official statistics published half-yearly by the Federal Economics Minister in the *Bundesanzeiger* only cover those investments abroad which are effected by the export of capital from Federal Germany. The net capital expenditures which are embraced by these statistics display a strong upward trend, especially in recent years: in 1961, they amounted to DM 3291 million; in 1966, DM 8236 million; in 1971, DM 19932 million; and in 1976, DM 47048 million. Thirty per cent of this total went to the developing countries.[1] The statistics are broken down by region and country, as well as by economic sector.

The increase in these investments is an incontrovertible indication of a substantial increase in production abroad. More cannot really be deduced from these statistics as they do not show, for example, what share of investment is destined for the establishment of production, and what share for the service sector. In addition, the regional distribution cannot be accurately derived from them as a portion of the investments made are executed through holding companies in third countries, which are then shown as investments in the country in which the holding company is domiciled. Statistics on investment abroad have, until now, only shown capital exports from the Federal Republic of Germany: these officially registered investments are considerably exceeded in individual countries by the

1. Bundesminister für Wirtschaft, *Runderlaß Außenwirtschaft betreffend: IV, 1; Vermögensanlagen Gebietsansässiger in fremden Wirtschaftsgebieten. Bundesanzeiger*, various issues.

actual amount of capital present, which is built up through the re-investment of profits and the local raising of capital.[1]

Establishing the geographical distribution and the development over time of Federal German production abroad is intended to serve as a basis of information and data which will allow an adequate treatment of the question as to how far the tendency towards a new international division of labour has advanced. The material which is presented in the course of the investigation is also of value in itself in that it provides detailed information on the extent of production and employment abroad which was not previously available. It necessitates a substantial upward revision of previous estimates and reveals the extent to which particular sectors are engaged in production abroad.

The foreign production of Federal German companies can be broken down as follows:

— production for the market of the country in which production takes place,
— production for third markets,
— production for the Federal German market.

The first case is the same as import-substitution industrialisation in that in many instances the new domestic production replaces what was formerly imported. Products manufactured at the new sites often replace those which were previously manufactured in other plants of the same company, such as in Federal Germany, and imported from there. Both the second and third cases represent production for export. In the second case the products are sold in other countries and not on the local or Federal German market; we should also make a distinction here between regional markets which to some extent present specific market conditions (e.g. the countries of the Andean Pact), and the unrestricted world market which is basically characterised by demand originating in the traditional industrial countries. In the third case former domestic production in Federal Germany is replaced by production abroad for the Federal German home market. In all three cases production abroad frequently

1. For example, these figures indicate a 1975 total for Mexico of DM 462.1 million, whereas the Deutsch-Mexikanische Industrie- und Handelskammer estimates the value of Federal German investments in Mexico at DM 1.0–1.2 billion (*Handelsblatt*, 31 March 1976). The figure for South Africa for the year-ending 1974 was DM 419 million. 'According to South African estimates total German investments reached DM 3.5 billion by the end of 1974.' (*Südafrika. Delegation des Bundesverbandes der deutschen Industrie* (Cologne 1975) p. 5.)

consists of partial manufacturing processes (subassembly, or final assembly for example) which have been extracted from the manufacturing process as a whole and transferred to the new sites because of the divisibility of the production process (cf. Introduction). The three cases also are often combined in the actual production process of an individual plant.

The replacement of former export production in Federal Germany by new production abroad represents just as much a process of relocation as does production abroad for the Federal German home market. It is not only the extension of production capacity abroad with a simultaneous reduction in capacity at home which leads to a change in the distribution of industrial production between the old and new sites, but also the retention of a constant domestic capacity with a simultaneous expansion abroad. However, the relocation of production does not only consist in the redistribution of sites at the level of individual Federal German companies; it also implies a world-wide redistribution of the production of entire sectors of the economy. This redistribution can force Federal German companies to shut down production, whilst at the same time it is not only Federal German companies who are undertaking the corresponding establishment of production at the new sites.

What is the significance of the three different cases above in the context of the tendency towards a new international division of labour? Let us recall those factors in the world-wide valorisation process of capital which have brought about this trend, which have already been discussed in Part I: availability of cheap labour, divisibility of the production process, developed systems of transport and communications.

In many instances these conditions render the replacement of domestic production by export-oriented production abroad both possible and necessary. However, this replacement is by no means restricted to the relocation of production as covered by case three in its narrow sense. In fact, at the present time, import-substitution industrialisation is also overwhelmingly the product of the conditions of the new international division of labour, for if it is the case that world market oriented production at the new sites has often become profitable through the availability of cheap labour, the divisibility of the production process and the development of transport and communications, this applies all the more for that part which can be regarded as import-substitution production in that it is sold on the respective home market and replaces former imports. One should not therefore counterpose production which replaces former imports and which is directed towards the retention and expansion of markets and is one particular form of production abroad to relocated world market oriented foreign production.

In general, production under the conditions of the new international division of labour means producing for the world market. Nevertheless, world market production can also be said to take place when production, which takes place at that site which offers the most favourable conditions for production in comparison with all other possible sites, is either partly or wholly, in the first instance or for the foreseeable future, destined for the respective home market.

The distinction which was suggested above between three types of production abroad is artificial to the extent that the three cases often combine or alternate, and that, furthermore, the switching of roles is envisaged from the outset. As a rule the actual manufacturing operations themselves display no differences as regards the eventual outlets for the products. Although some parts of production which has an import-substitution effect are protected from external competition by selective tariffs and quotas which confer a relative advantage on the domestic market for those companies producing internally, nevertheless the conditions of the new international division of labour are also increasingly compelling the reorganisation of production to secure that particular use of labour and the division of the production process which guarantees the optimal valorisation of capital aside from the benefits conferred by protective tariffs and quotas. In relation to a site to be chosen from the outset for world market oriented production (specifically for production destined overwhelmingly or exclusively for export) the existence of a protected home market is merely one additional factor to be taken into account, and only plays a key role for small areas of production abroad and only then for a few regions and sectors.

A large industrial enterprise will take account of the existence of this distinction in the way in which it expresses its policy: it will initially differentiate between national factories and world market factories only to discover subsequently that any national factory can always become a world market factory. The tendency towards a new international division of labour embraces all production sites, including those which were established before this tendency began to exert an influence, or which had previously escaped its effects because of specific circumstances. We should therefore add the possibility of a national factory becoming a world market factory to the possibility of establishing new export-oriented world market factories at new sites. Under present conditions this possibility must be increasingly incorporated in the plans for the establishment of plants which initially produce predominantly for the local market: every national factory must be at least potentially a world market factory. These possibilities taken together are a sign of the extent and dynamic of the process of the new global determination of sites for industrial production. This process represents, among others, a key (and we believe the central) explanation for the chronic mass unemployment in the traditional industrial countries.

We present a summary of the most important statistics on this theme to convey an overall picture of the extent of employment and production abroad by Federal German industrial companies, and its regional and sectoral distribution.

The number of companies in the study known to have production abroad outside the EEC amounts to 602.[1] Of these, 172 were in mechanical engineering, with 90 in other fields of manufacturing industry, precision engineering and optics had 84, chemicals 84, electrical engineering 63, ferrous and non-ferrous metals 45, stone, glass and ceramics 22, vehicle building 20, energy and mining 11, agriculture and forestry 11. These 602 firms were found to have (including the relatively few given up) 1760 manufacturing subsidiaries outside the EEC in the period 1961–76, which were broken down as follows: chemicals 502, mechanical engineering 368, electrical engineering 231, ferrous and non-ferrous metals 177, precision engineering and optics 176, other manufacturing industry 168, vehicle building 48, stone, glass and ceramics 46, energy and mining 31, agriculture and forestry 13 (Table II-1).[2]

1. Although on the one hand this figure is quite substantial and is higher than previous estimates, even when it is doubled to take into account producers in the EEC and textile and garment manufacturers, it still only represents a small fraction of the total of the 44 121 companies in manufacturing industry (1972) with ten or more employees (see *Statistisches Jahrbuch*, 1975, Table 14.3, p. 227). However, an estimate shows that at least half of the employees in Federal German manufacturing industry work in companies which also manufacture abroad.
2. Unless otherwise stated the figures in these tables are based on the authors' own survey data. The technical details of the construction and conduct of the survey can be found on pp. 282–8 of the German edition of this work. A number of limitations apply throughout, so that for example only those subsidiaries with a Federal German share-in-capital of 25% or more are included. Although British practice restricts the term 'subsidiary' to companies in which the parent has a holding of over 50%, and would refer to companies with a holding of 20%–50% as 'associates', we use 'subsidiary' throughout, both for ease of presentation and to indicate the fact that these companies do have a subordinate status.

Table II-1. *Number of Federal German companies, subsidiaries and plants by economic sector: 1961–76*

Economic sector	Companies covered	Subsidiaries: Existing in 1976	Subsidiaries: Given up 1962–76	Subsidiaries: Total	Plants of subsidiaries: Existing in 1976	Plants of subsidiaries: Given up 1962–76	Plants of subsidiaries: Total
Agric. & for.	11	11	2	13	11	2	13
En. & min.	11	29	2	31	33	2	35
Chem.	84	490	12	502	532	13	545
St., gl. & ceram.	22	40	6	46	41	7	48
Metal.	45	171	6	177	176	6	182
Mech. eng.	172	340	28	368	352	29	381
Veh.	20	46	2	48	47	2	49
Elec. eng.	63	220	11	231	253	11	264
Prec. eng. & opt.	84	167	9	176	183	9	192
Other	90	155	13	168	163	13	176
All sectors covered	602	1669	91	1760	1791	94	1885
Excluding agric. & for., en. & min.	580	1629	87	1716	1747	90	1837

Agric. & for. = agriculture and forestry; en. & min. = energy and mining; chem. = chemicals; st., gl. & ceram. = stone, glass and ceramics; metal. = ferrous and non-ferrous metals; mech. eng. = mechanical engineering; veh. = vehicle building; elec. eng. = electrical engineering; prec. eng. & opt. = precision engineering and optics; other = other manufacturing industry

Whereas the average number of foreign subsidiaries per company was 2.9, firms in the chemical industry had 6, ferrous and non-ferrous metals 3.9, energy and mining 2.8, vehicle building 2.4, mechanical engineering 2.2, precision engineering and optics, together with stone, glass and ceramics 2.1, other manufacturing industry 1.9, agriculture and forestry 1.2. Out of the total of 12 companies with twenty or more subsidiaries, 6 were from the chemical industry, 3 from the electrical engineering industry, 2 from the ferrous and non-ferrous metals industry and 1 from the mechanical engineering industry. Whereas the average number of subsidiaries per company for these 12 was 33.7, the majority of companies (namely 339) had only one manufacturing subsidiary abroad outside the EEC. A further 189 companies had between two and four subsidiaries so that 528 out of the 602 companies had between one and four subsidiaries, with an average of 1.6. These smaller foreign producers account for almost half of the foreign subsidiaries of the companies covered, with a total of 823 (Table II-2).

This result refutes the prevalent view that production abroad is only carried out by companies which operate in a large number of countries. These figures confirm that transnationally organised

Table II-2. *Federal German companies broken down by size (number of sudsidiaries) and economic sector: 1961–76*

	Size of firm (no. of subsidiaries)					No. of firms	No. of sub-sidiaries	Sub-sidiaries per firm
	1	2–4	5–9	10–19	> 20			
Agric. & for.	10	1	—	—	—	11	13	1.2
En. & min.	3	6	2	—	—	11	31	2.8
Chem.	31	31	10	6	6	84	502	6.0
St., gl. & ceram.	13	6	3	—	—	22	46	2.1
Metal.	24	11	5	3	2	45	177	3.9
Mech. eng.	100	58	9	4	1	172	368	2.2
Veh.	13	4	2	1	—	20	48	2.4
Elec. eng.	35	20	3	2	3	63	231	3.7
Prec. eng. & opt.	49	29	4	2	—	84	176	2.1
Other	61	23	4	2	—	90	168	1.9
All sectors covered	339	189	42	20	12	602	1760	2.9
No. of subsidiaries	339	484	257	276	404	1760		
Subsidiaries per firm	1	2.6	6.1	13.8	33.7	2.9		

See table II-1 for sector abbreviations

production forces capitals of all sizes to establish production abroad. Nonetheless the high concentration of domestic production also applies to foreign production: 937 subsidiaries are accounted for by 74 companies, of which 12 have 404. The large industrial concerns produce abroad almost without exception, whereas only about 1% of small companies do so.

The main task of the survey is to calculate the number of direct employees in Federal German production facilities abroad (subject to the limitations mentioned above). The number of actual subsidiaries is only a guide in the building up of a more complete picture of the extent and development of employment abroad. Table II-3 gives the breakdown of production and employment abroad by industrial and developing countries in each economic sector and indicates the broad spread of production through these different sectors.

Table II-4 attempts to indicate the relative significance of the individual sectors of the economy in relation to the total volume of employment and production maintained abroad by Federal German industry. In those branches covered (excluding agriculture and forestry, energy and mining), seven of the eight branches occupied at least one of the first four positions in the list. In addition to this indication of a wide spread of production it can be seen that

Table II-3. *Proven subsidiaries and employment of Federal German companies by economic sector and region: 1961–75/76*

	World			Industrial countries (excluding EEC)											
				Total			W. Europe			Non-European			E. Europe		
	I	II	III	I	II	III	I	II	III	I	II	III	I	II	III
Agric. & for.	13	5	133	1	—	—	—	—	—	1	—	—	—	—	—
En. & min.	31	20	4486	17	8	999	3	1	529	14	7	470	—	—	—
Chem.	502	371	131760	186	133	57358	73	54	8943	113	79	48415	—	—	—
St., gl. & ceram.	46	28	9433	26	16	4982	13	13	3765	13	3	1217	—	—	—
Metal.	177	87	48657	86	38	13809	34	19	8309	52	19	5500	—	—	—
Mech. eng.	368	219	51730	159	94	17786	54	39	9370	104	54	8266	1	1	150
Veh.	48	40	101988	12	11	11327	3	3	580	9	8	10747	—	—	—
Elec. eng.	231	179	154756	89	63	58708	46	41	41775	42	22	16933	1	—	—
Prec. eng. & opt.	176	116	32974	70	43	7782	34	25	3935	36	18	3847	—	—	—
Other	168	113	24871	63	40	5687	43	30	4293	20	10	1394	—	—	—
All sectors covered	1760	1178	560788	709	446	178438	303	225	81499	404	220	96789	2	1	150

Table II-3. (*cont.*)

	Developing countries																	
	Total			Mediterranean			Latin America			Africa (non-Mediterranean			W. Asia			S. & S.E. Asia		
	I	II	III	I	II	III	I	II	III	I	II	III	I	II	III	I	II	III
Agric. & for.	12	5	133	10	4	114	1	1	19	—	—	—	1	—	—	—	—	—
En. & min.	14	12	3487	4	3	236	6	6	2994	3	2	151	1	1	106	—	—	—
Chem.	316	238	74402	104	78	19457	153	122	42568	8	2	345	10	6	1957	41	30	10075
St., gl. & ceram.	20	12	4451	11	6	1281	3	3	2395	3	2	365	1	—	—	2	1	410
Metal.	91	49	34848	30	18	4568	42	23	24907	3	1	2876	3	—	—	13	7	2497
Mech. eng.	209	125	33944	56	38	6493	104	60	20758	6	5	598	1	—	—	42	22	6095
Veh.	36	29	90661	9	8	7537	18	14	76939	2	2	1506	2	1	839	5	4	3843
Elec. eng.	142	116	96048	47	43	26275	59	46	43706	2	1	87	8	5	2883	26	21	23097
Prec. eng. & opt.	106	73	25192	35	23	4661	46	32	8083	—	—	—	2	1	73	23	17	12375
Other	105	73	19184	33	24	3975	37	26	11584	11	6	1300	5	2	709	19	15	1616
All sectors covered	1051	732	382350	339	245	74594	469	333	233953	38	21	7228	34	16	6567	171	117	60008

Regional breakdown follows that of table II-8
See table II-1 for sector abbreviations
I = number of subsidiaries; II = number of subsidiaries for which employment was available; III = employment

Table II-4. *Rank order of economic sectors by (a) number of companies producing abroad, (b) number of subsidiaries abroad, (c) numbers employed in subsidiaries abroad*

	(a)	(b)	(c)
Agric. & for.	9	10	10
En. & min.	9	9	9
Chem.	3	1	2
St., gl. & ceram.	7	8	8
Metal.	6	4	5
Mech. eng.	1	2	4
Veh.	8	7	3
Elec. eng	5	3	1
Prec. eng. & opt.	3	5	6
Other	2	6	7

See table II-1 for sector abbreviations

different results are obtained depending on which of the three variables are considered: number of subsidiaries, number of companies producing abroad or the number of employees in each subsidiary. In this context the differences in the average size of company and the degree of concentration should also be taken into consideration, as well as the difference in the size of each economic sector.

Those Federal German companies covered by the survey normally controlled their associated undertakings by means of shares in capital. Table II-5 shows that 51.5% of associated companies – subsidiaries – are held through shares of 95%–100% of nominal capital (industrial countries 64.8%, developing countries 42%), 82.5% are held with 50% or more (industrial countries 90.7%, developing countries 76.3%) whereas those associated companies with less than a 50% holding account for 17.5% (industrial countries 8.9%, developing countries 23.6%).

10.2 An estimate of total employment abroad

The previous section set out the basis of an extensive empirical survey designed to test the existence and extent of the tendency towards a new international division of labour and presented a synopsis of its most important findings. In this section we attempt to estimate

Table II-5. *Share in capital, by region: 1961–76 (percentages)*

Share in capital	World	Industrial countries (excluding EEC)				Developing countries					
		Total	W. Europe	Non-European	E. Europe	Total	Mediter-ranean	Latin America	Africa (non-Mediter-ranean)	W. Asia	S. & S.E. Asia
25	3.4	1.7	1.8	1.7	—	4.6	4.2	2.7	3.4	3.7	12.1
26–40	8.9	5.2	6.7	4.1	—	11.5	9.5	8.0	17.2	37.0	21.2
41–49	5.2	2.0	1.8	1.7	100	7.5	4.9	8.0	13.8	7.4	10.6
50	13.5	12.9	6.7	17.9	—	13.8	19.9	9.4	10.3	18.5	13.6
51–65	6.9	5.5	6.7	4.7	—	7.9	8.8	6.6	27.6	—	9.8
66–94	10.6	7.8	7.7	8.0	—	12.6	14.1	12.6	10.3	18.5	9.1
95–99	5.6	3.1	1.8	4.1	—	7.4	5.9	10.6	—	7.4	2.3
100	45.9	61.7	67.0	57.9	—	34.6	32.7	43.2	17.2	7.4	21.2
Less than 50	17.5	8.9	10.3	7.5	100	23.6	18.6	18.7	34.4	48.1	43.9
50–100	82.5	91.1	89.7	92.5	—	76.4	81.4	81.3	65.6	51.9	56.1
95–100	51.5	64.8	68.8	62.0	—	42.0	38.6	53.8	17.2	14.8	23.5
No. of subsidiaries covered[a]	1560	650	285	363	2	910	306	414	29	27	132
Total no. of subsidiaries	1760	709	303	404	2	1051	339	469	38	34	171

Regional breakdown follows that of table II-8
a: Information on share in capital was obtained for this number of subsidiaries

the total direct foreign employment of Federal German industry, based on the findings already presented plus additional data.

The aim of this survey is to obtain a complete coverage of all production facilities abroad, and the total volume of employment in these plants. There is no procedure available which allows us to ascertain the percentage of the total which our survey has managed to embrace. For individual countries subsequent compilations based on official data could be obtained which in large measure confirmed the data which the survey had yielded. Federal German companies who produce in more than one country outside the EEC are almost totally covered. The total number of subsidiaries will also not be much higher than the number arrived at in the survey. Data on the numbers employed for at least one year could only be obtained for 72.5% (1975) of the subsidiaries. From the point of view of the initial aim of this survey this is the least satisfactory degree of coverage of the phenomenon under investigation.

In addition to the survey of individual subsidiaries with their own manufacture and employment in these subsidiaries, an additional survey was carried out in which total company figures for domestic and foreign employment were collected, with the inclusion of figures for the EEC countries.[1] For 1974 figures could be collected for 149 companies (149 out of 602) with a total employment of 1516379 (Table II-6). These 149 companies employed 336151 persons abroad, of which 107448 were in EEC countries. 197027 foreign employees were working in the domestic industry. The 149 companies, which all had production abroad, employed 47386 persons in non-manufacturing associated companies and establishments abroad, which amounted to 14.1% of employment abroad.[2]

The proportion of employment abroad for these companies was 22.2% of total employment, and the proportion of the employment of foreign workers (including foreign workers in the domestic industry) in total employment was 35.2%. What is interesting here is that this average figure hardly varies when companies are grouped together by size, large, medium or small. The size of firm had no impact on either the proportion of employment abroad, or

1. This additional survey does not include data on individual subsidiaries; companies supplied information on their *total* home and foreign employment, according to the categories in Table II-6.
2. The HWWA study assigns 15.4% of employees abroad in their sample of 27 companies to distribution companies. *HWWA-Report Nr. 31* (Hamburg 1975), Table 11, p. 31.

Table II-6. *Number of employees, domestic and abroad, for 149 Federal German companies: 1974*

Companies			Domestic employment		Employment abroad							
Size	No.	Total employment (1)	Total (2)	Foreign workers (3)	Total (4)	In EEC (5)	In non-manufacturing subsidiaries (6)	(4) as a proportion of (1)	(4) as a proportion of (2)	(3+4) as a proportion of (1)	(5) as a proportion of (4)	(6) as a proportion of (4)
								(%)	(%)	(%)	(%)	(%)
All	149	1516379	1180228	197027	336151	107448	47386	22.2	28.5	35.2	32.0	14.1
>5000 employees	38	1370804	1071372	179876	299432	101081	45257	21.8	27.9	35.0	33.8	15.1
1000–5000 employees	49	116963	86693	14012	30270	5126	1856	25.9	34.9	37.9	16.9	6.1
<1000 employees	62	28612	22163	3139	6449	1241	273	22.5	29.1	33.5	19.2	4.2

the proportion of foreign workers for those firms producing abroad (outside the EEC).[1]

It was possible to indicate the share of employment abroad, and the proportion of foreign employees as they developed over the period 1961–74 for 87 out of the 149 companies. The proportion of employment abroad increased from 7.9% in 1961, 11.5% in 1966, 19.5% in 1971 to 27.3% in 1974. The proportion of foreign workers employed increased from 10.7% in 1961, to 18.9% in 1966, 31% in 1971 and 39.4% in 1974. (See Table II-7.)[2] During this period the number of workers employed abroad rose by 505%, the numbers in Federal Germany by 49%, although the number of German workers in this rapidly expanding volume of employment rose by only 24%.

According to the evidence of the companies covered here, which only represent a portion of total foreign producers, the share of employment abroad has risen substantially throughout the period under study. As far as the available figures are concerned, the size of the company in question does not play a particular role in this overall process.

The following represents an attempt to provide an estimate of the total foreign employment of Federal German productive industry as a whole based on the findings of the empirical surveys conducted in the course of our investigation. In order to derive the proportion of foreign employment covered by our survey it was necessary to estimate the residual amount. The procedures employed are, admittedly, not particularly satisfactory. However, the attempt which we have made is superior to other, comparable, attempts in that it is based on actual employment figures and not such quantitative guides as reported direct investments or turnover figures which are systematically distorted.

In 1178 out of the 1760 subsidiaries for which employment figures could be obtained, 560788 employees were found to be employed (1975). (See Table II-3.) If one takes this as a representative sample then the corresponding proportional figure for the 1760 is 838000 (excluding EEC).[3] This figure may be somewhat high as those

1. This applies to all companies. However, for all industrial companies it is true that large firms taken together have a higher proportion of foreign employment than all the small- and medium-sized companies grouped together.
2. These figures indicate a shift from the employment of foreign workers in Federal Germany to the employment of foreign workers abroad.
3. These estimates are rounded up or down to the nearest thousand.

Table II-7. *Total employment, employment abroad, and foreign workers in domestic employment for eighty-seven Federal German companies: 1961, 1966, 1971, 1974*

Companies: Size	Companies: No.	Total employment (1)	Employment abroad (2)	Foreign workers in domestic employment (3)	(2) as a proportion of (1)	(2+3) as a proportion of (1)	Total employment (1)	Employment abroad (2)	Foreign workers in domestic employment (3)	(2) as a proportion of (1)	(2+3) as a proportion of (1)
		1961					1966				
					(%)	(%)				(%)	(%)
All	87	469852	37211	13037	7.9	10.7	553927	63766	40783	11.5	18.9
> 5000 employees	16	406293	33903	10825	8.3	11.0	481069	57210	36780	11.9	19.5
1000–5000 employees	33	52865	2817	1780	5.3	8.7	59743	5208	3116	8.7	13.9
< 1000 employees	38	10694	491	432	4.6	8.6	13115	1348	887	10.3	17.0
		1971					1974				
					(%)	(%)				(%)	(%)
All	87	770150	150111	88420	19.5	31.0	855941	225016	112404	26.3	39.4
> 5000 employees	16	678855	135306	79553	19.9	31.7	756970	203065	99614	26.8	40.0
1000–5000 employees	33	74913	12290	7371	16.4	26.2	81417	18353	11133	22.5	36.2
< 1000 employees	38	16382	2515	1496	15.4	24.5	17554	3598	1657	20.5	29.9

holdings whose employment figures were not ascertained may have had a lower than average figure.

If it is assumed that the selected 149 companies are a representative sample (Table II-6) then a projected figure of 793 000 is obtained for the 602 companies covered in the wider survey.[1] On this basis an estimate of 1 167 000 emerges for all manufacturing subsidiaries including the EEC (see Table II-6, Column 5) and 1 358 000 with the inclusion of non-manufacturing establishments (see Table II-6, Column 6). (Companies which produce only within the EEC and companies which only have non-manufacturing establishments abroad are not taken into account here.) These estimates are based on 1974 data. Taking a low estimate, the numbers employed rose by 5% to 1 426 000 in 1975. The foreign employment of the textile and garment industry, elsewhere estimated at 61 000,[2] and the building industry at 65 000[3] supplement these figures to 1 552 000. Thus a conservative estimate of the *foreign employment of Federal*

1. The question crops up here as to whether these estimates might not be too high as the companies covered by the additional survey may have a higher than average share of employment abroad. However, these estimates are still below those obtained from the data for almost three-quarters of the companies – see the previous paragraph. There is therefore no need for any concern about attempting to make an estimate on this basis.
2. See the study of the textile and garment industry in Part I.
3. On 31 December 1975 (the day chosen) the Hauptverband der Deutschen Bauindustrie collected figures for the number of workers employed on construction projects abroad: 'On the day chosen for the survey a total of 5000 German and 60 000 foreign workers were employed on the foreign construction sites of the German construction industry. Since several new sites have started work in the first few months of the current year these figures will now be somewhat higher.' (*Bauindustriebrief* 2–3 (February/March 1976), p. 14.) Employment for six selected companies:

	Total employees	At home	Abroad	Year
Beton- u. Monierbau	15268	6280	8988	1976[a]
Bilfinger & Berger	28700	6850	21850	1976[e]
Dyckerhoff & Widman	14955	12055	2900	1975[b]
Hochtief	26682	15232	11450	1975[c]
Holzmann	25800	14300	11500	1975[d]
Züblin	7300	5250	2050	1975[b]
	118705	59967	58738	

Sources
a: *Süddeutsche Zeitung* 10:12:1976
b: *Geschäftsbericht* 1975
c: *Handelsblatt* 23:11:1976
d: *Zwischenbericht* 31:8:1976
e: *Zwischenbericht* 31:3:1977

German productive industry is 1.5–1.6 million workers for 1975.[1]

These estimates leave two not inconsiderable areas out of account. Some economic sectors which do not belong to productive industry have a large share of their operations abroad, and employ correspondingly large numbers of people there. In addition to the various branches of commerce (including distribution) there are banks,[2] insurance and transport companies. But many other service sectors, ranging from engineering consultants to office cleaners, also migrate abroad often in the wake of manufacturing companies. The second area of foreign employment by Federal German companies not taken into account in the above estimate involves production with very small or no capital holding, which is controlled e.g. by licence arrangements. This comprises international subcontracting which accounts for a significant proportion of foreign operations in some spheres. The importance of subcontracting has already been estimated for the textile and garment industry in the case study presented in Part I.

1. It is realistic to assume that several firms and subsidiaries, as well as shareholdings of private individuals, are not covered here: if one adds 5%–10% for such cases then a figure of 1.7 million emerges. All these estimates exclude the indirect employment generated by Federal German production abroad.
2. According to Ursel Steuber's survey Federal German banks controlled twenty-six banks abroad at the end of 1975, and in addition had 231 'important' holdings abroad. Ursel Steuber, *Internationale Banken, Ergänzungsband 1976* (Hamburg 1977), Appendix 4.

11 ❧ Production and employment abroad by region

11.1 Summary of the regional distribution

Table II-8 gives an overall picture of the distribution of employment and production abroad of Federal German companies in the industrial and developing countries included in the survey in this study. The number of countries in which Federal German companies are engaged in production (outside the EEC and excluding textiles and garments) is seventy-seven. If one adds the eight EEC countries to this then an impression is created of a broad distribution of production over a number of countries. However, this impression requires some correction; in the form which is dealt with here (i.e. with capital holding) Federal German companies are not represented at all in the centrally planned economies outside of Europe, and scarcely in the centrally planned economies in Europe. In addition, forty-one out of the seventy-seven countries only have between one and four German subsidiaries, and a further seven countries between five and nine. The concentration in a few countries is illustrated by the fact that there are 819 subsidiaries in the four countries which have over a hundred (Brazil, Spain, USA, Austria); a further five countries have fifty or more (South Africa, India, Switzerland, Mexico and Argentina). Thus, 1181 out of the total of 1760 are in these nine countries.

A similar picture emerges as far as the distribution over the major geographical regions is concerned: there are 600 subsidiaries in Europe (305 in the industrial countries), 469 in Latin America, 232 in North America (excluding Mexico), 130 in Africa (excluding the African Mediterranean countries and including South Africa) and 34 in West Asia.

40.3% of subsidiaries are in the industrial countries with a total

Table II-8. *Proven subsidiaries (1961–76) and employment (1975) of Federal German companies by region and country*

	I	II	III
Industrial countries (non-EEC)	709	446	178438
W. Europe (non-EEC)	303	225	81499
Austria	181	148	54005
Finland	8	8	2406
Norway	6	2	2142
Sweden	33	24	12707
Switzerland	75	43	10239
Non-European	404	220	96789
Australia	39	26	9595
Canada	47	29	4886
Japan	39	25	10753
New Zealand	2	1	198
South Africa	92	46	18065
USA	185	93	42292
E. Europe	2	1	150
Hungary	1	—	—
Romania	1	1	150
Developing countries	1051	732	382350
Mediterranean	339	245	74594
Algeria	2	1	38
Egypt	3	2	451
Greece	47	34	6678
Israel	2	1	180
Lebanon	1	—	—
Malta	11	8	870
Morocco	10	5	571
Portugal	33	24	8753
Spain	186	141	46042
Syria	1	—	—
Tunisia	7	3	155
Turkey	18	15	7900
Yugoslavia	18	11	2956
Latin America	469	333	233953
Argentina	52	39	21883
Bolivia	1	1	42
Brazil	267	176	177798
Chile	13	12	2281
Colombia	15	10	2832
Dominican Republic	2	1	85
Dutch Antilles	1	1	31
Ecuador	5	2	123
El Salvador	4	3	372
Guatemala	7	6	713
Mexico	63	50	22433
Nicaragua	2	1	45
Peru	11	10	2062
Puerto Rico	3	3	143
Trinidad and Tobago	1	1	33
Uruguay	10	8	997
Venezuela	12	9	2074
Africa (non-Mediterranean)	38	21	7228
Angola	1	—	—
Botswana	1	—	—

Table II-8. (*cont.*)

	I	II	III
Cameroon	3	1	553
Congo	1	—	—
Ethiopia	1	—	—
Ghana	4	4	516
Ivory Coast	1	—	—
Kenya	1	1	30
Lesotho	1	—	—
Liberia	2	2	3160
Mozambique	1	—	—
Niger	1	1	133
Nigeria	9	7	2261
Rhodesia	2	—	—
Senegal	1	—	—
Sudan	1	1	98
Tanzania	1	1	200
Togo	1	—	—
Zaire	3	2	192
Zambia	2	1	85
W. Asia	34	16	6567
Iran	32	16	6567
Jordan	1	—	—
Saudi Arabia	1	—	—
S. & S.E. Asia	171	117	60008
Bangla Desh	1	1	220
Hong Kong	3	2	240
India	80	44	38480
Indonesia	21	17	3934
Malaysia	15	13	4229
Pakistan	3	3	1459
Philippines	2	2	456
Singapore	14	4	5748
South Korea	10	6	2296
Taiwan	5	4	692
Thailand	17	16	2254

The allocation of countries to either industrial or developing country groups follows the usual UN practice. It may be open to question in individual cases – for example the Republic of South Africa has many features which are peculiar to developing countries

I = number of subsidiaries; II = number of subsidiaries for which employment was available; III = employment

of 709 (Table II-8). These countries account for 31.8% of employment, a figure of 178438 workers in 1975.[1]

1051 subsidiaries can be found in the developing countries with 382350 employees (Table II-8). Whereas the average number of employees in the industrial countries per subsidiary is 400, this figure increases to 552 for the developing countries.

The distribution between the industrial and the developing

1. Taking the data from Table II-6 as a basis, 54% of all foreign employment is in industrial countries (including EEC).

Table II-9. *Number of subsidiaries by economic sector: 1961, 1966, 1971, 1974 and total*

	1961			1966			1971			1974			'Total' (1976)			Proportion of sectors of 'total' (%)		
	World	IC	LDC	World	IC	LDC	World	IC	LDC	World	IC	LDC	World	IC	LDC	World	IC	LDC
Agric. & for.	6		6	6		6	9	1	8	12	1	11	13	1	12	0.7	0.1	1.1
En. & min.	11	9	2	12	9	3	17	10	7	26	13	13	31	17	14	1.8	2.4	1.3
Chem.	238	94	144	302	110	192	401	142	259	467	167	300	502	186	316	28.5	26.2	30.1
St., gl. & ceram.	19	9	10	22	12	10	30	16	14	37	19	18	46	26	20	2.6	3.7	1.9
Metal.	92	45	47	112	56	56	139	70	69	163	83	80	177	86	91	10.1	12.1	8.7
Mech. eng.	168	71	97	214	89	125	265	117	148	311	137	174	368	159	209	20.9	22.4	19.9
Veh.	19	4	15	22	5	17	37	9	28	46	12	34	48	12	36	2.7	1.7	3.4
Elec. eng.	87	45	42	120	54	66	180	71	109	207	80	127	231	89	142	13.1	12.6	13.5
Prec. eng. & opt.	73	30	43	97	40	57	122	52	70	147	62	85	176	70	106	10.0	9.9	10.1
Other	58	28	30	89	44	45	118	51	67	147	54	93	168	63	105	9.5	8.9	10.0
All sectors covered	771	335	436	996	419	577	1318	539	779	1563	628	935	1760	709	1051	99.9	100.0	100.0
Proportion of IC and LDC (%)	100.0	43.4	56.6	100.0	42.1	57.9	100.0	40.9	59.1	100.0	40.2	59.8	100.0	40.3	59.7			
Proportion of 'total' (%)	43.8	47.2	41.5	56.6	59.1	54.9	74.9	76.0	74.1	88.8	88.6	89.0	100.0	100.0	100.0			

IC/LDC breakdown follows that of Table II-8
See Table II-1 for sector abbreviations

IC = industrial countries
LDC = developing countries

countries has changed only very slowly over the period: between 1961 and 1976 it changed by only 3.1% towards the developing countries (Table II-9). The number of manufacturing subsidiaries more than doubled in this period in the developing countries, but also doubled in the industrial countries. However, different methods of looking at the phenomenon reveal tendencies towards a shift in the significance of particular areas, as will be shown below.

The proportions of the various sectors of the economy represented in the number of subsidiaries display only slight differences between the industrial and the developing countries (see Table II-9). Industries such as chemicals, mechanical engineering and electrical engineering, which produce on a substantial scale abroad, do so in almost the same porportions in both the industrial and the developing countries. Although production abroad is concentrated in a small number of countries, these include both industrial and developing countries.

Of the 602 industrial companies producing abroad which are covered by this survey, in addition to any domestic or possible EEC production, 158 produce only in industrial countries outside the EEC, 267 only in developing countries, and 177 in both groups of countries. Accordingly there are 335 companies operating in the industrial countries and 444 in the developing countries.

Table II-10, from which these figures have been calculated, compares the data on the subsidiaries and numbers employed for those industrial and developing countries covered. The table confirms the data in Table II-9 insofar as the growth of manufacturing abroad between 1961 and 1976 was almost the same in both groups of countries, not only measured by the number of subsidiaries but also the number of employees which could be ascertained. There are only a few deviations at the level of individual branches of industry. For example, the electrical engineering industry almost doubled the number of its subsidiaries in the industrial countries, but increased them threefold in the developing countries; employment figures have changed correspondingly and are available for an above average number of subsidiaries in this branch.

What does this tell us about the tendency towards a new international division of labour? It proves, first of all, that a considerable growth in the number of production facilities, and an even stronger growth in the volume of employment abroad, has occurred: in the period from 1961 to 1976 this applies, however, to

Table II-10. *Number of subsidiaries and employees by sector: 1961, 1966, 1971, 1973, 1974, 1975, 1976*

(a) Industrial countries (excluding EEC)

	1961			1966			1971			1973			1974			1975			1976		
	I	II	III	I	II	III	I	II	III	I	II	III	I	II	III	I	II	III	I	II	III
Agric. & for.	—	—	—	—	—	—	1	—	—	1	—	—	1	—	—	1	—	—	1		
En. & min.	9	2	793	9	2	712	10	3	903	10	4	936	13	6	999	15	8	999	16		
Chem.	94	25	3687	110	42	7569	142	77	22883	153	101	37482	167	116	55373	178	133	57358	179		
St., gl. & ceram.	9	1	21	12	2	110	16	9	1427	19	13	3817	19	14	3776	17	16	4982	23		
Metal.	45	4	1144	56	10	2181	70	26	8321	76	31	11469	83	35	12828	83	38	13806	81		
Mech. eng.	71	20	6379	89	36	8515	117	60	12765	130	78	16518	137	88	17308	136	94	17786	143		
Veh.	4	2	2420	5	2	4096	9	5	6968	10	7	10280	12	9	11059	11	11	11327	11		
Elec. eng.	45	12	5424	54	16	7981	71	43	34577	72	46	39501	80	54	54562	83	63	58708	87		
Prec. eng. & opt.	30	8	750	40	16	2062	52	28	4951	60	35	6831	62	39	6963	63	43	7782	69		
Other	28	8	615	44	29	2255	51	35	3965	53	33	4618	54	38	5380	56	40	5687	60		
All sectors	335	82	21233	419	155	35481	539	286	96760	584	348	131452	628	399	168248	643	446	178438	670		

Number of Federal German companies:	335		
Number of subsidiaries in operation:	670	Number of plants in operation:	740
Number of subsidiaries given up:	39	Number of plants given up:	40
Total number of subsidiaries:	709	Total number of plants:	780

Table II-10. (*cont.*)

(b) Developing countries

	1961			1966			1971			1973			1974			1975			1976		
	I	II	III	I	II	III	I	II	III	I	II	III	I	II	III	I	II	III	I	II	III
Agric. & for.	6	—	—	6	—	—	9	2	38	10	3	48	11	4	113	10	5	133	10		
En. & min.	3	1	46	4	2	73	8	6	1417	8	6	2217	14	12	3268	13	12	3487	13		
Chem.	144	48	9292	192	89	18558	259	156	41375	290	186	62132	300	225	72371	311	238	74402	311		
St., gl. & ceram.	10	2	784	10	2	757	14	5	1183	14	7	3500	18	10	3890	18	12	4451	17		
Metal.	47	11	7777	56	18	12121	69	29	18670	78	40	30300	80	44	32978	86	49	34848	89		
Mech. eng.	97	19	2672	125	41	6072	148	72	18612	166	97	25870	173	105	29897	190	125	33944	197		
Veh.	15	6	15811	17	10	26554	28	20	55990	31	24	76104	34	28	89260	34	29	90661	36		
Elec. eng.	42	8	7137	66	17	10822	109	54	47130	124	72	62991	127	98	89389	130	116	96048	134		
Prec. eng. & opt.	43	14	2480	57	21	4680	70	36	10368	80	52	15688	85	60	25012	98	73	25192	97		
Other	31	7	2432	46	15	2638	68	36	10083	86	50	12754	94	64	17419	99	73	19184	95		
All sectors covered	438	116	48431	579	215	82275	782	416	204866	887	547	291604	936	649	363597	989	732	382350	999		

Number of Federal German companies: 444
Number of subsidiaries in operation: 999
Number of subsidiaries given up: 52
Total number of subsidiaries: 1051

Number of plants in operation: 1051
Number of plants given up: 54
Total number of plants: 1105

See table II-1 for sector abbreviations
I = number of subsidiaries; II = number of subsidiaries for which employment was available; III = employment

both the developing and the industrial countries. A vigorous and fairly steady expansion of manufacturing abroad is a clear indication of the growing effectiveness of the new conditions for the world-wide valorisation of capital. This general indication can be expanded and made more specific by the analysis of the operations of companies in individual regions and countries. As the following section shows in detail, there are for example not only individual countries, but in fact whole regions in which Federal German companies did not begin their own manufacturing until the end of the 1960s or the beginning of the 1970s. The new sites should be seen as a clear indication of the impact of the new conditions for the valorisation of capital, regardless of whether they are to be found in the Mediterranean region or South East Asia. The same can be said of the fact that a country such as the USA has begun to exhibit a strongly growing Federal German manufacturing presence over the last few years. The reasons for this are discussed below.

The new sites in a number of developing countries constitute a particularly distinct group as they demonstrate that the three factors raised in the introduction – availability of labour at low wages, divisibility of the production process and the access to and availability of developed systems of transport and communication – can be clearly identified as the main determinants of the distribution of these locations. World market production in the characteristic form of export-oriented production, often simply as semi-manufacture, can be found at many of these new sites and there are a number of signs that this type of foreign manufacturing is not only increasing absolutely but also relatively in importance.

The developments recorded in the official statistics also corroborate this tendency: whereas the share of foreign investments going to the developing countries remained steady at about 30% for many years, 38.1% of all net capital expenditures recorded in 1976 went to the developing countries.[1] In the first six months of 1976 the proportion of foreign investments in the electrical engineering industry going to sites in the developing countries even went as high

1. Calculated from Bundesminister für Wirtschaft, *Runderlaß Außenwirtschaft Nr. 11* (1977), *Bundesanzeiger*, 26 April 1977. We have already referred to the fact these statistics only cover part of total investments. The share going to the developing countries is usually too low because investments in developing countries which are made through affiliates in Canada, Switzerland or Luxembourg appear under the heading of industrial countries. Our own survey shows that the share of the developing countries in employment abroad by Federal German industry is 46%.

as 70%.[1] The bulk of the new manufacture is destined for markets outside the new producing countries – including the Federal German market – and replaces manufacture previously undertaken in Federal Germany.

11.2 Characteristics of the developing country regions

The tables reproduced in this section provide information on the distribution of the subsidiaries surveyed and employment in the individual branches over time, and subsidiaries in the individual branches according to regions in which the developing countries are to be found. These results are not presented in the text or discussed individually. The text is confined essentially to references which are of use in evaluating the data as regards the tendency towards a new international division of labour.

The global reproduction of capital makes use of the particular conditions for valorisation at the respective sites and in doing so establishes real relations between the various sites. A number of factors play a significant role in the competition between the production sites which include: low wages, tax concessions, subsidies, specific measures designed to promote export oriented production, 'political stability' (i.e. disciplining the work-force) – all of which are 'incentives to investment' which operate both in the industrial and in the developing countries. The relative importance of the individual 'incentives', which already vary from country to country and sector to sector, also vary in details as between the two main groups of countries. The structures of uneven development, unequal exploitation and dependency are reflected in these differences: these are structures which can be located geographically and which are expressed in the respective social formations, the character of the class society, both at the respective sites and on a world scale. For the actual choice of production it is always the totality of the conditions of production which is decisive. In the developing countries these are determined primarily by the almost unlimited availability of labour at low wages. Despite continued underdevelopment the technical and infrastructural preconditions for those types of production which are initiated in order to use cheap labour

1. 'Whereas investments in the developing countries rose by 37% for industry as a whole during this period, they increased by around 70% in the electrical engineering industry (DM 187.5 million).' (Zentralverband der elektrotechnischen Industrie, *Elektroindustrie aktuell* (Frankfurt–Main, November 1976).)

are already present at many sites. The fact that production can also be shifted to traditional sites of industrial production does not contradict the tendency towards a new international division of labour but is in fact itself an expression of the massive reflexive effect which this tendency is already having on the conditions for the valorisation of capital at the traditional sites.

The central focus of the following short presentation is the extent of the manufacturing operations of Federal German companies in particular regions. However, it should be borne in mind that the main centres of globally integrated industrial production looked at as a whole diverge from those of Federal German companies. The reader is referred to the study of free production zones in Part III for an amplification of this.

The Mediterranean countries

In recent years it has become increasingly clear that the EEC countries are organising the Mediterranean area into an economic zone which, together with a tendency towards differentiation within the existing EEC, is helping to create a particular kind of relationship between metropole and periphery. This is conditioned, for example, by the geographical proximity of the Mediterranean countries to the EEC and by the granting of associate status. As a consequence the Mediterranean countries are treated as one group here (Table II-11). The number of subsidiaries, which according to our information almost tripled in the period under consideration, grew rapidly in the 1960s but less rapidly for the region as a whole after the beginning of the 1970s.

Out of the 339 subsidiaries in the Mediterranean region 295 were in the European countries bordering on the Mediterranean. This excludes Italy which is an EEC country, although the particular conditions of the Italian south, the Mezziogiorno,[1] are comparable to the other Mediterranean countries in many ways.

Whereas the majority of older subsidiaries manufactured pre-

1. 'In all eighteen German companies with twenty-one plants are represented, employing 7000 people... The net rate of profit is higher than anywhere else in Europe. The financial assistance which is already provided, and which is to be increased by new legislation, offers considerable incentives for new investments. For example, according to the new law 30% of investments up to DM 10 million can be paid up in the form of lost contributions. Loans at preferential interest rates are available for 40% of the investment total.' (*FAZ/Blick durch die Wirtschaft*, 26 January 1976.)

Table II-11. *Mediterranean countries*

(a) Number of subsidiaries and employees by sector: 1961, 1966, 1971, 1973, 1974, 1975, 1976

	1961			1966			1971			1973			1974			1975			1976		
	I	II	III	I	II	III	I	II	III	I	II	III	I	II	III	I	II	III	I	II	III
Agric. & for.	6	—	—	6	—	—	7	1	19	8	2	29	9	3	94	8	4	114	8		
En. & min.	—	—	—	1	1	27	2	1	104	2	1	125	4	3	195	3	3	236	3		
Chem.	42	14	2586	63	30	6574	86	51	12120	97	68	17549	99	74	19026	104	78	19457	104		
St., gl. & ceram.	7	2	784	7	2	757	9	3	686	9	3	709	11	5	919	10	6	1281	10		
Metal.	15	3	604	21	8	1538	26	12	2374	28	16	3816	29	17	4433	29	18	4568	28		
Mech. eng.	22	5	810	29	10	1609	39	19	2960	51	35	5773	50	36	6281	54	38	6493	55		
Veh.	2	—	—	3	1	100	7	4	2951	8	7	6890	9	8	7392	9	8	7534	9		
Elec. eng.	12	3	3863	24	8	5945	37	20	14748	42	33	21557	42	38	25331	44	43	16275	45		
Prec. eng. & opt.	11	3	1280	16	7	1559	21	12	2336	24	18	3215	28	21	4221	31	23	4661	31		
Other	8	3	424	13	6	897	20	13	2150	27	21	3607	28	22	3839	31	24	3975	31		
All sectors covered	125	33	10351	183	73	19006	254	136	40448	296	204	63270	309	227	71731	323	245	74594	324		

Table II-11. (*cont.*)

(b) Subsidiaries in operation 1961–76 by sector

	Agric. & for.	En. & min.	Chem.	St., gl. & ceram.	Metal.	Mech. eng.	Veh.	Elec. eng.	Prec. eng. & opt.	Other	All sectors covered
Algeria	—	1	1	—	—	—	—	—	—	—	2
Egypt	—	1	1	—	—	—	—	—	—	1	3
Greece	1	1	11	—	4	10	1	9	3	7	47
Israel	—	—	—	1	—	1	—	—	—	—	2
Lebanon	—	—	1	—	—	—	—	—	—	—	1
Malta	—	—	—	—	—	1	—	3	6	1	11
Morocco	1	—	4	—	—	2	—	1	—	2	10
Portugal	2	—	11	2	2	3	—	8	3	2	33
Spain	3	1	62	7	20	35	5	19	19	15	186
Syria	—	—	1	—	—	—	—	—	—	—	1
Tunisia	2	—	—	—	1	—	—	—	—	4	7
Turkey	1	—	7	—	3	1	1	4	1	—	18
Yugoslavia	—	—	5	1	—	3	2	3	3	1	18
Total	10	4	104	11	30	56	9	47	35	33	339

Number of Federal German companies:	218		
Number of subsidiaries in operation:	324	Number of plants in operation:	349
Number of subsidiaries given up:	15	Number of plants given up:	15
Total number of subsidiaries:	339	Total number of plants:	364

See Table II-1 for sector abbreviations

I = number of subsidiaries; II = number of subsidiaries for which employment was available; III = employment

dominantly for the home markets of their respective locations, in recent years export-oriented production (often in the form of sub- or final manufacture/assembly) has grown in importance. World market factories have been established in the fields of electrical engineering, precision engineering and optics in Portugal; such plants are typical of foreign manufacturing in Tunisia and Malta and are functional in drawing in Greece, Turkey and Egypt as production sites. It is mainly smaller companies who use these relatively close sites to build up their export production.

Latin America

Latin America accounted for nearly half of Federal German foreign production facilities in developing countries with a total of 469. Of these, 382 were in Brazil, Mexico and Argentina, with the remaining 87 being spread over fourteen other countries; in eight countries there were only one to five subsidiaries in each (Table II-12). 54.2% of the known subsidiaries were already in existence in 1961, as compared with 37.8% in the other developing country regions. Official statistics on investment abroad show that a high, and of late increasing, share is going to Latin American countries. In December 1973, 42.3% of investments in developing countries were in Latin America – an absolute figure of DM 4080.6 million: by 31 December 1975 this share had risen to 44.6%, a total of DM 5482.8 million.[1] Inasmuch as these investments, the geographical distribution of which can usually be discerned from official figures, are used both for the expansion of existing plants and the construction of new ones are expressed both in the expansion of already existing plants and their work-forces, and in an increase in the number of subsidiaries. The expansion of existing plants accounts for a considerable proportion of the increase in employment in recent years. Average employment for those subsidiaries in which it could be determined increased from 637 in 1971 to 703 in 1975. These averages are substantially above those for other regions.

A number of Federal German subsidiaries were already in existence in Latin America before the tendency towards a new international division of labour began to exert an influence. These early subsidiaries were usually engaged in manufacturing for the

1. Bundesminister für Wirtschaft, *Runderlaß Außenwirtschaft Nr. 13* (1976), *Bundesanzeiger*, 14 April 1976.

Table II-12. *Latin America*

(a) Number of subsidiaries and employees by sector: 1961, 1966, 1971, 1973, 1974, 1975, 1976

	1961			1966			1971			1973			1974			1975			1976		
	I	II	III	I	II	III	I	II	III	I	II	III	I	II	III	I	II	III	I	II	III
Agric. & for.	—	—	—	—	—	—	1	1	19	1	1	19	1	1	19	1	1	19	1		
En. & min.	1	—	—	1	—	—	4	4	1252	4	4	1991	6	6	2899	6	6	2994	6		
Chem.	82	32	6384	100	49	10543	132	84	23552	141	99	34422	147	117	42109	149	122	42568	149		
St., gl. & ceram.	2	—	—	2	—	—	3	1	277	3	3	2390	3	3	2396	3	3	2395	2		
Metal.	23	7	7113	25	8	8654	29	13	13330	34	18	21576	34	21	23733	39	23	24907	42		
Mech. eng.	50	10	1343	63	22	2867	70	37	11368	74	42	14213	79	46	17150	91	60	20758	97		
Veh.	11	6	15811	12	8	25193	15	12	50927	17	12	65394	17	12	76845	17	14	76939	17		
Elec. eng.	25	5	3274	31	8	4827	47	26	24043	52	29	30933	52	37	41610	54	46	43706	56		
Prec. eng. & opt.	25	9	1053	21	12	2242	37	20	4128	39	26	6672	39	27	7692	43	32	8083	42		
Other	19	4	2008	23	6	1661	31	16	7466	32	21	8099	35	22	10386	35	26	11584	34		
All sectors covered	238	73	36986	288	113	55987	367	214	136362	397	255	185709	414	292	224839	437	333	233953	446		

Table II-12. (*cont.*)

(b) Subsidiaries in operation 1961–76 by sector

	Agric. & for.	En. & min.	Chem.	St., gl. & ceram.	Metal.	Mech. eng.	Veh.	Elec. eng.	Prec. eng. & opt.	Other	All sectors covered
Argentina	—	—	14	1	4	9	3	8	6	7	52
Bolivia	—	—	1	—	—	—	—	—	—	—	1
Brazil	—	3	61	1	33	87	14	27	24	17	267
Chile	—	—	9	1	—	—	—	1	1	1	13
Colombia	—	—	10	—	1	—	—	2	1	1	15
Dominican Republic	—	—	1	—	—	—	—	—	1	—	2
Dutch Antilles	—	—	—	—	—	—	—	—	—	1	1
Ecuador	—	—	3	—	—	—	—	1	1	—	5
El Salvador	—	—	3	—	—	—	—	—	1	—	4
Guatemala	—	—	6	—	—	—	—	1	—	—	7
Mexico	—	1	27	—	3	7	1	14	8	2	63
Nicaragua	—	—	1	—	—	—	—	—	—	1	2
Peru	—	1	8	—	1	—	—	1	—	—	11
Puerto Rico	1	—	1	—	—	—	—	—	1	—	3
Trinidad & Tobago	—	1	—	—	—	—	—	—	—	—	1
Uruguay	—	—	4	—	—	—	—	—	—	6	10
Venezuela	—	—	4	—	—	1	—	4	2	1	12
Total	1	6	153	3	42	104	18	59	46	37	469

Number of Federal German companies:	234		
Number of subsidiaries in operation:	446	Number of plants in operation:	466
Number of subsidiaries given up:	23	Number of plants given up:	26
Total number of subsidiaries:	469	Total number of plants:	492

See Table II-1 for sector abbreviations

I = number of subsidiaries; II = number of subsidiaries for which employment was available; III = employment

respective local markets, and in some cases for export to the markets of other Latin American countries. Since these exports displaced exports from Federal Germany this type of manufacturing could be assigned to the category of import-substitution. Despite the very many subsidiaries which did exist prior to 1961 the number expanded considerably during the period under consideration, and production rose in all sectors, as shown in Table II-12(a). The disadvantages associated with the policy of import-substitution manufacturing are become increasingly evident. A strong tendency towards the build up of export-oriented production can be seen both in the economic policies of individual countries and the manufacturing operations of foreign capital.[1] In Central America in particular, but also for example in Brazil, manufacture (subassembly) is being developed oriented towards the markets of the traditional industrial countries and utilising the three factors which have been specified as important determinants in the new international division of labour: abundant cheap labour, the divisibility of the production process and developed systems of transport and communications.

Africa

Federal German production abroad as covered by this study could be found in thirty-eight subsidiaries in Africa (excluding South Africa and Namibia and the African Mediterranean countries),[2] which were distributed over twenty countries with the main focus in Nigeria (Table II-13). The number of subsidiaries is clearly increasing and has tripled since 1961. If one takes the official statistics for Federal German capital assets in Africa (excluding the Mediterranean countries, South Africa and the Canary Islands) they show investments at the end of 1973 standing at DM 596.7 million, rising to DM 739.2 million by the end of 1975.[3] This is about the equivalent of one-quarter of the investments in Brazil. In addition, the increase over these two years was, at 23.9%, only slightly above the average for all developing countries, which stood at 22.7%. The

1. A special issue of the journal *World Development* with the title 'Latin America in the Post-Import-Substitution Era' deals with this development and contains contributions on Argentina, Brazil, Columbia, Mexico and Peru: *World Development*, 1/2 (1977).
2. This is therefore only a part of the African continent: in Africa as a whole the number of subsidiaries is much larger. We referred above to whether South Africa is correctly allocated.
3. Bundesminister für Wirtschaft, *Runderlaß Außenwirtschaft Nr. 13.*

Table II-13. *Africa (excluding Mediterranean countries and South Africa)*

(a) Number of subsidiaries and employees by sector: 1961, 1966, 1971, 1973, 1974, 1975, 1976

	1961			1966			1971			1973			1974			1975			1976		
	I	II	III	I	II	III	I	II	III	I	II	III	I	II	III	I	II	III	I	II	III
Agric. & for.	—	—	—	—	—	—	—	—	—	—	—	—	—	—	—	—	—	—	—		
En. & min.	2	1	46	2	1	46	2	1	61	2	1	101	3	2	167	3	2	151	3		
Chem.	4	—	—	4	—	—	4	—	—	6	1	196	6	1	228	7	2	345	8		
St., gl. & ceram.	—	—	—	—	—	—	—	—	—	—	—	—	2	1	165	3	2	365	3		
Metal.	1	—	—	2	1	1839	2	1	2517	2	1	2646	2	1	2763	2	1	2876	3		
Mech. eng.	1	—	—	1	—	—	3	2	82	3	2	113	5	4	349	6	5	598	6		
Veh.	—	—	—	—	—	—	—	—	—	—	—	—	2	2	455	2	2	1506	2		
Elec. eng.	1	—	—	1	—	—	1	—	—	1	—	—	1	1	88	1	1	87	2		
Prec. eng. & opt.	—	—	—	—	—	—	—	—	—	—	—	—	—	—	—	—	—	—	—		
Other	3	—	—	5	1	40	6	2	175	9	2	205	9	5	1156	10	6	1300	9		
All sectors covered	12	1	46	15	3	1925	18	6	2835	23	7	3261	30	17	5371	34	21	7228	36		

Table II-13. (*cont.*)

(b) Subsidiaries in operation 1961–76 by sector

	Agric. & for.	En. & min.	Chem.	St., gl. & ceram.	Metal.	Mech. eng.	Veh.	Elec. eng.	Prec. eng. & opt.	Other	All sectors covered
Angola	—	—	1	—	—	—	—	—	—	—	1
Botswana	—	—	—	—	—	—	—	—	—	1	1
Cameroon	—	—	—	—	1	—	—	—	—	2	3
Congo	—	—	1	—	—	—	—	—	—	—	1
Ethiopia	—	—	—	—	—	—	—	—	—	1	1
Ghana	—	—	—	1	—	2	1	—	—	—	4
Ivory Coast	—	—	—	—	—	—	—	—	—	1	1
Kenya	—	—	1	—	—	—	—	—	—	—	1
Lesotho	—	—	—	—	—	—	—	1	—	—	1
Liberia	—	—	—	—	1	—	—	—	—	1	2
Mozambique	—	—	1	—	—	—	—	—	—	—	1
Niger	—	—	—	—	—	—	—	—	—	1	1
Nigeria	—	1	2	1	1	2	1	—	—	1	9
Rhodesia	—	1	1	—	—	—	—	—	—	—	2
Senegal	—	—	1	—	—	—	—	—	—	—	1
Sudan	—	1	—	—	—	—	—	—	—	—	1
Tanzania	—	—	—	—	—	1	—	—	—	—	1
Togo	—	—	—	—	—	—	—	—	—	1	1
Zaire	—	—	—	—	—	1	—	1	—	1	3
Zambia	—	—	—	1	—	—	—	—	—	1	2
Total	—	3	8	3	3	6	2	2	—	11	38

Number of Federal German companies: 29
Number of subsidiaries in operation: 36
Number of subsidiaries given up: 2
Total number of subsidiaries: 38

Number of plants in operation: 36
Number of plants given up: 2
Total number of plants: 38

See Table II-1 for sector abbreviations
I = number of subsidiaries; II = number of subsidiaries for which employment was available; III = employment

main feature of development over the period under consideration is the tripling in the number of known subsidiaries. Production by Federal German subsidiaries is still, however, modest. On the one hand it should be remembered that our figures here only deal with a part of Africa: on the other hand, there are historical reasons as to why Federal German companies are as yet little represented in Africa in comparison to other countries. The former colonial powers (France, Britain and Belgium) have been able to safeguard a considerable amount of their influence and use it in the interests of their respective companies. In addition, so many potential sites have been opened up within the framework of the new international division of labour that they cannot all be integrated into the world-wide organisation of production at once but only as time progresses and region by region. Apart from their direct links with raw material extraction, export-oriented industrialisation by Federal German companies in Africa is only at an initial stage.

West Asia

Thirty-four subsidiaries were found to exist in West Asia which satisfied the critieria of this study: thirty-two were in Iran, sixteen of which employed 6567 workers (1975) (Table II-14). At the end of 1975, officially recorded Federal German investments in Iran amounted to DM 222.5 million; this was nearly DM 50 million more than in India and DM 50 million less than in Japan.[1] Out of the thirty-two subsidiaries in existence in Iran[2] in 1976 four existed in 1961, and nine by 1966. The rapidly growing footwear industry in Iran, in which three Federal German companies are involved, is displacing craft shoe manufacture. Shoes are now not only sold on the Iranian market but also in neighbouring countries and in Eastern Europe; they are also intended for export to Western Europe.[3]

The two subsidiaries in this region which are not in Iran are a 26 %

1. Bundesminister für Wirtschaft, *Runderlaß Außenwirtschaft Nr. 13.*
2. 'There are approximately fifty joint German-Iranian companies at the present time. Although German investments remain largely concentrated in the electrical and telecommunications, chemical and pharmaceutical industries and in manufacture of motor vehicles and machinery, more and more partnerships are being founded in the service industries, notably among consulting firms, which reveals growing interest in the acquisition of technical know-how and international experience.' (German-Iranian Chamber of Commerce, *Länderbericht 1975/76* (Hamburg 1976), p. 7.)
3. *FAZ/Blick durch die Wirtschaft,* 14 October 1974 and 15 September 1975.

Table II-14. *West Asia: number of subsidiaries and employees by sector: 1961, 1966, 1971, 1973, 1974, 1975, 1976*

	1961			1966			1971			1973			1974			1975			1976		
	I	II	III	I	II	III	I	II	III	I	II	III	I	II	III	I	II	III	I	II	III
Agric. & for.	—	—	—	—	—	—	1	—	—	1	—	—	1	—	—	1	—	—	1		
En. & min.	—	—	—	—	—	—	—	—	—	—	—	—	1	1	7	1	1	106	1		
Chem.	1	—	—	2	1	58	8	5	930	10	5	1271	10	5	1342	10	6	1957	10		
St., gl. & ceram.	—	—	—	—	—	—	—	—	—	—	—	—	—	—	—	—	—	—	1		
Metal.	1	—	—	1	—	—	1	—	—	2	—	—	2	—	—	3	—	—	3		
Mech. eng.	1	—	—	1	—	—	1	—	—	1	—	—	1	—	—	1	—	—	1		
Veh.	—	—	—	—	—	—	1	1	342	1	1	753	1	1	825	1	1	839	2		
Elec. eng.	1	—	—	4	1	50	7	2	266	7	2	259	8	4	1391	6	5	2883	6		
Prec. eng. & opt.	—	—	—	—	—	—	—	—	—	1	—	—	1	1	69	1	1	73	2		
Other	—	—	—	1	—	—	1	—	—	4	—	—	4	1	461	4	2	709	3		
All sectors covered	4	—	—	9	2	108	20	8	1538	27	8	2283	29	13	4095	28	16	6567	30		

Number of Federal German companies:	30		
Number of subsidiaries in operation:	30	Number of plants in operation:	30
Number of subsidiaries given up:	4	Number of plants given up:	4
Total number of subsidiaries:	34	Total number of plants:	34

See Table II-1 for sector abbreviations
I = number of subsidiaries; II = number of subsidiaries for which employment was available; III = employment

holding by Daimler-Benz in the Saudi Arabian National Automobile Company Ltd, Jeddah, which was established in 1975 in order to assemble Daimler-Benz vehicles,[1] and in Jordan, the Jordan Ceramic Industries, which has been producing tiles and sanitary equipment since 1976.

South and South East Asia

171 manufacturing subsidiaries located in eleven countries were found in South and South East Asia (excluding Japan): employment figures were obtained for 117 of these subsidiaries yielding a total of 60008 in 1975. Table II-15 provides a general statistical overview of the region. Almost half the subsidiaries (84 out of 171) are in the Indian sub-continent, the remaining half being spread over the other countries of South East Asia. South East Asia has only recently become accessible for manufacture by Federal German companies on any scale. According to our research there were only fourteen subsidiaries in the region in 1961, forty-six in 1971 and eighty-seven by 1976. In fact the establishment of more than forty subsidiaries in South East Asia since 1971 is a clear indication of the spread and development of the tendency towards a new international division of labour. The importance of developed systems of transport and communication for the inclusion of sites in South East Asia into the world-wide organisation of production is self-evident when the distance from Europe is considered. Details on production and working conditions in this area can be found in Part III.

Federal German world market factories were found in every country in this region which was covered by the survey, most of which operated 100% for export. A few examples, all of which were established recently, offer proof of this development. AEG-Telefunken has a 50% stake in a company producing semiconductors in the Philippines: the company commenced production in 1974 with an initial work-force of 300. Since 1975 Rodi & Weinberg has had a 51% stake in a company manufacturing watch-straps in Hong Kong (180 employees). An affiliate of Robert Bosch GmbH has been

1. 'Plans have now been finalised for the commercial vehicle assembler National Automobile Industry Company Ltd, Jeddah, which was found in 1975 in partnership with the Mercedes-Benz agents of many years standing, E. A. Juffali & Bros. Daimler-Benz has a 26% stake in this enterprise. Over the past year Daimler-Benz has supplied the Saudi Arabian market with around 7600 commercial vehicles – mostly heavy lorries.' (Daimler-Benz AG, *Geschäftsbericht 1975*, p. 56.)

Table II-15. *South and South East Asia*

(a) Number of subsidiaries and employees by sector: 1961, 1966, 1971, 1973, 1974, 1975, 1976

	1961			1966			1971			1973			1974			1975			1976		
	I	II	III	I	II	III	I	II	III	I	II	III	I	II	III	I	II	III	I	II	III
Agric. & for.	—	—	—	—	—	—	—	—	—	—	—	—	—	—	—	—	—	—	—		
En. & min.	—	—	—	—	—	—	—	—	—	—	—	—	—	—	—	—	—	—	—		
Chem.	15	2	312	23	9	1383	31	16	4773	36	23	8694	38	28	9666	41	30	10075	40		
St., gl. & ceram.	1	—	—	1	—	—	2	1	220	2	1	401	2	1	410	2	1	410	1		
Metal.	7	1	60	7	1	90	11	3	449	12	5	2262	12	5	2049	13	7	2497	13		
Mech. eng.	23	4	519	31	9	1596	35	14	4202	37	18	5771	38	19	6117	38	22	6095	38		
Veh.	2	—	—	2	1	1261	5	3	1770	5	4	3065	5	4	3743	5	4	3843	6		
Elec. eng.	3	—	—	6	—	—	17	6	8073	22	8	10242	24	18	20969	25	21	23097	25		
Prec. eng. & opt.	7	2	147	10	2	879	12	4	3904	16	8	5801	17	11	13030	23	17	12375	22		
Other	1	—	—	4	2	40	10	5	292	14	6	843	18	14	1577	19	15	1616	18		
All sectors covered	59	9	1048	84	24	5249	123	52	23683	144	73	37081	154	100	57561	166	117	60008	163		

Table II-15. (*cont.*)

(b) Subsidiaries in operation 1961–76 by sector

	Agric. & for.	En. & min.	Chem.	St., gl. & ceram.	Metal.	Mech. eng.	Veh.	Elec. eng.	Prec. eng. & opt.	Other	All sectors covered
Bangla Desh	—	—	—	—	—	1	—	—	—	—	1
Hong Kong	—	—	—	—	—	1	—	—	1	1	3
India	—	—	20	1	9	29	3	10	6	2	80
Indonesia	—	—	7	—	1	2	1	2	—	8	21
Malaysia	—	—	2	—	2	2	1	3	5	—	15
Pakistan	—	—	—	—	—	1	—	2	—	—	3
Philippines	—	—	1	—	—	—	—	1	—	—	2
Singapore	—	—	1	—	—	5	1	4	3	—	14
South Korea	—	—	4	—	—	—	—	1	4	1	10
Taiwan	—	—	1	—	—	—	—	2	1	1	5
Thailand	—	—	5	1	1	—	—	1	3	6	17
Total	—	—	41	2	13	41	6	26	23	19	171

Number of Federal German companies: 119
Number of subsidiaries in operation: 163
Number of subsidiaries given up: 8
Total number of subsidiaries: 171

Number of plants in operation: 169
Number of plants given up: 8
Total number of plants: 177

See Table II-1 for sector abbreviations
I = number of subsidiaries; II = number of subsidiaries for which employment was available; III = employment

assembling lenses and view-finders for cine-cameras in Taiwan since 1970 (530 employees). An affiliate of the Zeiss-Gruppe has been manufacturing spectacle rims, also in Taiwan, since 1975 with 130 employees, and has been making the lenses for them since 1976. The Becker Group has had a subsidiary assembling car radios there since 1975 (50 employees), and Schuhunion, which has a 100% holding in the Servas Far East Shoe Manufacturing Company, has been operating a plant for leather processing and shoe manufacture for export since 1973.

In South Korea, Siemens AG has a 46.8% stake in Gold Star Teleelectric, with the remaining portion being in Japanese ownership; component parts for telephone exchange equipment are assembled employing 1700 workers. In Thailand examples of smaller companies engaged in export manufacturing can be found, such as the Thai German Brush Factory (49% Federal German holding) in which 24 employees have been making paint brushes since 1975; the Thai Nakon Pewter Co. Ltd (25%) which has been making tin and pewter products since 1975; Gebrüder Schmeing has a 25% stake in a plant employing 150 workers which manufactures weaving shuttles and other articles.

Apart from the Varta Group battery factory, there are three 100% Federal German owned export manufacturers of components and condensors in Singapore. Brown Boveri Singapore (180 employees), Siemens Components (550 employees) and E. Hopt Singapore (230 employees).[1] Knives are made at two German undertakings; Henckel's J.A. Twinworks and WMF Singapore (100 employees). SKF Kugellagerfabriken of Schweinfurt (roller bearings/ball bearings), which itself belongs to SKF of Sweden, has also established a manufacturing subsidiary in Singapore.[2]

The Rollei Group is by far the largest Federal German company in Singapore in terms of production capacity. In 1974, employment

1. According to more recent sources (31 May 1976) the volume of employment in these affiliates has increased: at Brown Boveri to 220, at Siemens to 750 and at Hopt to 540. Preh Singapore is having a new component factory built. (*BfA/Nachrichten für Außenhandel*, 12 November 1976.)

2. 'If a highly skilled worker has to be paid DM 2500 a month in Bavaria, this figure is only 700 Singapore dollars in Singapore (1 Singapore dollar = DM 1.10). Semiskilled workers' wages are around 250–300 dollars a month (mostly women). But this isn't all. There is a forty-four hour week, and only seven days annual holiday. There is no labour turnover and absenteeism through sickness is almost zero. This is a golden field for cost and productivity conscious Western managers who themselves can earn from 40%–50% more than at home. But it is not without its dangers for jobs in the older industrial countries.' (*Süddeutsche Zeitung*, 20 November 1975.)

was 5800, and in 1975, 4400, working in five factories. The massive shift of production within this group which began in 1970 has created a situation in which two-thirds of the company's total output is now manufactured in Singapore. The company calculates that unit wage costs in comparison to costs in Federal Germany are in the ratio 1:11.[1] The company ran into serious difficulties between 1973 and 1975 and could only be kept going by massive government loans. Employment was drastically cut by mass redundancies in Germany and Singapore, with proportionally more jobs being lost in Federal Germany: from 2500 to 1550, as against 5800 to 4400 in Singapore. This year the company 'came out of the red'[2] in Singapore and it is quite possible that additional areas of production may be transferred there unless the company plumps for Indonesia.[3] These figures demonstrate that temporary difficulties do not substantially alter the necessity of production abroad.

In Malaysia, Federal German electrical engineering companies have established three 100% owned plants since 1972, all of which produce for export. A subsidiary of Robert Bosch GmbH assembles cine-cameras and vehicle parts with a total of 850 employees.[4] Nordmende makes television sets (250 employees) and Siemens assembles electrical components (350 employees). A plant which was 100% owned by Aesculap-Werke AG (now a majority holding of B. Braun, Melsungen) has been making surgical instruments since 1973 (180 employees). The Opti-Werke company manufactures zip-fasteners (150 employees) and since 1975 Jenaer Glaswerke (Zeiss-Gruppe) have had an 85% stake in a company involved in the working of optical glass (110 employees).

Most of these plants have commenced production recently and there are a number of indications, such as companies' prospective production plans, that the present stage is merely the beginning of a process which will gather momentum in the future.

1. 'The total pay roll for the 5500 employees in Singapore will amount to DM 11 million next year. In Brunswick almost DM 120 million would have had to be found for the same production.' (*Süddeutsche Zeitung*, 6 November 1973.) It is now intended to shut down the Uelzen works which first began production in 1970. (*Handelsblatt*, 4 July 1977.)
2. *Süddeutsche Zeitung*, 25 May 1976.
3. 'In addition the manufacture of some items from the photographic range, such as camera cases, could be transferred to Singapore. Transportation half way around the world does not lead to the incurral of particularly high costs: only 40–50 Pfennig per camera from Singapore to Germany.' (*Süddeutsche Zeitung*, 1/2 March 1975.)
4. 100% export according to Robert Bosch GmbH's company report for 1975, p. 2.

11.3 Employment and production by Federal German companies in individual countries

The aim of this study is to discover in what ways the development of production abroad by Federal German companies confirms the existence of a tendency towards a new international division of labour. In order to document the empirical basis of our analysis a full list of all firms known to be manufacturing abroad, their subsidiaries and the countries in which they manufacture has been compiled. In addition to data on sector, year of production commencement, percentage of direct and indirect formal share holding and capital participation by Federal German companies, and size as indicated by amount of employment, information is also given on the products of the respective companies. As a rule such information does not indicate the structure of production or the production technology: in many instances production in foreign plants is confined to assembly or subassembly, which should be borne in mind when studying the indicated products.

The list is by no means complete; the gaps are an indication of the fact that in a whole series of instances it was impossible to obtain the desired information. The data given here is based on a number of different sources. A certain amount was made available by Chambers of Commerce and companies. No guarantee can be given for the accuracy of these figures although we have tried to use only reliable sources and check the data used, as far as possible. Despite the fact there are bound to be some uncertainties and errors, the list can be regarded as by and large a reliable survey of the foreign production of Federal German companies (excluding textile and garment) outside the EEC.[1]

This general picture is exemplified here by a presentation of the foreign production of Federal German companies in a number of selected countries, which is intended to convey a more concrete picture of foreign production: this is further supplemented in the following chapter by observations on particular industrial branches.

The choice of countries is not a random one: it includes some of the most important countries in which Federal German investment

1. The entire list is given in Appendix II-A-1, on pp. 398–472 of the German edition of this book, to which the reader is referred. To obtain a typewritten English version free of charge, the reader may write to the authors (c/o Max-Planck-Institut zur Erforschung der Lebensbedingungen der wissenschaftlich-technischen Welt, Postfach 1529, 8130 Starnberg, Federal Republic of Germany).

has taken place. This also means that this sample is significant in quantitative terms, as a proportion of the total, and also that it will reveal some of the typical characteristics of foreign manufacturing, notwithstanding regional and national features.

Brazil

Brazil is an outstanding example of the establishment of industry at the new sites in almost all respects. Although Brazil already possessed a not inconsiderable industry at the beginning of the period under consideration, in which companies from Federal Germany were quite deeply involved, employment in Federal German subsidiaries increased, on a conservative estimate, by more than three times between 1961 and 1976. The utilisation of cheap labour, the divisibility of the production process and the existence of developed systems of transport and communication have led to Brazil gaining substantially in significance as a production site during the period under study.

We were able to find 267 manufacturing subsidiaries (of which 253 are still in existence and 14 have been abandoned) owned by Federal German companies.[1] 176 of them employed 177 798 workers (1975), almost a third of the employees recorded in the context of this study (Table II-16). According to Federal German official statistics 23.4% of all German investments in the developing countries were in Brazil.[2] With 15.1% Federal Germany followed the USA (32.1%) into second place amongst the officially recorded foreign direct investments in Brazil.[3] The Brazilian-German Chamber of Industry and Commerce gives the 'German share of post-war foreign investment' as 'around 20%'.[4] The difference can largely be explained by the fact that companies transact and administer their investments via third countries (such as Canada, Dutch Antilles, Bahamas, Switzerland, Luxembourg), which do not subsequently appear as German investments in the official statistics.

1. Jean Bernet, *Guia Interinvest – O Brasil e o capital internacional* (Rio de Janeiro 1973) records 212 Federal German companies with 449 listed subsidiaries. Many are accounted for by distribution companies, holding companies and companies with suspended business activities. This list also includes commercial undertakings, banks, insurance companies and other services, and also holdings of less than 25%.
2. Calculated from Bundesminister für Wirtschaft, *Runderlaß Außenwirtschaft Nr. 13.*
3. Hans Jolowicz, *Auslandsinvestitionen in Brasilien* (Hamburg 1974), p. 325, Table 24 (based on data from the Brazilian Central Bank, as at 30 June 1973).
4. Deutsch-Brasilianische Industrie- und Handelskammer, *Deutscher Beitrag zur Industrialisierung Brasiliens* (Rio de Janeiro–Sao Paulo 1971), p. 6.

Table II-16. *Brazil: number of subsidiaries and employees by sector: 1961, 1966, 1971, 1973, 1974, 1975, 1976*

	1961			1966			1971			1973			1974			1975			1976		
	I	II	III	I	II	III	I	II	III	I	II	III	I	II	III	I	II	III	I	II	III
Agric. & for.	—	—	—	—	—	—	—	—	—	—	—	—	—	—	—	—	—	—	—		
En. & min.	1	—	—	1	—	—	3	3	1229	3	3	1966	3	3	2784	3	3	2784	3		
Chem.	35	14	4478	39	18	5890	45	32	15345	52	38	22156	57	43	25882	58	46	25754	58		
St., gl. & ceram.	1	—	—	1	—	—	1	—	—	1	1	308	1	1	314	1	1	313	1		
Metal.	16	6	7013	17	7	8554	20	11	12980	25	16	21162	26	16	22676	30	18	23850	33		
Mech. eng.	38	9	1262	49	18	2698	55	29	8865	59	32	11093	63	35	13983	74	48	17478	82		
Veh.	8	3	14015	9	5	21356	11	9	43286	13	9	51957	13	10	61571	13	10	63071	13		
Elec. eng.	11	3	2720	12	4	3920	19	13	20523	22	15	26394	22	18	30752	25	22	31819	25		
Prec. eng. & opt.	13	7	800	16	9	1811	18	13	3126	19	15	5320	20	15	5918	23	17	6070	23		
Other	9	—	—	11	1	162	14	7	3534	14	8	4240	15	9	5524	16	11	6659	15		
All sectors covered	132	42	30288	155	62	44391	186	117	108888	208	137	144596	220	149	169404	243	176	177798	253		

Number of Federal German companies: 197
Number of subsidiaries in operation: 253
Number of subsidiaries given up: 14
Total number of subsidiaries: 267

Number of plants in operation: 269
Number of plants given up: 15
Total number of plants: 284

See Table II-1 for sector abbreviations

I = number of subsidiaries; II = number of subsidiaries for which employment was available; III = employment

According to a recent survey of 1000 important firms in all sectors, 49.5% are state enterprises, 28.4% local private companies and 22.1% foreign companies. (Of the fifty largest undertakings 82.7% are in state ownership, 12.6% in foreign ownership and 4.8% in local private hands.)[1] The state enterprises operate in the local infrastructural sectors and basic industries; the main focus of the foreign companies is manufacturing industry.[2] Those manufacturing companies controlled by local capital are highly dependent on foreign capital since they are either suppliers of the large foreign concerns or operate under licence.

The variety of types of production by Federal German companies in Brazil reflects the spread over the individual sectors. The chemicals industry, which takes first place in other Latin American countries, is exceeded in terms of the number of subsidiaries by mechanical engineering, and in terms of employment by vehicle building, electrical engineering, and ferrous and non-ferrous metals. Whereas the number of subsidiaries has doubled in non-ferrous and ferrous metals, mechanical engineering and the electrical engineering industry, it increased by 50% in the chemical industry in the period under consideration. This is also an expression of the time-lag in the establishment of production by suppliers of raw materials and capital-goods (especially for the vehicle building industry).[3]

The Brazilian mining industry is operated by state undertakings.[4] Thirty-five Federal German companies from the chemicals industry have subsidiaries, with the larger companies controlling several. In comparison to other developing countries there is a much greater variety of production. Of those companies operating in Brazil, Degussa and Merck each employ more than 1000 workers, Freudenberg and Henkel each more than 1500, BASF and Hoechst each

1. *Neue Zürcher Zeitung*, 17 July 1976. 'Private entrepreneurs in Brazil have long felt sandwiched between the big foreign companies and state concerns.' (*The Economist*, 31 July 1976, Brazil Survey.)
2. 80% of all foreign investment, and almost 100% of investment by the multinationals, is concentrated in the industrial sector. See Carlos von Doellinger and Leonardo C. Cavalvanti, *Empresas Multinacionais na Indústria Brasileira* (Rio de Janeiro 1975), p. 32.
3. See the results of a questionnaire on this in Bernd Olbricht, *Unternehmenspolitik bei Direktinvestitionen in Brasilien* (Baden-Baden 1974), p. 215.
4. Foreign companies have been entitled to prospecting rights since 1975. Oil reserves, in particular, are marked for exploitation. Although subsidiaries listed under 'energy and mining' belong to mining concerns (Saarbergwerke, Salzgitter), they in fact manufacture tools or operate in steel fabrication in Brazil. Such irritations are unavoidable in order to avoid double-counting and obtain a clear allocation of a company's subsidiaries.

more than 4000 and Bayer over 5500. A number of smaller companies also exist: a subsidiary of the Keramchemie company has thirteen employees, a subsidiary of Röhm GmbH has thirty-seven employees and Parsch do Brasil employs sixty-two workers.

In the stone, glass and ceramic sector Rosenthal has a 50% stake in Porcelana Renner S.A., with 300 employees.

Smelting and foundry operation are the main activities in the ferrous and non-ferrous metals branch. Mannesmann AG should be noted here; the company has a 72.3% holding in an integrated smelter, the production of which extends from the production of pig iron to fine steels and tubes.

As from 1978 the subsidiary of the Düsseldorf steel and tube concern Mannesmann will increase the production of basic steel by a quarter to 750000 tonnes per year, and the production of seamless and welded tube by a third to 400000 tonnes. Furthermore, CSM, at present the fifth largest Brazilian steelworks, will double its output of tubes within ten years.

After doing good business with steel and tubes Mannesmann has now turned to the field of capital-goods in Brazil. Demag AG, Mannesmann's mechanical engineering company based in Duisburg, has built a heavy engineering plant valued at DM 70 million not far from Belo Horizonte. The new Demag subsidiary will initially operate with 500 employees to produce foundry and smelting equipment and will reach a turnover of around DM 180 million per year by the early 1980s. The Duisburg company already have experience of manufacturing in Brazil: since 1975 the Movicarga plant, with 700 employees, has been making cranes and lifting equipment near Sao Paulo.

According to Demag chief, Otto Blank, 'Movicarga has already achieved a pleasing profit in the first two years of operation'.

There is no doubt that for a foreign investor such as Mannesmann Brazil is one of the last oases of early capitalism, if the company is in command of its affairs: and Mannesmann are. The company's Brazilian plant, which employs 14800 out of 109000 employees, already contributes 'more than its share to the group's profits'.[1]

Exports are destined to play a larger role in the long term. There are hopes for orders from other parts of South America and beyond, referring in this connection to the much more advantageous production costs as compared with Federal Germany.[2]

More than 4500 people are employed in several affiliates of Thyssen, in particular in the fields of casting, and also in iron-ore processing (57.7% stake in Ferteco Mineracao S.A.) and 41.96% in Companhia Siderúrgica da Guanabara.[3] Almost 2000 people are

1. *Die Zeit*, 15 April 1977: 'Paradies für Fremde. Das arme Brasilien bleibt für ausländische Unternehmen attraktiv'.
2. FAZ, 30 March 1977.
3. Under the title 'Massive expansion plans for the Brazilian steel industry' the *Neue Zürcher Zeitung* reported on 24 March 1976 on the plans adopted by Thyssen and Mannesmann for expansion in Brazil.

employed in a die-works and in the production of springs, struts and railway equipment in a subsidiary of Hoesch (Forjaria Sao Bernardo SA together with Krupp and Volkswagenwerk).

The mechanical engineering sector was the most strongly represented between 1961 and 1976 with seventy-six Federal German firms.[1] On average mechanical engineering is characterised by smaller subsidiaries. Employment figures were obtained for forty-eight subsidiaries; the average employment was 364 each. If one disregards the four large companies which each have more than 1000 employees the average falls to 209. The four large subsidiaries are: a minority holding by Gutehoffnungshütte in Mecanica Pesada SA, which employs 2700 and makes marine equipment, turbines and diesel engines; Rolamentos Schaeffler do Brasil, an affiliate of Industriewerk Schaeffler, which employs more than 1000 workers and manufactures rolling-mill equipment; Voith SA with 2500 employees making large industrial equipment, paper machines, pumps, transmissions, control systems and governors; and a subsidiary of Zahnradfabrik Friedrichshafen which employs more than 2000 people and makes transmissions, gears, steering systems – mainly for the vehicles industry.

In terms of employment, companies in the vehicle building industry are represented more than twice as strongly as any other branch of industry. Of the minimum of 63 000 employed in this sector almost 40 000 are employed by VW do Brasil (80% = Volkswagenwerk AG), which is not only the largest industrial establishment in Brazil but also the largest foreign industrial undertaking possessed by any Federal German company. In 1975 VW took 59% of the Brazilian car market and 44.7% of the commercial vehicle market. Including knocked-down (KD) production it produced 502 580 units and exported approximately 12% (59 172) primarily to South and Central America and Africa.[2] According to VW's figures 3800 suppliers and 170 000 Brazilian

1. Four companies have given up production in Brazil, and in 1976 eighty-two subsidiaries out of the total of eighty-seven were still in existence. The reasons for ceasing operations are various: bankruptcy of the German parent, sale of the holding, ceasing actual local manufacturing: only small companies were involved.
2. Volkswagenwerk AG, *Geschäftsbericht 1975* p. 38. Export is mostly in the form of knocked-down kits which are reassembled in the Philippines, South Africa, Portugal and recently Nigeria. The VW plant in Mexico is an important customer for parts, and there is also a daily flow of some 500 transmissions and 100–200 engines to the Federal Republic for the Passat model, as the Brazilian subsidiary can manufacture these cheaper than the German plant.

workers are now dependent on VW do Brasil, which started production in 1957 with less than 1000 workers.[1]

Production capacity is being extended further. The Taubaté works, opened in 1976, is intended to increase capacity by 50%. The full capacity of this plant will not be utilised initially. VW also wishes to extend its operations in the commercial vehicles sector and build two new models in a diesel version.[2] Expansion is not confined to Brazil alone. VW do Brasil is also pursuing plans for an assembly plant in Chile[3] and a larger assembly plant, and later full manufacture, in Iraq. This latter project is clearly being organised via the Brazilian subsidiary as it is being subsidised by the Brazilian government.[4]

Although VW do Brasil can introduce new model variations this does not mean that it has the capacity for independent technical development: this applies, for example, to the VW Brasilia model, and to the diesel versions of the Brasilia and Passat.

Volkswagenwerk also has other business interests in Brazil: it has a 38.25% stake in the Forjaria Sao Bernardo foundry which employs 650 people and makes castings for the vehicles industry. However VW's activities go far beyond the sphere of manufacturing industry:

> We are involved in fisheries, tourism, hotels, and the aerospace industry. I could list a whole series of other interests, afforestation and so on. On top of that comes the project which was mentioned – cattle raising in Brazil. We propose to use an area of around 144000 hectares of land to establish a large-scale project for cattle raising – that is, meat production. Of course this project includes things like a slaughterhouse, cold store, and preserving factory.[5]

The establishment of a cattle ranch for 110000 head of cattle in the Amazon region aroused particular criticism in the press which was concerned not only about the ecologically dubious exploitation of the Amazonian region[6] but also the support given by the Brazilian government to international capital at the expense of their hard-pressed small farmers and peasants.[7]

1. Volkswagenwerk AG, *VW in Brasilien* (Wolfsburg 1973), p. 10.
2. *Financial Times*, 17 March 1976.
3. *Handelsblatt*, 23 July 1975.
4. *O Estado de Sao Paulo*, 8 October 1974; *FAZ*, 16 June 1975.
5. *FAZ/Blick durch die Wirtschaft*, 24 October 1974: statement by the Chairman of the Management Board, Leiding, at the Annual General Meeting, 1974.
6. Rolf Pflücke, Franke Müller-May, 'Amazonien – Das letzte Kapitel der Zivilisationsgeschichte', *Bild der Wissenschaft* (March 1977), pp. 46–61.
7. The tax incentives on offer prove to be irresistible: 'For example, VW purchased 140000 hectares of virgin forest for the establishment of a cattle farm with 110000 head and an annual planned production of 20000 carcasses for which a total investment of DM 62

The significance of VW do Brasil for the whole combine is revealed by the fact that substantial profits have been shown and transferred for a number of years. 'In 1973 nearly DM 100 million profit were shown by VW do Brasil.'[1]

Daimler-Benz, with 15084 employees in the production of commercial vehicles and diesel engines, and with 3894 in a foundry (both wholly owned), is the second largest Federal German company in Brazil. Like VW, Daimler-Benz has been in production since 1957. In 1975 the production of commercial vehicles was increased by 16.1% and amounted to a total of 43600 units. In addition the number of diesel engines produced rose by 8% over the preceding year to 23105. The market share was about 45% for commercial vehicles over three tonnes, and 90% in the bus market. The company was 'once more able to substantially expand its exports'. Important markets, in addition to the Latin American countries, are the USA and several African countries.[2] In order to expand its sales in the USA, Daimler-Benz has concluded an agreement with the Fruehauf Corporation, the largest US manufacturer of lorry superstructures, which has its own service network in the USA for the sale of vehicles produced in Brazil.[3]

In addition to VW and Daimler-Benz, a number of smaller companies in the vehicles sector also operate in Brazil: a number of them are extremely dependent on the two large producers. The body manufacturer Karman has been in production in Brazil since 1960 and currently employs 1600 people there. Knorr-Bremse KG makes brakes and also diesel engines (1450 employees). Fichtel & Sachs has been manufacturing transmissions and other vehicle parts since 1959 (1100 employees). In addition companies which are nominally in other branches of industry operate exclusively or predominantly for the vehicle industry as suppliers. VDO do Brasil manufactures instruments (810 employees); Petri makes steering wheels and E. A. H. Naue upholstery and trim (200 employees); Triangeler

million was required: the company only had to raise a third of this sum from its own sources. Two thirds could be written off against tax.' (*Süddeutsche Zeitung*, 17 February 1975, pp. 8–11.)

1. *Süddeutsche Zeitung*, 27 May 1974.
2. Daimler-Benz AG, *Geschäftsbericht 1975*, p. 55.
3. *Süddeutsche Zeitung*, 4 May 1976. 'Daimler-Benz has sold around 1200 trucks in the USA in the last year, most of which were imported from Brazil. Only lightweight buses were supplied from Federal Germany.' (*Süddeutsche Zeitung*, 22 October 1976.) 'If one extrapolates the current rates of growth it will not be long before the Brazilian subsidiary will be producing more trucks and buses than the German parent company.' (*Handelsblatt*, 27 November 1976.)

produces various types of insulation materials. Since 1970 the 62% held subsidiary of Karl Schmidt GmbH (a Metallgesellschaft affiliate) has been manufacturing pistons for the motor industry (600 employees).

In addition Federal German electrical firms also supply the Brazilian assembly plants; this applies in particular to Robert Bosch GmbH which employs almost 8000 people in three plants and also makes power tools and radiators. It also manufactures packing machinery on a small scale. Varta AG has a one-third holding in Microlite do Brasil, which makes electrical components and employs 4800 employees. Part of the output of Osram is similarly intended for the vehicle industry: the firm has 1300 employees.

The electrical engineering industry is also represented by other types of manufacture. AEG-Telefunken has several plants producing products for communications systems, high voltage equipment, radio and television sets and typewriters (Olympia) employing almost 5000 workers. Siemens is engaged in the production of various types of condensors (3000 employees) and also has three plants producing a wide range of electro-technical products (almost 6500 employees). Transformatoren Union (Siemens) established a new Brazilian subsidiary in 1973 and assembles transformers at two sites (1200 employees).

Precision engineering and optics are also strongly represented in Brazil, although the establishments are smaller. Only Hartmann & Braun Brasilia (electrical measuring and regulating devices) employs more than 1000 people. Stumpp & Schüle do Brasil, in which Robert Bosch GmbH have a stake, manufacture technical balance springs. Günther Wagner Pelikan-Werke have been making office and drawing-office equipment in Brazil since 1932 and employ 410 workers at two locations. The Zeiss-Gruppe have four subsidiaries producing microscopes and working and processing glass (with a total of more than 1000 employees).

Amongst other manufacturing industries are, for example, the Artland Dörffler meat products factory with more than 700 employees. Melitta makes filters and filter papers (140 employees) and in addition has a stake in a cigar factory in Bahia via August Blase GmbH (1000 employees). Oetker is involved in food processing and has bought a coffee plantation. Reemtsma state that they have sold their cigarette factors in Santa Cruz do Sul, which employed more than 2000 people in 1975.

Figures for the size of shareholdings or capital stake were available for 234 out of the 267 holdings. Only 19.6% were less than 50%, whereas 80.4% were 50% or more and 52.1% were almost or wholly owned (95%–100%).

We do not deal in detail here with the various operations which are planned in the nuclear field. The construction of eight large reactors is envisaged, and in addition a uranium enrichment and a reprocessing plant.[1] The exploration and mining of uranium ore is being developed in cooperation with Federal German companies with the support of the Federal German government.[2]

We do not intend to analyse the connection between the industrial production of foreign companies in Brazil and their development on the one side, and the development on the social conditions of the population and the policies of those in power in Brazil on the other. There are a large number of studies which investigate the development of underdevelopment and dependency in the case of Brazil.[3]

The economic and political problems of the Brazilian state are not necessarily prejudicial to the conditions for the valorisation of foreign capital. They can, in fact, even improve and promote them. For example, attempts to reduce dependency on imports lead to support for the local production of capital-goods: as a consequence

1. 'The nozzle separation process is being developed in conjunction with Brazil (NUCLEBRAS). The Trenndüsenentwicklungs- und Patentverwertungsgesellschaft mbH company (50% STEAG, 50% NUCLEBRAS) has the exclusive rights to the patent for this process in Latin America.' (Ruhrkohle AG, *Geschäftsbericht 1975*, p. 50.)
2. 'Similarly one of the main hopes for both sides in the Brazilian deal is that German geologists will help discover substantial uranium reserves that they believe to exist in Brazil...German geologists are now farming out over the northern Amazon basin to seek new uranium deposits, with 80% of their exploration expenses subsidised by Bonn.' (Norman Gall, 'Atoms for Brazil, dangers for all', *Bulletin of the Atomic Scientists* (June 1976), p. 9.) 'Aloisio Chaves, Governor of Para State, has revealed that a new uranium deposit has been discovered in North Brazil. The deposit, the size of which was not specified, is not far from the border with Surinam and French Guyana and lies in the Amapa and Roraima provinces.' (*FAZ/Blick durch die Wirtschaft*, 12 July 1976.) (Gall deals with all the aspects of the German-Brazilian nuclear deal in his detailed article. He also discusses why the reactor manufacturers prefer to sell to some underdeveloped countries: 'At the same time, strong public opposition to nuclear power has spread from the United States to France, Germany, Japan and Sweden, compounding the inflation and delay...Both US and European reactor manufacturers have responded to inflation and delay at home by competing fiercely for export sales in third markets, especially in developing countries with authoritarian regimes that need not worry about public opposition to the siting of nuclear power plants.' (Gall, 'Atoms for Brazil', p. 9).)
3. See, Dieter Senghaas, 'Brasiliens assoziativ–kapitalistische Entwicklung' in *Weltwirtschaftsordnung und Entwicklungspolitik* (Frankfurt–Main 1977), pp. 118–52. Edmar L. Bacha, 'Issues and evidence on recent Brazilian economic growth', *World Development* 1/2 (1977), pp. 46–67.

the Brazilian government is paying almost half the costs of Krupp's new industrial equipment plant in Minais Gerais.[1] Foreign capital also benefits from the encouragement of exports as half of the exports of mining and industry are accounted for by the subsidiaries of foreign companies.[2]

India

After India gained political independence in 1947 British capital retained a significant influence: this was not however sufficient to prevent capital from other countries, in particular the USA and Federal Germany, from gaining access to the subcontinent and acquiring influence themselves. Within the framework of the new international division of labour industrial companies found themselves obliged to utilise India's plentiful supply of cheap labour and its technical infrastructure for the development of increasingly export-oriented production at a large number of locations.[3]

Indian capital, itself involved in the search for favourable investment opportunities,[4] is not inactive abroad in its own right, and also links up with the foreign capital which begins operations in India. In none of the firms for which we could establish the size of the foreign capital holding was this two-thirds or more, and majority holdings could only be found in 18.9%, which includes however

1. 'The government must take decisive measures to encourage equipment production inside Brazil...Government financial bodies have agreed to contribute 4 million sterling to this project, out of a total investment of 9.5 million sterling.' (*Financial Times*, 10 September 1975.)
2. Import restrictions on equipment unavailable in Brazil have been lifted; they can even be imported free of tariffs: see, The Economist Intelligence Unit, *Quarterly Economic Review, Brazil No. 2* (1976), p. 13. In the study conducted by Doellinger and Cavalvanti referred to above, out of the 318 undertakings covered (1973), 38.8% of the exports of these companies/undertakings were accounted for by state concerns, 9.8% by local private capital, and 51.4% by the affiliates of foreign companies: see Doellinger, Cavalvanti, *Empresas Multinacionais*, p. 75, Table IV.9. *Handelsblatt* reported on the encouragement of exports: 'The Council for Economic Development sets the highest priority on as strong a growth in exports as is possible. Around 35 billion Cruzeiros (DM 7 billion) is being held ready for the purpose of boosting exports to US $11.5 billion.' (*Handelsblatt*, 8 February 1977.) According to these figures, around 25% of the total value of exports was subsidised.
3. Between 1 January 1957 and 31 December 1973 agreements on financial and/or technical cooperation were made with following countries: Great Britain, 995; USA, 731; Federal Germany, 644; Japan, 381; Switzerland, 191; France, 167; Italy, 107; East Germany, 84. See Indo-German Chamber of Commerce, *Indo-German Collaboration*, 3rd edition (Bombay 1974), p. viii.
4. 'Capital in India, far from being in insufficient supply as theoretical orthodoxy would have it, is in fact in excess supply, as evidenced, among other things, by excess installed capacity.' (Andre Gunder Frank, 'Reflections on green, red and white revolutions in India', *Economic and Political Weekly*, 3 (1973), p. 123.)

large-scale operations by Bayer, Bosch, Gedore and Siemens. Important cooperation agreements also exist with companies in which there is less than a 25% holding (and which are therefore not dealt with here). Among these holdings is the 11.5% stake which Daimler-Benz has in the Tata Engineering and Locomotive Company Ltd, Bombay, which produced more than 25000 commercial vehicles in 1975.[1]

More than two-thirds of current 'Indo-German cooperation agreements' are confined to technical collaboration without any formal capital holding.[2] Similarly foreign companies make great use of production capacity in India for their world production without any commensurable investment of their own capital.[3]

Following the imposition of the state of emergency (which has since ended) India opened itself even more to foreign capital. During the state of emergency strikes were forbidden and labour legislation was suspended.[4] At the same time capital was increasingly encouraged by means of tax reductions and subsidies.[5]

Production was directed even more than previously towards

1. Daimler-Benz AG, *Geschäftsbericht 1975*, p. 54.
2. 'Out of the existing 344 Indo-German collaborations, 236 have been sanctioned as mere technical collaborations and 108 have been sanctioned as joint ventures. Out of the 108 Indo-German sanctioned joint ventures, 67 have still financial cum technical collaboration. The technical collaboration agreement has ceased to exist in 39 collaborations so that there remains only financial collaboration. In 2 cases, the financial collaboration has ceased to exist whilst the technical collaboration is still existing.' (*Indo-German Collaboration*, p. viii.)
3. As an example we mention the case of the firm established in Calcutta in 1975 for the production of truck mounted cranes: 'Foreign Collaboration. The Company has entered into collaboration with Messrs. H. Weyhausen GmbH of West Germany whereby the latter will furnish the Company with technical data and other information appertaining or related to certain specified products including Truck Mounted Hydraulic Cranes and accessories thereof ("the specified products") and will grant to the Company the sole and exclusive right and licence to manufacture and sell in India the specified products under their patents and registered designs and the nonexclusive right and licence to sell the specified products under the same patents and designs to other countries subject to certain limitation. The foreign collaborators have also agreed to purchase 25% of the Company's annual production of the specified products subject to certain conditions.' From a notification by the Atlas Hydraulic Equipment Ltd in *Economic and Political Weekly*, 30 (1976), p. 1110.
4. '"If a trade union official starts to grumble I, Mr K., can even punish him." This must be good news for any company.' (*FAZ/Blick durch die Wirtschaft*, 27 September 1975.)
5. 'The budget recognises that high levels of personal income and wealth taxation are counter-productive. It also recognises the need to leave companies with adequate funds to invest and to increase the attractiveness of shares vis-à-vis other investments. Also, for the first time, the so-called luxury items are given tax reliefs in order to stimulate domestic demand for these industries...Private investment is likely to respond to the incentives provided in the budget and to other policy changes.' (The Economist Intelligence Unit, *Quarterly Economic Review. India, Nepal No. 2* (1976), pp. 8–15.)

meeting the consumer wishes of an affluent minority and towards exports[1] which were encouraged by a number of measures. The basic needs of the mass of the population were totally neglected. The business press commented at the time: 'More discipline and higher profits'[2] and 'India continues to remain attractive for German direct investments',[3] a state of affairs which still seems to prevail.

Eighty subsidiaries were recorded as falling within the scope of the study, of which seven had ceased to operate. In 1975 employment in forty-four of these subsidiaries amounted to 38480 (Table II-17).

Calculated by the number of subsidiaries the main areas of Federal German production are in mechanical engineering and the chemicals industry, whereas reckoned by employment the electrical engineering industry takes first place. All the large chemicals combines are represented. Bayer has a 52.7% majority holding in Bayer India Ltd and manufactures pesticides, drugs and other chemicals (almost 1600 employees). Boehringer Ingelheim and Boehringer Mannheim are prominent amongst the drug manufacturers: both have almost 40% holdings in companies which each employ around 700 workers. (In addition to Boehringer Mannheim, Knoll AG has a 19.4% stake in Knoll Ltd.)

Buderus (Flick Group) operates in the metal fabrication sector and is involved in the manufacture of tubes. Gontermann-Peipers India produces iron and steel rolls (420 employees). Khatau-Junker Ltd (35% = Otto Junker GmbH) manufactures condensors (75 employees). The Krupp combine has a stake in several large companies: the Buckau Wolf New India Engineering Works (Krupp = 49.9%) assembles sugar-making equipment and conveyor belts in Pimpri; Koppers India (Krupp = 40%) is active in steel fabrication (around 100 employees); Widia India (Krupp = 52.4%) has been involved in the tool-making industry since 1967 (560 employees). In addition Polysius AG maintains a subsidiary which manufactures equipment for the production of iron-ore pellets.

Thirty of the subsidiaries are in mechanical engineering: collaboration ceased in four of them over the period. Most are middle-sized

1. In a study of Indo-German collaborations covering the years 1970–72, it was established that 57% of companies exported, principally those in which there was a Federal German Stake. In 1972, 9.6% of the companies exported more than 50% of their output. See Indo-German Chamber of Commerce, *Indo-German Joint Ventures. Export Situation* (Bombay 1973), pp. 4–7.
2. *FAZ/Blick durch die Wirtschaft*, 27 September 1975.
3. *FAZ/Blick durch die Wirtschaft*, 17 January 1976.

Table II-17. *India: number of subsidiaries and employees by sector: 1961, 1966, 1971, 1973, 1974, 1975, 1976*

	1961			1966			1961			1973			1974			1975			1976		
	I	II	III	I	II	III	I	II	III	I	II	III	I	II	III	I	II	III	I	II	III
Agric. & for.	—	—	—	—	—	—	—	—	—	—	—	—	—	—	—	—	—	—	—		
En. & min.	—	—	—	—	—	—	—	—	—	—	—	—	—	—	—	—	—	—	—		
Chem.	11	2	322	14	4	1082	18	7	3792	19	10	7184	19	12	7825	20	12	7961	19		
St., gl. & ceram.	1	—	—	1	—	—	1	—	—	1	—	—	1	—	—	1	—	—	—		
Metal.	6	1	60	6	1	90	9	3	449	9	4	1632	9	4	1699	9	5	2129	9		
Mech. eng.	17	4	519	25	9	1596	28	13	4184	28	13	4500	29	13	4665	28	14	4974	26		
Veh.	2	—	—	2	1	1261	2	1	1547	2	1	2016	2	1	2140	2	1	2140	2		
Elec. eng.	3	—	—	4	—	—	9	3	7541	10	3	8429	10	5	14568	9	5	15416	9		
Prec. eng. & opt.	4	2	147	5	2	879	5	2	3412	5	3	4811	5	3	5819	6	3	5807	6		
Other	—	—	—	2	2	40	2	2	57	2	2	58	2	2	53	2	2	53	2		
All sectors covered	44	9	1048	59	19	4948	74	31	20982	76	36	28630	77	40	36769	77	44	38480	73		

Number of Federal German companies: 70
Number of subsidiaries in operation: 73
Number of subsidiaries given up: 7
Total number of subsidiaries: 80

Number of plants in operation: 78
Number of plants given up: 7
Total number of plants: 85

See Table II-1 for sector abbreviations
I = number of subsidiaries; II = number of subsidiaries for which employment was available; III = employment

companies: where numbers of employees could be determined we found 850 in one subsidiary (a 39.4% holding of Kugelfischer) and 800 in another (a 27% holding of Eicher in a tractor and agricultural machinery manufacturer) – apart from these two cases the numbers employed were always less. A factory making drills in which Rohde & Dörrenberg have had a 42.7% stake since 1966 employs 500 people.

In the vehicles industry Hanomag-Henschel have a 26.6% holding in a subsidiary which has been assembling vehicles since 1957 (2140 employees), apart from the subsidiary of Daimler-Benz which we have already mentioned. Fichtel & Sachs AG are involved in a moped factory via their Zweirad-Union company.

Two companies stand out in the electrical engineering industry: Bosch and Siemens. Bosch has a 51% holding in Motor Industries Co. Ltd which makes fitting for diesel engines, sparking plugs and other vehicle parts in Bangalore and Nasik (9200 employees). In value terms 28% of output was exported in 1975.[1] Siemens India is also 51% owned by the Federal German company. It produces meters, electrical equipment, transformers and cable and has been in operation since 1964 (5200).

There are also a number of significant subsidiaries in the field of precision engineering. Stumpp, Schüle & Somappa (30% = Stumpp & Schüle) has been manufacturing springs since 1961 and employs nearly 700 people. A 25% holding of VDO-Adolf Schindling AG has been manufacturing vehicle instrumentation since 1964 (over 900 workers). Gedore Tools India, which manufactures a variety of tools, has been 51% owned by Gedore Werkzeugfabrik since 1961 (4200 employees).

The further expansion of industrial production in India will be determined to a not inconsiderable extent by the development of the political situation there. The conditions for the valorisation of capital in India are not fundamentally different from those of other South East Asian countries. However, India is also an important location for those parts of globally organised manufacturing which require higher levels of technical capacity.

1. Robert Bosch GmbH, *Geschäftsbericht 1975*. For a case study of this firm see Reinhard Koppe, *Deutsche Investitionen in Indien, dargestellt am Beispiel der Firma Mico-Bosch in Bangalore* (Constance 1974/75), unpublished.

Yugoslavia

Yugoslavia is a country in which forms other than formal capital holdings by Federal German companies in local industrial establishments are of importance in the utilisation of production capacity within the framework of the world-wide organisation of production sites.

The law on foreign investment, passed on 19 April 1973, prohibits holdings in excess of 49%.[1] Direct capital holdings have been permissible since 1968 and the first Federal German company, Kautt & Bux, purchased a stake in a commutator factory in 1969. We were able to find eighteen manufacturing associates with a capital share higher than 25% up to the time of writing. In the eleven of these for which figures were available employment was 2956 (1975) (Table II-18). A list dating from 31 January 1974 which was based on official statistics reveals ninety-seven holdings of which twenty embraced a Federal German involvement. However, a number of these were less than 25%, and one company (Helsa-Werke, Gefrees) belonged to the textile and garment industry.[2]

One of the forms in which Yugoslavian production capacity is used is that of cooperation between undertakings without any formal share in capital being held by one company in another. The register of long-term intercompany cooperation agreements for the period from 1968 to the end of 1975 shows 171 agreements, each governing one collaboration between a Yugoslavian and a Federal German undertaking for the manufacture of particular products. These range from 'electric shavers, coffee grinders, fruit presses, mixers' to 'parts and components for reaping machines of the FKM 2 H Typ Fella'.[3] A number of Federal German companies are represented here which do not otherwise feature as manufacturers abroad: the main reason for this is that such cooperation agreements facilitate the utilisation of the advantages of production abroad combined with a low injection of capital, calculable risks and extensive security through the Yugoslavian government. Thus, although direct capital holdings have been permitted since 1968 they are more the exception than the rule.

1. OECD, *Foreign Investment in Yugoslavia* (Paris 1974), p. 10.
2. *Foreign Investment*, pp. 38–56 (Annex I). For the ninety-seven holdings taken as a whole the median share is 83% Yugoslavian-owned, and 17% by foreign companies (p. 56).
3. From a list supplied by the Federal German embassy in Belgrade.

Table II-18. *Yugoslavia: number of subsidiaries and employees by sector: 1961, 1966, 1971, 1973, 1974, 1975, 1976*

	1961			1966			1971			1973			1974			1975			1976		
	I	II	III	I	II	III	I	II	III	I	II	III	I	II	III	I	II	III	I	II	III
Agric. & for.	—	—	—	—	—	—	—	—	—	—	—	—	—	—	—	—	—	—	—		
En. & min.	—	—	—	—	—	—	—	—	—	—	—	—	—	—	—	—	—	—	—		
Chem.	—	—	—	—	—	—	1	1	32	4	4	647	4	4	742	5	5	722	5		
St., gl. & ceram.	—	—	—	—	—	—	1	—	—	1	—	—	1	—	—	1	—	—	—		
Metal.	—	—	—	—	—	—	—	—	—	—	—	—	—	—	—	—	—	—	—		
Mech. eng.	—	—	—	—	—	—	—	—	—	2	1	736	2	1	779	3	1	952	3		
Veh.	—	—	—	—	—	—	1	—	—	2	1	773	2	1	849	2	1	840	2		
Elec. eng.	—	—	—	—	—	—	2	1	150	3	3	291	3	3	344	3	3	372	3		
Prec. eng. & opt.	—	—	—	—	—	—	1	1	46	1	1	52	1	1	60	2	1	70	3		
Other	—	—	—	—	—	—	1	—	—	1	—	—	1	—	—	1	—	—	1		
All sectors covered	—	—	—	—	—	—	7	3	228	14	10	2499	14	10	2774	16	11	2956	17		

Number of Federal German companies: 17
Number of subsidiaries in operation: 17
Number of subsidiaries given up: 1
Total number of subsidiaries: 18

Number of plants in operation: 17
Number of plants given up: 1
Total number of plants: 18

See Table II-1 for sector abbreviations
I = number of subsidiaries; II = number of subsidiaries for which employment was available; III = employment

In addition to those holdings of at least 25% covered by our survey the much smaller holdings in large enterprises along with licence agreements and other forms of cooperation are also of significance. Klöckner-Humboldt-Deutz AG gives its share in the enterprise Tovarno Automobilov in Motorjeve in Maribor which employs 6000 people and assembles cars and commercial vehicles as 1.2%. Daimler-Benz has a 5.9% stake in FAP FAMOS, which employs 12300 workers and produces lorries, buses, engines and transmissions at several locations.

Enterprises which do have a higher Federal German capital holding do not come anywhere near these employment totals. A Volkswagen assembly plant (VW = 49%) has the highest with 840 employees. This is followed by a holding of E. A. H. Naue (29.7%) which makes car seats. The largest chemical holdings employ a mere 100–200 people.

This low average capital involvement does not seem to fit in with how the Yugoslavian side envisaged matters:

> Belgrade is increasingly complaining about the investment activities of Federal German companies in Yugoslavia. Their interest in establishing joint ventures with Yugoslavian partners or in becoming involved, in terms of capital investment, has clearly waned and the upwards trend has come to a halt. In addition, the Yugoslavians seem to be disappointed by the fact that German firms have only made rare use of the opportunity to take up to a 49% stake in Yugoslavian enterprises.[1]

Attempts are therefore made to improve further the conditions for foreign capital: 'The new provisions will facilitate even more open and free investments by foreign capital and long-term tie-ups with the Yugoslavian economy.'[2] What is at stake is made quite clear: 'to find a satisfactory method of regulating the question of the repatriation of invested capital and generated profits'.[3]

East European countries

It is necessary to look at Eastern Europe in some detail in this section as the extent to which Federal German companies are active in the Eastern European socialist countries (excluding Yugoslavia) is woefully inadequately recorded in those empirical surveys which only take into account holdings in companies abroad when collecting data on foreign manufacturing. In fact, capital holdings have been

1. *Handelsblatt*, 18 May 1976.
2. *Handelsblatt*, 15 June 1976.
3. *Handelsblatt*, 8 June 1976.

possible in some East European countries for a number of years, and this possibility is spreading amongst the socialist countries. Federal German companies are known to have holdings in Hungary and Romania. However, this form of foreign operation is still of subordinate importance in the East European countries.

Other forms of operation which are not based on capital holdings, such as export-processing under subcontract, licence and marketing cooperation, are of greater significance both for the Federal German companies and the countries themselves. International subcontracting in general, and cooperation with Hungarian enterprises in particular, in the textile and garment industry are dealt with in Part I.[1]

In order to illustrate the kind of agreement concluded we cite here the example of a cooperation agreement drawn up with Polish enterprises in 1976. Most of the contracts are supply contracts which run for four or five years, and usually contain provisions for some form of exchange trade (compensatory trade) whereby Federal German companies supply capital-goods in exchange for semi-finished and finished goods. The branches involved are chiefly chemicals, equipment manufacture and foundry products: the main firms involved are BASF, Bayer, Hoechst, Krupp (Krupp-Koppers GmbH), Salzgitter and Uhde (77.5% = Hoechst).[2]

Because of its size and the high technology required a project for the gassification of coal has received particular attention. Another long-term raw materials project is intended to secure 10% of the long-term imports of copper into Federal Germany. Metallgesellschaft, Norddeutsche Affinerie (40% = Metallgesellschaft), Kabelmetall (= Gutehoffnungshütte) and Siemens are all involved in this project, which also envisages cooperation in the further stages of processing and manufacture. The copper is intended to be exported not primarily as a raw material but in the form of semimanufactured articles.[3]

1. The brochure 'Kooperieren mit Ungarn. 10 praktische Tips für Unternehmen in der Bundesrepublik' (Bonn 1974) is also extremely informative. As well as export processing, licensing and market cooperation, and additional 'specialisation cooperation' is distinguished: 'The areas of production of each company are closely connected through the specialisation cooperation. The intermediate products to be supplied by each party are needed at the right time for final assembly, regardless of whether this takes place for the product concerned in Hungary or in Germany, or both.' ('Kooperieren mit Ungarn', p. 23.)
2. See the list of fourteen supply and cooperation contracts in *Süddeutsche Zeitung*, 12 June 1976.
3. *FAZ*, 4 June 1976, 12 June 1976 and 18 June 1976.

Instead of companies putting in their own capital this is replaced by (state guaranteed) initial financing of the investment goods supplied ('the coal–chemicals plant will be paid for out of the "world-wide" sales of the products')[1] and the function of such capital holdings is taken care of by the fact that the supply contracts are long-term in nature.[2]

Projects for the manufacture of goods for third markets represent one fundamental step further in the direction of using Polish production capacity for world market production under the control of Federal German companies.[3] One extensive cooperation agreement is concerned with the supply of electrical filters for thermal generating plant: 'Common supplies of electrical filters, carrying the joint trade-marks of Walther-Köln and ELWO Pszczyna, have already reached Australia, Yugoslavia, Bulgaria and Egypt.'[4] The most important area for such supplies is the construction of plant. The construction of chemical plant and sugar factories[5] is envisaged, and contracts for the building of power stations have been concluded with Turkey and Libya.[6]

The cooperation agreements which have been cited here in the case of Poland can be interpreted as distinctive examples of the established forms of the international division of labour. Of course, in this as in many other instances cheap labour has been one of the principal factors which has induced Federal German companies to initiate manufacturing cooperation with enterprises in Eastern Europe. However, in addition there are even clearer examples of

1. *FAZ*, 4 June 1976.
2. 'The usual aim of these agreements, which exist in a variety of forms, is the combination of western capital and know-how with eastern labour and pre-production via the exchange of supplies and services. Often the agreements go as far as the supply of complete production installations by the west which are paid for, as regulated by long-term agreements, by the progressive sale of the products made...In economic terms these cooperation plans are very close to direct investment.' (*Neue Zürcher Zeitung*, 11 June 1976.) This also applies to the competition which German workers find themselves in: 'Poland's licence-producers are ready to take on those jobs abandoned by West Germany in the eventuality that, in the not far distant future, the level of wages in Germany will make it impossible to produce trucks and buses on a basis which covers their costs.' (*Handelsblatt*, 28/29 May 1976.)
3. 'Gierek: the range of goods produced in Poland is broad enough. The question is not simply one of exporting to Federal Germany, but should also include the possibility of joint exporting to third markets.' (*Der Spiegel*, 7 June 1976, p. 41.)
4. *Handelsblatt*, 4/5 June 1976. Special supplement 'Polen', p. v. Walther & Cie belongs to the Krupp combine.
5. *Süddeutsche Zeitung*, 12 June 1976.
6. *Handelsblatt*, 4/5 June 1976, p. v and x.

how production sites in Eastern Europe are drawn into the global reorganisation of production sites under the conditions of the new international division of labour.

Standard Elektro Lorenz (an ITT affiliate) has television sets which are intended for the world market assembled in Hungary:

Business involving technical and organisational know-how with partners in various parts of the world is gaining in importance. For example in the year under report a cooperation agreement has been concluded between the Hungarian foreign trade enterprise Elektroimpex and Orion, Radio- und Elektrizitätswerke which involves the manufacture of colour televisions. Within the terms of the agreement we shall be supplying the know-how for manufacture, tools and machinery and subsequently distributing the sets which are made in Hungary, with the aim of improving our competitiveness in the export field. Production started in spring of this year.[1]

The same applies in the case of a large mechanical engineering company:

The Gildemeister Group, which will continue to supply the market with its product line from Hamburg, will be having the lathes which were made there manufactured by a Hungarian cooperation partner after May 1977, so that they can once more be sold at a profit.[2]

Hence, those direct formal holdings of capital in foreign establishments only represent a small part of cooperation in the field of manufacture.

So far only one capital participation has come about with a Hungarian enterprise[3] although, up until 1976, 323 cooperation agreements had been signed between German and Hungarian partners.[4] The capital holding is in the Sicontact enterprise which was established in 1974 and in which Siemens has a 49% holding: the company operates in the field of the development of electrotechnical equipment and computer and systems technology.[5] The

1. Standard Elektro Lorenz GmbH, *Geschäftsbericht 1975*, p. 22.
2. *Handelsblatt*, 27/28 August 1976. Since then further extensive agreements have been made. 'Gildemeister will grant the Hungarian establishment the right to manufacture medium and large Universal lathes, at the same time as it is shutting down the production of these same machines in their own plant.' (Hungaropress, *Wirtschaftsinformationen* 22 (1976).) Many agreements for production under licence clearly represent shifts in production. One further example: 'Bosch has given the Hungarian manufacturing enterprise Jasberény a licence to manufacture refrigerators, which has put Hungary in a position to increase its exports of refrigerators within the socialist countries as well to the free market economies.' (*Cooperation* 2 (1977), p. 38.)
3. In fact *Handelsblatt* reports: 'According to figures from Bonn there are three joint ventures.' It is doubtful whether three manufacturing enterprises are involved.
4. *Süddeutsche Zeitung*, 22 October 1976.
5. *Süddeutsche Zeitung*, 13 July 1974.

Swedish Volvo company was the first Western country to take a holding in a cooperative enterprise, which it did shortly before Siemens: the company assembles cross-country vehicles.[1]

In 1973 in Romania a joint enterprise was established with the mechanical engineering company Resita which initially began with the production of marine drives for medium-speed diesel engines in 1975. The gear manufacturer Renk AG, which belongs to the Gutehoffnungshütte combine, has a 49% holding in this venture. The number of employees was put at 150 in 1975, and an increase to 300 is envisaged. '75% of the products of the joint enterprise are intended to be sold in Romania and the Comecon countries, with the remainder going to Western markets.'[2] Gutehoffnungshütte has concluded a licensing agreement with a Romanian enterprise through its commercial vehicle affiliate MAN for the construction of lorries; a proportion of the vehicles will be sold in Federal Germany, with MAN taking over the distribution.[3]

The shoe manufacturer Otterbeck KG, which employs 500 in two plants in Germany, will be having 'a Romanian partner manufacture almost half of Otterbeck's production on a subcontracting basis.'[4] 'In addition the possibility of setting up a plant in Bulgaria has also been sounded out'[5] which would not however imply a capital involvement as joint ventures are not supposed to be possible in Bulgaria.[6]

Although some forms of capital holding may develop in Eastern Europe in the next few years, for the foreseeable future this form of foreign manufacturing will be of less significance than the others mentioned above.

The examples given here show the existence of a number of different possibilities for Federal German companies by which they can integrate labour and production capacities in Eastern Europe into the world-wide organisation of production. In this context some of these cases, at least, show quite clearly that the tendency towards a new international division of labour is also expressed through and in economic relations with the East European countries.

1. *BfA/Nachrichten für Außenhandel*, 29 July 1974.
2. *GHH-Pressedienst*, 23 November 1973, pp. 1–3.
3. *FAZ*, 17 November 1975.
4. *Handelsblatt*, 14 November 1974.
5. *Handelsblatt*, 1 April 1975.
6. According to the President of the Bulgarian Chamber of Commerce and Industry, 'Joint ventures are not possible in Bulgaria'. (*Süddeutsche Zeitung*, 1 November 1975.)

USA

The USA provides a clear example of the possibility of the re-emergence of profitable conditions for industrial manufacture at one site because of the prior relocations of industry in the context of the new international division of labour. The chronic high levels of unemployment, pressure on real wages and government policies which attempt to encourage industrial investment in the wake of relocation in the industrialised countries all contribute to the improvement in the conditions for the valorisation of capital at these locations.

In all, 185 Federal German subsidiaries were found in the USA; employment was 43293 in 95 of them (1975) (Table II-19).[1] This development has recently become widely recognised because of Volkswagen's decision to produce in the USA. This decision will also force a number of VW's suppliers to commence or expand their production in the USA.[2]

Chemicals are particularly important: twenty-three companies have thirty-six subsidiaries in all, twenty-seven of which employed 29988 people (1975). All subsectors of the industry are represented, ranging from large-scale chemical production to washing powders and plant sprays, partly through holdings in existing US companies but more through the establishment of new plants, which are likely to be added to.

Examples of the wide variety of activities by companies in the electrical engineering industry include: Siemens, who have increased their employment from 609 in 1970/71 to 2500 by 1975. 'Current US production of 20% (of US turnover) will rise to 50% within three years.'[3] Bosch will double its manufacturing capacity for fuel injection equipment.[4] Nixdorf Computer Inc., Chicago, which came

1. Cf. the list published annually by the German-American Chamber of Commerce, *American Subsidiaries of German Firms.* The introduction to another list of foreign companies in the USA discusses why such lists can hardly be complete: 'Foreign firms both entering and operating in the US have adopted low-visibility profiles – occasionally going to great lengths to mask their foreign identity and almost always avoiding publicity of it.' (Jeffrey S. Arpan & David A. Ricks, *Directory of Foreign Manufacturers in the United States* (Atlanta–Georgia 1975), p. xi.)
2. *Der Spiegel*, 31 May 1976, p. 84.
3. *Süddeutsche Zeitung*, 4 June 1976. In the field of medical technology Siemens has a plant in Connecticut (since 1975) and California (since 1974): the former is expected to employ between 800–1000 over the next few years. Siemens justifies 'its involvement in the USA by the need to balance out foreign currency fluctuations and to gain access to production technology.' (*Süddeutsche Zeitung*, 13 October 1976.)
4. *Handelsblatt*, 21/22 May 1976.

Table II-19. *USA: number of subsidiaries and employees by sector: 1961, 1966, 1971, 1973, 1974, 1975, 1976*

	1961			1966			1971			1973			1974			1975			1976		
	I	II	III	I	II	III	I	II	III	I	II	III	I	II	III	I	II	III	I	II	III
Agric. & for.	—	—	—	—	—	—	1	—	—	1	—	—	1	—	—	1	—	—	1		
En. & min.	3	—	—	3	—	—	4	1	210	4	1	230	7	3	298	8	3	343	8		
Chem.	13	2	1236	16	5	2646	19	7	8735	23	13	17618	29	20	28864	35	27	29988	36		
St., gl. & ceram.	1	—	—	1	—	—	2	1	40	2	1	55	2	1	53	1	1	53	3		
Metal.	4	—	—	6	1	270	10	6	1395	12	7	1723	14	8	2106	14	9	2355	15		
Mech. eng.	27	3	43	32	8	305	42	17	1477	50	25	2332	53	28	2552	52	29	2823	60		
Veh.	1	—	—	1	—	—	3	1	227	3	1	306	4	2	190	3	3	300	3		
Elec. eng.	6	—	—	8	1	25	9	4	746	9	4	1040	13	6	4017	14	8	3886	19		
Prec. eng. & opt.	5	1	32	7	3	667	11	6	1237	13	8	2343	13	8	2236	13	9	2652	19		
Other	3	—	—	5	2	192	6	2	270	6	2	344	6	3	814	7	4	892	10		
All sectors covered	63	6	1311	79	20	4105	107	45	14337	123	62	25991	142	79	41133	148	93	43292	174		

Number of Federal German companies: 152
Number of subsidiaries in operation: 174
Number of subsidiaries given up: 11
Total number of subsidiaries: 185

Number of plants in operation: 203
Number of plants given up: 11
Total number of plants: 214

See Table II-1 for sector abbreviations
I = number of subsidiaries; II = number of subsidiaries for which employment was available; III = employment

into being through the purchase of the computer section of the Victor Comptometer Corp. (Nixdorf's former agents) on 1 January 1973 sells Nixdorf computers in the USA and maintains its own research department in Costa Mesa, California.[1] The company has 600 employees. In the meantime, 'independent manufacturing capacity is being prepared at the US distribution company in Chicago where a development project in software is also being fostered.'[2] Furthermore Nixdorf wishes to buy Entex Inc. of Burlington, Massachusetts, which employs 600 people in the manufacture of computer systems for the recording, pre-processing and transfer of data.[3]

The number of subsidiaries in the mechanical engineering is strikingly high (sixty in 1976), and includes both medium-sized and small companies. On average the subsidiaries are not large, as indicated by the fact that the total employment in twenty-nine subsidiaries was 2823 employees (1975). Production is primarily for the US market.

The operations of Ruhrkohle AG are worthy of note in the field of raw materials. It began to buy itself into coal-mining in the Eastern US coalfields, and in 1976 was already negotiating for the purchase of a third mining company. The large Federal German steel manufacturers are also pursuing plans for an involvement in US coal-mining corporations.[4]

The reasons why the USA has become an important site for Federal German manufacturing companies include the following factors: lower wage costs, sufficient skilled and often non-trade-union organised workers, good sites for export-oriented production, indirect and direct government investment assistance, 'political stability', and, in addition, the great importance of the US domestic market.

The present-day conditions for the valorisation of capital in the USA have to be understood as an expression of an advanced phase in the development of the new international division of labour. US companies have on average relocated their production to quite a considerable extent before Federal German companies to the new

1. Nixdorf Computer AG, *Geschäftsbericht 1974*, pp. 24 and 6.
2. *Süddeutsche Zeitung*, 27 December 1975.
3. *Süddeutsche Zeitung*, 7/8 April 1977.
4. 'American mining is interesting for foreign companies because there are enormous reserves in the US which will not be exhausted for a long period of extraction, and because American coal, geologically, is comparatively to cheap to mine.' (*FAZ/Blick durch die Wirtschaft*, 29 May 1976.)

sites abroad. This has led to the creation of chronically high open and hidden unemployment and stagnating or falling real incomes for workers. The USA has therefore become a favourable location for technologically advanced production for West European companies.

Changes in wage levels are particularly noticeable. Whereas in 1960 a worker in US manufacturing industry earned 2.66 dollars an hour and a Federal German worker in Germany 0.83 dollars an hour, this difference had been practically wiped out by 1976, with the US rate at 6.90 dollars and the German 6.70. These are average figures. In the case of textiles, footwear and garments wages are considerably higher in Federal Germany than in the USA.[1]

At the 1975 Annual General Meeting of Hoechst the following figures were given for the production of Trevira artificial fibres: 'Expressed as production costs per kilo in Deutschmarks it will be seen that the wage total needed in Federal Germany is 40% higher.'[2] Alongside changes in the value of the dollar, lower social benefits and more hours worked per worker per year also play their part. The pace of work is somewhat higher and working hours per year longer (fewer holidays and days off), and it is easier to dismiss workers.[3] The existence of different degrees of union organisation is also influential in the choice of site. The low level of union organisation is offered as an incentive to foreign companies: 'The southern states sell hard their tractable, mainly non-unionised labour force'.[4] Among the reasons given by a mechanical engineering firm for its decision to move to South Carolina were: 'reduced union influence, so that the plant can be operated as a non-union shop until 1975 under a local state law'.[5] This is not an isolated instance:

1. *International Economic Report of the President. Transmitted to Congress, January 1977* (Washington 1977), pp. 99–101. The 'Institut der deutschen Wirtschaft' in Cologne has carried out an international cost comparison which came to the following results: 'Hourly labour costs in the last year in Federal Germany rose from DM 15.66 to DM 17.00. In the USA, which took first place in 1975 with DM 16.10, labour costs were only DM 16.00 per hour in 1976.' (*Süddeutsche Zeitung*, 25 January 1977.)
2. *FAZ/Blick durch die Wirtschaft*, 31 July 1975.
3. This is discussed in terms of 'flexibility' 'which management in the USA normally possesses in order to adjust output and employment to changing needs.' (*FAZ/Blick durch die Wirtschaft*, 19 June 1976). 'In the latest phase of an investment push into the US Britain's ICI is putting US $ 70 million into a herbicides plant near Houston, partly because freedom to hire, fire and move workers from job to job makes for higher productivity in the US than in Britain.' (*Business Week*, 12 April 1976.)
4. *Economist*, 29 November 1975.
5. H. Jürgen Schlichting & Hans-J. Krüger, *Deutsche Niederlassungen in den USA* (Frankfurt–Main 1975), p. 150.

'Numerous companies, including Federal German ones, have settled in the South East of the USA – in the Southern states, the former Confederacy – not least because the trade unions are traditionally weak there and only 5% of the work-force is unionised.'[1]

A full listing of the 'investment incentives' on offer from the various US states fills four printed pages.[2] Up to 65% of machinery and equipment can be financed from public funds, with the addition of numerous tax concessions, provision of sites, and help in the training of skilled workers.[3] The Federal states are particularly keen to attract foreign capital: 'Several US states are just as concerned to attract foreign investors through cheap loans, land, tax holidays and similar incentives as the European countries were to attract US capital... Many of them have established foreign agencies in Brussels and other centres the main task of which is to bring in foreign investment.'[4] Such conditions also make the USA attractive for export oriented production. *Business Week* reported that 'more and more foreign companies will produce in the US for export to other markets all over the world.'[5] Export from the USA attracts additional tax advantages.[6] All these benefits are the expression of a political system which is friendly to capital and which is therefore happily embraced by foreign investors: 'Foreigners who invest in the US have other motives besides market growth, of course. One is their uneasiness about the future of private enterprises in their own nations because of government regulations, labor's growing role in corporate management, and in the case of Italy and France, leftist political trends.'[7]

1. Schlichting & Krüger, p. 69.
2. Schlichting & Krüger, pp. 37–40.
3. Schlichting & Krüger, pp. 35 ff. In one case not only did the state of South Carolina pay for the training of workers at a Technical Education Center but 'beyond that paid 50% of the first, 40% of the second and 30% of the third month's salaries of every worker who passed the examination.' (Schlichting & Krüger, p. 154.)
4. *The Economist*, 29 November 1975.
5. *Business Week*, 12 April 1976. For example, a mechanical engineering subsidiary exported 30% of its production in 1973 to South America, and also a number of specialised machines to Federal Germany. (Schlichting & Krüger, p. 151.)
6. Schlichting & Krüger, p. 94.
7. *Business Week*, 12 April 1976.

12 ❧ Structural features of production and employment abroad

12.1 Production and employment abroad by industrial branch

Although the aim of this part is to provide a comprehensive survey of the extent of employment and production abroad by Federal German companies, its development over time[1] and regional distribution, it is not possible to provide a full or even systematically comparative analysis of those specific factors which lead to the adoption of production abroad in individual branches of industry. Initially a rough breakdown into ten branches was made, of which eight belonged to manufacturing industry (excluding the textile and garment industry). The Federal German companies covered in this survey were allocated to a branch along with all their subsidiaries according to which branch characterised the bulk of the group's operations. Under this procedure VW do Brasil's ranch belongs to the vehicle building industry: similarly, the pharmaceuticals (Byk Gulden) and baby foods (Milupa) operations undertaken by Varta are classified under electrical engineering. This procedure is not entirely satisfactory but is necessary to avoid double-counting.

Only a relatively crude breakdown of manufacturing industry seemed viable for the purpose of surveying production abroad in its entirety. An analysis of individual branches requires a much more differentiated basis and would break down manufacturing by production process or product group (at least at the level of the ISIC three-digit categories).

As a rule both the home and foreign production of the same company fit into the same branch, although there is often no complete manufacture abroad but merely assembly or subassembly operations. However, there are a number of exceptions to this rule.

1. With the limitation which applies throughout: excluding the EEC and the textiles and garment industry.

(Such examples of vertical and horizontal integration can also be seen in the domestic economy.) In particular, companies in the basic materials industries diversify vertically (iron and steel, chemicals) by becoming involved in the production of raw materials. For example, Thyssen has a large stake in iron-ore mining in Liberia, and Bayer is involved in South Africa in the production of fluorspar; Hoechst is also involved in the extraction of ferrous silica in South Africa. VW's stake in a foundry through VW do Brasil is another example of the extension into the manufacture of pre-products. Commercial companies become involved in the manufacture of the products which they sell, one particular example being in the production of animal feeds in the countries of South East Asia. There are other patterns of diversification and integration abroad. A trading concern, which also works on projects for industrial equipment, has bought a stake in a glass factory in Zambia, and a publisher has a holding in a toy factory in Hong Kong.

However, such diversifications do not by and large lead to large inaccuracies in the allocation of firms to a branch (e.g. of combines of the Varta type). Similarly, they are not of great significance in showing that foreign production is not simply confined to a few branches of industry.

Table II-20 provides an overall picture of foreign manufacturing broken down according to the branches of manufacturing industry, their principal regional distribution and development over time. We have already established above that different shares of the various industrial branches in production abroad are obtained depending on whether the index chosen is the number of companies producing abroad, the number of subsidiaries, or the number of employees (see Table II-4). Accordingly, the respective first places are occupied by the mechanical engineering industry, the chemical industry and electrical engineering in turn.

The average number of subsidiaries per country in which subsidiaries were found for each branch of industry represented there is as follows: mechanical engineering 10, chemicals 9.7, vehicle building 2.6, ferrous and non-ferrous metals 2.5. Of course the average size of undertaking varies considerably. In vehicle building average employment in each subsidiary was 2459, in electrical engineering 866, whereas in chemicals it was 372, mechanical engineering 236 and other manufacturing industry 222.

These differences do not only express variations in technical

Table II-20. *Branches of manufacturing industry by region: 1961–76*

	Countries of production	Federal German companies	Subsidiaries (1961–76)	Plants (1961–76)	Employees (1975) . . .	. . . proven in subsidiaries	Number of subsidiaries in 1961	1966	1971	1973	1974	1975
	(1)	(2)	(3)	(4)	(5)	(6)	(7)	(8)	(9)	(10)	(11)	(12)
CHEMICALS												
World	52	84	502	545	131760	371	238	302	401	443	467	488
Industrial countries	11	55	186	220	57358	133	94	110	142	153	167	178
W. Europe	5	38	73	74	8943	54	48	54	67	69	71	71
Non-European	6	39	113	146	48415	79	46	56	75	84	96	107
E. Europe	—	—	—	—	—	—	—	—	—	—	—	—
Developing countries	41	65	316	325	74402	238	144	192	259	290	300	310
Mediterranean	10	38	104	107	19457	78	42	63	86	97	99	104
Latin America	15	43	153	158	42568	122	82	100	130	141	147	149
Africa	8	4	8	8	345	2	4	4	4	6	6	7
W. Asia	1	9	10	10	1957	6	1	2	8	10	10	10
S. & S.E. Asia	8	22	41	42	10075	30	15	23	31	36	38	41
STONE, GLASS & CERAMICS												
World	19	22	46	48	9433	28	19	22	30	33	37	34
Industrial countries	6	14	26	27	4982	16	9	12	16	19	19	17
W. Europe	3	9	13	14	3765	13	5	7	10	13	13	12
Non-European	3	8	13	13	1217	3	4	5	6	6	6	5
E. Europe	—	—	—	—	—	—	—	—	—	—	—	—
Developing countries	13	14	20	21	4451	12	10	10	14	14	18	17
Mediterranean	4	10	11	11	1281	6	7	7	9	9	11	10
Latin America	3	2	3	4	2395	3	2	2	3	3	3	2
Africa	3	3	3	3	365	2	—	—	—	—	2	3
W. Asia	1	1	1	1	—	—	—	—	—	—	—	—
S. & S.E. Asia	2	2	2	2	410	1	1	1	2	2	2	2
FERROUS & NON-FERROUS METALS												
World	27	45	177	182	48657	87	92	112	139	153	163	169
Industrial countries	9	26	86	90	13809	38	45	56	70	76	83	83
W. Europe	4	18	34	34	8309	19	18	21	28	31	33	33
Non-European	5	21	52	56	5500	19	27	35	42	45	50	50
E. Europe	—	—	—	—	—	—	—	—	—	—	—	—
Developing countries	18	33	91	92	34848	49	47	56	69	77	80	86
Mediterranean	5	17	30	30	4568	18	15	21	26	28	29	29
Latin America	5	19	42	42	24907	23	23	25	29	34	35	39
Africa	3	3	3	3	2876	1	1	2	2	2	2	2
W. Asia	1	3	3	3	—	—	1	1	1	2	2	3
S. & S.E. Asia	4	8	13	14	2497	7	7	7	11	11	11	13
MECHANICAL ENGINEERING												
World	33	172	368	381	51730	219	168	214	265	296	311	326
Industrial countries	10	96	159	163	17786	94	71	89	117	130	137	136
W. Europe	4	45	54	55	9370	39	28	38	47	51	50	48
Non-European	5	74	104	107	8266	54	43	51	70	79	86	87
E. Europe	1	1	1	1	150	1	—	—	—	—	1	1
Developing countries	23	129	209	218	33944	125	97	125	148	166	174	190
Mediterranean	7	44	56	60	6493	38	22	29	39	51	50	54
Latin America	4	82	104	108	20758	60	40	63	70	74	79	91
Africa	4	4	6	6	598	5	1	1	3	3	5	6
W. Asia	1	1	1	1	—	—	1	1	1	1	1	1
S. & S.E. Asia	7	36	42	43	6095	22	23	31	35	37	38	38

Table II-20. (*cont.*)

	Countries of production (1)	Federal German companies (2)	Subsidiaries (1961–76) (3)	Plants (1961–76) (4)	Employees (1975) . . . (5)	. . . proven in subsidiaries (6)	Number of subsidiaries in 1961 (7)	1966 (8)	1971 (9)	1973 (10)	1974 (11)	1975 (12)
VEHICLE BUILDING												
World	19	20	48	49	101988	40	19	22	37	41	46	45
Industrial countries	4	7	12	12	11327	11	4	5	9	10	12	11
W. Europe	1	3	3	3	580	3	1	1	2	2	3	3
Non-European	3	6	9	9	10747	8	3	4	7	8	9	8
E. Europe	—	—	—	—	—	—	—	—	—	—	—	—
Developing countries	15	17	36	37	90661	29	15	17	28	31	34	34
Mediterranean	4	8	9	10	7537	8	2	3	7	8	9	9
Latin America	3	12	18	18	76939	14	11	12	15	17	17	17
Africa	2	2	2	2	1506	2	—	—	—	—	2	2
W. Asia	2	1	2	2	839	1	—	—	1	1	1	1
S. & S.E. Asia	4	3	5	5	3843	4	2	2	5	5	5	5
ELECTRICAL ENGINEERING												
World	39	63	231	264	154756	179	87	120	180	199	207	213
Industrial countries	11	35	89	108	58708	63	45	54	71	72	80	83
W. Europe	5	25	46	56	41775	41	28	32	43	44	44	46
Non-European	5	20	42	51	16933	22	17	22	28	28	35	36
E. Europe	1	1	1	1	—	—	—	—	—	—	1	1
Developing countries	28	46	142	156	96048	116	42	66	109	127	127	130
Mediterranean	7	27	47	52	26275	43	12	24	37	42	42	44
Latin America	9	22	59	67	43706	46	25	31	47	52	52	54
Africa	2	2	2	2	87	1	1	1	1	1	1	1
W. Asia	1	6	8	8	2883	5	1	4	7	7	8	6
S. & S.E. Asia	9	14	26	27	23097	21	3	6	17	22	24	25
PRECISION ENGINEERING & OPTICS												
World	32	84	176	192	32974	116	73	97	122	140	145	161
Industrial countries	8	46	70	73	7782	43	30	40	52	60	62	63
W. Europe	3	24	34	36	3935	25	16	22	29	33	33	34
Non-European	5	29	36	37	3847	18	14	18	23	27	29	29
E. European	—	—	—	—	—	—	—	—	—	—	—	—
Developing countries	24	61	106	119	25192	73	43	57	70	80	93	98
Mediterranean	6	32	35	45	4661	23	11	16	21	24	28	31
Latin America	10	30	46	47	8083	32	25	31	37	39	39	43
Africa	—	—	—	—	—	—	—	—	—	—	—	—
W. Asia	1	2	2	2	73	1	—	—	—	1	1	1
S. & S.E. Asia	7	21	23	25	12375	17	7	10	12	16	17	23
OTHER MANUFACTURING INDUSTRY												
World	43	90	168	176	24871	113	58	89	118	138	147	154
Industrial countries	9	45	63	66	5687	40	28	44	51	53	54	56
W. Europe	4	36	43	46	4293	30	21	35	40	39	40	40
Non-European	5	14	20	20	1394	10	7	9	11	14	14	16
E. Europe	—	—	—	—	—	—	—	—	—	—	—	—
Developing countries	34	62	105	110	19184	73	30	45	67	85	93	98
Mediterranean	8	29	33	35	3975	24	8	13	20	27	28	31
Latin America	9	19	37	40	11584	26	19	23	31	32	35	35
Africa	10	6	11	11	1300	6	3	5	6	9	9	10
W. Asia	1	5	5	5	709	2	—	1	1	4	4	4
S. & S.E. Asia	6	13	19	19	1616	15	1	4	10	14	18	19

World, industrial countries, W. Europe: excluding EEC countries
Africa: excluding Mediterranean countries

structure but also the different competitive conditions, and accordingly the different reasons why production was initially established abroad. The following cases attempt to demonstrate this point.

The *chemical industry*, which includes petro-chemicals, pharmaceuticals and rubber manufacture, has 502 subsidiaries in fifty-two countries, which is by far the highest number of subsidiaries. The industry accounts for half the number of companies with twenty or more subsidiaries, with a total of twelve (Table II-2). The chemical industry already had a not inconsiderable presence abroad at the beginning of the period under consideration here: nonetheless, the number of subsidiaries doubled in this period from 94 to 186 in the industrial countries, and 144 to 316 in the developing countries (Table II-20). Production was also increased in existing subsidiaries: employment rose from 26082 to 44921 in the 129 subsidiaries for which data was available between 1966 and 1975.

The great majority of subsidiaries in the chemical industry are involved in the final production ('formulation') of preparations with the main emphases being on human and veterinary medicaments, agricultural chemicals (pesticides, fertilisers) and cosmetics. Using chemical basic materials obtained from other sources (often imported within the combine) the preparations are mixed, put into their various forms in which they eventually appear on the market and packaged. The technology employed is relatively simple and extensively standardised. Part of the production process is labour-intensive[1] or alternatively can be performed either mechanically or manually depending on the size of the batch in question, and the level of wage costs.

However, these production conditions are not sufficient to explain why an extensively decentralised process, with production at several sites, is preferred to centralised production. As well as the moderate investments required for each individual plant, manufacture at many sites is favoured as the local production of chemical preparations is especially encouraged. In addition to the usual 'incentives', products manufactured domestically can enjoy a protected market through design copyright, testing procedures and appropriate tariff policies which keep competing products at bay and allow the setting of

1. 'Consider the pharmaceuticals sphere, in which raw materials' costs do not play a large part but where the final production is labour-intensive: in our firm the bulk of this type of production is already located abroad.' (*Wirtschaftswoche*, 6 June 1975, p. 16.)

monopoly prices. In combination with intra-company transfer pricing for pre-products this set of factors makes it possible for companies to take advantage of very substantial and lasting opportunities for profit with relatively modest expenditures in the manufacture of standard preparations. This can include export to neighbouring countries whose internal markets are too small to warrant their own production.

Such a globally widespread distribution of manufacture can also be found in the production of cleansers and detergents, cosmetics and adhesives as well as in pharmaceuticals and agricultural chemical products. This applies in the case of companies such as Beiersdorf, Henkel and Wella. Taking Beiersdorf as an example we found sixteen manufacturing subsidiaries outside the EEC with a total work-force of 2764 (1975); Beiersdorf employs 6063 people in Federal Germany and 4950 abroad (1975). Since 1973 the number of employees abroad has risen by 759, whereas at home it has fallen by 431. Most of the European subsidiaries, and those in Argentina, Chile, Mexico and Australia, were established before 1970, with, in addition to Finland, sites in Canada, USA, Guatemala and Columbia being added after 1970. The 1974 Company Report provides some information on the company's policy as far as production abroad is concerned: 'Including the sales of our licencees, total foreign business was 14% above home business. It follows from this that more than 80% of all the products sold throughout the world, outside Federal Germany, which have been manufactured according to our processes or under our trade mark are made abroad.'[1] In the first six months of 1976 total receipts from home sales rose by 10.6%, and from foreign sales by 24%.

The relocation of production exclusively in order to utilise cheap labour abroad is only gradually beginning to take on significant dimensions for wide sections of the chemical industry. Labour-intensive sections of the production process already exist abroad as a result of a policy of organising production on a global basis which has been pursued for some years. We have already referred to the industry's interest in the extraction and processing of raw materials. The large involvement of the big Federal German chemical concerns, which are among the biggest in the world, in the US chemicals industry can be explained, on the one hand, by the fact that it is

1. *Handelsblatt*, 2 September 1976.

advantageous to supply the world's largest individual market for chemical products from within[1] and, on the other, by the possibilities for technical collaboration with US concerns from which the German companies can benefit. As a result Federal German companies have established a number of joint ventures with US corporations such as Dow Chemical and Monsanto fairly early in their US involvements.

172 foreign manufacturers were noted in the *mechanical engineering industry*: 96 of them produced in the industrial countries included in the survey and 129 in the developing countries. A not inconsiderable proportion was accounted for by small and medium-sized companies. The number of subsidiaries increased by 200 from 168 in the period under study. The increase was equally strong both in the developing countries and the industrial countries (Table II-20).

There are now twenty-three developing countries with subsidiaries carrying out the generally technically advanced production undertaken by Federal German engineering firms. Part of this production developed from sales' agencies and service facilities. However, the relocation of production is being increasingly pushed ahead to take advantage of differences in wage costs. This production is oriented towards exports to a growing extent, whether it takes place in the Eastern European countries or in the developing countries. Although the share of mechanical engineering imports into Federal Germany from the developing countries is still small, it has increased sixteenfold between 1962 and 1974.[2] Furthermore a recent questionnaire reveals that almost one-third of all mechanical engineering companies see locational advantages in the developing countries for the world market production of their products.[3]

We have already referred to the case of the production of lathes in Hungary, with the simultaneous termination of their manufacture in Federal Germany. According to the Gildemeister company's own

1. The Foreign Manager of BASF expressed himself in the following terms: 'Big customers are not prepared to rely on supply from overseas.' (*Der Spiegel*, 31 May 1976.)
2. Rolf Dick, *Maschinenbau unter Wettbewerbsdruck aus Entwicklungsländern?*, Kieler Arbeitspapiere Nr. 44 (Kiel 1976), p. 3, Diagram 1.
3. 'In fact it appears as if wage differences between the industrial and the developing countries are having an increasing influence on the choice of site. Thus 58% of companies indicate – chiefly more frequently by reference to wage costs than obstacles to trade – that it is more profitable for them to manufacture products from their range abroad when these products are destined for the local market. 29% of companies also see international locational advantages in the developing countries for products from their range.' (Rolf Dick, *Maschinenbau unter Wettbewerbsdruck*, pp. 19–22.)

figures, production in Hungary is around 40% cheaper: the German employment of this firm was cut by 550 in 1976, and was to be further cut in 1977.[1]

> The Gildesmeister Group, which will continue to supply the market with its product line from Hamburg, will be having the lathes which were made there manufactured by a Hungarian cooperation partner after May 1977, so that they can once more be sold at a profit...Production is scheduled to begin in Brazil in the second half of 1977. Employment is intended to reach 800 in two years.[2]

The pressures which force companies to seek the benefits of low cost production at the new sites under the conditions of the new international division of labour are especially evident in the mechanical engineering industry. It is already being debated whether the capital-goods industry in general, and mechanical engineering in particular, can be restricted to technical development at home, and production on the basis of this development abroad ('the export of blueprints'). On the other hand, it is emphasised that advanced and further technological development cannot be made suitable for application in production unless it can be tested 'on site' in actual mass production. But even if this is the case, there still remains a large area open for the relocation of the manufacture of standard items and components. The results of our survey, and the concrete examples cited, show that this scope for relocation is exploited and how this is accomplished.

Road vehicles are the predominant product group in the foreign operations of the *vehicle building industry*. In addition to the larger manufacturing plants, such as those belonging to VW or Daimler-Benz in Brazil, there are a large number of smaller (assembly) plants. Many countries encourage local production and protect it from competing imports by high tariffs and import quotas. This is one reason why pure assembly, as well as manufacture, is undertaken abroad. Semi- and completely knocked-down (KD) vehicles can be shipped for final assembly anywhere in the world. Some of the parts are frequently already produced in the country where assembly is to take place, and the KD kits imported without these parts. If the proportion of local parts exceeds 40% of the final vehicle, the imported part ceases to count as an imported vehicle: this provides a point of transition from mere assembly to local production, which nevertheless remains dependent on the import of

1. *Handelsblatt*, 31 December 1976.

2. *Handelsblatt*, 27/28 August 1976.

Table II-21. *Foreign production of road vehicles, five companies: 1975 (excluding EEC)*

Country	Capital holding (%)	Year of start	Number of employees[a]	Assembly or manufacture	Annual output[a]	Export
BMW						
New Zealand	—	—	—	A	Cars	—
South Africa	100	1972	662	A	Cars	—
Portugal	—	—	—	A	Cars	—
Thailand	—	—	—	A	Cars	—
Daimler-Benz						
South Africa	26.7	1966	2468	M	10701 Cars 5580 CV.	—
Spain (with VW)	26.84	1955	4052	M	13584 CV. 8676 D. eng.	2342 transporters
Turkey	36	1968	1077	M	1068 Buses	—
Turkey	undecided	after 1976	—	A	CV.	—
Yugoslavia	5.9	1971	12300	M	6300 CV.	—
Argentina	100	1954	3900	M	6723 CV.	—
Brazil	100	1957	15084	M	43600 CV. 23105 D. eng.	South & Central America, USA, Africa
Peru	—	1975	—	A	CV.	—
Venezuela	—	—	—	A	Cars	—
Ghana	—	—	—	A	CV.	—
Nigeria	40	1979	—	A	(7500) CV.	—
Zambia	15 (with DEG = 25)	1978(?)	(400)	A	CV.	—
Iran	30	1969	839	M	14200 D. eng	—
Iran	—	—	—	A	600 Veh., buses	50% of buses to Arabian countries
Saudi Arabia	26	1976	(450)	A	(5000) CV.	—
India	26.2	1957	2140	M	CV.	—
India	11.5	—	—	M	25269 CV.	—
Indonesia (with VW)	33.3	1971	1213	A	2226 CV.	—
Malaysia	—	before 1973	—	A	CV.	—
Singapore	26	1971	140	A	1431 Cars (4800) CV.	—

VW (with Audi-NSU)						
Australia	100	1954	1920	A	15300 Veh. (given up 1976)	—
New Zealand	—	—	—	A	—	—
South Africa	98.7	1951	5307	M, A	49885 Veh.	—
Algeria	—	after 1976	—	A	—	—
Portugal	—	—	—	A	—	—
Spain (with Daimler-Benz)	26.84	1955	4052	M	see Daimler-Benz	see Daimler-Benz
Syria	—	after 1976	—	A	—	—
Turkey	—	—	—	A	—	—
Yugoslavia	49	1972	840	A, MP	13276 Veh.	—
Brazil	80	1951	38533	M, MP	502580 Veh.	59172 veh.; parts especially to Mexico & Fed. Germany; KD sets to Africa & Asia
Costa Rica	—	—	—	A	—	—
Mexico	100	1954	9871	M, MP	106937 Veh.	USA; parts to Brazil; export = 30%
Peru	—	—	—	A	—	—
Uruguay	—	—	—	A	—	—
Venezuela	—	1967	—	A	8000 Veh.	—
Ghana	—	—	—	A	—	—
Kenya	—	—	—	A	—	—
Nigeria	40	1975	1303	A	5873 Veh.	—
Senegal	—	—	—	A	—	—
Indonesia (with Daimler-Benz)	33.3	1971	979	A	see Daimler-Benz	—
Iraq	—	1977/78	—	A	—	to Arabian countries (planned)
Malaysia	—	—	—	A	—	—
Pakistan	—	—	—	A	—	—
Philippines	—	—	—	A – 60% local production	—	—
Singapore	—	—	—	A	—	—
Thailand	—	—	—	A	—	—

Table II-21. (*cont.*)

Country	Capital holding (%)	Year of start	Number of employees*	Assembly or manufacture	Annual output*	Export
Klockner-Humboldt-Deutz (with Magirus-Deutz)						
Japan	< 50	1963	218	M	Eng.	—
South Africa	majority	1970	330	A	Veh., eng.	—
USSR	—	after 1977	—	M	(50000) Eng.	—
Algeria	—	1974	—	M	Eng., tractors	
Greece	100	1956	221	A	Buses	—
Yugoslavia	8	1971	6489	M	CV., eng.	—
Argentina	< 50	1959	1682	M	CV., eng.	—
Zaire	100	1975	—	A	CV.	—
Iran	—	—	—	A	1200 Buses	Partial export
Gutehoffnungshütte (MAN, Büssing)						
Austria	< 50	1950	2025	M	CV.	—
Australia	94.5	1964	195	A	250–300 CV.	—
South Africa	100	1970	320	A	CV.	—
South Africa	24.5	1970	1000	A	CV.	—
Turkey	< 50	1966	780	M	CV.	—
Argentina	50	1961	350	M	D. eng.	—
Peru	—	—	—	A		—

A = assembly; CV. = commercial vehicles; D. = diesel; eng. = engines; M = manufacture; MP = manufacture of parts; veh. = vehicles
a: Planned figures in parentheses

particular parts. Production is normally carried out under licence. In addition control can be exercised through a capital holding, which may vary in size: as a rule vehicle manufacturers normally have a higher stake in their manufacturing subsidiaries than in mere assembling firms.

Table II-21 provides a picture of the production outside the EEC of road vehicles abroad by five companies from the car industry (BMW, Daimler-Benz, VW) and the commercial vehicles sector (MAN including Büssing, a constituent of Gutehoffnungshütte, and Magirus-Deutz, a constituent of Klöckner-Humboldt-Deutz). Opel and Ford–Cologne are wholly-owned subsidiaries of General Motors and Ford respectively and both are fully integrated into these companies' globally organised production. For their part Opel and Ford-Cologne have no capital holdings in companies outside of Federal Germany. Models which are built in Federal Germany within the overall framework of the parent's world-wide division of labour are assembled or finished in a number of countries (Opel: Belgium, Switzerland, Portugal, Zaire, South Africa, Iran, South Korea, Malaysia; Ford: Belgium, South Africa).[1]

The trend is towards the replacement of assembly by manufacture abroad. Whereas it has only been possible in the past to assemble technically complex products such as cars at many sites, but not to fully manufacture them, it is now becoming possible, within the context of the new international division of labour, to engage in complete manufacture. The transition from assembly to complete manufacture can take place progressively within the overall framework of the global reorganisation of production.

The further expansion of manufacturing abroad is planned, and in part already implemented. The decision by VW to construct an assembly plant in USA,[2] which was finally agreed to by the trade union representatives on the company's Supervisory Board, gave the signal. But as early as 1974 a report from Daimler-Benz stated: 'Changed competitive circumstances could lead to Daimler to revise its basic principle according to which production abroad was only contemplated if no reduction in output at home was entailed. This rethinking process will chiefly affect labour-intensive and less

1. Götz Weihmann, 'In Deutschland produziert, im Ausland montiert: Autos aus der Kiste', *ADAC-Motorwelt* 7 (1976), pp. 6–8.
2. The new plant in New Stanton was officially taken over by VW on 5 October 1976, and began production late-1977/78.

technically demanding products.'[1] It later emerged that 'Daimler-Benz intends to establish additional production facilities in the Third World, especially in countries rich in raw materials.'[2]

A report by two research institutes into the markets for the car industry recommended:

Companies should increasingly transfer self-contained labour-intensive manufacture to low wage countries and establish links with other European countries for those areas of manufacture which requires the use of skilled workers. The future prospects for the Federal Republic as a site lie more with the development of new models and methods of production than with established forms of production and assembly.[3]

This casts doubts on the value of prognoses which were derived from the extrapolation of already existing trends and which foresaw for the period 1973 to 1985 a loss of 15700 jobs to the developing countries against a gain of 39000 jobs through increased exports to the developing countries in the vehicles sector.[4] Notwithstanding these predictions, in 1974 the Western automobile industry had 551 manufacturing and assembly plants in eighty-one countries, as compared with a presence only in fifty-five in 1964.[5]

The *electrical engineering industry* is represented in thirty-nine countries outside the EEC (Table II-20). Electrical engineering companies have not only been very active abroad for some years[6] but in fact represent the industry with most operations abroad measured by the number of its employees. Employment figures could be ascertained for 179 of the 231 subsidiaries and totalled 154756 (1975): An estimate of total employment for all subsidiaries excluding EEC countries could be put at around 200000, and 250000 with the inclusion of the EEC. These figures compare with a total employment of the whole of the electrical engineering industry in

1. *Süddeutsche Zeitung*, 18 July 1974. Since then negotiations for the purchase of the commercial vehicle manufacturer Euclid Inc. in the USA by Daimler-Benz have progressed to an advanced stage. See *Süddeutsche Zeitung*, 22 October 1976.
2. *FAZ/Blick durch die Wirtschaft*, 30 October 1974.
3. *Süddeutsche Zeitung*, 10 July 1975. (Report on studies carried out by the Rheinisch-Westfälisches Institut für Wirtschaftsforschung in Essen, and the Institut für Weltwirtschaft in Kiel.)
4. Hugo Dicke, Hans H. Glissmann, Ernst-Jürgen Horn & Axel D. Neu, *Beschäftigungswirkungen einer verstärkten Arbeitsteilung zwischen der Bundesrepublik und den Entwicklungsländern*, Kieler Studien Nr. 137 (Tübingen 1976), p. 96.
5. *La division internationale du travail. Vol. I: Les tendences actuelles* (Paris 1976), p. 234.
6. According to Siemens' own statistics their total employment in 1914 was 82000; of these some 17000 worked abroad, with 16000 of this total in three countries, namely Britain, Russia and Austria.

Federal Germany (including those companies with no production abroad) of 999 200 (1975 average). Federal German electrical companies are the market leaders in many countries, especially in such areas as information technology, transformers, cables and electrical installations. Companies such as Siemens, AEG-Telefunken and Osram number among those oligopolies which operate on a world scale and which can divide up markets through effective cartel agreements.[1]

Between 1961 and 1976 the number of subsidiaries increased from 45 to 89 in the industrial countries covered by our survey, and from 42 to 142 in the developing countries (Table II-20). In this process, export-oriented production abroad has grown rapidly in significance in recent years. The industry itself differentiates between 'national factories' and 'world market factories'. 'The world market factories have gained in importance in the 1970s. In a clear division of labour with the German parent establishment they produce selected manufactures for the world market.' World market factories not only complement the traditional division of labour within a company but in fact point towards a new global division of labour: 'Every national factory can always of course eventually become a world market factory.'[2]

Federal German electrical engineering world market factories are engaged in the production of both consumer goods and intermediate products. In the first category are those plants making radios and televisions located in Austria, Portugal, Northern Ireland and Taiwan (Grundig) and Malaysia (Nordmende);[3] there are also plants which fit into this category involved in manufacturing cine-cameras, lenses and projectors in Malaysia, Taiwan and Italy (Bosch). The second category includes, in particular, the manufacture of active and passive components.[4] In addition to the larger concerns a host of smaller companies have also transferred their production to such countries as Portugal, Malta and Tunisia.

1. Cf. Kurt Rudolf Mirow, 'Nach dem Gesetze der Wölfe – Das Welt-Elektro-Kartell', *Technologie und Politik – aktuell-Magazin* 5 (Reinbek 1976), pp. 143–205.
2. Quote from a written statement of an electrical engineering concern, February 1976.
3. 'World production of smaller items is being increasingly shifted to the Far East. The site advantages and government support are so substantial that no company can remain outside this trend for very long...According to Mende, the positive aspects of Nordmende's foreign operations entail long-term dangers to jobs in Germany's home electronics industry.' (*Süddeutsche Zeitung*, 6 August 1974.)
4. The development of world market production for this product group is dealt with in detail in Part III.

Both the construction and the removal of manufacturing plant can be accomplished very rapidly in the area of production. Only short training periods are required for the workers employed, and the technical equipment is frequently quite basic. This allows a swift change of site which means that the companies involved can escape both the demands of the local work-force and governments.

As estimated above the volume of direct employment abroad in the electrical engineering industry is 250000 (1975). Those subsidiaries covered by our survey have almost doubled in number since 1966: the increase in production in existing subsidiaries should be added to this. Employment figures are known for 32 subsidiaries for the years 1966 and 1975. Employment in these subsidiaries rose from 19256 in 1966 to 34178 in 1975 – an increase of 77.5%. By contrast employment inside Federal Germany fell again in 1976[1] despite the fact that representatives of the industry assessed the developments for the industry for that year as being positive. The results which further rationalisation has brought about, with the corresponding loss of jobs, are now being expressed in terms of reduced wage costs.[2] Siemens, Federal Germany's largest employer, has shown falls in employment every year in Germany since 1971, with rising employment abroad. In the ten years between 1966 and 1975 the number of employees in Germany fell from 218000 to 207000 and rose from 39000 to 89000 abroad.[3] In 1975/76 turnover over the first eight months increased by 9%: in Germany employment fell by 6%, and abroad by 1% over the first eight months.[4] If Osram[5] is included the

1. According to official figures average domestic employment was as follows: 1973 – 1089300; 1974 – 1089800; 1975 – 999200; 1976 – 964500. (*Wirtschaft und Statistik* 5 (1977), p. 299.)
2. 'The German electrical engineering industry may grow by 7%–8% this year . . . The profit outlook has improved with an increase in plant utilisation to 84% . . . Wage costs per unit of output are even falling . . . However, imports have also risen by 28.8%.' (*Süddeutsche Zeitung*, 22 October 1976.)
3. Siemens AG, *Geschäftsbericht 1974/75*, p. 61. (Figures are for 30 September in each year.)
4. 'Growth amounted to 9% on a comparative basis: 6% for domestic business, 13% for foreign business. It is expected that turnover (including Osram) will reach DM 20.5 billion for the whole year, and exceed DM 10 billion for the first time for foreign subsidiaries. Excluding Osram the number of employees has fallen by 4%, with a stronger fall at home (−5%) than abroad (−1%).' (*FAZ*, 10 July 1976.) Up to 30 June 1976 the fall in Germany amounted to 6%, with a drop of 1% abroad: see *Süddeutsche Zeitung*, 13 August 1976.
5. On the occasion of the closing of Osram's financial year early in 1976 (1 January–30 September) because of its merger with Siemens, *Handelsblatt* spoke of a 'radical course of slimming and rejuvenation treatment' in the Osram group. In terms of the number of employees this meant the following: 9455 people are employed inside Germany, which is 6000 less than the 1973 total; the number of employees abroad was 500 less than the 1973 figure and amounted to 8500. See *Handelsblatt* 20 October 1976.

total number of Siemens' employees abroad has actually increased to 96 000.

In order to illustrate the process of structural change in the electrical engineering industry we look briefly at two examples of how the decision on future production sites was made in two companies. In 1974/75 Grundig employed 23 490 workers in Germany and 9042 abroad; this represented an increase of 327 in Germany and 1092 abroad over the preceding year.[1]

Whereas the company's plants in France produce almost exclusively for the home market, export production has reached significant proportions in the plants located in Italy, Northern Ireland and Austria, and amounts to 95% in Portugal, with Federal Germany being named as the most important importing country.[2] Radios and televisions have been produced at Braga (Portugal) since 1965, with employment building up to 2300. A new colour television factory has also now been established in Taiwan and is expected to employ 1000 workers.[3]

Robert Bosch GmbH employs the term 'regional company' to describe its foreign subsidiaries: these produce primarily for the local country or region. Accordingly the company's annual report observed: 'We have expanded the capacities of our manufacturing plants according to the needs of the respective markets.'[4] This applies to plants in Belgium, France, Sweden and the USA. The plants in Spain, by contrast, export a quarter of their production, in Italy more than a half, and one plant in Switzerland (power tools) exports 94% of its production. Although other plants, in particular those making electrical parts for vehicles, have a lower percentage exported, some of this production is exported by being fitted into vehicles which are themselves exported (Brazil, Mexico). Pure 100% export production can be found in Bosch plants in Taiwan and Malaysia, which produce lenses, view-finders and vehicles. Although Bosch's Indian subsidiary (51% stake) produces mainly for the local market, its exports are as much as 28% of output; fuel injection pumps, to take one example, are exported in large numbers to

1. Until March 1976 the fall in employment in Germany had reached 22 496 from 23 490 in the previous year. See Grundig AG, *Geschäftsbericht 1975/76*, p. 32.
2. Details from Grundig AG, *Geschäftsbericht 1974/75.*
3. *Süddeutsche Zeitung*, 22 October 1976. 'The financial year for Grundig AG, Fürth, was "excellent" and the current year will also be "exceptional". Grundig was able to increase its world turnover by 16% to DM 2.39 billion, although the industry had to put up with falls in sales for the first time ever in 1975.' (*Süddeutsche Zeitung*, 16 October 1976.)
4. Robert Bosch GmbH, *Geschäftsbericht 1975*, p. 22.

Federal Germany. Out of a total of more than 9000 workers in this plant, approximately 3000 work for export.

The number of employees in Germany itself has fallen sharply: in 1971 it was 84 166, by 1975, 70 276 (mid-year figures). During the same period the number of employees in the 'regional companies' – which means employment abroad – increased from 24 883 to 35 277.[1]

This process is even more marked in some instances in the smaller branches of industry. For example in the *footwear industry* a report dated March 1975 stated: 'Hopes for a gradual pushing back of imports have suffered a set-back in 1974. Imports rose by 13.3% to 155 million pairs, in value terms by as much as 24.9% to short just of DM 1.8 billion. This reflects an above average level of imports of high value leather shoes, which German manufacturers have in fact contributed to themselves by transferring production abroad. A number of well-known German firms now produce either through cooperation agreements or joint ventures in Iran, Brazil, Spain and Taiwan.'[2] As a consequence we read one year later: 'Despite its long process of contraction the shoe industry has confounded hopes of recovery in 1975. Employment fell by 10% to 55 600. Output fell, once more, by 8% to 107 million pairs. The number of footwear factories dropped by 41 to 511.'[3] Forecasts for the home shoe industry up to 1985, based on previous trends and data, run as follows.

> As far as the footwear industry is concerned, it can be expected that it will also be subject to an increased pressure to readjust itself because of imports from developing countries, which may endanger up to one-third of the jobs in this industry. However the effect of import-competition from the non-developing countries may be even more serious, and around 60% of all the jobs existing in 1973 can be viewed as being threatened from this source.[4]

Such prognoses are unsatisfactory *per se* inasmuch as they represent mere extrapolations of a process without reference to a specific point of time within the further development of the process.

1. Robert Bosch GmbH, *Geschäftsbericht 1972*, p. 30, and *1975*, p. 31.
2. *FAZ*, 10 March 1975. 'The import ratio now amounts to just short of 63%, which means that the domestic industry is now supplying less than 40% of the home market. The employers' federation considers that these imports consist 20% of products produced abroad by the Federal German industry itself.' (*Süddeutsche Zeitung*, 12 April 1977.)
3. *Süddeutsche Zeitung*, 26 March 1976. In 1971 the Federal German footwear industry still employed 84 000 people.
4. Dicke, Glissmann, Horn and Neu, *Beschäftigungwirkungen*, pp. 102–3.

12.2 The increase in production abroad: 1961–76

Our survey was not structured in a form which permitted an analysis of historical developments.[1] Although we requested information on the start of production in each of the foreign subsidiaries, this is not a complete enough basis for a full description of the historical development of foreign production: one reason is that this question was sometimes only partly or unreliably answered;[2] furthermore this data only relates to those subsidiaries which have been in production in the period 1961–76 outside the EEC. Production abroad prior to this period and which may have been discontinued (especially after the Second World War) is not taken into account. Table II-22 should be studied with these limitations in mind. Despite its shortcomings it makes clear that the vast majority of foreign manufacturing subsidiaries have been established within the last two decades, with a trend towards an acceleration of this tendency over this period. Of the 602 companies which now produce abroad only 86 produced abroad before 1955 with 174 subsidiaries (in comparison to the 1340 subsidiaries whose year of production commencement is known).

Table II-23 shows (on a cumulative basis) the number of subsidiaries by region and sector for 1961, 1966, 1971 and 1974. These figures should not be compared with Table II-22 as it is assumed here that where the year of commencement was not known (but which it is assumed was sometime prior to 1976 as per the conditions adopted by the survey) these subsidiaries were already in production in 1961. This assumption was made as it has a conservative impact on the hypothesis that production grew strongly during the period under consideration. Thus, if it assumed that 771 out of the 1760 subsidiaries covered were already in production in 1961, this figure includes 420 for which the year in which production started could not be ascertained, and which had either started production in or before 1961, or sometime later. It is therefore permissible to suppose that the number of subsidiaries not only doubled, as Table II-23 shows, but in fact trebled or even quadrupled. (The same

1. Some of this material is brought together in Lawrence G. Franko, *The European Multinationals* (London 1976). See in particular Chapter II, 'The origins of continental European multinational enterprises', pp. 23–44. 'Some companies in some industrial sectors did venture abroad at an early stage, though usually for special reasons other than high domestic costs or shortage of labor.' (Business International, *Germany in the Seventies* (Geneva 1973), p. 103.)
2. In some cases the year of recommencement of operations is given if production was interrupted by the war.

Table II-22. *Number of companies and subsidiaries, beginning of production, by economic sector*

	Until 1900		Until 1915		Until 1925		Until 1935		Until 1945		Until 1955		Total (1976)	
	C	S	C	S	C	S	C	S	C	S	C	S	C	S
Agric. & for.	—	—	—	—	—	—	—	—	—	—	—	—	11	13
En. & min.	—	—	—	—	1	1	1	1	1	1	2	2	11	31
Chem.	2	2	3	5	8	13	14	21	15	28	26	69	84	503
St., gl. & ceram.	1	1	1	1	1	1	3	3	3	3	4	5	22	46
Metal.	—	—	—	—	1	1	1	1	4	4	7	11	45	177
Mech. eng.	2	3	2	3	4	5	4	5	5	6	16	20	172	360
Veh.	1	1	1	1	1	1	1	1	1	1	4	8	20	48
Elec. eng.	2	3	3	6	5	8	6	9	6	13	9	25	63	231
Prec. eng. & opt.	1	1	3	3	5	5	6	8	6	9	11	19	84	175
Other	1	1	4	4	4	4	5	7	5	9	7	15	90	168
All sectors covered	10	12	17	23	30	39	41	56	46	74	86	174	602	1760

See Table II-1 for sector abbreviations
C: companies; S: subsidiaries

Table II-23. *Number of subsidiaries by economic sector region: 1961, 1966, 1971, 1974*

(a) Industrial countries (excluding EEC)

	World				Industrial countries												Total			
					W. Europe				Non-European				E. Europe							
	1961	1966	1971	1974	1961	1966	1971	1974	1961	1966	1971	1974	1961	1966	1971	1974	1961	1966	1971	1974
Agric.&for.	6	6	9	12	—	—	—	—	—	—	1	1	—	—	—	—	—	—	1	1
En. & min.	11	12	17	26	2	2	2	1	7	7	8	12	—	—	—	—	9	9	10	13
Chem.	238	302	401	467	48	54	67	71	46	56	75	96	—	—	—	—	94	110	142	167
St., gl. & ceram.	19	22	30	37	5	7	10	13	4	5	6	6	—	—	—	—	9	12	16	19
Metal.	92	112	139	163	18	21	28	33	27	35	42	50	—	—	—	—	45	56	70	83
Mech. eng.	168	214	265	311	28	38	47	50	43	51	70	86	—	—	—	1	71	89	117	137
Veh.	19	22	37	46	1	1	2	3	3	4	7	9	—	—	—	—	4	5	9	12
Elec. eng.	87	120	180	207	28	32	43	44	17	22	28	35	—	—	—	1	45	54	71	80
Prec. eng. & opt.	73	97	122	147	16	22	29	33	14	18	23	29	—	—	—	—	30	40	52	62
Other	58	89	118	147	21	35	40	40	7	9	11	14	—	—	—	—	28	44	51	54
All sectors covered	771	996	1318	1563	167	212	268	288	168	207	271	336	—	—	—	2	335	419	539	628

Table II-23. (*cont.*)

(b) Developing countries

	Mediterranean				Latin America				Africa (non-Mediterranean)				W. Asia				S. & SE. Asia				Total			
	1961	1966	1971	1974	1961	1966	1971	1974	1961	1966	1971	1974	1961	1966	1971	1974	1961	1966	1971	1974	1961	1966	1971	1974
Agric.&for.	6	6	7	9	—	—	1	1	—	—	—	—	—	—	1	1	—	—	—	—	6	6	9	11
En. & min.	—	1	2	4	1	1	4	6	2	2	4	6	—	—	—	1	—	—	—	—	3	4	8	14
Chem.	44	65	87	98	82	100	127	141	5	5	5	6	1	3	8	10	16	23	31	38	148	196	258	293
St., gl. & ceram.	7	7	9	11	2	2	3	3	—	—	—	2	—	—	—	—	1	1	2	2	10	10	14	18
Metal.	16	20	25	28	23	25	29	36	1	2	2	2	1	1	1	2	8	8	10	11	49	56	67	79
Mech. eng.	23	29	39	50	52	65	72	79	1	1	3	5	1	1	1	1	25	32	36	39	102	128	151	174
Veh.	2	3	7	9	11	12	15	17	—	—	—	2	—	—	1	1	2	2	6	6	15	17	29	35
Elec. eng.	13	25	38	42	27	32	48	52	1	1	1	1	1	4	7	8	3	6	18	24	45	68	112	127
Prec. eng. & opt.	11	16	21	28	26	30	36	37	—	—	—	—	—	—	—	1	7	10	12	16	44	56	69	82
Other	9	14	20	28	23	25	29	33	4	5	6	10	2	3	3	5	1	3	9	17	39	50	67	93
All sectors covered	131	186	255	307	247	292	364	405	14	16	19	31	6	12	22	30	63	85	124	153	461	591	784	926

See Table II-1 for sector abbreviations

systematic inaccuracy should be noted in Chapter 11 in the figures on the development of manufacture abroad in the regions and individual countries.)

Following the Second World War Federal German companies were not allowed to invest abroad until 1952: after this date they were permitted to do so if the investment 'had the effect of yielding foreign exchange both swiftly and enduringly, or saved foreign exchange.'[1] These restrictions had been dismantled by 1959, and after that date direct investments[2] abroad were encouraged.[3] However, the official statistics did not show a steep increase in direct investments abroad until the mid-1960s: 1961 – DM 3291 million; 1966 – DM 8236 million; 1971 – DM 19932 million; 1975 – DM 47048 million.[4]

1. Bundesminister für Wirtschaft, *Runderlaß Außenwirtschaft* Nr. 15, 30 January 1952. Cf. M. Holthus (ed.), *Die deutschen multinationalen Unternehmen* (Frankfurt–Main 1974), pp. 8–14.
2. Direct investments were defined as 'those capital investments which are undertaken by an investor with the intention of obtaining a direct influence over the business operations of the company in receipt of the capital or those investments which add new assets to a company in which the investor is already considerably involved.' ('Die deutschen Direktinvestitionen im Ausland', *Monatsbericht der deutschen Bundesbank* (December 1965), p. 19.)
3. We do not go any further here into the promotion and encouragement of investment abroad. Cf. on this subject Henry Krägenau, 'Entwicklung und Förderung der deutschen Direktinvestitionen', in Hans-Eckart Scharrer (ed.), *Förderung privater Investitionen* (Hamburg 1972), pp. 470–597; and Heinrich Jüttner, *Förderung und Schutz deutscher Direktinvestitionen in Entwicklungsländern* (Baden-Baden 1975).
4. In Chapter 10 we have already referred to the fact that these figures do not represent all foreign investments: however, they do give an approximate picture of development over time.

13 ❧ The economic and political determinants and consequences of increased production abroad

13.1 Remarks on the reasons for production abroad

A progressive internationalisation of production for Federal German companies can be empirically demonstrated from the above survey and study for the period from 1961 to 1976. However, this in itself does not prove whether and to what extent the production and employment which has been found to exist abroad is the expression of the conditions for the valorisation in a new phase of capitalist development, the expression of a tendency towards a new international division of labour. We maintained above that this new phase began approximately in the 1960s; the substantial increase in production abroad, the integration of new sites and the relocation of manufacturing processes which were previously reserved for domestic production are trends which emerge quite clearly from our analysis, and are strong indicators of the tendency which we claim to exist. The results of the supplementary survey showed, for example, that the share of foreign employment increased rapidly in those Federal German companies covered after the end of the 1960s, whilst employment in Germany itself virtually stagnated (Table II-7). Furthermore, the presentation of the individual regions and branches of industry (Chapters 11 and 12.1) revealed the existence of foreign manufacturing which can only be explained as the result of the exigencies imposed by the conditions of the new international division of labour.

The rapid increase in manufacturing abroad by Federal German companies is beyond dispute. However, in evaluating this phenomenon it is important to ask to what extent former imports from Federal Germany have been replaced by production abroad. There is no doubt that a number of instances can be found where production operates to replace exports: isn't this then a simple case of import-substitution of a type which we have long been acquainted with? And if so what connection has this with a new international division of labour? It would be a fundamental mistake to try to understand the current relocation of production for the substitution of former exports as being subsumed under anything *other* than the conditions of the new international division of labour. These are the same conditions which both facilitate and compel export-oriented and import-substitution production at the new sites. Both occur within the context of the constant world-wide restructuring of industrial production by transnationally operating corporations.

The dynamic of the process consists in the fact that sites at which production for the local market is commenced are, at the same time, also sites for production for export. In the terminology of a large electrical company: 'any national factory' can develop into a 'world market factory'. Although world market factories operating particular processes with a standard technology for the purpose of exporting the final or intermediate products made represent an especially clear case of the effects of the conditions of the new international division of labour, nonetheless, a number of plants engaged in foreign manufacturing for Federal German companies initially produced mainly for the local market and later turned to individual products or semi-manufacture for export using the local specific locational advantages. 'National factories' which are currently being constructed are conceived as potential 'world market factories' from the very outset. As a consequence the possibility of supplying the world market now also determines the choice of site for those factories which initially produce for the local market and which therefore replace imports (import-substitution). Since by international comparison Federal German industry exports a high share of domestic production[1] it should not appear as surprising if companies which are manufacturing at advantageous sites abroad should not attempt to replace exports from Germany with production from this new source. Nevertheless, since the export ratio of Federal German manufacturing industry has been increasing for a number of years with only minor fluctuations, a process to which the capital-goods industries have made a key contribution, then some

1. The export ratio, measured by the share of foreign sales as a proportion of total sales in the industry (where foreign sales are measured as direct sales to customers abroad and to German exporters, if this can be established) was 23.1% for the period mid-1973 to 1975 for manufacturing industry and 33.3% for the capital-goods industry. Calculated from *Statistisches Jahrbuch 1976* (Stuttgart–Mainz 1976), p. 246, Table 14.12.

explanation is needed. As the connection between foreign production and foreign trade has not been extensively analysed in this study only a few factors can be mentioned, without any assessment of their quantitative importance. The high export of capital-goods may be connected with a type of shift from one economic phase to another: the world-wide construction of manufacturing plant at new sites has led to a strong demand for capital-goods with the new sites initially taking up production in the field of pre-products and consumer goods. The production of manufacturing plant for the capital-goods industry is normally relocated later. Another factor also plays a role in the evaluation of export ratios, namely the supplying of one establishment by another within the same company which is increasing within the context of the spread of the new international division of labour. Inasmuch as these supplies cross national borders they are not differentiated from other imports or exports in official statistics.[1]

In the course of adapting to the conditions of the new international division of labour the functions (and the specific advantages) of 'national factories' combine with those of 'world market factories'. This is of particular significance inasmuch as it serves to extend the potential for the relocation of industrial production both quantitatively and qualitatively. It is not only the rapidly growing number of sites for pure export production which compete with sites in Federal Germany, but in fact *all* sites whose production is initially intended for the local market but which can be extended to produce for export. Relocation of production not only takes place in the case of manufacturing processes which are specifically allocated to export-oriented factories but also in the case of *any* kind of production which could be undertaken abroad.

The potential for relocation which is the consequence of this is, in political and economic terms, the most important product of the spread and intensification of the new international division of labour.

1. In addition to supplies within a company we should add those supplies and services from other companies abroad which are embodied in the export figures when the end-product is finally exported. A member of the Krupp Management Board stated on this subject: 'For example, increased exports of turn-key plant comprise a large amount of supplies and services which are not performed or which do not originate in Federal Germany but are purchased abroad or even executed in the country of destination with foreign labour. This means that German exports result in constantly less employment in German factories. Increasing exports with declining employment and the loss of domestic market shares have finally had their ultimate effect: less employment, more unemployed.' (*Süddeutsche Zeitung*, 20 April 1977.)

13.2 The promotion of investment abroad

For Federal German companies the promotion of increased foreign production also numbers among the conditions of the valorisation of capital in the current phase of capitalist development. A complex system of legal and fiscal instruments has been created for the direct encouragement of investment abroad[1] although we can only provide a slight indication of their quantitative impact here. The most important instruments are summarised below.

The Federal German government guarantees capital equipment and profits against 'political risks' (expropriation, wars, revolution/civil disturbances, freezing of payments, moratoria, impossibility of conversion or repatriation of assets). Treuarbeit AG and Hermes Kreditversicherung AG are the competent bodies acting on behalf of the Federal German government. The investor is responsible for 5 % of any eventual damages or losses incurred and pays 0.5 % of the sum insured as a premium.

Private investors abroad can obtain finance from a number of quasi-official sources. The DEG states its preconditions for the provision of finance for investment as 'entrepreneurial involvement of a German productive establishment, collaboration between undertakings with a German partner, satisfactory profitability, positive contribution to the development of the country'.[2] The Kreditanstalt für Wiederaufbau (Bank for Reconstruction and Development) is empowered to grant establishment loans from the European Recovery Program at advantageous conditions.[3] The Kreditanstalt also provides loans – as the DEG – to national and regional development banks which Federal German companies can also resort to.[4] (For example, one capital aid agreement states: 'In the use of this sum

1. See Horst Goltz, *Förderung privater Kapitalanlagen (Direktinvestitionen) in Entwicklungsländern* (Cologne 1975); Henry Krägenau, 'Entwicklung und Förderung der deutschen Direktinvestitionen', in Scharrer (ed.), *Förderung privater Direktinvestitionen* (Hamburg 1972), pp. 470–597.
2. From a DEG notice (June 1976). In 1975 the loaned or committed resources of the DEG (DM 313.5 million) were composed of 78 % of their own funds and 22 % of trustee funds. The authorised capital of the DEG was increased to DM 600 million in 1976. See DEG, *Geschäftsbericht 1975*, p. 15. The DEG is dealt with in detail in Chapter 8.4 where we make clear what 'a positive contribution to the development of a country' really means.
3. 'Within the framework of the European Recovery Program economic plan, between DM 20 and 25 million are annually granted for the promotion of investment and settlement of German companies in developing countries.' (Goltz, *Förderung privater Kapitalanlagen*, p. 119.)
4. See Goltz, pp. 271–7, for a detailed survey.

the requirements of companies established in Pakistan with German capital holdings will be treated with goodwill.')[1] Funds are available for investment in those countries with EEC associate status from the European Investment Bank in Luxembourg. Finally we should also note the World Bank and the International Finance Corporation (IFC) in Washington. The statutes of the IFC state that the organisation promotes 'the establishment or expansion of private profitable industrial concerns in member-states by the granting of loans and the assumption of share-holdings'.[2]

There are also a large number of fiscal instruments for the encouragement of investment abroad. Double taxation agreements have been concluded with a number of countries[3] which are intended to prevent the double taxation of profits, but which in practice lead to lower average levels of taxation. The Developing Countries Tax Act is of some significance: according to this law, which superseded the Development Aid Tax Act on 1 January 1974 after a long debate on the definition of tax-privileged investments abroad, 100% of the capital investment in the group of especially backward developing countries[4] and 40% in the other developing countries, can be deducted from taxable profits as a reserve which can be released after the sixth year at an annual rate of one-sixth (one-twelfth in the case of labour-intensive manufacture) to increase profits. The estimated reduction in tax receipts amounted to DM 208 million in 1976, rising to DM 294 million in 1978.

Additional instruments for the promotion of such investments are international agreements relating to the encouragement of investments and the mutual safeguarding of investments:[5] projects for technical assistance for infrastructural improvements, particularly in the field of transport and communications; a variety of opportunities (mostly free) for information on investment conditions, up to the

1. Goltz, p. 117.
2. Quoted from Goltz, p. 94.
3. Up until 1975 double taxation agreements were in force with seventeen countries, with another twenty-three planned. See Goltz, pp. 280–90.
4. According to the law Group 1 (least developed countries) includes the following: Ethiopia, Afghanistan, Bangla Desh, Bhutan, Botswana, Burundi, Dahomey, Guinea, Haiti, Yemen (Arab Republic), Yemen (Democratic Republic), Laos, Lesotho, Malawi, Maldives, Mali, Nepal, Niger, Upper Volta, Ruanda, Sikkim, Somalia, Sudan, Tanzania, Chad, Uganda, West Samoa.
5. Up until 1975 thirty-six such agreements were in force with a further nine signed. See Goltz, pp. 288–90.

minutest detailed investment advice and consultancy;[1] grants and aid in the training of German and local workers.[2]

The majority of these special measures only apply to the developing countries, which usually embraces the non-EEC Mediterranean countries.

The following extracts show how employers' organisations and individual companies seek to present production abroad, often in collaboration with economic research institutes.

Mastering structural change, preferably well in advance, is the real function of the entrepreneur in a free market system, especially if he is in full agreement with the system and wishes to see it preserved . . . When looked at from this perspective, many of the contradictions of capitalism are in reality the contradictions of an economic policy which obstructs those changes urged by the free market, instead of facilitating and encouraging these changes . . . If businessmen are one day no longer prepared to take on market risks then nothing would be lost by replacing them by bureaucrats and their companies would be ripe for socialisation.[3]

Precisely which structural change is being referred to here is expanded on below.

One way out, which would assist companies at home and also the developing countries, would be the relocation of particularly labour-intensive parts of the production process to locations where wages are so low that the increase in transport costs is of no importance. One could also transfer the entire production but leave research and development, and the marketing organisation here.[4]

In a publication by an employers' organisation we find the following concluding passage, to which dozens of similar passages could be added:

Direct investment in low wage countries encourages the necessary concentration of the resources of the German economy in those sectors of the economy with a higher level of technological and entrepreneurial demands.[5]

1. The DEG, the Statistisches Bundesamt and the Bundestelle für Außenhandelsinformation are among the most important sources of information.
2. 'Grants for training:

   apprentices or unskilled workers in developing countries: Under certain conditions payment will be made up to the value of DM 250 per person per month for training costs (re-evaluation of this sum in progress: likely increase in these rates).

   trainees in Germany: training up to managerial and skilled positions. Under certain conditions assumption of travelling costs, costs of language tuition, maintenance grant.'

   In addition 'technical aid' creates the infrastructural preconditions for the valorisation of capital at many locations, which we have merely brushed on here.
3. Herbert Giersch, 'Wandel unserer Wirtschaftsstruktur im Zuge weltwirtschaftlicher Veränderungen', *Deutscher Industrie- und Handelstag, Standortvorteil Ausland* (Bonn 1973), pp. 14–24.
4. Giersch, p. 16.
5. Willy Kisselmann, *Errichtung von Fertigungsstätten in Niedriglohnländern* (Cologne 1975), p. 7.

Many companies have experienced creeping socialisation in their plants for a number of years and fear further developments in this direction – even if in homeopathic doses – until the company falls completely under the domination of the socialising cadres.[1]

Similar threats to relocate production are made at numerous points.

The trade unions too cannot run away from asking their members the question: Would you rather have a secure job, or would you rather earn more now and go on the dole tomorrow? I fear that we will have to take leave of many of our most cherished customs in the very near future. One of these is that the overwhelming majority of employees have been able to enjoy real increases in their standard of living year after year... What we need is the consensus of all those involved – government, trade unions and firms – on the economic benefits of overseas involvements by firms... In the long run we can only retain highly sophisticated technology in the Federal Republic, that is, the manufacture of products with a high technology content. Simple mass production will become unprofitable here as wage costs are becoming too high. Everything under this threshold will have to be transferred abroad.[2]

Up until the recession which set in 1974 the argument as to the relation between wage cost differences and production abroad was quite gladly played down in public statements, and the pressure to secure markets abroad was given prime place. In a public hearing before the Federal German Parliamentary Committee for Economic Cooperation the Arbeitsgemeinschaft Entwicklungsländer (Study Group on Developing Countries) of the leading employers' organisations stated as late as November 1974: 'The motive to use lower production costs, especially lower wage costs, has played a subordinate role in the policy of German companies up to now.'[3]

But only one month later an internal organisational publication stated: 'The most notable incentive for relocation is the difference in wage costs compared with Federal Germany. Very large wage differences of in the order of 12:1 in the case of unskilled labour exist in the developing and low wage countries when compared with the Federal Republic.'[4]

1. Kisselmann, p. 6.
2. From a statement of the then Chairman of the Management Board of Gutehoffnunghütte AG, von Menges, quoted in *Der Spiegel*, 11 February 1974, pp. 47–8.
3. Ausschuß für wirtschaftliche Zusammenarbeit, Stenografisches Protokoll der 31 und 32 Sitzung am 11 und 12 November 1974, p. 196.
4. Kisselmann, *Errichtung von Fertigungsstätten*, p. 8. By contrast the result of a more recent study gives rise to the impression that 'securing of sales through greater proximity to the market' is the 'main reason for investment abroad': 'Approximately 30% of firms expressed this view.' This result is by no means so surprising since it clearly does not simply

The significance of this 'incentive' had naturally already been accurately perceived. At the beginning of 1974 the President of the Deutsche Industrie- und Handelstag was unambiguous in his assessment of this factor:

The enormous increase in wage costs together with the rise in the cost of imports is leading to a situation in which some types of industrial production will no longer be feasible in the highly industrialised countries, and hence no longer in Federal Germany. . . A long process will get under way in which the international division of labour will adapt to these changed circumstances. For us this implies specialisation in highly skilled, technically perfected production on the one hand, and on the other, the relocation of production which requires less skilled labour to countries with a lower level of wages.[1]

The attitude of the national trade unions and their international confederations towards the new world determination of industrial sites would require a separate presentation which is not offered here.[2]

13.3 The movement of jobs from Federal Germany

In the face of the serious and chronic levels of unemployment in the traditional industrial countries[3] public discussion is increasingly turning towards the question as to the extent to which investment

relate to investment in manufacturing companies but also includes trading concerns. See H. Baumann, 'Direktinvestitionen der Industrie im Ausland', in *Ifo-Schnelldienst* 3 (1977), pp. 5–9.

1. Otto Wolff von Amerongen, beginning of 1974 at the Hannover Industrie- und Handelskammer, quoted in Peter G. Rogge, 'Geänderte Standortqualitäten der Bundesrepublik Deutschland im internationalen Wettbewerb' (Basle 1974), mimeo, pp. 16–7. Cf. also Bundesverband der deutschen Industrie, *Zur Gestaltung der wirtschaftlichen Beziehung zwischen Industrie- und Entwicklungsländern* (Cologne 1976).
2. In place of undertaking such a study here we refer to a number of works, which in turn also provide numerous references to the relevant literature. 'Zur Internationalisierung der westdeutschen Wirtschaft', *WSI-Mitteilungen* 4 (1976), pp. 230–34; Ernst Piehl, *Multinationale Konzerne und internationale Gewerkschaftsbewegung* (Frankfurt–Main 1974); Kurt P. Tudyka (ed.), *Multinationale Konzerne und Gewerkschaftsstrategie* (Hamburg 1974); Gerhard Leminsky & Bernd Otto (eds.), *Gewerkschaften und Entwicklungspolitik* (Cologne 1975); Eckart Hildebrandt, Werner Olle & Wolfgang Schoeller, 'National unterschiedliche Produktionsbedingungen als Schranke einer gewerkschaftlichen Internationalisierung', *Prokla* 24 (1976), pp. 27–57.
3. This should not simply be taken to mean officially recorded unemployment. In addition to short-time working there is also the export of unemployment by the reduction in the number of foreign workers; people, mainly women, who have no change of finding a job but cannot claim unemployment benefit or social security; young people forced to stay on at school because there are no training places available; pensioners who are forced into early retirement. 'What is noticeable is the reduction in the employment of foreign workers between 1973 and the end of 1975 – down by 25% or 662400 to 1932600.' (*Süddeutsche Zeitung*, 17 September 1976.)

abroad, and consequently production abroad, are leading to the destruction of jobs at home. We cannot deal in detail with the link between production abroad and the development of the domestic labour market in the context of this analysis. We have already presented results in Part I for this phenomenon in the textile and garment industry. Below are the results of a survey of the rest of manufacturing industry, which could function as the basis of a more extensive analysis.

The extent of employment abroad has previously been underestimated, one reason being that insufficient attention was paid to small and medium-sized firms. According to an estimate made by the HWWA, employment abroad in manufacturing industry amounted to some 600000 in 1971 or 7.1% of domestic employment in Federal Germany;[1] in contrast, our results yield a figure of 1500000[2] for 1975/76, which is equal to more than 20% of domestic employment in manufacturing.[3] (If one assumes an annual rate of growth of 10% for employment abroad than the figure would have been 1000000 in 1971 on this basis.)

We now turn to the results of our supplementary survey (see Tables II-6 and II-7). The following figures were obtained for 149 of the 602 firms covered for 1974: the share of employees abroad was 22.2%[4] rising to 35.2% if foreign workers working in Germany are included. It was possible to trace the development between 1961 and 1974 for 87 firms out of this 149: the share of employment abroad was as follows: 1961 – 7.9%; 1966 – 11.5%; 1971 – 19.5%; 1974 – 26.3%. The share of foreign employees was: 1961 – 10.7%; 1966 – 18.9%; 1971 – 31%; 1974 – 39.4%. Between 1961 and 1974 the number of workers employed abroad increased by 505% whereas the employment of Germans in Germany increased by 24%. These figures are a clear indication of the fact that employment abroad by Federal German companies first became of real quantitative importance at the end of the 1960s.

1. M. Holthus (ed.), *Die deutschen multinationalen Unternehmen* (Frankfurt–Main 1974), p. 146, Table 36.
2. Our own estimate (cf. Chapter 10) from which agriculture, forestry, mining, energy and construction have been excluded for comparability.
3. In an official publication from August 1975 the foreign employment of US manufacturing industry was put at 3293000 for 1970, or 17.1% of home employment. See US Senate: Committee on Foreign Relations, *Direct Investment Abroad and the Multinationals' Effects on the United States Economy* (Washington 1975), p. 14, Table 2–4c.
4. A survey carried out by the IfO-Institut für Wirtschaftsforschung which covered around one-fifth of industry came to the following results: Measured in relation to numbers

The number of persons employed in Federal German manufacturing industry increased from 7 608 000 in 1967 to 8 115 000 in 1973, and then fell back to 7 816 000 (1974), 7 246 000 (1975) and 7 192 000 (1976) (third quarterly seasonally adjusted figures).[1] There were therefore a million fewer jobs in manufacturing industry in Germany in 1976 than in 1973. Figures for 1976 for a number of companies reveal rising turnover and profits, with still declining employment in Germany.[2] Whereas investment has been made abroad for the purpose of expansion, investment in Germany itself has been for replacement and rationalisation which, with a constant or even growing capacity leads to a reduction in the number of jobs available.[3]

Falling or stagnating employment in Federal Germany, and rising employment abroad have characterised developments in many

employed in Federal Germany the number of employees in foreign subsidiaries rose from 12.3 % (1965) to 28.1 % (1975).' (H. Baumann, *Direkinvestititionen*, p. 6.) Our figures drawn from our own supplementary survey which also covered around one-fifth of all manufacturing industry yielded a percentage of 28.3 % for 1974: see Table II-6.

1. Figures from the Deutsches Institut für Wirtschaftsforschung and from data from the Statistisches Bundesamt. The figure for the third quarter of 1976 is higher than that for the first quarter for the first time since the third quarter of 1973 – by 0.2 % (14 000). See Arthur Bonaß, 'Erstmals wieder leichte Zunahme der Beschäftigenzahl in der verarbeitenden Industrie', *DIW Wochenbericht* 49 (1976), pp. 455–7.
2. Proof of this development can be found in the case of the three chemical concerns BASF, Bayer and Hoechst. At BASF turnover increased by 19.4 % in the first six months of 1976, with pre-tax profits up by 117 %, and a fall in employment of 2.2 % (*BASF Presseinformation*, August 1976). At Bayer, turnover over the same period increased by 24 %, pre-tax profits by 102.7 % and the number of employees fell by almost 1000 to 63 370 (*FAZ*, 2 September 1976). Hoechst also announced impressive increases in turnover and profits, with a fall in employment of 1888 to 88 320 (*Süddeutsche Zeitung*, 29 September 1976).
3. In individual companies domestic production capacity has been even drastically cut back in some cases. We cite two typical examples here: 'In order to reduce surplus structural capacity in certain mass production processes AEG-Telefunken Berlin/Frankfurt wishes to shut down three plants by 1977. 1150 employees will have to be made redundant. As Cipa stressed, the decision to make these shut-downs was forced on the company by the world surplus capacity in these product groups.' (*Süddeutsche Zeitung*, 22 October 1976.) On the total work-force of the undertaking: 'Whereas total employment abroad rose by 800 it fell by 1000 at home.' (*Süddeutsche Zeitung*, 18 February 1977.) A report on SKF Kugellagerfabriken, Schweinfurt, stated: 'The work-force fell from 10 000 to just under 7000 within the last three years. The work-force at Schweinfurt clearly feels itself to be the victim of a system which is oriented towards the optimal distribution of manufacturing within the multinational SKF concern. This system was introduced under the maxim that no production losses would occur in any one area of operation, but this intention could not be adhered to given the developments in the business cycle and the tough competition prevailing on the roller bearing market.' (*FAZ*, 19 October 1976.) 'A further reduction of personnel from the present level of 6700 at the Schweinfurt plant of SKF is necessary when seen against the background of the structural and the cyclical problems in the bearing industry.' (*Süddeutsche Zeitung*, 13 October 1976.)

companies for a number of years, especially the large combines.[1] This development is often obscured in the case of such combines as they constantly expand by taking over other firms which is only then noticed in spectacular cases, and only shows up in the figures for one or two years until the consequences of the merger are fully worked out.[2]

The reduction in employment at home combined with increased employment abroad can also be seen in the results of the IfO-Institut survey 'Prognose 100' carried out in November/December 1976, in which 297 mostly large companies participated.

In view of the unutilised capacity (utilisation stood at 81.2% in the IfO economic study, seasonally adjusted in January 1977 in contrast to a norm of 88%) and an increase in output by firms of the order of 5%, manufacturing industry has no room for increasing employment (−0.5%)...

No increases in employment are envisaged for 1978 either: as in 1977 the anticipated modest rise in output will be attainable simply out of productivity increases...

Manufacturing industry is planning an annual average reduction in employment of 0.3% between 1976 and 1981. It should be noted that the first year's employment was already low because of the recession...

Having got over the world recession industry seems to be expanding its operations abroad. The number of firms wishing to expand more abroad than at home has increased since the last survey.

The fact that Federal German industrial involvement in manufacturing facilities abroad is passing through an expansive phase can be seen not only in real turnover forecasts but also employment plans. According to the plans of those companies which participated in 'Prognose 100' the number of employees abroad will increase more rapidly than in Germany both for the total of respondents and for the main industrial groups. A slight acceleration in the pace of this process can also be

1.

	Workers in Federal Germany by thousands					Workers abroad by thousands				
	1971	1973	1974	1975	1976	1971	1973	1974	1975	1976
AEG-Telefunken	146	150	144	133	132	21	25	26	29	30
BASF	78	87	89	89	89	15	21	22	23	24
Bosch	90	82	79	70	72	25	31	35	35	34
Daimler-Benz	127	134	130	129	133	20	22	25	27	28
Hoechst	97	105	107	105	104	45	52	72	77	79
Mannesmann[a]	73	91	91	85	84	12	19	21	23	25
Siemens[b]	234	222	221	207	208	72	81	88	89	96
Volkswagenwerk	160	161	142	118	124	42	54	62	59	59

a: As of 1973 with Demag. b: As of 1976 with Osram.

2. Such as Mannemann's take-over of Demag, Siemens' of Osram, AEG's of Hartmann & Braun and Bayer's of Metzeler.

discerned as compared with the previous year, when it should be remembered that the starting level was low because of the world-wide recession.[1]

The President of the Federal Confederation of German Industry was in full agreement with this assessment when he stated in September 1976 that German industrial investment abroad will have doubled within a decade.[2]

The figures which we have obtained and the additional information cited allow the building up of an overall picture of the development of employment of Federal German manufacturing industry at home and abroad over time: looked at as a whole there was a sharp drop at home and a marked increase abroad. However, this does not allow us to deduce the extent to which employment abroad has replaced employment in Germany. Although in 1975/76 we can observe the 1.5 million workers abroad in relation to the less than 7.5 million in Germany it is impossible to say with any confidence how large the latter figure would be if the former had been smaller. The question as to whether and to what extent jobs have been 'exported' through manufacturing abroad has taken on the status of much more than an academic discussion in the USA. The relocation of domestic production and the associated export of jobs has been particularly criticised by the trade unions and has also been the subject of congressional hearings, investigations and debates.[3] Nevertheless no effective limitation and control has been placed on manufacture abroad.

In addition one cannot overlook the methodological difficulties which lie in the way of providing an unobjectionable quantitative determination of the link between production abroad and the development of the domestic labour market. Although the evidence for the shift of jobs is presented in the form of national, and hence partial, employment statistics the existence of a world market for

1. Shalom Apeloig, 'Industrie rechnet mit Fortsetzung des gedämpften Konjunkturaufschwungs', *IfO-Schnelldienst* 10 (1977). 'Corporate investment in Germany today is directed toward rationalisation and reduction in work costs rather than toward job foundation.' (*Business International*, 3 September 1976, p. 284.)
2. From a statement issued by the Vereinigte Wirtschaftsdienste, 13 September 1976.
3. The trade unions have claimed that 900 000 jobs have been lost by US production abroad: on the other hand management claims that an additional 500 000 domestic jobs have been created by the overseas operations of multinational concerns. 'The middle ground between the two extremes leaves the analysis undefined in the sense that the results go from negative – job destruction – to positive, indicating job creation...a situation in which no reliable estimates can be derived.' (Roberto Marchesini, *Impact of Multinational Corporations on Domestic Employment* (Ann Arbor 1976), p. 110.)

labour and the current level of integration of capital as it expands on a world-wide basis means that one cannot in theory determine the particular employment effect for one individual country.

The partial empirical evidence cited includes, first of all, data on the development of employment at home and abroad. In addition we should include statements from companies indicating their plans to expand production capacity abroad whilst investing in rationalisation and reducing jobs domestically (see Chapter 6.3). It should also be noted that the product structure of imports has fundamentally changed. In value terms the share of Federal German imports accounted for by manufactures has risen from 44.2% in 1960 to 61.7% in 1975, despite the substantial increases in the prices of imported raw materials. By volume the import of manufactured goods from outside the EEC has increased by 61%, that of raw materials has fallen by 5% between 1970 and 1975.[1] The change in the structure of imports from the non-European developing countries corresponds to this. In 1966 the products of the group of miscellaneous manufacturing industry (e.g. wood and metal articles, textiles, leather) accounted for 23.3% of Federal German imports; by 1975 this figure had risen to 32.6%.[2]

These empirical indicators of a substitution of production at home by production abroad can also be supplemented by a consideration of a theoretical nature. The world market for sites for industrial production as it has been created tends to abolish the distinction between domestic and foreign production (and hence between domestic and foreign employment) for those companies which operate on a transnational basis. The former chairman of the Management Board of the largest Federal German domestic and foreign company in terms of employment stated:

> Without doubt the most crucial precondition for the genesis, existence and growth of a multinational company is *that it thinks multinationally*. What does this mean? In the first instance that the cultivation and development of the world market is its primary corporate goal, and that this becomes the guiding thread of its operations, with all the conceptual and actual implications which this entails. But primarily that the multinational corporation is aware of the fundamental balance which has to exist between the different markets in which it operates.[3]

1. Figures calculated or taken from *Statistisches Jahrbuch 1976*, Tables 17.2 and 17.3.
2. DIW, *Industrielle Fertigwaren aus Übersee* (1976), in *DIW Wochenbericht* 34 (1976), p. 313, Table 3.
3. Gerd Tacke, 'Wesen und Aufgabe der multinationalen Unternehmen'. (Lecture given to the Bavarian Banking Foundation, Munich 1972, mimeo, pp. 13–14.)

National markets can only be correctly understood as submarkets integrated into a coherent world market. This applies both for the markets for goods and capital and for the markets for industrial sites and labour-power. The empirical data which has been collected and put together therefore expresses the conditions for the valorisation of capital on the world market, and the changes in these conditions, which underlie the observable processes.

13.4 Outlook for the development of production abroad

The present study attempts to extend the knowledge of the existing extent and form of the internationalisation of industrial production taking as an example companies from Federal Germany. The question then naturally follows on from this as to what might be conjectured as far as future developments of this phenomenon are concerned.

We stated at the outset that the internationalisation of production is without exception an expression of the current phase of the world-wide development of the conditions of the valorisation of capital. We showed that it was not only large companies which transferred production abroad; nor only companies in a few branches with labour-intensive processes. On the contrary, a substantial and so far neglected part of manufacture abroad is accounted for by small and medium-sized companies mostly from the chemicals, electrical engineering, mechanical engineering and vehicle building industries. Looked from the perspective of Federal Germany's industrial structure it is not simply marginal but central sectors which are affected. No longer is it simply a question of sport-shoes, fashion jewellery, toys, spectacles and cameras; we now find such products as electrical equipment, cars, machine tools and pharmaceuticals manufactured at sites distributed throughout the world. We also revealed that the relocated processes cannot always be designated as being labour-intensive. Both relatively labour-intensive and relatively capital-intensive manufacturing processes are relocated if production costs at the new sites are lower, which is a function of general working conditions and not merely wage costs. In short: the condition for the maintenance of a firm's competitiveness is the discovery and utilisation of the most favourable production sites on a world-wide basis.

The expression 'relocation of production' is seen far too narrowly when it is simply understood as meaning the replacement of domestic production for the Federal German home market. It is much more a question of production for the whole world market which frequently means, as far as Federal German companies are concerned, the replacement of former export production in Germany by production abroad. In addition to the relocation of production for the home market we also therefore see the relocation of former export production *and* the replacement of goods formerly made in Germany by German companies by goods now made abroad by non-German companies. These individual processes and their mutual interaction added together constitute the overall process of the world-wide structural change in industrial production.

How will production abroad by Federal German companies develop in the future? Those companies which already produce abroad will extend their activities. This applies both for expansion at sites where production is already under way and for new production at new sites. Corporate policy will tend towards investment in production capacity abroad with the aim of expansion, and simultaneous investment in rationalisation schemes at home: that is, a further increase in employment abroad, and a further contraction in employment at home.

The further spread and intensification of the new international division of labour will be bound up with more shifts in production. The compulsion to undertake such relocations will persist as long as the conditions of the new international division of labour determine the global process of the valorisation of capital. This development will only be put into reverse if these conditions undergo a decisive change, which would be tantamount to putting into question the prevailing world capitalist mode of production. However, the processes which could contribute to such a change may themselves be the creation of the economic, social and political consequences of the new international division of labour.

Part III

The world market oriented industrialisation of the developing countries: free production zones and world market factories

Introduction

The aim of this case study is to examine free production zones and world market factories in Asia, Africa and Latin America. Free production zones and world market factories represent a new element in the international division of labour, being production sites for the *industrial* utilisation of the labour-forces of the developing countries for the purpose of world market oriented production. The industrial utilisation of the labour-forces of the underdeveloped countries for world market oriented production takes place in world market factories. The factory of the free production zone is the world market factory.

The world-wide tendency towards the industrialisation of the underdeveloped countries is one partial process within the structural tendency towards a new international division of labour. The aim of this case study is, firstly, to present empirical material which has been systematically collected on the process, chiefly taking the example of the free production zones in order to show how the tendency towards a new international division of labour is revealing itself as a partial process of industrialisation in the developing countries – namely, as world market oriented industrialisation. Secondly we intend to show that the actual development of the world market for production sites intensifies the tendency towards a new international division of labour by means of the supply of new sites onto the world market, and through the competition between these sites. Thirdly we examine in detail the conditions for investment and working conditions in the free production zones. This analysis will show very clearly to what the extent the specific conditions at these sites, such as low wages, long working hours, high intensity of work, short duration of employment, ban on organisation into unions etc., affect workers throughout the world. Fourthly we analyse some of the effects which the process of world market oriented industrialisation under consideration has on the socio-economic development of the developing countries. We put forward the thesis here that this specific type of industrialisation, which is determined and directed by the interests and logic of the valorisation of capital, serves to intensify the tendency towards the uneven and dependent development of the underdeveloped countries of Asia, Africa and Latin America.

The restriction of the empirical study predominantly to the free production zones is based both on methodological arguments and the practical exigencies of undertaking the required empirical research. The process of the world market oriented industrialisation of the underdeveloped countries as determined by the rationality of the valorisation of capital is found in its ideal-typical form, or to put it more concretely, in its most undisguised and brutal expression, in the free production zones. In terms of the actual research process itself the restriction is justified on the grounds that the necessary statistical material on the process under investigation was at least accessible for the free production zones and could therefore be subjected to analysis. The study was also expanded to include, where comparable, empirical material on world market factories at other sites (outside the boundaries of the free production zones).

The analysis of working conditions in the free production zones and world market factories is an integral part of this study. Changes in the international division of labour are first and foremost regional and occupational movements in the employment of workers. These changes and their effects on the living conditions of working people throughout the world are the principal focus of this study.

Although this study cites and interprets evidence for the thesis that a tendential change in the international division of labour is under way insofar as this change can be observed in the industrialisation of the underdeveloped countries, the statistical material does not provide details of change through time, and is mainly derived from and applicable to 1975. For the majority of the underdeveloped countries in Asia, Africa and Latin America, manufacturing industry producing for the world market simply did not exist in the mid-1960s.

Table III-1. *Countries included in the investigation*

Asia and Pacific	Africa	Latin America
Afghanistan	Algeria	Argentina
Bahrain	Angola	Barbados
Bangla Desh	Benin	Bolivia
Burma	Botswana	Brazil
Fiji	Burundi	Chile
Hong Kong	Cameroon	Colombia
India	Central African Rep.	Costa Rica
Indonesia	Chad	Dominican Rep.
Iran	Congo, Dem. Rep.	Dutch Antilles
Iraq	Egypt	Ecuador
Jordan	Equatorial Guinea	El Salvador
Kuwait	Ethiopia	Guatemala
Lebanon	Gabon	Guayana
Malaysia	Gambia	Haiti
Maldives	Ghana	Honduras
Nepal	Guinea-Bissau	Jamaica
Oman	Ivory Coast	Mexico
Pakistan	Kenya	Nicaragua
Papua New Guinea	Lesotho	Panama
Philippines	Liberia	Paraguay
Qatar	Libya	Peru
Saudi Arabia	Madagascar	Puerto Rico
Singapore	Malawi	St Lucia
South Korea	Mali	Trinidad and Tobago
Sria Lanka	Mauritania	Uruguay
Syria	Mauritius	Venezuela
Taiwan	Mozambique	
Thailand	Morocco	
Turkey	Niger	
Un. Arab Emirates	Nigeria	
Western Samoa	Rwanda	
Yemen	Senegal	
Yemen, Dem.	Sierra Leone	
	Somalia	
	South Africa	
	Sudan	
	Swaziland	
	Tanzania	
	Togo	
	Tunisia	
	Uganda	
	Upper Volta	
	Zaire	
	Zambia	

The data for 1975 is therefore an expression both of the stage of development reached by that date and the progress of the development, measured against the base-level of zero of a few years previously.

This investigation is based on information from 103 countries: 33 in Asia (including the Pacific region), 44 in Africa and 26 in Latin

America (including the Caribbean area). The statistical material originates mostly from the following sources:

(1) Material/information from Ministries, Chambers of Trade and Commerce and embassies in the countries named in the list of countries.
(2) Information from the administrations of the free production zones, and planning and development authorities in numerous countries.
(3) Information from companies in the free production zones (especially Malaysia).
(4) National reports by the statistical offices of a large number of countries, in particular the German Statistisches Bundesamt, the Bundestelle für Außenhandelsinformation and the US Department of Commerce.
(5) National surveys, miscellaneous analyses and statistics from the UN Secretariat, the UNCTAD Secretariat, UNIDO, the International Labour Office (ILO), the UN Economic Commissions for Asia and the Pacific Region, Africa, Latin America and Europe, the Secretariat of the European Community (EEC), GATT (General Agreement on Trade and Tariffs), the OECD and the World Bank.
(6) Reports, analyses and statistics from the business press, in particular *Handelsblatt, Nachrichten für Außenhandel, Financial Times, The Times, Le Monde Diplomatique, Africa, African Development, Far Eastern Economic Review, Business International, Business Asia, Business Latin America, Business Europe, Latin America, Latin American Economic Report.*

14 ❧ Free production zones in Asia, Africa and Latin America: a survey

14.1 The new production sites: free production zones

World market oriented production cannot be undertaken at every location in the developing countries where there happens to be an unemployed work-force. Profitable industrial production for the world market requires an adequate provision of industrial inputs and a sophisticated infrastructure as well as a labour-force. These factors are not necessarily available at those sites where there is an abundant supply of unemployed labour. In addition, profitable industrial production for the world market in the developing countries requires the lifting of the national restrictions on international transfers which exist in most developing countries as a result of their chronic balance of payments deficits. In fact, it is the function of free production zones to fulfil the requirements for profitable world market oriented industrial production in those places in the developing countries where unemployed labour is available and suitable for industrial utilisation.

The surveys, feasibility studies and promotional literature of UNIDO (United Nations Industrial Development Organisation) provide a clear picture of the technical, organisational and legal provision of the free production zones in the developing countries. The promotion of free production zones and assistance in their planning and construction has become one of UNIDO's major activities, within the overall framework of their programme for the promotion of export-oriented industries in the developing countries. The concept of the free production zone, as promoted by UNIDO, and in the form in which it has found world-wide application largely because of the efforts of UNIDO,[1] is outlined in their basic

1. UNIDO, *Industrial Free Zones as Incentives to Promote Export-Oriented Industries*. Training Workshop on Industrial Free Zones, ID/WG 112/3 (28 October 1971).

document *Industrial Free Zones as Incentives to Promote Export-Oriented Industries.*

Disregarding those sections of the document which preach the possible benefits of free production zones for the developing countries (see Chapter 17) it is clear that UNIDO conceives of free production zones from the perspective of their function in the valorisation process of capital. The selection of sites and the establishment of free production zones, their provision with equipment and infrastructure, the removal of trade and currency restrictions and the granting of investment incentives are all justified, derived and advocated from the point of view of the interests of private companies.

The document quite clearly begins from the problems of the valorisation of capital – problems which are currently being exacerbated by increasing international competition. Five spheres are identified in which free production zones provide opportunities for increasing the profitability of production.

Foreign manufacturers with world markets, particularly being pressed by the increasing level of labour cost on the one hand and the sharpening of international and national competition on the other, are constantly seeking ways and means to cut down or minimise their manufacturing and distribution costs...Should they advance their base of manufacturing to a suitable Free Zone, some of the following reasons could bring decisive merits in this direction.

(a) Cutdown of raw material transportation costs;
(b) Cutdown of finished products transportation costs;
(c) Cutdown of labour costs;
(d) Availability of abundant qualified labour power;
(e) Reduction of initial investment cost and consequently lower percentage of so-called sleeping capital, through the available fiscal and and physical incentives, common and general services and other preferential treatments provided in the zone etc.[1]

As a basic structure for free production zones UNIDO recommends the following technical equipment and commercial and financial incentives:

— Full exemption of duties and taxes, for a certain given period, on all machineries and production equipments as well as on the raw materials and components required for production activities in the zone...
— Income tax exemption of 5 to 10 years...
— A special period of holiday or reduction of rates on other direct and indirect taxes, surtaxes, surcharges etc. payable by enterprises if not located in the free zone.

1. UNIDO, p. 8.

- Freedom of foreign exchange control with a guarantee of the same status in the future, and with the assurance of free repatriation of earned profits up to a certain fixed annual rate of percentage.
- Preferential financing facilities, such as the provision of short, medium and long term loans with advantageous rates of interest, provided they are required for the establishment of the industries in the zone, including the construction of non-standard factory buildings.
- Preferential tariff rates on transportation costs between the zone and the sea-or-airports of arrival or departure in the country, as well as on the cost of utilities, rents of ground and buildings (standard factory buildings), common and general services charges, etc.
- Possibilities of renting or purchasing pre-constructed standard factories and office buildings or spaces, according to the wishes of the industries. This could relieve the investors from spending their investment capital on long term fixed assets, or in other words, minimise their amount of sleeping capital.
- The availability of work and repairshops, canteens, medical services or clinics, banking services, post and telecommunication services, petrol stations, patrol and security services, public warehouses, transportation and forwarding agent services, cooperative insurance services, recreation facilities etc. all established in the zone for the benefit of the inhabitants and their workers, would amount to a considerable portion of reducing the work as well as the initial investment costs of the investors had these to had to be made available by themselves, and brings a kind of physical incentive to the investors.[1]

As will be shown later almost all the free production zones operating in developing countries are equipped with those features suggested by UNIDO. It is this combination of features, together with production exclusively for the world market, which distinguishes free production zones from other industrial sites in developing countries and at the same time endows the zones with their special enclave character. The provision of a modern infrastructure and the granting of tariff, tax and currency related privileges facilitate the utilisation of labour in regions where – outside the limits of the free production zones – none of the preconditions for profitable production are present apart from the labour-force. The screening off of the free production zones from their surrounding under-developed environment, which is nonetheless the source of their labour-force, and their physical encirclement with fences and sometimes watch-towers – initially for customs' purposes but also for the control of the employees – visibly reveals the enclave nature of the zones.

The following extracts have been taken from official brochures as supplied to potential investors by the respective authorities. They

1. UNIDO, pp. 16–17.

describe the function and the conditions of one zone in Asia, one in Africa and one in Latin America.

Masan Free Export Zone, South Korea

Ready-made industrial estate makes your investment simplier, freer and more profitable than anywhere else.

The Masan Free Export Zone is a specially designed, 175 hectare, industrial free zone where foreign-invested firms can manufacture, assemble or process export products using tax free raw materials and semi-finished goods, most or all of which may be imported for the purpose. The zone embodies the ideal investment climate Korea offers, along with the most liberal incentives, the best facilities and every convenience to foreign investors.

The application of pertinent laws and regulations are waived or eased in regard to the business activities of foreign-invested firms in the zone. Once admitted, occupant-enterprises are not required to obtain the permissions, licences, registrations, etc. prescribed by law for some types of business operating outside the zone. In addition, occupant-enterprises are treated on the same footing as public utilities in relation to the handling of labor disputes.

Plant sites and buildings (standard factory buildings) may be either leased or purchased by occupant-enterprises. The zone provides ample water and power, and will have its own port facilities. To facilitate business operation in the zone, forwarding, shipping, stevedoring, warehousing, packing, maintenance and repair service facilities, among others, are being established within the zone.

The Administration Office is empowered to grant the various permissions and approvals necessary to take up occupancy, to induce foreign investment and technology, to construct plants, and to conduct export and import activities and other related business activities. Besides the Administration Office, the following government and non-government agencies will be stationed in the zone in order to simplify and expedite administrative services for foreign investors.

(a) Foreign Exchange Bank,
(b) Customs Office,
(c) Post and Telecommunication Office,
(d) Exit and Entry Control Office,
(e) Employment and Labor Office,
(f) Dispensary,
(g) Airline and Travel Agents.

Occupant-enterprises have the option of constructing their own factory buildings by leasing or buying plant sites, or of purchasing or leasing standard factory buildings...

No restrictions, except the requirement for initial approval, will be imposed on imports of raw materials and equipment necessary for the production of export products.

No duties or taxes will be imposed on raw materials, parts, semi-finished goods and equipment brought in for export production.

Export products are exempted from export inspection, except for a very few cases...

Income, corporate, property and property acquisition taxes will be exempted during the first 5 years while a 50% reduction will apply for the subsequent 3 years...The remittance overseas of profits and dividends by foreign investors is guaranteed from the first year of business operations...

Low cost labor is abundant and will provide an excellent advantage for products from the zone to compete on international markets. Highly qualified work forces, both male and female, all with at least a primary education and easily trainable, will be continually available from surrounding towns. The average cost of labor in Korea is about 50% that of labor in Hong Kong, 30% of that in Japan and roughly the same as that in Taiwan. The Administration will provide assistance in recruiting and training workers. Enterprises may also send workers overseas for training.[1]

Mauritius Export Processing Zones, Mauritius

Mauritius offers a labour force: Young, plentiful literate, adaptable.

An export processing zone, by combining the features of a free trade zone with those of an industrial estate, performs multilateral functions. It ensures to the manufacturer for export the smooth and speedy conduct of business in an atmosphere which is highly conducive to efficient industrial processing. By creating a number of such zones over the island, Mauritius wishes to offer to the investor, in various suitable localities where the necessary infrastructure facilities exist, a site which is particularly suited to the nature of his industrial activities. This variety of sites is intended to ensure optimum conditions of work as regards temperature, access to raw materials, supply of labour etc. No matter where the zone is situated, transport to the harbour or airport is no problem in view of the short distances involved and the excellent road network. Steps have been taken to ensure priority of treatment and particularly favourable conditions of work to investors within the zones to guarantee success in their enterprise and help them meet their export targets. The administrative machinery, which is centrally located in the Ministry of Commerce and Industry, has been geared to this requirement and legislative measures have been taken to fulfil these aims (Export Processing Zones Act, 1970)...Manufacturers in MEPZ are known as export enterprises and benefit from the following advantages, benefits and facilities:

(1) Complete exemption from payment of import duty on capital goods (that is, machinery, equipment and spare parts).

(2) Complete exemption from payment of import and excise duty on raw materials, components and semi-finished goods (except spirits, tobacco and petroleum products).

(3a) Corporate Income Tax holiday for a minimum of 10 years and a maximum of 20 years, depending on the merits of each case.

(3b) Exemption from payment of Income Tax on dividends for a period of 5 years.

(4) Immediate issue of import licences for machinery and raw and semi-finished materials and of export licences for the finished products.

(5) Completion within 24 hours of Customs inspection of incoming or outgoing commodities.

(6) Loans at preferential rates (from commercial banks) for the importation of raw materials.

1. Office of the Masan Free Export Zone Administration, Republic of Korea, *The Masan Free Export Zone. Korea Invites Foreign Investment and Entrepreneurship.*

(7) Electric power at preferential rates (see Costs of Factors – Electricity).
(8) Exemption from payment of crane and other harbour handling dues chargeable by Government on imported contents of export products.
(9) Export finance at preferential rates of interest.
(10) The issue of permanent residence permits to promoters and shareholders as warranted by the size of their interest.
(11) Priority, wherever possible, in the allocation of investment capital by the Development Bank of Mauritius.
(12) Provision of reinforced factory buildings (preferably 2 to 3 storeys high) for use by industrialists.
(13) Loans of up to 50% of total building cost for a 10 year period.
(14) Provision of an office and creation of a Committee to deal promptly and exclusively with applications in respect of industries falling within the Export Processing Zones.
(15) Reshuffling of labour legislation as under:
  (i) Exemption of industries in the Zones from some provisions of the Termination of Contracts Service Ordinance.
  (ii) Minor amendments to labour legislation to enable manufacturers to meet export targets.
  (iii) Creation, in due course, for the benefit of employees, of a National Pensions Scheme. (In the meantime, employers will be expected to provide normal retirement benefits)...

The most important wealth of Mauritius is its people. They combine the inherent resourcefulness of their forebears with the progressive outlook of a young nation. Mauritian labour is adaptable and intelligent. Wage rates are relatively low for both men and women. A properly managed firm can obtain the productivity in quality and output attainable in any developed market economy.[1]

Zona Franca Industrial y Comercial Palmaseca and Buenaventura, Colombia

Plentiful labor at low cost in the hub of the Americas.

The essential aim of Free Zones is to make available factory space and other facilities to export manufacturers at a low cost and with a minimum of controls and red-tape, so that they will be induced to take advantage of the ample supply of low-cost labor. To investors are offered the tax concessions of a free trade area and the facilities of an industrial park. Procedural requirements are reduced considerably by having representatives from the government agencies concerned work together in the Zone in dealing with such matters as foreign exchange, customs clearing and licensing. The Zones therefore offer an expedient means for making use of Colombia's low-cost, efficient labor force in manufacturing operations to expand existing markets or open up new ones...

Manufacturing for export within the Free Zones should be special interest to companies with labor-intensive operations. The combination of extremely low-cost, easily trained labor, excellent transportation facilities and geographic proximity to major markets in the United States and Europe is worth investigating. The following are salient points to consider:

1. Ministry of Commerce and Industry, *Mauritius Export Processing Zones* (1972), pp. 6–9, 20.

An ample supply [of labor] is available, with wages ranging from US $ 0.13 to US $ 0.24 per hour actually worked (including legal benefits) for unskilled workers. This compares favourably with rates in most Free Zones throughout the world.

The Zones will be designed to reduce red-tape to a minimum, as it is realised that their success will depend largely on their ability to turn goods around rapidly and efficiently. For example, cargo aircraft landing at Palmaseca will be cleared directly to the Zone, with all customs procedures taking place under Zone management and within the territory of the Zone. The Free Zone at Buenaventura will offer similar facilities for unloading cargo from ships. The business climate of Colombia is attractive for export manufacturing. The country has for some years been trying to diversify its exports and welcomes any new manufacturing enterprise aimed at markets in the United States, Europe, and the Far East. Foreign exchange and control restrictions will not apply to the Free Zones at Buenaventura and Palmaseca. Living conditions for management families in the Cauca Valley are of good quality by international standards, with good schools, universities, clubs and pleasant suburban communities.

Enterprises establishing in the Free Zones will be allowed to import and export freely all types of goods such as equipment, furniture, manufactured and semi-manufactured goods, parts and raw materials, without restrictions, bonds, licences or taxes of any type...

Freedom from exchange controls is especially important, not only to guarantee freedom of international commerce, which is important for export industries, but also for remitting of profits, return of capital to country of origin and payments to foreign companies for royalties and services. There will be no restriction or limitation for any of these operations inside the Free Zones...

Both Free Zones afford all services expected in highgrade industrial parks. These services and utilities are: water, electricity and sewers, paved roads and sidewalks, police and fire protection and other amenities. Telephone and other communications are available to all parts of the world.

Warehouse and production buildings are being constructed of steel and concrete, with standard specifications comparable to those of the United States. Size of factory buildings varies from 16500 to 33000 square feet and there are ample facilities for future expansions.[1]

These extracts make it quite plain that despite the very variable conditions in each of the countries in which the zones are located the zones themselves display hardly any differences in their conditions. The identity of the zones reflects the identity of their function as production sites in developing countries for the optimal utilisation of the labour-forces of those countries for world market oriented industrial production.

Definitions of free production zones which emphasise their freedom from tariffs do not only inadequately grasp the fact that it is the utilisation of labour and not the exploitation of customs privileges which is the main function of the zones, but in fact fail

1. Zona Franca Industrial y Comercial Manuel Carvajal Sinisterra (Palmaseca)/Zona Franca Industrial y Comercial de Buenaventura, *Two New Free Zones in Colombia* (1973), pp. 3–10.

to understand the phenomenon altogether.[1] Customs privileges are just one of the many preconditions for the profitable utilisation of labour for world market oriented industrial production.

The new production sites go under a variety of designations: the most frequent are 'free export zone', 'free industrial zone', 'free trade zone', 'free zone', 'export processing zone', and 'export industrial zone'. The term 'free production zone', which is used in this study, refers to all those production sites (zones) in developing countries, whose major function is the industrial utilisation of labour in those countries for world market oriented production.

14.2 Transnational organisation of production: world market factories

The factory is the site of the industrial utilisation of labour-power. The industrial utilisation of labour-power for world market oriented production has led to the establishment of a new kind of factory: the world market factory.

The concept of the world market factory will be used in this study to identify those plants which have been established within the framework of the transnational organisation of manufacturing for the purpose of utilising an available labour-force. Usually vertically integrated into transnational enterprises, world market factories produce, assemble or finish components, intermediate products or final products in processes which allow for the profitable utilisation of the labour-force available at the respective sites. In the transnationally integrated economy, any production which is part of this

1. For example, the designations 'industrial export free zone', 'industrial free zone', 'export processing free zones', and 'processing free zone' refer primarily to the extent of the customs and other privileges for export and other industrial manufacture. See UNIDO, *Notes on the Training Workshop in Industrial Free Zones as Incentives to Promote Export-Oriented Industries Organised by UNIDO in Cooperation with the Department of Industry and Commerce of the Republic of Ireland, the Irish Industrial Development Authority and the Shannon Free Airport Development Company* (*SFADCO*). ID/WG 112/21 (March 1972), pp. 6–7.

An UNCTAD definition also ignores the significance of the utilisation of the labour-force and stresses the duty-free aspect: 'An export-processing free zone is an enclave within a national customs territory, usually situated near an international airport and/or port, into which foreign capital goods, components and materials are brought without being subject to customs requirements. The imported products are processed within the zone, then exported elsewhere, without intervention from the customs authorities of the host country. The payment of customs duties is not required unless these products – or the final goods in which they are incorporated – enter the national customs territory of the host country (this is the exception rather than the rule, insofar as the entire production of such zones is normally export-oriented).' (UNCTAD, *Some Aspects of the Operations of Export-Processing, Free Zones in Developing Countries*, TD/B/C.2/149 (11 April 1975), p. 2.)

economy takes place under the conditions of the world market, and is thus necessarily production for the world market. For practical reasons, the concept 'world market factory' will be used in this study in a more limited sense to identify those factories in which the labour-force is utilised to produce for the world market – i.e. the external market.

Factories located in free production zones are world market factories (in the limited sense explained above). Nevertheless in a number of developing countries world market factories are also located outside free production zones, given that the conditions for the industrial utilisation of the labour-force for world market oriented production can be found outside the zones. These conditions are to be found at the following locations:

(a) sites that have been constructed for domestic industrial production and therefore possess the necessary infrastructure, and
(b) sites where the necessary services are already available and can be used for industrial purposes, primarily airports and ports.

The term 'world market factory' in this study therefore refers both to factories within free production zones and factories outside these zones which, nonetheless, (1) clearly meet the criteria of 'production for the world market undertaken for the most part in order to utilise the available labour-force', and (2) also share the customs privileges and technical characteristics of firms producing within the zones: the great majority of world market factories are owned and operated by foreign firms, although one should add to those the local subcontracting firms which also fulfil the criteria for world market factories. However, in this study world market factories outside of free production zones are only taken into account insofar as the necessary empirical material was available, which applies mainly to foreign controlled firms.[1]

1. World market factories are often identified by the term 'offshore plants'; similarly, terms like 'offshore production' and 'offshore sourcing' are used to indicate world-wide utilisation of the labour-force and means of production. See: T. S. Chang, *The Transfer of Technology: Economics of Off-Shore Assembly. The Case of Semiconductor Industry,* UNITAR Research Reports 11 (1971); J. M. Finger, *Tariff Provisions for Off-Shore Assembly and the Foreign Exchange Earnings of Developing Countries,* Discussion Paper Series (Department of the Treasury, Office of the Assistant Secretary for International Affairs, Research Office; Washington 1971); Richard W. Moxon, *Offshore Production in the Less Developed Countries. A Case Study of Multinationality in the Electronics Industry,* New York University, Graduate School of Business Administration, Institute of Finance, The Bulletin (July 1974), pp. 98–9. It is no accident that world market factories go under different names inside the developing countries: for example, 'enclave factories' in Trinidad and Tobago, 'empresas maquiladoras' in Mexico, and 'bonded factories' in Malaysia.

The industrial utilisation of the labour-forces of the developing countries for world market production is by no means a characteristic simply of large or multinational firms. Transnational organisation of production takes place regardless of the size of the firm.

14.3 Free production zones and world market factories in Asia, Africa and Latin America 1975: regional distribution and employment

The industrial utilisation of the labour-force in the developing countries for world market oriented production was found to exist in thirty-nine of the 103 countries included in the study in 1975. Production took place in free production zones in twenty-five of these countries, and in nine out of these twenty-five world market factories also existed outside the zones: world market factories were in operation outside a zone in fourteen further countries. Free production zones were under construction in another seven countries, and world market factories outside zones in five countries. Thus, at the time the survey was conducted a total of fifty-one out of the 103 developing countries covered revealed the existence of a process of world market oriented industrialisation in at least its initial stages. Thirty-nine countries had world market factories in operation either within or outside free production zones, and in twelve countries world market factories were under construction. (See Table III-2.) The regional distribution of free production zones is given in Tables III-3 and III-4, and that of world market factories in Tables III-5 and III-6.

The overall regional distribution of free production zones and world market factories outside the limits of a zone in the developing countries is as follows: in 1975 free production zones and world market factories outside free production zones were either in operation or under construction in seventeen of the thirty-three Asian countries, thirteen of the forty-four African countries and twenty-one of the twenty-six Latin American countries. Free production zones were in operation or under construction in thirty-six countries in 1975; fifteen in Asian countries, six in African countries and fifteen in Latin American countries. World market factories outside of a free production zone were in operation or under construction in twenty-eight countries; eight Asian countries, eight African countries and twelve Latin American countries.

Table III-2. *Location of free production zones and world market factories (outside free production zones) by region: up to 1975*

		No. of countries			
		Total	Asia	Africa	Latin America
1	FPZs in operation	25	11	5	9
2	Total no. of WMFs in operation	23	8	4	11
3	WMFs in countries with no FPZs in operation before 1975	14	4	3	7
4	*Sum 1+3*	39	15	8	16
5	Total no. of FPZs under construction[a]	11	4	1	6
6	FPZs in countries with no WMFs in operation before 1975	7	2	1	4
7	WMFs under construction[b]	5	0	4	1
8	*Sum 6+7*	12	2	5	5
9	*Sum 4+8*	51	17	13	21
10	WMFs (inside and outside FPZs) under consideration[c]	11	6	5	0
11	*Sum 9+10*	62	23	18	21

Source: author's compilation
FPZ: free production zone WMF: world market factory
a: Only countries in which FPZs were not in operation before 1975
b: Only countries in which WMFs were not in operation before 1975
c: Only countries not included in groups 1–9

Table III-3. *Location of free production zones in Asia, Africa and Latin America: 1975*

State of operation	Asia	Africa	Latin America
FPZs in operation	Bahrain Hong Kong India[a] Jordan South Korea Lebanon Malaysia[a] Philippines[a] Singapore Syria Taiwan[a]	Egypt Mauritius Senegal Togo Tunisia[a]	Brazil[a] Dominican Rep. El Salvador Guatemala Haiti[a] Colombia Mexico[a] Panama Puerto Rico[a]
FPZs under construction[b]	Indonesia Thailand Western Samoa[c] Yemen, Dem.[c]	Liberia[c]	Chile[c] Honduras[c] Jamaica Nicaragua Uruguay[c] Venezuela[c]

Source: author's compilation
FPZ: free production zone
a: These countries also had world market factories outside the FPZs in operation before 1975
b: Only those countries are listed in which FPZs were not in operation before 1975
c: These countries also had no world market factories in operation before 1975

Table III-4. *Free production zones by region: 1975*

Region	FPZs in operation: No. of countries	FPZs in operation: No. of zones	FPZs under construction: No. of countries: Total	FPZs under construction: No. of countries: With no FPZs in operation before 1975	FPZs under construction: No. of zones: Total	FPZs under construction: No. of zones: In countries with no FPZs in operation before 1975
Asia	11	48[a]	11	4	20	5
Africa	5	7	3	1	8	1
Latin America	9	24[b]	7	6	11	9
Total	25	79[a, b]	21	11	39	14

Source: author's compilation
FPZ: free production zone
a: Including industrial districts in Hong Kong (7) and industrial estates in Singapore (14)
b: Including industrial parks in the northern border zone of Mexico (11)

Table III-5. *Location of world market factories (outside free production zones) in Asia, Africa and Latin America: 1975*

State of operation	Asia	Africa	Latin America
WMFs in operation	India[a] Indonesia Iran Malaysia[a] Philippines[a] Taiwan[a] Thailand Turkey	Ivory Coast Morocco Swaziland Tunisia[a]	Barbados Brazil[a] Costa Rica Dutch Antilles Haiti[a] Jamaica Mexico[a] Nicaragua Puerto Rico[a] St Lucia Trinidad and Tobago
WMFs under construction[b]		Botswana Ghana Lesotho South Africa	Ecuador

Source: author's compilation
WMF: world market factory
a: These countries also had free production zones in operation before 1975
b: Only those countries are listed in which WMFs were not in operation before 1975

Table III-6. *Location of world market factories (outside free production zones) by region: 1975*

	WMFs in operation: Total no. of countries	WMFs in operation: No. of countries with no FPZs in operation before 1975	WMFs under construction: no. of countries with no WMFs (inside and outside FPZs) in operation before 1975
Asia	8	4	0
Africa	4	3	4
Latin America	11	7	1
Total	23	14	5

Source: author's compilation
FPZ: free production zone WMF: world market factory

The data in Table III-4 show that in 1975 a total of seventy-nine free production zones were in operation in the developing countries; forty-eight in Asia, seven in Africa and twenty-four in Latin America. These figures include only those production sites which are or were planned for world market oriented manufacturing and in which the greater part or all of production is for the world market. A further thirty-nine industrial sites – conceived as free production zones – were under construction in 1975; twenty in Asia, eight in Africa and eleven in Latin America.

The majority of all production sites designated as free production zones are physically separated, fenced off, from their surrounding environment. They are usually autonomous units; a few have been incorporated into airports, sea ports or commercial free zones. The size of the zones ranges from less than 10 hectares (e.g. Tanjong Kling Free Trade Zone, Malacca, Malaysia: 7 hectares, 4 factories, 2000 employees in 1975) to more than 1000 hectares (e.g. Bataan Export Processing Zone, Mariveles, Philippines: 1300 hectares, 23 factories, 8000 employees in 1976).[1]

The industrial areas of Hong Kong, Singapore and the northern border area of Mexico are special cases. Hong Kong and Singapore are free ports; that is, the entire territory functions as a free zone. In this study we have included only those industrial sites in Hong Kong and Singapore in which the bulk of industrial production is for the world market. Moreover, we have only considered those firms which are controlled by foreign capital. In Mexico the northern border area has been declared a duty free region for world market oriented manufacturing. The major sites for world market oriented foreign firms (almost exclusively US firms) – the industrial parks in the border cities of the zone – are also taken into account in this study. The sites in Mexico, Hong Kong and Singapore all fulfil the basic functions of free production zones.

Tables III-7 and III-8 show the extent to which the industrial utilisation of the labour-force in the developing countries for world market oriented production in free production zones and world market factories had developed by the middle of the 1970s. According to our (by no means complete) statistics at least 420000 workers in Asia, 40000 in Africa and 265000 in Latin America, making a total of 725000, were working in world market factories both inside and outside free production zones in the developing

1. Further data on the size of individual zones can be found in Table III-18, Column 3.

Table III-7. *Free production zones in operation in Asia, Africa and Latin America: commencement of operation, employment*

Country	Free production zone	Commencement of operation	Employment	
			Year	Number
Asia				
Bahrain	Mina Sulman	1972[a]	1975	2770
Hong Kong	Hong Kong	1965[b]	1975	59607[c]
	Kwung Tong			
	Tsuen Wan/Kwai Chung			
	Sam Ka Tsuen			
	San Po Kong			
	Cheung Sha Wan			
	Chai Wan			
	Wong Chuk Hang			
India	Kandla	1965	1975	649
	Santa Cruz	1974	1975	600
Jordan	Aqaba Port	n.a.		n.a.
Lebanon	Beyrouth	n.a.		n.a.
Malaysia	Prai	1973	1975	6823
	Prai Wharves	1972		
	Bayan Lepas	1972	1975	15608
	Sungei Way	1972	1975	6446
	Ulu Klang	1974	1975	4414
	Telok Panglima	n.a.	1975	1918
	Batu Berendam	1972	1975	3307
	Tanjong Kling	1972	1975	1949
Philippines	Bataan	1973	1976	8177
Singapore	Singapore	1967[d]	1974	105000[e]
	Bunkit Timan			
	Jurong Town			
	St. Michael's			
	Tiong Bahru			
	Redhill			
	Ayer Rajah			
	Tangling Halt			
	Kallang Basin			
	Toa Bayoh			
	Ang Mo Kio			
	Chai Chee			
	Bedok			
	Indus Road			
	Woodlands			
South Korea	Masan	1972	1975	21100
	Iri	1974	1975	50
	Gumi	1973	1975	11100
	Gurudong	n.a.	1975	80000
	Gurudong	n.a.		
	Gurudong	n.a.		
	Bupyong	n.a.		
	Juan	n.a.		
	Juan	n.a.		

Country	Free production zone	Commencement of operation	Employment	
			Year	Number
Syria	Damascus	n.a.	1975	231
Taiwan	Kaohsiung	1966	1975	41017
	Nantze	1970	1975	13160
	Taichung	1971	1975	7966
Africa				
Egypt	Port Said	1976		n.a.
Mauritius	Plaine Lauzun	1971 }	1975	9952
	Coromandel	1976 }		
Senegal	Dakar	1976	1976	150
Togo	Lomé	n.a.		n.a.
Tunisia	Mégrine	n.a.		n.a.
	Ben Arous	n.a.		n.a.
Latin America				
Brazil	Manaus	1968	1973	27650
Colombia	Barranquilla	1969	1974	5000
	Buenaventura	1973		n.a.
	Palmaseca	1973	1975	600
	Cucúta	1974		n.a.
Dominican Rep.	La Romana	1969 }		
	San Pedro de Macorís	1973 }	1975	6500
	Santiago	1974 }		
El Salvador	San Bartolo	1975	1975	6143
Guatemala	Santo Tomás de Castilla	1975		n.a.
Haiti	Port-au-Prince	1974		n.a.
Mexico	Zona Fronteriza	1966[f]	1975	74676
	Tijuana			n.a.
	Mexicali			n.a.
	Nogales			n.a.
	Cd. Juárez (2)			n.a.
	Cd. Acuña			n.a.
	Piedras Negras			n.a.
	Nuevo Laredo			n.a.
	Reynosa			n.a.
	Matamoros (2)			n.a.
Panama	Colón	1974[g]	1975	1300
Puerto Rico	Mayaguez	1974[h]	1975	481

Source: author's calculation
a: Free port in operation since 1960
b: Export-oriented industrialisation since the beginning of the 1950s, production for the world market by foreign firms since the mid-1960s
c: Employees only in foreign firms
d: Production for the world market by foreign firms since 1967
e: Estimate
f: Start of production for the world market by foreign firms
g: Free port in operation since 1948
h: Commercial activities since 1961

Table III-8. *Employment in free production zones and world market factories in Asia, Africa and Latin America: last available year*

Country	Total	Employment in FPZs	Employment in WMFs	Year
Asia				
Bahrain	2770	2770		1975
Hong Kong	59607	59607		1975
India	1249	1249	n.a.	1975
Indonesia	11191		11191	1975
Iran	n.a.		n.a.	
Jordan	n.a.	n.a.	n.a.	
Lebanon	n.a.	n.a.	n.a.	
Malaysia	40465	40465	n.a.	1975
Philippines	9827	8177	1650	1976
Singapore	105000	105000		1974
South Korea	112250	112250		1975
Syria	231	231		1975
Taiwan	62143	62143	n.a.	1975
Thailand	16700		16700	1974
Turkey	n.a.		n.a.	
Africa				
Egypt	n.a.	n.a.	n.a.	
Ivory Coast	2800		2800	1974
Mauritius	9952	9952		1975
Morocco	n.a.		n.a.	
Senegal	150	150		1976
Swaziland	2500		2500	1976
Togo	n.a.	n.a.		
Tunisia	24000	n.a.	n.a.	1974
Latin America				
Barbados	3000		3000	1975
Brazil	27650	27650	n.a.	1973
Colombia	5600	5600		1975
Costa Rica	n.a.		n.a.	
Dominican Rep.	6500	6500		1975
Dutch Antilles	n.a.	0	n.a.	
El Salvador	6143	6143		1975
Guatemala	n.a.	n.a.		
Haiti	25000	n.a.	n.a.	1973
Jamaica	6100		6100	1971
Mexico	84308	74676	9632	1974
Nicaragua	n.a.		n.a.	
Panama	1300	1300		1975
Puerto Rico	96726	481	96245	1975
St Lucia	3500		3500	1976
Trinidad and Tobago	n.a.		n.a.	
Asia	*c.* 420000			
Africa	*c.* 40000			
Latin America	*c.* 265000			
Total	*c.* 725000			

Source: author's calculation
FPZ: free production zone WMF: world market factory

countries in 1975. More than 500000 of the 725000 employees worked inside a free production zone.[1] In some of the zones the number of workers had reached a total of several tens of thousands.

The employment statistics are for 1975 for most of the countries; for four countries the figures are for 1976, for five for 1974, for two for 1973, and for one country for 1971. The justification for aggregating these figures into one 1975 total is that other evidence shows that the number of employed in 1975 was not lower in those countries for which the figures for an earlier year are taken. The data on the total number of employees in free production zones and world market factories outside free production zones should be understood as an expression of the lower limit of the magnitude which the industrial utilisation of the labour-force of the developing countries for world market production – both inside and outside free production zones – had reached by that time.

Since we make no attempt to give a quantitative estimate of the employment totals in the free production zones and world market factories for which employment figures were not available, some remarks on those areas not covered are necessary: Table III-8 contains data for only twenty-seven of the thirty-nine countries in which, by 1975, free production zones and world market factories outside the zones were in operation. No data was available on the number of employees in the world market factories for the remaining twelve countries. Among these twelve are five for which there are indications that the total production in world market factories is anything but small – Iran, Morocco, Costa Rica, Guatemala and Nicaragua.[2] For many countries for which the employee figures are given it was only possible to obtain data for a part of the total employment. This was the case in India, Taiwan and Brazil. For these countries employment data was only available for the free production zones themselves. However, even with such incomplete data on the activities of the export-oriented firms operating outside free production zones in these countries, one is forced to the conclusion that the number of employees in world market factories

1. For two countries, Tunisia with 24000 workers (1975) and Haiti with 25000 workers (1973), it was not possible to distinguish between workers in world market factories inside free production zones and those outside the zones.
2. See e.g.: Bundestelle für Außenhandelsinformation, Marktinformation, *Iran: Industriestruktur* (June 1976); Bundestelle für Außenhandelsinformation, Rechtsinformation, Marokko, *Die Investitionsförderungsgesetze* (June 1975); *FAZ/Blick durch die Wirtschaft*, 14 February 1976, 'Autozulieferungen jetzt auch für den Export'; *Business International*, 23 August 1974, 'Central America attracts international investors'.

outside the zones is very considerable.[1] (The total number of employees in the manufacturing export sector in Brazil has been estimated at 412000 in a study by Tyler for example.)[2] The figures for employment in world market factories outside the zones is, insofar as the data was available at all, only partially complete. Finally, it should also be noted that, except in a small number of cases, the employment figures only included employees working for foreign firms. The employment figures for world market production in domestically owned subcontracting firms are not taken account of for the most part. Table III-8, for example, gives the figure of 59607 employees for Hong Kong. This figure is based solely on the number of employees in world market oriented foreign-owned manufacturing plants. A significantly larger number of workers are, however, employed in Hong Kong firms which also produce essentially for the world market. In 1971, there were 677000 workers in Hong Kong employed in manufacturing.[3]

Other factors which should be taken into consideration when interpreting the data on employment is that we have only taken account of manufacturing firms which produce *solely* for the world market at a particular site, and for the most part we have only considered firms which produce at a particular location in order to utilise the available labour-force. We have excluded employment in the world market oriented manufacturing operations of foreign companies which, at any particular site, are partly or predominantly for a domestic market (e.g. the automobile industry in Brazil and Mexico). We also excluded employment in the manufacturing operations of foreign companies in the developing countries (outside of free production zones) which even though producing exclusively for the world market do so at these particular locations not primarily because of the availability of labour but in order to obtain raw materials and/or energy supplies. This applies to the majority of oil refineries, for example.[4]

1. See e.g. for Brazil: Bundestelle für Außenhandelsinformation, *Regionale Entwicklung in Brasilien I, II, III and IV* (December 1974 and February 1975); for India: Deutsch-Indische Handelskammer, *Deustch-Indische Gemeinschaftsunternehmen*; for Taiwan: Business International Corporation, *Investing, Licensing and Trading Conditions Abroad* (Taiwan 1976).
2. See William G. Tyler, *Manufactured Export Expansion and Industrialisation in Brazil* (Tübingen 1976), p. 172.
3. See Trade Development Council, *Industrial Investment in Hong Kong* (Hong Kong 1974/75), p. 19.
4. Three of the world's five largest refining centres are located in developing countries (one in the Caribbean, one in West Asia and one in Singapore).

The statistical results discussed above (Tables III-2 to III-8) reveal, on the one hand, that the industrial utilisation of the labour-forces of the developing countries in the sites and plants covered by our definition was a world-wide phenomenon by the middle of the 1970s and was by no means limited to a few countries. On the other hand certain regional concentrations are evident. The main areas for world market factories (both inside and outside free production zones) are South East Asia and the Caribbean region (including Mexico), with only a few countries from northern and southern Africa being represented. In this context, the specific centre-periphery relationships are very clear: Japan to South East Asia, Western Europe to Africa, and the USA to the Caribbean region. These specific patterns of dependency are also reflected in the data on the origins of foreign capital in these regions (Table III-18, Column 7). The concentration of production in particular areas is essentially a result of the international competition of capital, since when the utilisation of the local labour-force for world market production proves to be profitable for a particular firm at a particular location their international competitors are forced to follow. The regional distribution also reflects the availability of or enforcement of guarantees for investment of a more explicitly political character, i.e. military dictatorships and anti-trade-union governments which play a particularly important role.[1]

From Table III-9, which contains the statistical data on population and gross national product for the 103 countries included in the study, it is evident that there is no correlation between the regional distribution of free production zones and world market factories on the one hand and the distribution of the potentially economically active population (indicated by total population) and the respective level of economic development (insofar as GNP is an indicator) on the other. In 1975 the industrial utilisation of the developing countries' labour-forces for world market production could be found in countries with large populations and a relatively high per capita GNP (e.g. Mexico) as well as in countries with large populations and low per capita GNP (e.g. Indonesia), countries with a small population and relatively high per capita GNP (e.g. Dutch Antilles), and countries with a small population and low per capita GNP (e.g. Haiti). It is not surprising that there is no correlation between these two factors on the one hand and the existence of world market

1. See Chapter 14.1.

Table III-9. *Developing countries in Asia, Africa and Latin America: free production zones, world market factories, population, gross national product per capita: 1974, 1975*

Asia			Africa			Latin America		
Country	Population 1974 (mill.)	GNP per capita 1974 (US $)	Country	Population 1974 (mill.)	GNP per capita 1974 (US $)	Country	Population 1974 (mill.)	GNP per capita 1974 (US $)
FPZs in operation 1975								
Bahrain	0.2	2250	Egypt	36.4	269	Brazil	104.2	799
Hong Kong	4.2	1409	Mauritius	0.9	369	Colombia	24.0	425
India	586.0	116	Senegal	4.3	259	Dominican Rep.	4.6	539
Jordan	2.6	267	Togo	2.2	191	El Salvador	4.0	354
Lebanon	2.8	893	Tunisia	5.6	494	Guatemala	5.2	466
Malaysia	11.7	572				Haiti	4.5	142
Philippines	41.5	250				Mexico	58.1	891
Singapore	2.2	2015				Panama	1.6	909
South Korea	33.5	401				Puerto Rico	3.0	2182
Syria	7.1	397						
Taiwan	15.8	n.a.						
WMFs in operation 1975[a]								
Indonesia	128.0	120	Ivory Coast	4.8	552	Barbados	0.2	837
Iran	32.0	1034	Morocco	16.9	295	Costa Rica	1.9	791
Thailand	41.0	231	Swaziland	0.5	319	Dutch Antilles	0.2	1530[c]
Turkey	38.3	539[b]				Jamaica	2.0	875
						Nicaragua	2.1	524
						St Lucia	0.1	480[b]
						Trinidad and Tobago	1.0	1244
FPZs under construction 1975								
Western Samoa	0.2	280	Liberia	1.7	252	Chile	10.4	796
Yemen, Dem.	1.6	109				Honduras	2.9	282
						Uruguay	3.0	873
						Venezuela	11.6	1374
WMFs under construction 1975[a]								
			Botswana	0.7	353	Ecuador	7.0	416
			Ghana	9.6	289			
			Lesotho	1.0	102			
			South Africa	24.9	1142			

			FPZs/WMFs under consideration 1975					
Bangla Desh	75.0	100	Gambia	0.5	188			
Fiji	0.6	720	Kenya	12.9	172			
Pakistan	68.2	125	Malawi	4.9	113			
Sri Lanka	13.7	196	Nigeria	61.3	274			
Un. Arab Emirates	0.2	13500	Sierra Leone	2.7	165			
Yemen	6.5	73						
No FPZs and no other locations for WMFs in operation, under construction or under consideration, or no information 1975								
Afghanistan	18.8	81	Algeria	16.3	510	Argentina	25.1	1317
Burma	30.3	83	Angola	5.8	501	Bolivia	5.5	210
Iraq	10.8	675	Benin	3.0	126	Guyana	0.8	423
Kuwait	0.9	6710	Burundi	3.7	73	Paraguay	2.6	423
Maldives	0.1	90	Cameroon	6.3	247	Peru	15.4	639
Nepal	12.3	93	Central African Rep.	1.6	175			
Oman	0.7	1250	Chad	3.9	94			
Papua New Guinea	2.7	368	Congo, Dem. Rep.	1.3	445			
Qatar	0.1	5830	Equatorial Guinea	4.3	147			
Saudi Arabia	8.7	1877	Ethiopia	27.2	83			
			Gabon	0.5	1289			
			Guinea-Bissau	0.5	283			
			Libya	2.3	3568			
			Madagascar	6.8	176			
			Mali	5.6	76			
			Mauritania	1.3	203			
			Mozambique	9.0	344			
			Niger	4.5	130			
			Rwanda	4.1	68			
			Somalia	3.1	81			
			Sudan	17.3	123			
			Tanzania	14.8	123			
			Uganda	11.2	134			
			Upper Volta	5.9	81			
			Zaire	24.2	153			
			Zambia	4.8	513			

Sources: UN, *Demographic Yearbook 1974* (New York); UNCTAD, *Handbook of International Trade and Development Statistics 1976* (New York 1976); author's calculation
FPZ: free production zone WMF: world market factory
According to the succession of countries in the vertical subdivision, each country is listed only once
a: WMFs outside FPZs
b: Gross national product per capita 1973
c: Estimate for 1973

oriented manufacturing on the other since the preconditions for industrial production for the world market are not a function of the level of economic development in any individual country but rather exist, or can be brought into existence, in any part of the world.

Table III-7 indicates the years in which production began in the free production zones. The year in which production began in world market factories outside free production zones is given – if known – in Column 2 of Table III-18. Industrial production in developing countries for the world market, especially production by foreign firms, did not exist until the middle of the 1960s. In 1966 there were world market factories in operation[1] in four countries: Hong Kong, Taiwan (in one of the first free production zones of the developing countries, Kaohsiung),[2] South Korea and the northern border zone of Mexico. The first free production zone in Colombia, Barranquilla, was established in the same year. In 1967 foreign firms first began to relocate industry to Singapore on a large scale;[3] in 1968 the free zone of Manaus in Brazil was established. In 1969 the first of three free production zones began to operate in the Dominican Republic. A second zone (Nantze) was put into operation in 1970 in Taiwan and a third followed in 1971 (Taichung). 1971 was also the year in which the first free production zone in Mauritius entered the world market for sites for industrial production. By 1971 free production zones were in operation in a total of nine countries. Between 1972 and 1976 the number of new zones increased rapidly. During this same four year period most of the world market factories located outside free production zones were also established. World market oriented industrialisation, more specifically, the industrial utilisation of the labour-force of developing countries for world market production which is recorded in the figures here, became established in a matter of a very few years. Whereas scarcely any industrial production for the world market existed in Asia, Africa and Latin America in the mid-1960s, by the middle of the 1970s world market factories were in operation in seventy-nine free production zones in

1. The free zones of Kandla, India, and Mayaguez, Puerto Rico, were put into operation before 1966, but significant production did not take place until 1975.
2. 'We have the copyright for these free export zones and we've been sending experts abroad to help other countries to build similar ones – free of charge.' (L.Lu, Industrial Development and Investment Center, Taiwan; see *Far Eastern Economic Review*, 9 January 1976.)
3. 'The story of large foreign manufacturing investments to Singapore began in 1967, with the coming in of multinational electronics corporations. When these corporations established operations in Singapore they were followed by others.' (Ministry of Culture, Singapore, *Singapore 1974*, p. 127.)

thirty-nine countries and in many sites outside the zones, employing in all 725000 workers according to our statistics. There were free production zones and world market factories outside the zones under construction in a further twelve countries. An additional group of eleven countries, six in Asia, and five in Africa, were giving active consideration to the construction of free production zones or world market factories at other sites (Table III-2).

We can summarise our findings so far as follows:

(1) The industrial utilisation of the labour-forces of the developing countries for world market oriented production in world market factories both inside and outside free production zones, a process which only began in the mid-1960s, had reached significant proportions by the mid-1970s.

(2) Although the regional distribution of free production zones and world market factories outside such zones clearly reveals areas of concentration, the industrial utilisation of the labour-force in the developing countries for world market oriented production is not limited to just a few countries, but is rather a world-wide phenomenon.

(3) The industrial utilisation of the labour-force in developing countries for world market oriented production is correlated neither with a given size of population nor with a given level of gross national product per head of population.

(4) Free production zones fulfil, in a particular manner, the requirements for the profitable industrial utilisation of the labour-forces of the developing countries for world market oriented production at the location at which this labour-force is to be found.

(5) The number of countries that offer free production zones on the world market for production sites for this type of production is growing.

14.4 Terms of investment and investment incentives

The provision of all the zones with infrastructure and utilities conforms more or less to the standards recommended by UNIDO. Without exception, transport and communication facilities, factory buildings, energy and water facilities, and a central administration or a central investment authority are an integral part of the zones' basic layout. Almost all zones have either direct access to a sea port or airport or such facilities are incorporated directly into the zone itself. Facilities for containerised transport are also available at most sites along with telephone and telex facilities. Nearly all zones offer standardised factory buildings. Energy and water facilities are adequate for the needs of all types of manufacturing in most zones. Other basic services and utilities which are often available include maintenance and repair services, training facilities, sewage systems etc., workers' dormitories and workers' compounds. More specific types of installation and services are often available depending on the particular demands of the firms which are operating in the zone.

The above list of utilities and infrastructural items which are available at most free production zones clearly shows precisely what technical conditions have to be met before manufacturing for the world market can be got under way in the developing countries. Once these general preconditions have been fulfilled, and given that labour exists in the required quantity and quality, the remaining technical and economic preconditions for industrial production are the concern of the firm. The means of production – machines, tools, intermediate products and raw materials – are imported into the production sites by the firms. These inputs are not necessarily obtained either from local producers or from other firms inside the zones, even if they may be locally available.

The whole range of investment policies, concessions, and incentives which exist for the firms in most zones, when not already part of the investment laws of the particular country, are usually based on particular legal codes which are intended to define the status of the free production zones and of the firms producing within them. The high degree of similarity which such codes display from country to country and the similarity which they all bear to the UNIDO recommendations is striking. A survey of the key clauses of the particular regulations and incentives will be sufficient to indicate the investment policies and conditions which firms will encounter in the free production zones. It is necessary to distinguish between conditions which apply to actual production, privileges granted to capital and investment incentives, especially financial incentives.

Firms operating in free production zones are obliged to fulfil only one requirement: the products produced, assembled or finished in the zones must be exported. Delivery or sale to the domestic market of the country where the zone is located is, with very few exceptions, forbidden. This restriction applies in all the zones; but since the firms only produce in the free production zones for the express purpose of utilising the local labour-force for world market oriented production this obligation fully conforms with the firms' intentions. Further obligations, in particular requirements for a minimum amount of investment or for a particular type of industry, also exist in a few cases.[1]

The most important privilege granted to capital in free production zones is simply the lack of any restrictions on foreign investment and on capital transfers. In almost all zones there are hardly any restrictions on foreign investment; foreign capital is allowed 100% ownership in almost all zones. This is the case even in those countries where substantial restrictions are placed on foreign capital outside the zones. Almost all zones offer the guarantee of unrestricted capital transfer, i.e. both (a) the unlimited repatriation of profits, which as rule is possible as early as the first year of operations, and (b) the unlimited repatriation of the initial investment, which as a rule is possible after only three years operation.

The unlimited duty-free, tax-free, and quota-free import of investment goods, replacement parts, raw materials, intermediate goods, and other inputs is a fundamental element of free production zones. In many cases, the period of customs' exemption is unlimited. The possibility for unlimited import even exists in most cases where raw materials, intermediate products, and other inputs could at least be provided to some extent by the local economy.

Investment incentives are granted in every free production zone – without exception. Financial incentives include, in particular, tax exemptions, investment subsidies, and subsidised prices for inputs and services. The tax exemption for firms in free production zones applies to income and profit taxes, other business taxes (especially corporation tax) and sales taxes, as well as tax exemptions for local and provincial taxes. Tax regulations in different zones range from overall low rates of taxation[2] to limited periods of tax reductions[3] to total and unlimited exemption from all forms of taxation.[4]

1. In the free production zones in South Korea, for example, an initial investment of US $ 50 000 is required. For admission to the industrial free zone at Dakar, the creation of at least 150 jobs is required. Environmental protection regulations apply in a small number of zones.
2. This is true, for example, in Hong Kong. The 'profits tax' rate is 15% ('standard rate of 15%'). Trade Development Council, *Industrial Investment in Hong Kong* (Hong Kong 1974/75), p. 27.
3. For example, firms in the Malaysian free zones can enjoy tax exemptions of up to ten years duration. Federal Industrial Investment Authority, *Malaysia – A Basic Guidebook for Potential Investors* (1973), pp. 93–4.
4. Total tax exemption is granted in the free zones in Egypt, for example. 'Activities and projects in free zones are completely exempt from exchange control regulations, and all

Almost all zones offer investment subsidies, chiefly in the form of preferential credit and interest subsidies on investment credit.[1] Investment incentives are granted in many zones in the form of subsidised rates for energy and water supplies,[2] for transport services,[3] and rent subsidies for factory buildings,[4] etc. In a few cases subsidies in the form of funds for the training of the labour-force[5] and sometimes even subsidies for the payment of wages themselves are offered.[6]

A third form of political investment incentive (and in this instance political is meant in its most literal sense) consists in restrictions and/or the suspension of the political and social rights of the workers who work in the zones. This means the suspension of the validity and application of labour legislation otherwise observed in the countries, the elimination of minimum wage ordinances, exemption from the obligation for firms to pay social security contributions and restrictions on trade union rights.[7]

World market factories outside the free production zones can also, almost without exception, take advantage of investment incentives and special regulations. In particular, world market factories are almost always granted duty-free status. The so-called 'drawback

general tax laws for an unlimited period.' (General Authority for Arab and Foreign-Investment and Free Zones, *How to Invest in Egypt* (Cairo 1975).)

1. For the purchase of prefabricated, standardised factory buildings or for the construction of other factory buildings in the export-processing zones on Taiwan, for example, credit up to 70% of the purchase price or construction costs is granted for ten years at subsidised interest rates. The Export Processing Zone Administration, *Investor's Guide* (1975), p. 6.
2. Electricity at subsidised rates is offered, for example, in the export processing zones in Mauritius. Ministry of Commerce and Industry, *Investing in Mauritius: Investment Incentives* (January 1975).
3. For example, export firms in the northern border zone of Mexico can make use of cheap transportation rates. Mexico Institute of Foreign Trade, *Different Fiscal Incentives and Comments to the Law of Foreign Investment and Registry of Technology* (1975), p. 28.
4. Subsidised rents for factory buildings as well as for land are, for example, offered in the electronics export-processing zone Santa Cruz, Bombay. Development Commissioner, *Santa Cruz Electronics Export Processing Zone.*
5. The government of Singapore grants subsidies for training programmes for example. Singapore International Chamber of Commence, *Investor's Guide* (1975), p. 17.
6. Subsidies for the payment of wages are offered in the free production zones in Chile currently under construction. 'La empresa empleadora puede acogerse a la franquicia de subsidio a la maño de obra, con lo cual costo para la empresa se reduce a US$50 mensuales.' (*Decreto Ley*, No. 1.055 (June 1975).)
7. In South Korea, for example, investment capital is attracted by the possibility of a sixty hour working week and the guarantee of protection against labour disputes and strikes. 'The working hours may be extended to sixty hours per week by mutual agreement. An extended work week has become a common practice in manufacturing and export industries.' 'Foreign investors are given special protection from unwanted labor disputes.' (Economic Planning Board, *Guide to Investment in Korea* (1975), pp. 48 and 50.)

system' and the 'manufacturing-in-bond system' are the most common arrangements. According to the 'drawback system' the duties paid on imports to the world market factories are refunded at the time when the products are exported. The 'manufacturing-in-bond system' allows the processing of goods imported free of duty.[1] World market factories outside the free production zones also enjoy these investment incentives, again chiefly exemption from tax and the unrestricted transfer of capital, in all countries where they exist. The following extracts from the Nicaraguan investment law (The Off-Shore Assembly Law), a typical example of such legislation, clearly illustrate the conditions under which world market factories outside free production zones can operate:

> Industrial plants engaged in production for export outside the Central American area will be granted with the following privileges: Total or partial exoneration of customs duties assessables necessary for installation, operation and production of such industrial plants. Exoneration of taxes assessable on assets and income, and any other taxes assessable to the operation, production and sales of the enterprise. The law on foreign investments guarantees the foreign capital, settled in the country, freedom of movement and acknowledgement of the right to make profits and send them to his own country at any moment. . . Foreign companies will enjoy an equitable treatment and in no case less favorable than national companies.[2]

1. See UNCTAD, *The Use of Free Zones as a Means of Expanding and Diversifying Exports of Manufactures from the Developing Countries*, TD/B/C.2/125 (18 June 1973), p. 6.
2. Banco Central de Nicaragua, *Nicaragua – A Market for Offshore Assembly*.

15 • The structure of production in free production zones and world market factories

15.1 The industrial utilisation of the labour-force as the key determinant of the structure of production in free production zones and world market factories

Up to now free production zones have been identified as production sites for the industrial utilisation of the labour-forces of the developing countries for world market oriented production. This definition is concrete enough both to identify the function of such zones and to permit an overall assessment of the geographical distribution of such zones and their development over time. The concept 'industrial utilisation of the labour-forces of the developing countries' should be defined more precisely, however, as the industrial utilisation of *cheap* labour in the developing countries since this is the chief determining factor of the structure of production in free production zones in the context of the transnational organisation of capitalist production.

'Cheap labour' is a term borrowed from the language of the business press, but is one which precisely characterises the conditions on the labour markets of the developing countries. Labour in the developing countries is cheap because the workers in these countries are forced – after several centuries of uneven capitalist development – to sell their labour-power at a price which is much lower than the price which prevails in the traditional industrialised countries. Even if we accept the supposition that the reproduction costs of labour in the developing countries are substantially lower than in the developed countries (and this assumption is often contested), wages still do not often cover the costs of the reproduction of the workers.

The utilisation of this practically unlimited supply of cheap labour is the main reason for and major force behind the increase in production for the world market in the free production zones. More concretely, the availability of *cheap* labour is the main reason for the relocation of production for the markets of the industrialised countries from sites in these countries to the free production zones, which represent the new production sites in the developing countries for production for the markets of the industrialised countries. The forces and aims behind these relocations of production are not difficult to recognise:

(a) they can be systematically deduced from the conditions of the world market,
(b) they are present and observable in the specific conditions of the zones,
(c) they are simply assumed by every investor and substantiated by the experiences of every worker in the zones, and
(d) they are part of the current knowledge of any observer of the international economy.

Nevertheless, it is not easy to gather empirical evidence for the phenomenon itself. Therefore, in this study we employ the method of systematically documenting quotations from the business press, reports from UN institutions and international business consultancy organisations, and from investment authorities in the developing countries in order to provide an empirical basis for our investigation. As any attempt to make a schematic or indirect presentation of the evidence would strongly dilute its character, a word-for-word reproduction of selected documents is therefore unavoidable, although this entails some repetition as the material is arranged by country.

Hong Kong

Fairchild Semiconductor: using Asia as a source of supply

Fairchild produces in Asia mainly to supply markets outside of Asia proper. In fact 90% of all production volume comes from the Far East, and 85% of Far Eastern output goes back to the US, with the remaining 15% sold on the Asian market. But this pattern is rapidly changing. By mid-1973, the US share of output will be reduced to 70%, 15% will be diverted to the European Economic Community (through the company's German office), and Asia will retain its present 15%. A large portion of the goods transported to the US is involved in intercompany trade and does not go directly from the production facility to end-users. Furthermore, all of the raw materials used in Southeast Asian production – e.g. packaging, chips, wire and plastic – are sourced from the US.

Ten years ago, Fairchild came to Hong Kong obviously seeking a source of cheaper labor. Semiconductor plants were later established in Korea (1966), Singapore (1968), and Okinawa (1969).[1]

Malaysia

Malaysia: a pell-mell rush by foreign business

It sounds like a capitalist dream: a country and land with ample oil, cheap labor and land, a booming economy, and a stable government. The country is Malaysia, and foreign companies are flocking there as if it were the last prime investment site on earth...There, electronics companies, in particular, are finding an untapped source of nimble-fingered women willing to assemble integrated circuits for less than $2 a day. The US's National Semiconductor Corp, which already is turning out Malaysian-assembled electronic components, is just one company scouring the countryside for further pockets of cheap labor. Competition will be stiff. The US's Teledyne, West Germany's Siemens, Japan's Toshiba, and Britain's Plessey all plan Malaysian plants by yearend.[2]

Philippines

Bataan zone taking shape

Most of the zone factories produce items with a high labour component such as garments, shoes and electronics. (The largest factory, however, is a Ford car body stamping plant built for US $39 million and employing only 300 workers.) For most foreign investors, the reduced labour cost is the big attraction. An American electronics executive here says labour in the US would cost him US $7 an hour. Assembly line workers at Bataan say they receive 9 Pesos a day plus a 2 Peso cost of living allowance.[3]

Singapore

Singapore: Asia's new boom town

Lured...by Singapore's stability, central location and low-cost, highly motivated labor force, an estimated 500 foreign companies have set up shop in Singapore since 1965. They include such multinational giants as General Electric, Philips, Beecham, Ingersoll-Rand and Dainippon. American firms lead the pack with an aggregate investment of over $400 million. 'We came out here because it's faster and less expensive,' says Heinz Gelles of McGraw-Hill Far East Publishers. 'It would take us five years to produce an encyclopedia in the US that takes only one year.[4]

1. Business International Corporation, *Organising for Asia/Pacific Operations* (1972), p. 32.
2. *Business Week*, 30 March 1974.
3. 1 US $ = 7.50 Pesos. *Far Eastern Economic Review*, 20 August 1976.
4. *Newsweek*, 19 February 1973.

South Korea

Electronics: cheap labour attracts foreigners

One of the most remarkable success stories of South Korea's industrialisation has been the electronics industry. Beginning in 1958 with the assembly of radios from imported components, it now employs more than 100000 men and women in about 400 factories. It was not until 1966, however, that world manufacturers began to appreciate the advantage of using Korea's abundance of cheap, diligent labour to solve the growing cost difficulties of such a labour-intensive industry. First into the field were three American companies – Motorola, Signetics and Fairchild. That small beginning soon became a flood, with the Japanese leading the way. Today there are 168 Japanese electronic companies operating in Korea through 139 joint ventures and 29 wholly Japanese investments.[1]

Taiwan

Letter from Kaohsiung

The KEPZ (Kaohsiung Export Processing Zone), which alone accounts for almost 7% of the country's total exports, is more or less a microcosm of the Taiwan economy. Thus the Japanese, Americans and Overseas Chinese are the biggest investors; about half of the raw material and equipment imports comes from Japan while 50% of the exports goes to the US. One Chinese official explained: 'It's as if the EPZs were made for the Japanese – they use our cheap labour to produce exports to the US.'[2]

Mauritius

Mauritius Export Processing Zones pulling in the foreign investors

The Mauritius Export Processing Zones (MEPZ), set up by the government in 1970, continue to attract foreign investors from America, Australasia, Britain, France, Germany, Japan, India, Hong Kong and so on. The products manufactured in these zones include electronic components, knitwear, model boats, soft toys, polished diamonds, garments etc. Companies with technical know-how and marketing outlets found the MEPZ ideally suited for light industries of great labour/skill intensity where the value-added factor was substantial. In fact Mauritius has a large reserve of human resources easily adaptable to new modern techniques of production. Wage scales are much lower than for similar categories in developed countries. There is also a vigorous well financed local private sector keen to enter into joint venture arrangements with foreign investors.[3]

1. *The Times*, 26 September 1975.
2. *Far Eastern Economic Review*, 13 December 1974.
3. *African Development*, July 1976.

Tunisia

DEG arranges business trips to Tunisia

As the DEG explains, the European precision instruments and electrical engineering industry has discovered Tunisia as an attractive and cheap production site. The large supply of dextrous and easily trained workers, wages of DM1.50 per hour including social benefits, ten year tax holiday, unlimited transfer of capital and duty-free import and export within the EEC are the main reasons... German industry has so far established more than forty successfully operating plants – especially garment and shoe factories.[1]

Brazil

Burroughs in Brazil

One company that is finding Brazil a profitable export base is Burroughs, which is manufacturing made-in-Brazil products for the US and other world markets... The electronic components from Burroughs Brazil are all shipped back to the US, where they are integrated into the memory cores of Burrough's computer hardware. Air cargo is used both ways, but lower labor costs and quality work in Brazil have made the transportation and training expenses involved worthwhile... A number of factors lured Burroughs to Brazil for its electronic venture – in addition to its successful office machinery experience. Land in the Sao Paulo suburbs was reasonably priced and real labor productivity is high. Labor, even in Sao Paulo, is still inexpensive by world standards. Burroughs had also found in its office machinery venture that workers are easily trained, and Brazilian women are particularly responsive to training requiring manual dexterity.[2]

Dominican Republic

How companies view Dominican Free Trade Zone

La Romana free trade zone is operated and managed by Gulf & Western Americas under a 30-year contract with the Dominican Government. Since it came on stream in 1971 it has attracted about 14 firms, most of which are of US origin. Besides the fiscal exemptions, La Romana has a low-wage work force, and this appears to be the zone's main attractive point. Wage rates average nationally (including 28.07% fringe benefits) $0.77 an hour for semi-skilled workers and $0.51 an hour for unskilled. This is considerably lower than some of the island's Caribbean neighbours.[3]

1. *Nachrichten für Außenhandel*, 6 August 1976.
2. Business International Corporation, *Nationalism in Latin America* (New York 1970), p. 63.
3. *Business Latin America*, 8 May 1974.

Guatemala

The basic characteristic of industries operating under the 'drawback system' is that they make use of the abundant and economically advantageous labor factor, *highly desirable for international corporations* requiring labor intensive activities.[1]

Haiti

Over the last ten years and especially since the year 1967 a new type of industry has emerged from the Haitian economic panorama. This industry which is of the labour-intensive kind, manufactures export products with imported inputs and, therefore is known as the re-export industry. There are several reasons for the growth of the re-export industry in Haiti: (a) the availability of a large pool of inexpensive labour (legal minimum wage, $1.00 per eight hour day); (b) the nearness of Haiti to the US market and the existence of an adequate transportation system between Haiti and the USA; (c) the general trend to transfer labour-intensive industries to underdeveoped countries because of international competition.[2]

Mexico

Mexico's booming border zone: a magnet for labor-intensive American plants

Since the initiation of Mexico's Border Industrialisation Program in 1965, a considerable number of US assembly plants have been established in Mexico, mainly along the US border, which were attracted by labor rates considerably below those in the US. At present, over 470 border plants ('maquiladoras') are in existence with a total investment estimated at close to $1 billion. In addition, there are some 60 recently established in-bond plants in the interior of Mexico. Electric and electronic products account for 40% of the total and textiles for 20%. A number of plants manufacture timber products, foodstuffs, sports equipment and toys, as well as a variety of other products...

Low wage rates, combined with productivity rates that compare favorably with those in the US, are the principal motivating forces for US firms to establish assembly plants in Mexico.[3]

The above excerpts provide adequate proof of the fact that there are four prime factors involved in the decision to relocate world market production to free production zones (given that other investment incentives and conditions in the free production zones are taken into account):

(1) the availability of a practically unlimited supply of labour,
(2) the utilisation of an extremely productive labour-force,

1. Centro Nacional de Promocion de Las Exportaciones, *The Free Industrial Development Zone of Santo Tomas de Castilla and the 'Drawback System'*.
2. UNIDO, *Training Workshop in Industrial Free Zones as Incentives to Promote Export-Oriented Industries*, 24 March 1972, Bernhard Fatton, Haiti.
3. *Inter-American Economic Affairs*, 1 (1975), Peter G. Van der Spek, Manager, International Economic Research, Brunswick Corporation.

(3) the utilisation of an extremely cheap labour-force,
(4) the utilisation of an extremely 'compliant' labour-force.

Taken together, these considerations imply the utilisation of that particular group of workers in the world which is forced to sell its labour-power regardless of the wage, or the job, on pain of starvation.

However, even the cheapest labour-force can only be employed in manufacturing if the skill structure of the labour-force corresponds with the requirements of the industrial processes to be established. The unemployed labour-force at the sites of the free production zones is predominantly unskilled or semiskilled. Accordingly, a structure of production has arisen in the free production zones which is chiefly characterised by a product and process technology requiring mainly unskilled or semiskilled labour. This, however, does not imply, as is often claimed, *only* labour-intensive production. Capital-intensive production is equally as open to operation by unskilled and semiskilled workers, a fact that can be clearly seen in the case of the textile industry. Moreover, production in free production zones is by no means limited to assembly. Modern production technology allows the separation and allocation of operations to unskilled and semiskilled labour at all levels of production. It is precisely those production processes that can be operated on either a capital-intensive, i.e. automated, or labour-intensive basis, i.e. performed manually, which are often allocated to an unskilled labour-force in world market factories since both automation as well as the employment of unskilled labour requires the breaking down of the labour process into its most rudimentary parts.[1]

15.2 Industrial mono-structures

Of the twenty-nine ISIC Major Groups of manufacturing industry, all but two (beverages and tobacco) are represented in the production structure of the free production zones. This would seem to indicate

1. 'Using the low cost labor of the LDCs for manufacturing is simply a way to capitalise fully on these other competitive strengths. In this perspective, locating a factory in a LDC which permits minimum production costs is no different from choosing the most efficient manufacturing technology – a practice which firms take for granted.' (Nathaniel H. Left, 'International sourcing strategy', *Columbia Journal of World Business* (1974), p. 72.)

a wide spectrum of products but is in fact deceptive as the entire range cannot be found in any individual zone. Only a few of the product groups are represented within any one zone, and generally with only particular part-manufacturing processes. This applies especially to production processes in the Major Groups 381 (metal products), 382 (machinery), 383 (electrical machinery) and 384 (transport equipment). On the other hand the data does indicate that overall the utilisation of cheap labour in the developing countries can be found in almost all industrial branches.

The greater part of production in free production zones – both individual plants and within the zones as a whole – can be designated as non-complex. Some steps towards complex or partially integrated manufacturing can be seen in the textile and garment industry, but only infrequently in other branches, and only in a small number of zones.[1] The most important product groups are textiles and garments, metal products, electrical products, precision engineering, optical equipment, sports goods and toys. The major portion of production is associated with the consumer goods industry. A very high proportion of total production in free production zones is related to the textiles and garment industry, and the electrical engineering industry (Table III-10). In 1975, 59000 employees in textiles and garments and 108000 employees in the manufacturing of electrical products were at work in the world market factories of Hong Kong, Taiwan, Tunisia, El Salvador and Mexico – five countries for which the distribution of employment in world market factories by industry is available. These two sectors together accounted for 167000 of the 226500 employees, with the result that 74% of all employees in these zones worked in textiles and garment production (26%) or in the electrical engineering industry (48%).

One fact worthy of note is that the employment structure of foreign firms in Hong Kong and the northern border zone of Mexico exhibits a very similar pattern. Up to 80% of the total labour-force is employed in either textiles and garments or in the electrical

1. Examples of highly technical, partially integrated production processes are the manufacturing of watches (Singapore Time PTE. Ltd), oil rigs (Marathon Le Tourneau Offshore PTE. Ltd), machine tools (Hilgepore PTE. Ltd) in Singapore and the manufacturing of X-ray equipment (Kehrli X-Ray SDN. BHD.) in Malaysia. The Singapore Time PTE. Ltd is the first integrated world market factory established by the Japanese firm Seiko. The Singapore plant of Seiko will combine all production processes from the production of simple, basic materials such as brass or steel rods and coils to the final assembly.

Table III-10. *Free production zones in selected countries: employment in the industrial branches of textiles and garments, and electronics: 1975*

		Employment in free production zones					
Country	Total	Textiles and garments ISIC 321–322	Share of total employment (%)	Electrical products ISIC 383	Share of total employment (%)	ISIC 321–322 and ISIC 383	Share of total employment (%)
Hong Kong[a]	59607	12372	21	27993	47	40365	68
Taiwan	62143	14572	23	29300	47	43872	70
Tunisia[b]	24000	17700	74	2600[c]	11	20300	85
El Salvador	6143	660	11	1900	31	2560	42
Mexico	74676	13440[d]	18	46634	62	60074	80
Total	226569	58744	26	108427	48	167171	74

Source: author's calculation
a: Only foreign firms
b: Figures for 1974
c: Including metal products
d: Including footwear and leather products

engineering industry in the Mexican border zone. Both Hong Kong and Mexico belong to that group of developing countries in which world market oriented industrialisation began relatively early and was relatively advanced by 1975. However, the fact that these countries exhibit the same industrial structure as can be found in the zones of other developing countries is an indication of the fact that the process of world market oriented industrialisation, even at sites where the preconditions for complex production are already present in some initial form, will not allow complex production to develop if the specific calculations of companies do not make these sites appear strategically favourable for complex production.

In a survey on the subcontracting activities of US firms in developing countries published by the United States Tariff Commission[1] the following production processes were listed as being typical of free production zones and world market factories: subassembly and assembly of radios and radio parts, television receivers and parts for television receivers, record players, assembly of toys, assembly of scientific instruments, sewing together of precut

1. United States Tariff Commission, *Economic Factors Affecting the Use of Items 807.00 and 806.30 of the Tariff Schedules of the United States,* Report to the President (Washington 1970), pp. 91–149.

parts of gloves and sports balls,[1] and the sewing up of precut materials and assembly of metal frames for suitcases.[2]

15.3 Relocation of production in the electrical engineering industry: the production of electronic components

As is indicated by the employment figures given above for electrical engineering firms operating in the free production zones of the five countries mentioned, the relocation of production to developing countries in this branch of industry has reached considerable proportions. In 1975 the electrical engineering industry had established world market factories in twenty-three countries, including world market factories in free production zones in fourteen countries. The total number of employees in world market factories in these twenty-three countries had reached 691 160 by 1975. Assuming the same distribution of employees as in the five countries analysed above (48 % in the electrical engineering industry), the total number of employees in electrical engineering world market factories in the developing countries may be estimated at 332 000. Evidence that this estimate is not unrealistic can be derived by the number of electrical engineering plants listed in Column 5 of Table III-18. In addition, the information which is available for a number of other countries (i.e. Malaysia, Singapore and South Korea) roughly corroborates this estimate: 332 000 workers is equivalent to 6 % of the total employment in the electrical engineering industry in the EEC,[3] the USA and Japan which together accounted for 5.5 million employees in 1972.[4] This figure is all the more significant when one recalls that the very first world market factory in the

1. 'Leather covers, centers, cotton yarn, cement, and latex are manufactured in US plants, then shipped to plants in Haiti and/or Jamaica where the covers are sewn on. The balls are then returned to the United State's plant for further minor processing...The principle reason reported for the use of foreign assembly facilities for the production of baseballs and softballs is the reduction in the product costs through the use of foreign labor.' (United States Tariff Commission, *Economic Factors*, p. 120.)
2. 'The US producer of luggage...chose to use its foreign production facilities as an alternative to expanding its US plant. Taking account of the cost of all factors of production, it was found to be somewhat less costly to assemble the articles abroad than to produce them wholly in the United States in an expanded facility.' (United States Tariff Commission, *Economic Factors*, p. 121.)
3. Not including Belgium and the Netherlands.
4. The employment figures for the electronics industry in the USA, the EEC countries and Japan were drawn from: UN, *Yearbook of Industrial Statistics, 1974 Edition*, Vol. I (New York 1976).

electrical engineering industry was established in the developing countries as recently as 1966.

The electrical engineering industry is one the few branches for which surveys of the structure of production in world market factories exist: principally the surveys already mentioned by Chang and Moxon and a study by the secretariat of UNCTAD.[1]

The UNCTAD study lists the foreign employment in world market factories ('offshore operations') for leading firms in the electrical engineering industry of the USA, Western Europe and Japan (Table III-11) involved in the manufacture of electronic components. Between 1971 and 1974 employment in electronic component manufacturing in world market factories in developing countries increased from 22000 to 80000. This development is a classic example of the relationship between technical innovations and the valorisation of capital, and its effect on world-wide socio-economic development.

Two factors in the product and process technology of semiconductors are of significance in explaining why the relocation of certain production processes has taken place on such a scale:

(1) the development of three generations of semiconductors in the short span of a few years (silicon dioxide, integrated and later fully integrated circuits),
(2) the development of a product which requires, on the one hand, a highly mechanised and automated production process but which on the other hand is not easily mechanised in certain of its phases.

There are basically three production phases in the manufacture of semiconductors: production of the masks, production of the wafers, and assembly and testing. The first two phases are usually of necessity mechanised and/or automated, whereas the third phase is difficult to mechanise.

The soldering of the wires and the assembly into the capsule represents a significant portion of the production process which is being relocated to the developing countries.

1. T. S. Chang, *The Transfer of Technology: Economics of Offshore Assembly. The Case of Semiconductor Industry.* Richard W. Moxon, *Offshore Production in the Less Developed Countries. A Case Study of Multinationality in the Electronics Industry* (New York 1974). UNCTAD, *International Subcontracting Arrangements in Electronics between Developed Market-Economy Countries and Developing Countries* (New York 1975), TD/B/C.2/144.

Table III-11. *Location and employment of offshore operations of major firms in electronic component manufacturing: 1971, 1974*

Firms	Location in developing countries	Number of employees 1971	Number of employees 1974	Main products manufactured
United States firms				
Fairchild	Hong Kong	2000	3000	Semiconductors,
	South Korea	2000	6000	ceramic resistors
	Singapore	1500	3800	
	Mexico	650	n.a.	
	Indonesia		500	
Motorola	South Korea	2800	4500	Semiconductors,
	Mexico	1000	n.a.	test equipment
	Malaysia		3000	
	Hong Kong		300	
Texas Instruments	Singapore	1500	4000	Semiconductors,
	Taiwan	1000	3000	memory arrays,
	Malaysia		2500	parts of calculators,
	El Salvador		1800	control products
National	Singapore	1000	4000	Semiconductors
	Malaysia		2500	
	Thailand		2000	
	Indonesia		1500	
	Hong Kong		500	
Hewlett Packard	Singapore	500	1800	Memory arrays,
	Malaysia		800	semiconductors, parts and sub-assembly of calculators
Teledyne	Hong Kong		1600	Semiconductors
	Singapore		1300	
	Malaysia		400	
Intersil	Singapore	100	400	Semiconductors
Litronix	Malaysia		1500	Semiconductors
	Mauritius		850	
	Singapore		600	
American Micro	South Korea		2500	Semiconductors
	Mexico	500	n.a.	
Airco	Singapore	850	1300	Fixed carbon resistors,
	Mexico	211	n.a.	coil forms
Industrial Electronics	Singapore	n.a.	1200	Semiconductors
	Malaysia		300	
Monsanto	Malaysia		1000	Semiconductors
	Indonesia		500	
R.C.A.	Malaysia		1500	Semiconductors
	Taiwan	650	1500	
	Singapore	600		
General Electric	Singapore	500	1000	Capacitors, semiconductors
Advanced Micro Devices	Malaysia		600	Integrated circuits
West European firms				
Siemens	Singapore	250	1000	Semiconductors
	Malaysia		800	
S.G.S.	Singapore	500	2000	Semiconductors
Carter's	Hong Kong	3000	2000	Semiconductors
	Philippines		2000	
	Malaysia		1000	
Philips	Taiwan	850	1000	n.a.
	Hong Kong		850	
Plessey	Malaysia		n.a.	Semiconductors

Table III-11. *(cont.)*

Firms	Location in developing countries	Number of employees 1971	1974	Main products manufactured
Japanese firms				
Hitachi	Malaysia		500	Semiconductors
Toshiba	Korea	n.a.	800	Semiconductors
	Malaysia		150	
Toko Electronics	Republic of Korea		n.a.	Transformers and coils, semiconductors
	Malaysia		350	
Matsushita	Malaysia		300	Printed circuit boards, variable resistors, electrolytic capacitors
Sanyo	South Korea	n.a.	1000	Semiconductors, parts of electronic calculators
	Malaysia		n.a.	
Nippon Electronics	South Korea	n.a.	2000	n.a.
Tyodo Electronics	South Korea	n.a.	500	n.a.
Naito Electronics	Malaysia		180	Semiconductors
Seiko Electronics	Malaysia		7	Electrolytic capacitors (trial production)

Source: UNCTAD, *International Subcontracting Arrangements in Electronics between Developed Market-Economy Countries and Developing Countries* (New York 1975), TD/B/C.2/144/Supp. 1, pp. 17, 18.

The wafer, which is the heart of the semiconductor, is fabricated in the United States. It is then flown, together with other components, to, say, Singapore, where labour costs for assembly are about a tenth of American ones. Under magnification, the gold threads are soldered to the terminal, and the finished semiconductor is flown back to the United States.[1]

The proportion of those phases which are not easily mechanised has hardly been reduced with the development of the technology of the semiconductors themselves into the second and third generations. Phases of the production processes which can be mechanised/ automated or performed manually are carried out predominantly by hand provided that this can be done by semiskilled or unskilled workers: the main reason for this is the extremely swift change in semiconductor technology which exposes the heavy outlays on equipment to the risk of rapid obsolescence. To avoid this risk many firms try to perform these phases of the process with unskilled and semiskilled cheap labour.

. . . even if automation appears to be the lowest cost alternative, it will not be used unless management is sure that it can recover the heavy investment through a long period of production of the same product with the same process . . . One company that did automate its semiconductor production was Philco in the late 1950s. At the

1. UNCTAD, *International Subcontracting Arrangements in Electronics*, p. 7.

time, the company had a technological lead, but the technology quickly became obsolete and its production facilities of little use. But automation is economic for a few high volume standardised products, and one company interviewed now makes a few products in automated US plants that were once made offshore.[1]

The use of manual processing in semiconductor production is important to producers who supply a rapidly changing market characterised by new technology, product innovation, and swift obsolescence of products. Manufacturers state that such rapid changes in the market discourage economical automation of product lines; automation would tend (1) to prevent product innovation because of the investment required, and (2) slow the advance of technology vital to maintaining their competitive position with regard to imports.[2]

Both technical considerations and the need to valorise the capital invested (avoidance of the risk of rapid obsolescence of equipment) are the key factors in the existence of a relatively high degree of manual labour in the manufacture of semiconductors. What is decisive for the large amount of relocation of production to the developing countries is the basic maxim of the valorisation of capital: the utilisation of cheap labour.

Low labour cost is the most obvious important reason for selecting a particular country. The wage differential is the most advantageous at Korea, Taiwan, Singapore, Hong Kong and Mexico in that order. The productivity of assembly labour seems as the US experience and often better, after a brief learning period.[3]

US firms utilising item 806.30 in the processing of semiconductors state that the major reason for foreign assembly is the advantage of using lower-wage foreign labor. They state that intense competition with foreign producers of semiconductors requires that US firms seek the same wage costs available to foreign firms.[4]

The crucial criteria for the selection of a specific site are indicated by the following extracts from Moxon's and UNCTAD's studies.

The comments of managers also indicated that they often are searching for specific kinds of labor offshore. Managers from companies making computer memories, for example, often said that in the United States they could not find enough workers willing to do the tedious assembly work required. Such manufacturers need large numbers of workers having good dexterity and eyesight, and the right kind of mental attitudes. They cited as reasons for their move abroad the high turnover, poor productivity, and poor quality standards by their US workforce. Similar comments were made by some manufacturers of components and consumer electronics products. All managers interviewed agreed that offshore workers were better suited to these kinds of jobs, were more productive, and were less prone to errors.[5]

1. Moxon, *Offshore Production*, pp. 48 and 49.
2. United States Tariff Commission, *Economic Factors*, p. 128.
3. Chang, *The Transfer of Technology*, p. 26.
4. United States Tariff Commission, *Economic Factors*, p. 127.
5. Moxon, *Offshore Production*, p. 29.

Another important consideration for the setting up of offshore manufacturing centres in electronics is the immediate availability of labour at a particular location. Availability does not only mean numbers. The labour force must have a basic education if possible, be easily trainable and not widely dispersed. In Hong Kong and Singapore the labour force is concentrated in special housing schemes near to production centres.

Finally it is worth noting that most of the employment created so far by electronics manufacturing in developing countries has been for female labour. There are two main reasons for this: firstly, wage rates for female workers are normally lower than for male workers of similar grade and skills; secondly, it seems that much of this work – semiconductor assembly for example – is carried out with a higher degree of efficiency by female than by male workers.[1]

Moxon's study presents the case of the distribution of the production of a large US producer of semiconductors. All the masks and wafers are manufactured in plants in the USA. The soldering and assembly for simple semiconductors and for integrated circuits takes place almost exclusively in South East Asia, whereas this phase of production for the fully integrated circuits takes place exclusively in the USA. In the case of simple circuits the testing occurs mostly in the developing countries; a small amount of testing of integrated circuits takes place in plants outside the USA, whereas the testing of the fully integrated circuits is carried out exclusively in the USA (see Table III-12).

The manufacturing of electronic components in developing countries in fact consists to a great extent in the performance of single, elementary operations, which allow the profitable (cost minimising) substitution of labour for machines. What appears in the statistics as the manufacture of a highly sophisticated technical product in the developing countries consists in reality in the execution of a few routine operations (though physically and mentally demanding), mainly soldering and assembling, under a microscope by cheap, semiskilled labour.

Technically sophisticated integrated production processes for the manufacturing of electronic components are not carried out in the developing countries; moreover, there appears to be no significant tendency to suggest that such a development will occur. All Singapore's efforts to achieve an integrated production structure in the field of semiconductor manufacturing have until now merely led to a limited degree of forwards integration (testing, packaging, direct shipping to the customer). The technically demanding manufacture

1. UNCTAD, *International Subcontracting Arrangements in Electronics*, pp. 20–1.

Table III-12. *Offshore production pattern of one large semiconductor company*

Manufacturing operations	Diodes: glass package	Transistors		Integrated circuits			
		Plastic encapsulated	Metal can package	Digital applications	Linear applications	MOS memory	Hybrid integrated circuits
Mask making and wafer fabrication							
Location[a]	US	US	US	US	US	US	US
% offshore[b]	0	0	0	0	0	0	0
Assembly of circuit chip into package							
Location[a]	Far East	Far East & US	Far East	Far East & US	Far East & US	US	Far East & US
% offshore[b]	100	80	100	90	80	0	20
First year of off-shore production	Before 1965	Before 1965	1967/68	1969/70	1969/70	—	1969/70
Testing and marking							
Location[a]	Far East	Far East & US	Far East & US	Far East & US	US	US	US
% offshore[b]	100	80	10	10	0	0	0
First year of off-shore production	1967/68	1969/70	1969/70	1969/70			

Source: Richard W. Moxon, *Offshore Production in the Less Developed Countries. A Case Study of Multinationality in the Electronics Industry* (New York 1974), p. 43
a: Location of plants performing this manufacturing step
b: Percentage of the company's total production of this product done in offshore plants

of wafers and masks still does not take place in Singapore.[1] Recent changes in semiconductor technology – large circuits and miniaturisation – indicate merely an extension of the type of production structure already found in world market factories rather than a change. The replacement of electro-mechanics by electronics, now taking place in many branches of industry, is leading on the one hand to a significant increase in the manufacture and use of electronic components, and on the other hand, to the further relocation of production from the traditional industrial sites to world market factories at the new sites. The former stage (electro-mechanical equipment) relied on skilled labour: fitters, lathe operators, millers, electricians etc. In contrast the assembly of electronic components can be undertaken with unskilled or semiskilled workers.

1. 'The Economic Development Board in Singapore has been trying to promote the upgrading of skills and technology in the electronics industry. In the semiconductor sector, forward integration into testing, finishing, warehousing and direct shipping to customer instead of via the US parent is becoming more common. But the policy of encouraging backward integration into wafer manufacture has not been successful because of economic and technological considerations.' (*Financial Times,* 8 October 1976: 'Singapore'.)

16 ❧ The labour market and working conditions in free production zones and world market factories

16.1 Unemployment and underemployment in the developing countries

Working conditions in free production zones and world market factories can only be understood in the context of the conditions which prevail on the labour markets of the developing countries, which are part of the integrated capitalist world market for labour. It is therefore necessary to obtain an overall understanding of this submarket of the world labour market, and in particular of the extent of unemployment and underemployment. In 1975 the ILO presented for the first time aggregated estimates of the extent of unemployment and underemployment in the developing countries (see Table III-13).[1] According to their report about 5% of the economically active population in developing countries[2] (about 700 million people in 1975) were probably unemployed and about 36% were probably underemployed. In absolute figures that means that in 1975 about 33 million persons were unemployed and 250 million underemployed in the developing countries. Of these 283 million, 55 million lived in the large cities and urban areas in the developing countries. The total estimated number of unemployed and underemployed people in the developing countries (283 million) was about double the total number of persons employed in manufacturing in the developed *and* the developing countries (141 million persons in 1970): or about three and a half times the number of persons working in the manufacturing industries in the western developed countries (1970: 77 million).[3]

1. ILO, *Employment, Growth and Basic Needs. A One-World Problem* (Geneva 1976), pp. 18–19. Report of the Director-General of the ILO for the 'World Conference on Employment, Income Distribution and Social Progress and the International Division of Labour', 1975.
2. Not including the People's Republic of China and the other socialist countries in Asia.
3. The employment figures for the manufacturing industries were drawn from: UNCTAD, *Handbook of International Trade and Development Statistics 1976*, p. 386.

Table III-13. *Preliminary estimates (in millions) of unemployment and underemployment in developing countries, by region: 1975*

Region	Unemployment[a]				Underemployment[b]				Total			
	Total		Urban		Total		Urban		Total		Urban	
	(No.)	(%)	(No.)	(%)	(No.)	(%)	(No.)	(%)	(No.)	(%)	(No.)	(%)
Asia[c]	18	3.9	6	6.9	168	36.4	20	23.2	186	40.3	26	30.1
Africa	10	7.1	3	10.8	53	37.9	7	25.1	63	45.0	10	35.9
Latin America	5	5.1	5	6.5	28	28.9	14	22.8	33	34.0	19	29.3
Oceania					1	49.0			1	49.0		
Total	33	4.7	14	8.0	250	35.7	41	23.3	283	40.4	55	31.3

Source: ILO, *Employment, Growth and Basic Needs. A One-World Problem* (Geneva 1976), p.18.
a: Defined as 'persons without a job and looking for work'
b: Defined as 'persons who are in employment of less than normal duration and who are seeking or would accept additional work' and 'persons with a job yielding inadequate income'
c: Excluding China and other Asian centrally planned economies.

Figures on the extent of unemployment and underemployment in individual countries, which are available as estimates for some countries and as census results for others, reveal that the aggregated figures reported by the ILO only indicate the lower limit of the extent of unemployment and underemployment in the developing countries. An estimate by the Indian Government of unemployment in India in 1971 yielded a figure of 18.7 million persons.[1] In Indonesia, the estimate for 1974 was 4 million unemployed and 28 million underemployed;[2] this meant that from a potential working population of 45 million only 27% were in full-time employment. In 1975 unemployment and underemployment in the Dominican Republic was estimated at 40%;[3] 'open unemployment' in El Salvador was estimated at 20% in 1971;[4] in 1975, unemployment in Colombia was estimated at between 10% and 15%;[5] unemployment in Puerto Rico in 1974 was 13.9%, with the underemployed adding another 19.5%.[6] In 1975, unemployment in both Mauritius[7] and Tunisia[8] was estimated at 15%.

1. See UN, Economic and Social Commission for Asia and the Pacific (ESCAP), *Economic and Social Survey of Asia and the Pacific 1974* (Bangkok 1975), p. 130.
2. See Bundestelle für Außenhandelsinformation, Mitteilungen, *Indonesien*, August 1974, p. 4.
3. See *Financial Times*, 24 September 1975, 'Dominican Republic'.
4. See Bundestelle für Außenhandelsinformation, *El Salvador* (1975), p. 2.
5. Statistisches Bundesamt, *Kolumbien* (1975), p. 7.
6. See Economic Development Administration, *Puerto Rico Labor Profile* (1975), pp. 4, 5.
7. See *Nachrichten für Außenhandel*, 30 July 1975, 'Mauritius awaits German investors'.
8. See *Financial Times*, 16 June 1976, 'Tunisia'.

The existence of a large unemployed pool of labour (separated from the means of production as a result of the spread of capitalist relations of production) and the associated existence of acute poverty in developing countries forces the unemployed to work at virtually any price (i.e. at any wage). Within the world-wide integrated capitalist economy the unemployed labour-force in the developing countries constitutes an industrial reserve army which can be mobilised at any time. The total size of the reserve army in the developing countries, as stated above, easily exceeds the total number of people employed in manufacturing in Western Europe, USA and Japan.

The industrial utilisation of labour-power in free production zones and world market factories is now being marketed – on the world labour market – by the governments of many countries using the same modern advertising techniques employed in promoting or selling any other commodity. Productivity, loyalty, mobility and skill are the major slogans in the competition between the developing countries to sell their workers on the world labour market. The chief selling point is of course that the quantity is large and the price is low.

In a brochure entitled *Malaysia: Opportunities for European Investments*, the Federal Industrial Development Authority of Malaysia is trying to attract investors with the following arguments.

Labour rates in Malaysia are amongst the lowest in the region and female factory workers can be hired for approximately US $1.50 a day. The labour force is generally English speaking and the literacy rate is extremely high. Large multinational US corporations like Hewlett Packard, Motorola and National Semiconductor which have invested in labour intensive manufacturing projects in Malaysia have found labour so easy to train and so productive that within less than a year have not only expanded their operations in Malaysia but also set up new factories to produce more sophisticated products than their original investments.[1]

In a full page advertisement placed by the government of the Philippines in *The Times* under the headlines 'Seven good reasons why you should be looking to the Philippines now' the following appeared.

Our labour force speaks your language. Whether you're talking electronic components, garments or car-manufacturing. National literacy was placed at 83.4 per cent in 1973 (English is the medium of instruction), which brings the Philippines closest to the Japanese standard among all the Asian countries. The

1. Federal Industrial Development Authority, *Malaysia: Opportunities for European Investments*, p. 2.

generally high level of education of the Filipino worker makes him highly adaptable, easy to train in new skills. (You might even find that the government has pre-trained your workers for you in one of its skill centres.)[1]

The Board of Investment of Thailand advertises in a brochure *15 Powerful Reasons Why You Should Invest in Thailand.*

One of the major factors which recommends Thailand to the investor over other countries in the region is its abundant supply of cheap and trainable labour. The minimum wage for unskilled labour in the Bangkok metropolis and the six surrounding industrial provinces was fixed at 20 baht per day (US $1.00) as of late 1974. Although this is still an extremely low wage, it is 20 per cent higher than in late 1973, showing that public and private sectors are aware of the rising costs of living facing Thai workers. Outside Bangkok the minimum wage has recently been set at 16 baht per day in the North and Northeast and 18 baht in the South of Thailand.

The Thai people are naturally clever with their hands, and they are very quick to learn new processes, even when these require considerable concentration, adaptibility and initiative. The managers of two firms which require high precision work – Cosmo Watch Dials and National Semiconductor – have praised the dexterity as well as the quick trainability of their Thai workers. National Semiconductor sent a group of workers to learn electronic skills in Penang. The workers were all able to complete the six month course in three month's time. Thai women are every bit as skillful as the men, and are often preferred to men due to their perserverance. Women work side by side with men on many jobs where a sex distinction might be made in other countries. They are given equal pay for equal work as a general rule. Foreign investors should realise that the Buddhist religion and Thailand's social history have ensured that the relationship between employer and employee is normally more that of guardian and ward than of master and serf. In other words, it is easy to win and maintain the loyalty of the workforce as long as they are treated with kindness and due courtesy.[2]

The Economic Planning Board in South Korea offers the labour-force of South Korea to the potential investor in terms of the following attractions.

Korea's labour force is one of her primary resources. Due to a comprehensive educational system, over 90 per cent of the people are literate. If it is possible to stereotype, Koreans tend to be extremely bright, aggressive and individualistic. Traditionally, a major problem in Korea has been underemployment. A substantial portion of the labour force is seasonal and part-time. This has resulted in a relatively low average wage system by western standards. Now, due to the rapid increase in technical and vocational schools, skilled workers are available in almost all fields.[3]

The following text is an excerpt from an advertisment of the

1. *The Times*, 12 June 1975.
2. The Office of the Board of Investment, *15 Powerful Reasons Why You Should Invest in Thailand*, p. 13.
3. Economic Planning Board, *Guide to Investment in Korea*, pp. 45–6.

Ministry for Commerce and Industry of Mauritius in the *Financial Times*.

Companies with technical know-how and marketing outlets found the MEPZ ideally suited for light industries of great labour/skill intensity where the value added factor was substantial. In fact, Mauritius has a large reserve of human resources easily adaptable to new and modern techniques of production. Wage scales are much lower than for similar categories in developed countries.[1]

The administration of the Industrial Free Zone of Santiago, Dominican Republic, advertises its workers with the following text.

Above everything, Santiago is an ideal center for the operation of an industrial free zone because of its labor. The worker from this region, man or woman, is intelligent, cooperative, disciplined, ready to be trained, having lived in a community with a century old industrial tradition.[2]

The authorities of the Free Zone of Cartagena, Colombia, use a wage cost comparison as their main inducement.

Low cost labour: this is without doubt the chief incentive offered by the ZFIC as the salaries are more or less the same as those that prevail in the industrial zones of the Far East (US $2.10 a day including social security). Local people are easily trained by experts who are suitably equipped to do so. Male and female workers are easily obtained due to the high rate of unemployment, rapid increase of population and the emigration from the rural zones to the cities.[3]

The following text is taken from an advertisement by the Central Bank of Nicaragua.

Labor is abundant and cheap in Nicaragua, due in part to the fact that urban population has grown more rapidly than the creation of new jobs. Wages are relatively low and the minimum salary per day is lower than the minimum salary per hour in the USA.[4]

The Economic Development Administration of Puerto Rico advertises as follows in Federal Germany.

Puerto Rico has 921 000 workers, a half of which are under thirty-five years old. Indeed, this labour reserve is one of the island's richest industrial resources. At the present time more than 100 000 persons are available for immediate *hiring* – employers in Puerto Rico report that at least five candidates apply for each job offered. The island's labour-force is characterised by a high mobility; workers go where jobs can be found.[5]

1. *Financial Times*, 18 June 1976.
2. Corporation Zona Franca Industrial de Santiago, Inc., *Zona Franca Industrial*, p. 3.
3. Zona Franca Industrial y Comercial de Cartagena, *Investor's Guide*, p. 1.
4. Banco Central de Nicaragua, *Nicaragua – A Market for Off-Shore Assembly*, p. 5.
5. Commonwealth of Puerto Rico Economic Development Administration, *Arbeitskräfte, Berufsbildung, Löhne.*

The following implications can be drawn from such extracts, which could be multiplied many times over for other countries.

(1) They clearly indicate the conditions under which the labour of the developing countries is offered on the world labour market.
(2) They show that the unemployed labour-force of the developing countries is organised as an industrial reserve army of labour on a world-wide basis.
(3) They reveal the extent of the competition between different working populations on the world labour market.
(4) The existence of such notices is itself an expression of the globally integrated labour market.

16.2 The structure of employment in free production zones and world market factories

The following represents an analysis of the most important aspects of the structure of employment in free production zones and world market factories. A systematic treatment of all the relevant aspects of the structure of the labour-force and the type of employment available in free production zones and world market factories is not possible because of insufficient empirical data.

The most outstanding characteristics of the structure of employment in the free production zones and world market factories can be summarised quite briefly:

(1) The overwhelming majority of the employed are:
  (a) women;
  (b) aged between sixteen and twenty-five years;
  (c) unskilled or semiskilled;
  (d) employed as production workers.
(2) Investment per workplace is, on average, relatively low.
(3) There are no significant differences in the employment structure between free production zones that have been in operation for several years and those that have been established more recently.

In the majority of free production zones, more than 70% of the total employed are women. The following figures give a more detailed picture of the high proportion of female workers. Of a total employment of 13874 in the Free Zone Bayan Lepas, Malaysia, at the end of 1974, 11533 (83%) were women.[1] In the Masan Free Export Zone (MAFEZ), South Korea, in April 1975, 14434 of 20212 (71%) employed were women.[2] In the Export Processing Zones of Taiwan – Kaohsiung, Nantze and Taichung – out of 62143, 49080 (79%) of those employed in September 1975 were women. The high proportion of women in the three Zones was independent of the total size of the labour-force in the Zones. In Kaohsiung, 80% or 32892 out of 41017 were women, in Nantze 78% or 10328 out of 13160 were women and in Taichung 74% or 5850 out of 7966.[3] In the Export Processing Zones of Mauritius, various sources indicate that the proportion of women in the Zones' workers is more than 80%.[4] In the world market factories of Mexico's northern border zone, women also accounted for about 80% of total employment.[5] A similarly high proportion of female workers can also be assumed to prevail in the free production zones and world market factories in almost all developing countries. References which support this generalisation can be found in the figures supplied by or valid for individual companies, branch employment statistics, job notices etc. and also from the fact that the same product and production structure exists in most zones and world market factories.

As the following statistics on the age distribution of employees in Taiwan's Export Processing Zones clearly show,[6] the majority of the women employed belong to the fourteen to twenty-four age group. Of 46145 female production workers in Taiwan's three Zones in September 1975, 2016 belonged to the fourteen to fifteen age group, 20836 to the sixteen to nineteen group and 17285 to the twenty to twenty-four age group. Of the female production workers, 87% were under twenty-five years of age. In the Kaohsiung Zone, 91% (28262 out of 31152) of the female production workers were under twenty-five years of age. The proportion of male production workers between the ages of fourteen and twenty-four was, at the same time, 61% in the three Zones in Taiwan (5481 out of 9054); 81% of the total number of male workers belonged to the fourteen to twenty-nine age group (7328 persons). The age structure of

1. Statistics issued by the Penang Development Corporation.
2. See *Business Asia*, 11 July 1975, p. 222.
3. See Export Processing Zone Administration, Kaohsiung, *Export Processing Zones Essential Statistics* (1975), pp. 20–2.
4. See *Financial Times*, 26 June 1974, 18 June 1976; *FAZ*, 20 December 1976.
5. *The Times*, 17 August 1976.
6. See Export Processing Zone Administration, *Essential Statistics*, pp. 20–2.

employees in the Masan Free Export Zone in South Korea and in the Free Zones in Malaysia was very similar. Of the employees in Masan, 80% belonged in 1974 to the eighteen to thirty age group.[1] Also in 1974, 80%–85% of the female workers in the Free Zone Bayan Lepas in Malaysia were between eighteen and twenty-four years of age.

The proportion of workers in this age group who worked directly in production (operators) had reached a total of 100% in many factories.[2]

The following figures on the proportion of employees working directly in production in the Free Zones of Taiwan and Malaysia reveal the unusually high average percentage of production workers in the total work-force, a characteristic of the employment structure of all free production zones and world market factories. In Taiwan's[3] three Zones in September 1975, 55 199 out of a total of 62 143 employees (89%) were working directly in production. In the Kaohsiung Zone, the proportion of production workers reached 90% (37 008 out of 41 017). In the Free Zones of Penang – Bayan Lepas, Prai and Prai Wharf (including Pulau Jerejak) – in 1973, 11 885 out of a total of 14 028 or 84% of the employees worked directly in production.[4]

As the following figures show, investment per worker in free production zones and in world market factories outside the zones is generally low. In the Export Processing Zones of Taiwan, 260 firms had invested US $118.8 million. The average investment per worker was US $1912 (September 1975).[5] Among the branches represented the figures for investment per worker were as follows: electronics US $1822; electrical engineering (excluding electronics) US $2875; textile industry US $1163; garment industry US $763; metal products industry US $4314; precision instrument manufacture US $4552; manufacture of plastic products US $1727; engineering US $5233. The total investment of the 256 foreign manufacturing firms operating in Hong Kong (employing 70 421 workers) amounted to US $295 million in February 1975.[6] This represents an average

1. See 'A fact-finding survey of the Masan Free Export Zone', *AMPO Japan–Asia Quarterly Review* 2 (1976), p. 67.
2. Statistics issued by the Penang Development Corporation.
3. *Essential Statistics*, pp. 20–2.
4. See statistics issued by the Penang Development Corporation.
5. *Essential Statistics*, pp. 6–7.
6. See 'Hong Kong '75: Industrial Investment', *Far Estern Economic Review*, 28 March 1975.

capital investment per worker of US $4189. Individual industries showed the following capital investment per worker: electronics US $1961; electrical engineering (excluding electronics) US $5653; textile and garments US $5279; metal products manufacturing US $5602; and manufacturing of synthetics and toys US $2470. In the world market factories in the northern border zone of Mexico, the average investment per worker was US $840 – for the electrical engineering and electronics industry US $690; garments and shoes US $890; and furniture US $1100.[1]

As is evidenced by the above statistics on age, sex and skill, the structure of employment in free production zones and world market factories is extremely unbalanced. One particular type of worker is selected from the practically unlimited supply of unemployed labour and recruited into employment in the world market factories: young female workers. The criteria for selection are quite clear. The workers who are chosen are those who

(1) work for the lowest wages,
(2) are the most productive (can be expected to work at a high intensity) and
(3) are unskilled and semiskilled.

In developing countries – as in the industrialised – the price of female labour-power is lower than the price of male labour-power. In manufacturing (cf. Chapter 5.3) women's wages are frequently half of the male wage. Women have to sell their labour-power at the lowest possible price because under the conditions of underdevelopment women have even less possibility than men to change their living conditions: or to put it more bluntly, they have fewer possibilities of guaranteeing their day to day physical survival. In addition to the great wage differentials another major reason for the employment of women is the higher intensity at which they will work, a fact made evident in the following extracts.

The kinds of specified labor force demanded are for instance, wiring using a microscope for manufacturing memory planes for computers, spot welding in case of manufacturing radio receivers and television sets. As a consequence, workers with good visual power and deft handed workers are needed. Besides when a condition of relatively cheap wage is added, a required labor is a young female worker in Asian countries, where wage differentials between male and female workers still exist.[2]

1. See Secretaría de Indústria y Comercio. Quoted from Victor Manuel Bernal Sahagún, *The Impact of Multinational Corporations on Employment and Income: The Case of Mexico*, Working Paper, ILO (Geneva 1976), pp. 183–4.
2. Masami Tamaoki, *The Role of Industrial Free Zones. Case Studies in Asian Countries*, UNIDO (1972), p. 12.

Most manufacturers prefer female workers because they have a longer attention span than males and can adjust more easily to long hours on an assembly line. In addition, they are willing to accept lower pay and are said to have more agile hands, which is especially important in electronics.[1]

There has been some criticism of the fact that most zone industries, especially in the textile and electronic factories, employ mainly women. Some 85% of the workers are women, and efforts are being made to switch the trend... This trend is not necessarily due to the fact that women in Mauritius receive lower wages than men, but rather because industrialists have found that women are more adaptable than men to most of the skills required.[2]

Terms like 'more adaptable' and 'willing to accept lower pay' express nothing other than that women are forced to accept lower wages and a higher intensity of work than men.

The figures provided above on investment per worker can be interpreted as follows in the context of the structure of employment in the zones. Free production zones and world market factories employ mainly unskilled and semiskilled workers to execute tasks in highly subdivided and decomposed manufacturing processes, processes which, with few exceptions, require a relatively small capital investment (machines and equipment) per worker. Apart from factory buildings, repair and maintenance facilities and assembly lines, the capital equipment per worker consists, in the case of the manufacture of semiconductors for example, of a microscope, a soldering iron and a few small tools. In radio and television receiver assembly, the equipment for each work-place is also restricted to a few basic tools and testing equipment. Assembly is performed largely manually. In the garment industry, the necessary equipment consists chiefly of a sewing machine. Relatively high investment can be found in only a few branches, in particular textiles and some other branches – i.e. ship-building, precision engineering and optics. Whereas the textile industry employs almost solely unskilled and semiskilled workers despite its capital intensity, complex manufacturing operation such as ship-building and precision engineering require a relatively higher share of skilled workers.

There are no indications of any fundamental changes taking place in the employment structure of the free production zones. In the final analysis the expansion of production in world market factories is a function of the increased application of a manufacturing

1. 'Pressure on wages in Taiwan', *Far Eastern Economic Review*, 2 July 1976.
2. *Financial Times*, 18 June 1976, 'Mauritius'.

technology which is designed to break down operations into their most rudimentary parts within more and more product groups and industrial branches, to enable the profitable utilisation of an unskilled labour-force to take place. An expansion of production therefore implies primarily the employment of an unskilled and semiskilled labour-force. The proportion of unskilled and semi-skilled workers in world market factories – even in regions in which the world market oriented industrialisation process is highly advanced, for example in Hong Kong, Singapore and Taiwan – is almost exactly the same as in other, recently established free production zones. The demand for the particular type of worker – young female labour – remains the determining factor in the labour market.[1]

Even in those regions in which a concentration of world market factories had developed to such an extent that the availability of young unemployed women has been drastically reduced, no change in the structure of employment occurs. Instead the firms react almost without exception by relocating production to new sites where this particular type of worker can still be easily hired.[2]

1. 'Posters advertising job vacancies are again appearing in large numbers in working-class housing estates. These, however, generally seek the services of young female workers, indicating an increased labour demand in manufacturing (and particularly in the expanding denim factories).' (*Far Eastern Economic Review*, 5 March 1976, 'Hong Kong '76').

   'In the Taichung export processing zone alone, some 37 plants manufacturing electronics, timepieces, optical goods, garments, machinery, musical instruments, and plastic products are undertaking expansions. This already has created 2600 new jobs, of which 2300 are for women and only 300 for men.' (*Business Asia*, 26 March 1976, p. 100.)
2. An example presented by Baerresen in an investigation of world market factories in the northern border zone of Mexico clearly demonstrates how firms select workers. 'The experience of the manager of a certain plant in Ciudad Juárez is indicative of this situation. When the manager was ready to start production he placed a three-day advertisement for workers in a local newspaper. On the first day 2000 applicants appeared. From these applicants he selected 300 persons whom he tested for dexterity. Of this number, 280 persons made scores over 20, which is considered a high score. He hired the 90 workers he required. This manager had previously started five similar plants in the United States where the average dexterity score of applicants is between 14 and 16 and where he is happy to hire anyone with a score of over 16. The large supply of available Mexican workers permits employers to select workers with attitudes and physical skills that can reduce equipment costs. For example, electronic firms can hire young women who with their unaided eyesight can perform delicate assembly operations. For these operations in the United States available workers are usually older women for whom microscopes and magnifying glasses must be provided.' (Donald B. Baerresen, *The Border Industrialisation Programme of Mexico* (Lexington 1971), pp. 32–3.)

16.3 Super-exploitation of the labour-force

Table III-14 provides an overview of hourly wage rates in manufacturing in selected countries in Asia, Africa and Latin America. Average wages in the free production zones and world market factories are approximately the same as those shown in the table.[1] The table shows clearly that wages in the new production sites in the underdeveloped countries are extraordinarily low. In 1975 for an eight to ten hour working day and a forty-eight hour working week unskilled/semiskilled workers were paid a wage of US $1–2 per day, and frequently less than US $50 per month. In many countries, among them India, Indonesia, South Korea, Malaysia, the Philippines, Taiwan, Thailand, Mauritius, Brazil, Guatemala, Haiti, Honduras and Colombia, the wages of unskilled/semiskilled workers in 1974/75 came to less than 25 cents per hour.

The following examples illustrate in detail the wages actually paid in the free production zones and world market factories. In Hong Kong in 1974 the *daily* rates in the garments industry were US $3.15, in the electronics industry US $2.36 for female workers, in the plastic industry US $2.56 for female workers and in the toy industry US $3.34.[2] In 1976 in the Export Processing Zone in Bombay unskilled workers were paid an average of US $25 per *month* (including fringe benefits), semiskilled workers US $33, and skilled workers US $50.[3] In 1974 in Malaysia in the electronics industry semiskilled workers were earning US $1.45–1.75 per day.[4] In 1975 in the Export Processing Zone of Bataan in the Philippines wages averaged US $36 per *month*. The *daily* wage for unskilled workers was US $1.20, for semiskilled workers it was US $1.48–1.77, and skilled workers were receiving US $1.77–2.22.[5] In 1976 in the electronics industry in South Korea wages came to roughly US $1.50 per day for

1. It is frequently argued that foreign companies pay wages above the respective average wages in developing countries. Given the organisation of production in these companies, which ensures utilisation of the labour-force for the whole working day and the high intensity of labour, the assumption seems justified that a higher nominal wage is in many cases really a lower real wage (reproduction of a more exhausted labour-force). However, in the world market factories set up in the underdeveloped countries to enable utilisation of cheap labour, even the nominal wages often fall below the wages paid in domestic industry.
2. See Trade Development Council, *Industrial Investment in Hong Kong* (Hong Kong 1974), p. 25.
3. See Santa Cruz Electronic Export Processing Zone, *Investment Opportunities in Electronics Export* (Bombay 1976), p. 7.
4. Statistics from the Penang Development Corporation.
5. See Export Processing Zone Authority, *Bataan Export Processing Zone: An Introduction.*

Table III-14. *Hourly wages in manufacturing, selected countries of Asia, Africa and Latin America: last available year*

Country	Unskilled workers (US $)	Semi-skilled workers (US $)	Skilled workers (US $)	Average wage (US $)	Year
Asia					
Bahrain	n.a.	n.a.	n.a.		
Hong Kong	0.43	0.61	n.a.		1975
India	0.15	0.21	0.31		1974
Indonesia	0.23	0.34	0.56		1973
Iran	0.34	0.41–0.47	0.93–1.49		1974
Jordan	0.50	n.a.	1.88		1975
Lebanon	n.a.	n.a.	n.a.		
Malaysia	0.16–0.18	0.18–0.23	0.36–0.42		1974
Philippines	0.15	0.19–0.23	0.23–0.28		1975
Singapore	0.38	0.41	0.72		1974
South Korea	F n.a.	n.a.	n.a.	0.21	1974
	M n.a.	n.a.	n.a.	0.43	1974
Syria	n.a.	n.a.	n.a.		
Taiwan	F 0.23	0.25	n.a.		1974
	M 0.25	0.34	n.a.		1974
Thailand	0.15	0.31	0.61		1975
Turkey	n.a.	n.a.	n.a.	0.63	1974
Western Samoa	0.39	n.a.	0.61		1974
Yemen, Dem.	n.a.	n.a.	n.a.		
Africa					
Botswana	0.37	0.51	0.69		1975
Egypt	n.a.	n.a.	n.a.	0.32	1975
Ghana	n.a.	n.a.	n.a.	0.22[a]	1975
Ivory Coast	0.41	0.44–0.53	0.57–0.77		1975
Lesotho	0.19	0.22–0.53	0.79–2.26		1974
Liberia	0.15–0.25	0.25–0.40	0.50–1.00		1975
Mauritius	F 0.09	0.11	0.13		1975
	M 0.20	0.24	0.29–0.46		1975
Morocco	0.34	0.56	0.94–1.31		1975
Senegal	0.45–0.51	0.55–0.65	0.70–0.91		1975
South Africa	F 0.34	0.38	0.75		1974
	M 0.46	0.60	1.05		1974
Swaziland	0.26	0.34	0.46–1.07		1974
Togo	n.a.	n.a.	n.a.		
Tunisia	0.39	0.43	0.63–0.68		1975
Latin America					
Barbados	0.51–0.58	n.a.	0.73–0.97		1974
Brazil	0.25–0.36	0.58–0.82	1.17–1.40		1975
Chile	0.39	0.78	1.14		1975
Colombia	0.16–0.24	0.24–0.40	0.40–0.60		1973
Costa Rica	0.39	0.42	0.54		1975
Dominican Rep.	n.a.	n.a.	n.a.	0.45	1974
Dutch Antilles	1.65	1.75	2.11		1975
Ecuador	0.39–0.49	n.a.	0.76–0.98		1976
El Salvador	0.26–0.50	0.26–0.75	0.50–1.50		1975
Guatemala	0.21–0.38	0.44–0.63	0.50–0.75		1975
Haiti	0.16	0.40–0.50	0.70–0.80		1975
Honduras	0.25	0.35–0.40	0.60–0.80		1975
Jamaica	0.80	n.a.	2.29		1975
Mexico	0.56–0.85	n.a.	n.a.		1975
Nicaragua	n.a.	0.27	0.90		1975
Panama	0.50	n.a.	0.75		1975
Puerto Rico	n.a.	n.a.	n.a.	1.32[a]	1975
	n.a.	n.a.	n.a.	2.24	1974
St Lucia	0.31	0.31	1.00		1976
Trinidad and Tobago	n.a.	n.a.	n.a.	0.71	1974
Uruguay	n.a.	n.a.	n.a.	0.44[a]	1975
Venezuela	n.a.	n.a.	2.96	0.53[a]	1974
				1.51	1974

Source: author's compilation
a: minimum wage

foremen and toolmakers.[1] In Thailand at the end of 1974 unskilled workers in world market factories were being paid US $1.00 per day.[2] In Nicaragua in 1975 world market factories in the electronics industry were paying unskilled/semiskilled workers US $0.27 per *hour*; skilled workers were getting US $0.90 per hour.[3] In the Costa Rica export-processing industry unskilled/semiskilled workers were paid US $3.14–3.35 per *day*, skilled workers an average of US $4.31 per day.[4] In 1974 in the Dominican Republic wages in the free production zones were US $0.25–0.40 per *hour* for unskilled and semiskilled workers.[5] The lowest wages were paid in the Export Processing Zones in Mauritius. In 1975 unskilled female workers were paid US $0.70 per *day* and semiskilled female workers US $0.88 per day.[6]

Table III-14 reveals the wage differential between men and women.[7] In 1974 in the world market factories in South Korea female workers were earning an average of US $0.21 per hour, less than half the male wage which stood at US $0.43 per hour. In Mauritius in 1975 unskilled/semiskilled female workers also received less than half of the male wage. In Taiwan and South Africa the differential was between one-quarter and one-third. In Singapore in 1975 average female wages were 58% below the male average.

> The average woman in Singapore's labour force is earning less than her male counterpart, and by a substantial margin. For instance, in 1975, the latest available comprehensive survey of wage rates revealed that men workers were earning an average S $1.78[8] an hour with women earning 42% below the men's rate. In none of the industries were women earning more than men. For instance: ...in the traditionally female dominated textile industry [women were earning] – S $1.04/hour, 43% below the male rate of S $1.49/hour; in the garments industry – 96 cents/hour, 34% below the male rate;...and pharmaceuticals – 50% less than the male rate.[9]

The wages paid to workers in the world market factories in the free production zones and in other industrial sites in the under-

1. See DEG, *Reisebericht Korea*, p. 8.
2. See the Office of the Board of Investment, *15 Powerful Reasons*, p. 13.
3. See Banco Central de Nicaragua, *Nicaragua – A Market for Off-Shore Assembly*, p. 5.
4. Oficina de Planificación y Política Económica, 9 October 1975.
5. See Corporaciòn Zona Franca Industrial de Santiago, Inc., *Zona Franca Industrial*, pp. 4–5.
6. See Ministry of Commerce and Industry, *Factor Costs*, January 1975.
7. To the extent that Table III-14 only shows one wage rate (in the majority of cases) this, as a rule, refers only to male or only to female workers. It was not possible to specify this.
8. 1 US $ = S $2.51 (Singapore dollars).
9. *Asia Research Bulletin*, 28 February 1977, p. 293.

developed countries are often insufficient to cover the reproduction costs of the work-force.[1] It is hardly necessary to prove this. Wages ranging from US $30–100 per month will not cover the cost of reproduction, that is physical reproduction let alone the psychic recovery, of workers exhausted by highly demanding work in industrial production 'even' in the underdeveloped countries. This can be seen quite easily if wages are set against the costs of basic foodstuffs. If the worker is unable to secure his or her reproduction by other means, such as obtaining extra food from their family via the above mentioned subsidising function of the rural sector, the consequence is simply that the worker is all the more swiftly exhausted and replaced by another worker, either at the same site or may be at another site elsewhere: the first phenomenon can be seen in the high rates of labour turnover at particular sites, and the second in the frequent relocation of industrial production.

Table III-15 presents data on the average hours of work in manufacturing industry in underdeveloped countries. In most of the countries where free production zones and world market factorie are in operation the standard working week is forty-eight hours. The difference between this figure and the standard working week of forty to forty-four hours in the traditional industrialised countries is only a partial reflection of the real prolongation of the working day in the new production sites in the developing countries. The high number of weeks worked in the year, the large amount of overtime and the low number of days off serve to prolong the total annual working time still further, so that the labour-force in some world market factories works up to 50% more hours per year than the traditional industrial countries. For example, working hours in manufacturing industry in Hong Kong often amount to more than sixty hours per week.[2] In the world market factories in South Korea

1. The wages actually paid not infrequently fall below the rates set as the minimum rates by the respective administration or below the rates stipulated in the wage agreements. Deductions from wages are frequently made for transport, work clothes, training etc., sometimes contrary to the law and in violation of wage agreements.
2. 'There is no legal restriction on the hours of work for men over the age of 18 years. Consequently many men work ten hours a day with a rest period of one to two hours although three-shift working, enabling machinery to be used 24 hours a day, is common...Women and young persons aged 16 and 17 may work eight hours a day plus two hours overtime up to an aggregate of 300 hours overtime per year. Working hours for these persons are limited to 48 hours per week.' (Trade Development Council, *Industrial Investment in Hong Kong*, p. 25.)

Table III-15. *Average working hours in manufacturing, selected countries of Asia, Africa and Latin America: last available year*

Country	Hours per week	Year	Country	Hours per week	Year
Asia			Latin America		
Bahrain	n.a.		Barbados	40	1974
Hong Kong	48–60	1974	Brazil	48	1975
India	48	1974	Chile	n.a.	
Indonesia	40	1974	Colombia	48	1973
Iran	n.a.		Costa Rica	48	1975
Jordan	48	1975	Dominican Rep.	44	1974
Lebanon	n.a.		Dutch Antilles	n.a.	
Malaysia	48	1975	Ecuador	44	1976
Philippines	48	1975	El Salvador	44	1975
Singapore	44	1974	Guatemala	45	1975
South Korea	48–60	1975	Haiti	48	1975
Syria	n.a.		Honduras	44	1975
Taiwan	48	1974	Jamaica	48	1975
Thailand	48	1974	Mexico	48	1975
Turkey	n.a.		Nicaragua	48	1975
Western Samoa	40	1974	Panama	48	1975
Yemen, Dem.	n.a.		Puerto Rico	48	1974
Africa			St Lucia	40	1976
Botswana	45	1975	Trinidad and Tobago	40	1974
Egypt	42	1975	Uruguay	48	1975
Ghana	45–48	1976	Venezuela	48	1975
Ivory Coast	40	1975			
Lesotho	n.a.				
Liberia	n.a.				
Mauritius	45	1975			
Morocco	48	1975			
Senegal	40	1976			
South Africa	45	1975			
Swaziland	48	1974			
Togo	n.a.				
Tunisia	48	1975			

Source: author's compilation

the usual working week of the factory worker is sixty hours.[1] 'Total productive hours per year amounts to approximately 2800,' compared with 1860 on average in Federal Germany.[2] Workers in South Korean industry are required to work seven day, eighty-four hour weeks – i.e. a twelve hour shift each day without rest days.[3] In Thai manufacturing industry a nine hour working day with only one day

1. 'The standard working week is 48 hours; eight hours a day for six days. The working hours may be extended to 60 hours per week by mutual agreement. An extended work week has become a common practice in manufacturing and export industries.' (Economic Planning Board, *Guide to Investment in Korea*, p. 48.)
2. DEG, *Reisebericht Korea*, p. 8.
3. Cf. *Herald Tribune*, 13 February 1976: '7-day, 84-hour work weeks: Seoul's economic miracle is a heavy burden on workers'; *Handelsblatt*, 22 June 1976: 'A 6-, often 7-day work week, with a 12-hour day, common also in industry is praised as a patriotic act.'

off per month is often required.[1] Even if those working times may be exceptional, nonetheless the following conditions are the rule for workers in free production zones and world market factories in the developing countries:

(1) at least forty-eight hours per week,
(2) at least fifty weeks per year,
(3) very few holidays, and
(4) frequently a great deal of overtime.

Working time per year in most underdeveloped countries therefore exceeds that of the production sites in the traditional industrialised countries by at least 20%–30%. According to the DEG, the annual working time of a factory worker in Malaysia is 2288 hours,[2] in Tunisia 2226 hours,[3] and in Ecuador – where the standard working week is forty-four hours – 2152 hours.[4]

As indicated in reports from individual companies and analyses of particular branches of industry, productivity in world market factories in free production zones and at other sites (i.e. output per worker) is only marginally lower per time unit, and often substantially higher for the whole working year compared with productivity at the traditional industrial sites. Various surveys on investment conditions published by the DEG state that labour productivity in the world market factories in the underdeveloped countries is only a little below that of comparable processes in Western Europe, and that in view of the longer annual working time the annual performance of the workers in underdeveloped countries is often much higher than in comparable Western European production. According to investigations carried out by the United States Tariff Commission, the productivity of workers in world market factories belonging to US firms approximates, by and large, to that of workers in the same job classifications in the United States.[5] For the garments industry the report states that Mexican and Caribbean workers in many cases produce as many pieces per worker-hour as US workers.[6] For the

1. 'In manufacturing a 48-hour week is commonly worked but this is not standard. Some industries and trades work nine hours a day with only one day off each month for labourers.' (Board of Investment, *Investing in the Dynamic Growth of Thailand* (1974), p. 46.)
2. DEG, *Malaysia: Eckdaten für Privatinvestitionen* (1976).
3. DEG, *Tunisia.*
4. Cf. DEG and Bundestelle für Außenhandelsinformation, *Ecuador: Investitionsbedingungen* (Cologne 1976), p. 27. The DEG indicates the working time per year in the Federal Republic of Germany as being 1760 hours (shoe industry), 1840 hours (average) and 1860 (electrical engineering).
5. See United States Tariff Commission, *Economic Factors*, p. 171.
6. United States Tariff Commission, p. 172.

electronics industry it is stated that 'foreign labor in world market factories required 8 % more man-hours than the man-hours required by US workers to assemble such articles as radios, phonographs, television receivers and subassemblies and semiconductors'.[1] 'Foreign labor required 3 % less man-hours than was required by US workers to assemble such diverse articles as luggage, baseballs, toys, footwear, gloves, photographic equipment and scientific instruments.'[2]

Baerresen reports that in the US world market factories in Mexico productivity per worker is in some cases considerably higher than in comparable US plants. In the packaging of metal links, worker productivity was 40 % higher than in comparable plants in the United States; in the electronics industry labour productivity was 10 %–25 % above that in similar US plants; the productivity of seamstresses was up to 30 % higher than in US plants.[3] According to Baerresen, managers of American world market factories in Mexico who had also worked in US world market factories in South Korea reported that productivity in South Korea was up to between 20 %–40 % higher than that of the Mexican workers.[4] In discussions with the authors, production managers in US and Federal German world market factories producing textiles, clothing and electronics in free production zones in Malaysia unanimously reported that an operating time of a few months productivity per worker was the same as in their respectively domestically located comparable plants. The management of an integrated Japanese textile factory in Malaysia employing 1900 workers (80 % of them women) reported in 1974 that after a training period of not more than two weeks the productivity of labour was the same as in Japanese factories. In the electronics industry – according to Moxon – productivity in world market factories located in underdeveloped countries is generally higher than in comparable industrial processes in the USA.[5]

However, what is registered as productivity of labour (measured

1. United States Tariff Commission, p. 172.
2. United States Tariff Commission, p. 173.
3. See Baerresen, *The Border Industrialisation Programme*, p. 33.
4. Baerresen, p. 33.
5. Richard W. Moxon, *Offshore Production in the Less Developed Countries*, p. 61. ('The great majority of American electronics companies with offshore plants have been very satisfied with the results obtained, and have continued to expand their offshore operations. They have generally found a low-cost source of workers who are more productive than those in the United States, and have been able to manufacture products of the required quality.')

as output per worker), and what, when compared with productivity at traditional sites, turns out to be approximately the same or even higher is in fact – because of the different technical organisation of production – the expression of the much higher intensity of work which is often forced upon workers in the underdeveloped countries. The difference in the organisation of production between the traditional sites and the underdeveloped countries, where manual operations are frequently substituted for partially mechanised or partially automated operations, means that achieving an *equal* productivity per worker is equivalent to an *unequal*, namely higher, intensity of labour in processes with higher proportions of manual operations.

The remaining working conditions in free production zones and world market factories exhibit three main characteristics: social insecurity, shift work, and inadequate provision for safety at work.

Although, in theory, there is some legal provision for social security in most countries, workers in free production zones and world market factories are in practice not covered by such schemes: the lot of most of these workers is *social insecurity*. In case of sickness, social benefits are generally confined to further payment of the daily wage for a period of fourteen or, at most, thirty days. Failure to return to over a longer period because of illness almost always entails the loss of employment. Social provision is also totally inadequate for older workers. On reaching a certain age they are, as a rule, replaced by younger workers and receive practically no social security benefits. Although companies in most free production zones have to contribute to social security schemes for the workers they employ, the latter in fact receive almost no benefits from such schemes, partly because 'older' workers in reality simply means workers who have been rapidly worn out by the physically and psychically demanding work, and partly because the total insurance contributions are extremely low (on average less than 10% out of a monthly wage of often less than US $50). Moreover, in some free production zones companies are exempted even from such minimum obligations.[1] No form of unemployment benefit is provided for workers employed in free production zones and world market factories. On redundancy, workers receive, at best, a

1. Thus in a leaflet on factor costs from the Ministry of Commerce and Industry in Mauritius (1975) the column 'indirect costs for social benefits' simply states 'none'.

redundancy payment equal to one month's wage per working year, but even this is frequently withheld from them.[1]

All the promotional literature published by the free production zones, as well as the brochures which supply information to potential investors from bodies such as UNIDO, quite explicitly point out the low cost of fringe benefits, which in effect means the releasing of companies from the obligation to provide adequate social security for their employees. The cost of fringe benefits, in particular social security contributions, paid holidays, provision of working clothes, a works canteen and paid transport to and from work, normally add up to a mere 20% to 30% of the wage. In Korea, for example, they are 15% of the payroll total, in Senegal 25%, in Tunisia 38%, in the Dominican Republic 28%, in Haiti between 8% and 14%, and in Nicaragua 25%. Only when we arrive at the free production zones of Colombia do we find a percentage as high as 83%, a rate which approximates to the fringe benefits paid in the traditional industrial countries. However, since the average hourly rate in Colombia is only between US $0.24 and 0.40 the absolute amount of fringe benefits supplied is not at all adequate for the social security of the work-force.

Extended shift work – in plants that operate twenty-four hours a day, seven days a week, including holidays – is a predominant feature in the operation of free production zones and world market factories. Women are required to work on night shifts, even in countries where labour legislation nominally forbids night work for women.[2]

A number of reports point to the inadequate space and safety

1. At the occasion of a large-scale redundancy in 1974 Taiwan workers were tricked out of their redundancy payments by forcing them, through various means, not to turn up at their place of work at the appropriate time, e.g. by cancelling transport to the factory. Cf. *Far Eastern Economic Review*, 2 July 1976, 'Pressure on wages in Taiwan'.
2. Thus for instance the Malaysian 'Decree of Employment' states: 'Women may be employed to work up to 10.00 p.m. Women shift workers may work between 10.00 p.m. and 5 a.m. with the approval of the Minister of Labor. Where a woman has worked a night shift she must have 11 hours consecutive rest before she is required to assume work on the following day'. (Federal Industrial Development Authority, *Labor and Wage Rates* (1973), p. 7.)

   The Labor Law in Thailand contains the following provision regarding protection of labour: 'Except for shift work women may not be required to do dangerous or exerting work between the hours of 0.00 and 6.00 a.m.' (Thai Trade and Investment Center, Frankfurt–Main, *Wirtschaftsrecht in Thailand* (1976), p. 48.)

   The decree about Export Processing Zones in Mauritius provides the following regulations: 'A woman may be required to work between the hours of ten at night and five in the morning, but she shall not be required to assume work before a lapse of 12 hours.' (*The Export Processing Zones Act 1970*, p. 7.)

provisions in plants in free production zones and world market factories. A report on the Masan Free Export Zone, for example, listed insufficient ventilation, especially in areas with particular hazards such as lead working, workshop temperatures up to 35–38 °C, causing skin diseases, overcrowded work-rooms, insufficient attention to safety in asbestos processing and other hazards.[1] In the textile factories of the free production zones in South Korea[2] and Malaysia[3] the main causes of the widespread premature invalidity of the labour-force are the inadequate protection against noise and insufficient ventilation. Long periods at work with the microscope, often an entire shift, together with poor lighting bring about myopia and eye disease.[4] Workers who are affected by these illnesses and complaints almost inevitably lose their jobs and are replaced by fresh labour.

If one examines the interaction of the working conditions described above – the low wages, long hours, high intensity of work, social insecurity and, in many cases, additional burdens such as shift work (night work) and the lack of safety – it becomes clear that the industrial utilisation of labour in free production zones and world market factories in underdeveloped countries constitutes *super-exploitation.*

Super-exploitation in this context means essentially working conditions and a level of exploitation which actually impair the reproduction of the labour-force. Low wages, long hours and high intensity of work mean that the physical and mental recovery and reproduction of the labour-power expended in the labour process is not guaranteed or accomplished. In many cases wages are not even sufficient to pay for the minimum of physical subsistence. In addition, the long duration and high intensity of work (often under conditions which are a hazard to health) lead to the premature exhaustion of the labour-power which the workers can offer. The provision of the periods of rest which workers need to recuperate

1. 'A fact-finding survey on the Masan Free Export Zone', *AMPO Japan–Asia Quarterly Review* 2 (1976), p. 66.
2. See *The Times,* 26 September 1975, 'Textiles; controversy over older industry': 'Some of the factory noise levels are frighteningly high and unless rapidly improved will create permanent disability among workers.'
3. Authors' own findings made on location.
4. See, for example, *Far Eastern Economic Review,* 2 July 1976, 'Pressure on wages in Taiwan': 'Bad lighting in electronics factories has reportedly caused myopia and other eye diseases, though the personnel director of one American firm contends that conditions in most of the larger factories are acceptable.'

(breaks, days off, annual paid holidays) is more the exception than the rule. Furthermore, wages and fringe benefits do not even begin to cover the costs of reproduction of those workers whose capabilities and energies have been prematurely exhausted and who are then dismissed from employment.

A comparison of the work and the working conditions in the new production sites in the underdeveloped countries and in the traditional industrial countries shows very clearly that the industrial utilisation of the labour-forces in the free production zones and world market factories constitutes super-exploitation. In exchange for equal work, but frequently in exchange for harder, dirtier, more monotonous and more dangerous work than in manufacturing industry in the traditional industrial sites and for work which yields products which can compete on the world market with products from traditional industrial sites, workers in the free production zones and in world market factories are paid a wage which on average amounts to between a tenth and a fifth of that at the traditional sites.

Working conditions which represent a synthesis of Manchester capitalism and the forms of the capitalist organisation of work of the last quarter of the twentieth century compel the labour-force in free production zones and world market factories in the underdeveloped countries, on the one hand, to achieve levels of productivity and intensity of labour which corresponds to the most advanced current levels in the world, and on the other hand, to tolerate wage levels which are not much higher than those which prevailed in Manchester capitalism's heyday.

16.4 The enforcement of working conditions in free production zones and in world market factories

The continued maintenance of working conditions in the free production zones and world market factories which, as described above, enforce an exceptionally high productivity and intensity of labour, and yet do not ensure the immediate reproduction of the labour-force is achieved principally through the following mechanisms:

(1) competition between workers; in other words, the existence of a practically inexhaustible industrial reserve army,
(2) restrictive labour legislation and the suppression of trade unions and strikes,
(3) the use of military force when the above mechanisms fail.

The existence of a practically inexhaustible industrial reserve army in the underdeveloped countries means that there is a constant and a large supply of workers forced to sell their labour-power for virtually any wage and regardless of the working conditions. One indication of the rate at which workers are replaced and of the constant utilisation of newly recruited labour is the high turnover in the world market factories in the free production zones and world market factories at other industrial sites. A monthly turnover of 5%–10%, which means the total replacement of the entire work force within a period of one or two years, is a widespread phenomenon.[1]

If companies cannot recruit enough workers under the set conditions of any particular site they simply use the industrial reserve army which can be found at new sites.[2]

Although the existence of a practically unlimited industrial reserve army in the new industrial locations means that fresh workers are always available despite the low wages, long hours and high intensity of work, this does not mean that workers who are assembled at particular factories do not try to organise and change the conditions under which they work through collective action. For this reasons the obstruction and suppression of trade unions as well as other workers' organisations, the banning or suppression of strikes and restrictive labour legislation are part of the mechanisms

1. The following examples from the electrical engineering industry and the textile and garment industry in Singapore show that even at a site with a regionally limited reserve army a constant turnover of the work-force takes place:

   'Mister John Lu, director of the Singapore Textiles Industries (the only fully integrated textile factory in Singapore) and South Grant Textiles estimates that his labour turnover is five to ten per cent a month. "We need to get new people at all times", he says.' (*Financial Times*, 8 October 1976.)

   'One leading local electronics manufacturer told Business Asia that high absenteeism and staff turnover are the company's major problems. Absenteeism runs at an estimated 10% – but with a monthly turnover of around 7% of the 2500 workers, the firm cannot afford to discipline the regular absentees because of difficulties in finding replacements.' (*Business Asia*, 16 July 1976, p. 227.)

2. 'Mild tremors shook the electronics industry here this month when National Semiconductors sacked 1000 of its 4000 employees. Workers caught by the retrenchments were shocked as their employers had only recently agreed to implement the full National Wages Council (NWC) recommendation for 1974...That the axe fell on Singapore and not elsewhere indicates that factors were uppermost in the retrenchments. National Semiconductors possesses a chain of factories in Southeast Asia, including Bangkok, Penang, Malacca and Indonesia, but thus far, no news of any similar sackings has been reported. In fact, the very day when the *Straits times* reported the sackings, National Semiconductors' sister company in Malacca was advertising for more workers and, as the advertisment put it, this was due to "rapid expansion". A few days later, Malacca plant manager Peter Pang announced that the company intended to increase the number of workers from the present 2800 to 5000 next year.' (*Far Eastern Economic Review*, 23 August 1974, 'Singapore's victim of success'.)

which are central in the prevention of any action on the part of workers at the new sites. It therefore comes as no surprise that the list of countries in which free production zones or world market factories are in operation or under construction closely resembles the list of countries in which trade unions are either completely banned or curtailed, so that strikes or other actions of organised industrial struggle are largely suppressed. In Bahrain, Iran or Thailand, for example, they are prohibited. In Hong Kong, India, Malaysia, the Philippines and South Korea, the unions are either politically divided and their ability to undertake action commensurably reduced, or they are corrupted politically and forced into political acquiescence, as in the case of Indonesia, Singapore and Egypt. Strikes are prohibited and are suppressed in the majority of countries in which free production zones and world market factories are in operation, as in India, Indonesia, Malaysia, the Philippines, Singapore, South Korea, Egypt, Tunisia, Brazil and Haiti. The following quotations from official reports, from the business press, and from trade union statements on the situation of the trade union movement, on the right to strike and on labour legislation in South Korea and Malaysia reveal the extent to which workers in export-oriented industries are prevented from organising the defence of their interests in the new production sites in the underdeveloped countries.

The history of the labor movement in Korea is short: in that time, there have been few labor disputes. However, as the economy grows and living standards rise, more demands for increased salaries can be expected. Nevertheless, strikes, sabotages, lockouts, and other forms of labor violence are very few in Korea because when labor disputes arise, such agencies as the Office of Labor and the Central and Local Labor Committees mediate at the request of either party (or both parties), as stipulated in the Labor Disputes Adjustment Law. This law prohibits the use of violence or destructive acts in labor disputes.

In this connection, it should be noted that the Government takes special concern in the fair and fast solution of whatever labor disputes may arise in foreign-invested enterprises. For instance, the Government has recently enacted a special law governing labor union movement and arbitration of disputes which arise in these enterprises. This law stipulates that the organisation of a labor union in a foreign-invested enterprise must be reported to the Office of Labor, and in case of labor disputes, the Office will take arbitration measures for a fast and just conciliation. Thus, the Government takes direct responsibility and control of matters pertaining to labor union activities and disputes in the foreign investment enterprises: it is therefore hoped that labor union problems will be minimised and whenever possible, eliminated.[1]

1. Fine Instruments Center, *Guide to Electronics Industry Investment in Korea*, pp. 26–7.

If South Korea's 11 million strong labour force is a key to the country's development, it is also a potential source of trouble. Wage rates are among the cheapest in the world. Strikes are prohibited by law and the trade unions are a shadow of their western counterparts...

Today there are 17 industrial unions but their total membership is only 550000. The strict labour laws permit the government to break up any union which it considers has become a threat to the safeguarding of public order...On December 27 1971 the government introduced a series of emergency measures including the outlawing of strikes. Since that date the penalty for striking has been a prison sentence for up to seven years.[1]

The extent to which workers in the zones and world market factories are deprived of their rights, and how this has been codified in specific labour laws, is illustrated very clearly by the provisions of the Malaysian Industrial Relations Act.

The Government's policy regarding industrial relations is aimed at maintaining industrial peace and harmony with justice so as to create a favourable climate for investment, industrial expansion and growth opportunities.

Some of the main features of the Industrial Relations Act 1967, which is designed to achieve this objective are:

(a) protection of the legitimate rights of employers and workers,
(b) procedure to be followed in the submission of claims and collective bargaining,
(c) provisions for speedy and just settlement of trade disputes by conciliation or arbitration if not resolved through direct negotiation,
(d) power for the Minister of Labour to intervene and to refer disputes to the Industrial Court established under the Act. Awards by the Industrial Court are legally binding,
(e) prohibition of strikes or lock-outs for causes connected with negotiation of trade unions, or on matters connected with management functions,
(f) management functions pertaining to promotions, transfers, retrenchments etc. are not negotiable,
(g) safeguard for pioneer industries during their first five years of existence or for any such extended period against unreasonable demands of trade unions.[2]

Provisions also exist in the law [Industrial Relations Act, 1967] which protect industries, enjoying 'pioneer' status from unreasonable demands from workers for more attractive conditions of employment than the minimum provided in the law. Such protection normally extends over a period of 5 years or for such further periods as may be decided by the Government. These protective provisions seek to place the terms and conditions of employment on a more equitable basis, where employers are given greater expectation of securing a more contented and industrious labour force, which, in turn, contributes to stability and productivity; while workers are assured of minimum standards of protection and benefits.[3]

1. *The Times*, 26 September 1975, 'Electronics: cheap labour attracts foreigners'.
2. Federal Industrial Development Authority (Malaysia), *Labour and Wage Rates*, pp. 13–14.
3. The Hon. Datuk Lee Sun Choon, Minister of Labour and Manpower (Malaysia), 'Technical manpower, labour availability and stability', in Federal Industrial Development Authority of Malaysia, *Investment Opportunities in Malaysia*, Proceedings of International Seminar, October 27–29, 1975, p. 44.

Although the law allows trade unions to be established in Malaysia, their efforts to represent the interests of the labour-force in the free zones are prevented from the very outset by governmental measures, such as not allowing trade unions to operate in new industries and preventing all trade union activities within the area of the free zones.

When we were actively involved in organising the workers in Sungei Way Free Trade Zone, the Registrar of Trade Union intercepted and demanded that we seek his permission each time we wanted to organise a factory. We didn't do so because we felt that the registrar was unnecessarily interfering in our affairs and furthermore if employers come to know our plans beforehand they could place unnecessary obstacles. Next when we invited the workers in Penang to a general meeting, the registrar said that we had no right to hold the meeting. However, we held the meeting as scheduled and nearly 1500 attended. Having failed to daunt the determination of the officials and the enthusiasm of the workers by the above methods the registrar finally ruled that the EIWU can't cater for workers in the Electronics Industry.[1]

The government of our country has created a climate for trade unions which on the brim looks rather sober but when this created climate is analysed one would find that trade unions in our country do not in any respect have freedom of organisation and association. Wherever possible when given the opportunity it is often preached that they encourage the formation of one single trade union for a particular trade or industry but to our knowledge till to-date it has not been practised.[2]

1. Electrical Industry Workers' Union (Malaysia), *Problems Faced by the EIWU in Organising the Unorganised Electrical Workers* (1974).
2. Electrical Industry Workers' Union (Malaysia), *Country Report Submitted at 1st Asian Electrical Multinational Semina* (May 1974), pp. 7–9.

17 ❧ The impact of world market oriented industrialisation on the socio-economic development of developing countries

17.1 Declared objectives and actual results of world market oriented industrialisation

As we showed in Chapter 14, the function of the free production zones is to provide the technical, organisational and legislative preconditions for the industrial utilisation of the labour-forces of the developing countries for world market oriented production. The complete fulfilment of the specific preconditions for the profitable utilisation of cheap labour in underdeveloped countries in world market oriented manufacturing industry is only attained through the provision of industrial infrastructure, services and utilities at those sites in underdeveloped countries where cheap labour is available and through the granting of trade, currency and fiscal concessions which allow the unimpeded flow of goods and capital. Hence, the promotion, construction and operation of free production zones has but one function – to fulfil the economic requirements of the valorisation of capital through the intermediary of national as well as supranational public bodies. The extracts from the many reports cited above demonstrate quite clearly that both the national and supranational institutions themselves consider it their task to exercise these functions in the interests of the valorisation of capital.[1] At the same time the exercise of these functions is regarded as furthering policies which can overcome underdevelopment. Seen from this perspective free production zones and world market factories function essentially as vehicles, whose ultimate aim is the attainment of the main goals of development policy. According to the statements of the governments of almost all underdeveloped countries where free production zones are under construction or in operation or in which world market factories at other sites have been or will be

1. Cf. Chapter 1.1.

located, as well as in the relevant statements of UNIDO (the most important international institution active in this field), three basic goals are named as being attainable through the medium of free production zones and world market factories:

(1) the creation of new jobs and consequent elimination of unemployment,

(2) the training of a skilled industrial work-force and access to modern technology,

(3) access to increased foreign exchange receipts and a wider scope within which developing countries can conduct their foreign trade policies.

UNIDO has expounded the following set of goals which can be achieved through the establishment of free production zones.

The creation of an Industrial Free Zone is commonly considered by a combination of several reasons, such as:

(a) a part of an overall industrial development programme of the country or of a certain region of the country;

(b) a measure for solving the employment problem by the creation of new labour opportunities;

(c) stimulation of development of export oriented industries, to increase export volume and foreign exchange receipts;

(d) acquirement of modern industrial techniques from abroad through which the level-up of the domestic industrial standard may be achieved;

(e) encouragement of new industrial investments from domestic, as well as foreign capital markets;

(f) means of a concentrated and rational development of infrastructure with the industrial free zone acting as an industrial pole.[1]

That the governments of the countries in which free production zones and world market factories at other sites are under construction or in operation by and large share this view of the goals which can be accomplished by export industrialisation is shown in the following statements from the Chairman of the Board of Investments of the Philippines and from the Industrial Estates Administration of South Korea:

The objectives for promoting and developing the export sector are fairly straightforward:

(1) To generate employment opportunities and relieve the country's unemployment and underemployment situation...

(2) To improve the balance of payments position, more particularly, to cover the foreign exchange requirements of our development plans.

(3) To increase the local content of Philippine exports by encouraging domestic processing of primary products formerly exported in raw form.

1. UNIDO, *Industrial Free Zones*, p. 7.

(4) To diversify the markets for Philippine exports.[1]
The purpose of establishing free export zones is to induce foreign investment, promote exports, increase employment opportunities and develop technology, thereby contributing to the development of the national economy.[2]

Despite these stated objectives experience so far and foreseeable trends would seem to suggest, in fact quite unambiguously, that export-oriented industrialisation as it is at present developing in free production zones and world market factories does not solve the problem of unemployment, train a skilled labour-force or provide access to modern technology. Although it might appear as if industrialisation of this type could assist in solving the problem of unemployment, in fact, apart from a few countries, the creation of the specific job opportunities in export-oriented production cannot be equated with a general reduction in unemployment. The exceptionally unbalanced employment policy pursued in the free production zones and world market factories[3] is not capable of effecting a reduction of unemployment among the male population as a whole or among older men and women.

Once the reserves of the specifically selected labour-force have been fully exhausted production is expanded at other sites or is shifted to sites where this specific type of labour is still available. As a consequence no change in the structure of employment can be discerned. However, the enclave character of world market oriented production is still more important in its negative effects on employment. The vertical integration of this form of production into the world market and its horizontal lack of integration and separation from the respective national economy is closely linked with effects on the structure of employment which actually impede the development of the local economies concerned. The system of industrial enclaves gives rise to internal migration by the working population, in particular on the part of young workers who move to sites where world market production is located. As a result, unemployment in the new industrial sites is in most cases not reduced, and in turn serves to aggravate the underdevelopment of the rural areas. The

1. Paper submitted by Governor Conrado Sanchez, Jnr, Board of Investments, Philippines, for the Meeting of Experts on 'Improved Cooperation for the Development and Promotion of Exports from Developing Countries', OECD Development Centre, Paris, 25–28 March 1974.
2. The Industrial Estates Administration, Masan, *A Case Study of the Masan Free Export Zone.* Regional Expert Working Group Meeting on Industrial Free Zones (UNIDO), Barranquilla, 23 September to 1 October 1974.ID/WG. 185/2, p. 4.
3. Cf. Chapter 16.2.

multiplier effect which world market oriented production exercises through the creation of additional jobs in other sectors of the economy is rather limited. The lack of horizontal integration of world market oriented production means that other types of production in the respective national economies are only induced to a very limited extent. The only exception is the supply of industrial inputs which are of necessity local in origin and of utilities and infrastructure. However, even though world market oriented production does provide some job opportunities from this source, the effect on the domestic economy as a whole is still often largely negative as it entails a drain of technicians and skilled workers from sectors of the domestic economy to servicing functions for the free production zones as well as necessitating the employment of foreign specialists.

In addition, the integration of production in world market factories into the capitalist world market, and the dependence of this production on corporate strategies which are imposed externally, exposes the new industrial sites to large fluctuations in employment.[1]

Although aggregate employment in the free production zones and in the world market factories may have grown to substantial figures, although a further increase may be expected, and although employment may temporarily be high in the particular industrial sites, the

1. Thus in the foreign-controlled world market factories in Hong Kong within ten months, i.e. February to December 1975, the size of the work-force fell by 15% – from 70421 to 59607 employees. Employment in electronics had declined from 34668 to 24146, while in the watch-making industry it had increased from 4668 to 5391 over the same period, and in the electrical engineering industry (excluding electronics) from 1769 to 3847. Cf. *Far Eastern Economic Review*, 28 March 1975, 'Hong Kong '75', and 5 March 1976, 'Hong Kong '76'.

According to a report in *Business Week*, 17600 workers were dismissed in the world market factories in Mexico between mid-1974 and mid-1975. From the beginning of 1976 rehiring started again. See *Business Week*, 23 February 1976, 'New duty-free zones that aid US industry'.

The fluctuations even in the so-called growth branches are shown by the following report about the employment situation in the electronics industry of Singapore. 'The electronics industry, worldwide, is highly competitive, particularly at the semiconductor end which embodies the core of electronic technology. Market and technological developments have subjected the industry to wide cyclical fluctuations every three years or so. From the second half of 1974 to almost the end of 1975, the downturn in the industry coincided with the general world recession to hit the industry with its severest recession so far. Singapore was perhaps the worst affected offshore location. Some two thirds of the 20000 workers retrenched in Singapore during this period were from the electronics industry. Figures for 1975 are not yet out, but a recent newspaper report estimated the size of the workforce in September 1976 at 32000, down from a peak in early 1974 of nearly 50000, and after nearly six months of upturn and heavy rehiring.' (*Financial Times*, 8 October 1976, 'Electronics sector shows resilience'.)

employment effects of world market oriented production are not such as to offer any solution to the problem of employment, or rather the problem of unemployment which confronts the underdeveloped countries. The inherent structural limitations of world market oriented production mean that even a rapid growth in the phenomenon cannot create a pattern of domestic development which is conducive to the solution of the problems of unemployment and underemployment in underdeveloped countries. To summarise: the employment effects of world market oriented production are extremely disruptive. Their multiplier effects are minimal and often unbalancing in their consequences on the respective domestic economies. Last but not least, they are not stable (as far as the individual sites are concerned) even in the short term, but are exposed to large fluctuations originating in the world market.

The training of skilled workers and the transfer of modern technology through world market oriented production in the free production zones and world market factories is very limited in scale. The application of modern manufacturing technology for the purpose of decomposing highly complex processes into elementary operations which can be performed by unskilled labour in fact implies that the level of skill in world market factories will not be raised, as it is precisely these elementary operations which are allocated to the labour-forces in the free production zones and world market factories. The data on the skill structure, even in those zones which have been in operation for a number of years, shows that the labour-force is predominantly unskilled and has only been trained to perform specific operations. The content of training is therefore restricted to a few relatively limited tasks.

In the majority of the world market factories training schemes are limited to the following areas:

(a) Most workers are trained only to perform specific elementary functions which correspond to specific phases of the chosen production process; examples are the assembly of components, the control of automatic looms, and the operation of punching machines. Training for jobs requiring semiskilled qualifications which can also be utilised outside the original job allocation, such as welding, is provided to a much more limited extent.

(b) In the sphere of production, skilled workers are predominantly employed in subsidiary operations, such as tool-making or maintenance. Training for the required skills is only provided when skilled labour is not on hand or cannot be drawn from other occupations. This is the only real training which can be said to exist, and is confined almost exclusively to male workers.

(c) Similarly, training for technical and office staff is only on a very limited scale. Technical staff is trained predominantly for such duties as production control, supervision, internal transport, maintenance and so on, and office staff for such activities as accounting, payroll accounting and the like, depending on the particular requirements of the respective plant or production unit. Training schemes are thus restricted to the needs of the partial processes performed in each plant. This type of training is not designed to impart comprehensive knowledge, i.e. familiarise the trainee with all the technical or administrative and organisational aspects of operations (such as buying, marketing and transportation) at the level of the enterprise or company as a whole.

(d) Research and development does not take place in world market factories. This means that no training is provided in what is the most important sector for generating modern product and process technology.

Exceptions may be found in particular branches of industry, such as engineering and ship-building, where production in individual instances demands the training of a higher proportion of skilled workers. However, there are no indications to suggest that for the majority of world market factories the tendency is anything other than towards a production structure typified by non-complex production with the subdivision of the production process into partial operations designed for the industrial utilisation of a cheap labour-force and with only the most minimal effects on the skills of the workers.

The same basic phenomenon also applies to a large extent to the transfer of technology. Although one of the declared goals of underdeveloped countries, access to modern technology hardly ever takes place through the medium of world market oriented manufacturing. As with the case of training, access to modern technology is from the outset limited by the same factors: that is, the degree to which world market factories only involve partial operations.[1]

1. Thomas W. Allen, in an investigation into the effects of US investment in South East Asia on transfer of technology, comes to the following conclusion: 'When process-technology

Even when world market oriented production does involve the use of complex modern technology, this by no means implies access to such technology for the developing country concerned. Again the main cause is that the development of such technology (as well as its advancement: research and development) does not occur on site.[1] Nor can there be any access to new technology as long as new manufacturing processes are controlled centrally by foreign companies. The high number of foreign staff employed in work involving complex techniques or high technology is a strong indication of the continuance of external control.

is examined, it is apparent most projects are mainly assembly in character or require only general machinery. Significant existence of major processes requiring complex or developed machinery and techniques was apparent in only 16 out of the 39 metal-based projects examined, and in 32 of all 100 projects. However, all plants did involve subsidiary operations requiring general machinery of one type or another. The electronic industry yields a similar picture – a precision product with mainly assembly facilities. This is determined to a considerable extent by the nature of the processes, with pre-assembly stages involving very high technology which normally needs to be close to the main research and development centre. Some of the projects appeared to have extended the process-mix however, and these were mainly producers of components for television, transistors, etc. Such industries seem to have a good technological impact. . . On the whole, however, product- and process-embodied technology transfer does not appear to have been of great significance in United States operations. Where product-technology is involved in the complex products, the product-lines are normally limited and assembly operations only are involved. Most of the processes adopted also involve machinery/techniques which can be readily obtained from other sources, although the actual inputs (e.g. the wafers for semiconductors) in some cases could only come from the involvement of a foreign company. The assembly state is only the culmination of the underlying research and development.' (Thomas W. Allen, *Direct Investment of United States Enterprises in South East Asia; A Study of Motivations, Characteristics and Attitudes* (Bangkok 1973), pp. 32–4.)

1. 'In the developing countries there is hardly ever any decentralisation of research, and new manufacturing processes are handled centrally by the parent company. Research and development in multinational enterprises is run on the assumption that scientific knowledge is for internal circulation only, so that international dissemination of technology only takes place within the firm.'

'The concentration of research and development in multinational enterprises and its further concentration in the parent companies of these enterprises are accounted for the economies of scale in research and development, the desire to reduce the technical and commercial risks of experimental work on new products, and the availability of research facilities. This explains why in 1966 only about 6% of total research and development expenditure by American multinational enterprises in the manufacturing sector was done abroad; probably almost none of the 6% was done in subsidiaries in developing countries.' (ILO, *The Impact of Multinational Enterprises on Employment and Training* (Geneva 1976), p. 25.)

In a study of technology transfer in the electronics industry in South Korea, Kun Mo Chung comes to the conclusion that there is in fact no technology transfer via world market factories: '*The technology transfer through offshore activities by foreign firms has not been effective until now.* The main reason was that most offshore operations have been through wholly-owned subsidiaries which carry out only routine assembling and testing.' (Kun Mo Chung, 'Commercial transfer of foreign technology to the electronics industry in Korea', *Asian Economics* 13 (1975), pp. 22–3.)

The following report regarding the technical dependence of South Korean industry on Japan makes it evident that even in a country in which world market oriented manufacturing industry has reached significant levels, technical dependency has not decreased but in fact increased.

The technical dependency of Korean industry on Japan has increased in the past few years, a speaker of the Economic Planning Board (EPB) told the press in Seoul. The licence fees paid by Korea to Japan over the period 1962–75 came to US $36.72 million. As the EPB spokesman indicated this corresponded to 55.4% of all the licence fees paid by Korea abroad. This proportion had dropped from 50·9% in 1970 to 45.4% (1973); but in 1974 it again rose to 59.0% and in 1975 to as high as 63.6%.

This is a development viewed with regret in Seoul because, as the EPB spokesman stated, Japan allows Korean industry to buy licences primarily for older technological processes. This development, however, might weaken the Korean exporting industry. For this reason the EPB has been encouraging Korean industry to diversify its import of licences. Of the 581 licences imported over the period from 1962 to 1975, 93.3% were applied in Korean industrial manufacturing and mining, 1.2% in agriculture and fishing and 5.5% in the service and infrastructure sectors according to the EPB spokesman. Korea has imported Japanese technology mainly for its textile industry, for the electrical engineering and electronics industries, for the chemical industry and for engineering.[1]

As developments in the balance of payments and trade for countries in which free production zones and world market factories have been in operation for quite some time show, world market oriented production on this basis has no discernible positive effects on the external payments situation of these countries. Developing countries expect to get increased foreign currency receipts from the world market oriented manufacturing industry whose products are not sold on the domestic markets of the countries in which industries are located as the companies involved are obliged to use foreign currency to pay wages, fees, buy industrial inputs and pay for the use of infrastructure and the purchase of local raw materials (i.e. exchange their country's currency for local currency). However the other side of the balance reveals those expenditures incurred in connection with the construction and operation of the free production zones which are in turn effected in foreign currencies. In fact the balance of payments effects are frequently negative rather than positive.

Firstly, the foreign currency receipts from all the three items

1. *Nachrichten für Außenhandel*, 14 July 1976, 'Zunehmende technische Abhängigkeit von Japan'.

specified (wages, fees, raw materials) are quite small in view of the low wages and salaries, so that even with quite high employment the amounts of foreign currency which companies need to bring in to match their wages bills are also low. Subsidising fees, tariffs and prices for the supply of industrial inputs and for the utilisation of the infrastructure (subsidies being one of the incentives for investment) again does not lead to high foreign currency earnings. Often the foreign currency expenditures on the construction and operation of the respective installations are considerably higher than the receipts. Finally, the sale of domestic raw materials to the world market factories is not a source of any significant currency inflow. The possibility of importing raw materials without having to pay customs duties or taxes (again one of the main features of the free production zones) as well as the transnational organisation of production counteracts any tendency to utilise domestic raw materials on any considerable scale. Raw materials are largely imported.[1]

Foreign currency *outflows* for underdeveloped countries are not only incurred for the actual construction of the free production zones – site preparation, construction and operation of utilities, provision of factory space and buildings – but also for the supply of the free production zones and world market factories with industrial inputs (especially energy and water) and other infrastructural items such as roads, ports, airports, and container facilities.[2]

The following data gives an indication of the order of the foreign currency inflows accruing from the payments of wages and of the foreign currency outflows incurred in the development and maintenance of the sites. In the Masan Free Export Zone in South Korea, the world market factories located in the Zone with an average total

1. Finally, even the tariff policy of the industrialised countries influences the proportion of domestic raw materials used. Since in subcontracting many countries do not demand duty to be paid for the proportion of re-imported raw materials and semifinished products contained in the imported products, companies are often willing not to use domestic raw materials in world market production in underdeveloped countries so as to minimise customs duties when re-importing to the industrialised countries. (In its effects this is a protectionist policy employed by the industrialised countries.)
2. As the following example indicates, this may even include the construction of nuclear power stations: 'The Philippines Government announced last week that contracts have been signed by the state-owned National Power Corporation with Westinghouse Electric Corp. to construct two nuclear power stations near Manila. The reactors, which will produce a total of 1240 megawatts when completed, are to be built in Bataan Province. Although it was announced as a means of reducing Philippines oil dependency, it is likely that most of the power will be used to serve the needs of foreign multinationals, including Ford and Exxon, who are located in the nearby Mariveles Free Export Zone and surrounding industrial areas.' (*The Elements*, April 1976, 'Nuclear Export'.)

employment of 21 000 workers (21 100 in September 1975) and an average wage of US $2.00 per day have an annual wage bill of US $14.7 million. The Industrial Estates Administration of Masan made investments up to the end of 1973 amounting to US $16.3 million for the development of the factory sites and infrastructural installations (see Table III-16). If one assesses the proportion of the foreign currency expenditures conservatively as representing about one-third, then the foreign currency actually spent amounts to roughly US $5 million.

Table III-16. *Masan Free Export Zone, total investment in million US$: end–1973*

Site preparation	7.064
Industrial water	0.488
Port construction	2.103
Dredging	1.161
Public utilities	1.007
Standard factories	3.095
Dormitories	0.787
Other facilities	0.557
Total	16.262

Source: The Industrial Estates Administration, Masan, *A Case Study of the Masan Free Export Zone*, p. 9.

By March 1973 approximately 700 million Pesos had been spent on investments for the development and construction of the Bataan Export Processing Zone in the Philippines. Total state investments for equipping the Zone were estimated at 1000 million Pesos.[1] Assuming the total annual employment amounts to 10 000 workers (8177 in March 1976) and the average daily wage to US $2.00 the world market factories located in the Zone must pay an annual wage bill of about US $7 million. The proportion of foreign currency expenditures in the state investments paid out is very probably several times higher than the annual wage bill. The data given above refer, as indicated, solely to the investment cost for the development and equipment of the free production zones with installations. Not insubstantial amounts of foreign currency are also required for current expenditure for the operation and maintenance of the infrastructure and service facilities.

The financing of investments for the construction and equipment of the world market factories does not necessarily ensure a subse-

1. Teodoro Q. Peña, *Industrial Free Zone Activities in the Philippines*, p. 45.

quent compensating capital inflow from abroad. Investment credits are often available on the domestic capital market, the governments frequently offering the investors special subsidies (investment incentives) for financing their capital outlays.

The crucial determinant of the actual amount of currency receipts from production in the free production zones and world market factories is however the fact that, even with increasing exports from the zones and factories, equivalent currency inflows for the countries concerned do not necessarily follow. The ratio of exports from the zones to imports into zones and how this ratio develops depends essentially on intra-company transfers (transfer pricing) between the factories in the zone and their head offices. It is the overall strategy of the company or corporation which determines how such transfers are to be priced – in other words, the import prices of raw materials, semifinished products, etc. and the prices for the processed and finished goods exported. Even if such overall strategies embraced the possibility that it might prove profitable to set low import and high export prices, which would produce a large surplus on exports from the zones, this does not necessarily imply any corresponding net foreign currency inflows for the countries concerned as foreign companies are guaranteed the unlimited transfer of profits from the operations in the zones. A surplus in the balance of trade of the zones and world market factories and a corresponding surplus in the balance of trade of the respective country would, if all the earnings were transferred, correspond to an equivalent deficit on transactions on the capital account. And since earnings are exempted from tax (limited or unlimited tax holidays) foreign currency is not earned through the profits earned in the country either.

Only three sources of currency receipts are in fact available to the countries from this type of world market oriented production: the sale of their workers' labour-power, the sale of services and the sale of raw materials. The sale of cheap labour and of subsidised services may, at best, bring in foreign currency receipts roughly equivalent to the necessary foreign currency expenditures incurred, but the difference, if any, is hardly likely to bring about any general improvement in these countries' balance of payments. Only the increased utilisation of domestic raw materials might provide additional currency inflows, but this again depends on the specific conditions at each site.

17.2 Use of land, labour and capital

The previous section raised the question as to what were the immediate effects of world market oriented industrialisation through the free production zones and world market factories on the labour market, on technological development and on the balance of payments of underdeveloped countries. As this analysis made clear, there is nothing to indicate that the major problems confronting the underdeveloped countries can be solved through world market oriented industrialisation, even if this process were to advance rapidly. The process of world market oriented industrialisation will not resolve employment problems by reducing unemployment, nor will its secure access to modern technology and nor will it resolve balance of payments' problems by increasing the respective countries' net earnings from international payments transactions. In addition, there is also the question of the overall impact of world market oriented industrialisation in the socio-economic development of underdeveloped countries.

For underdeveloped countries world market oriented industrialisation means in the first instance the provision of land, resources, labour and capital.

The development of free production zones (i.e. preparing the site for occupancy) begins with the acquisition (expropriation) of the land and the provision of other resources. The choice of site will mainly be determined by factors related to the location of the labour-force, proximity to cities and towns, by the distance to the main outlets for the products, and by the availability or possibility of providing international transport facilities, primarily ports and airports. The selection of sites is often made in complete disregard for existing economic structures or the ecological effects of industrial production at the new sites. In many cases it involves the forced displacement of the rural population from areas in agricultural use.

The following extracts are taken from a report by Emmanuel O. Fernandez on the development of the Phividec Industrial Estate in the Province Misamis Oriental in the South Philippines, and its consequences for the local population. The Phividec Industrial Estate is an industrial free zone under construction in which both light and heavy industry will be located. A sintering plant for the Japanese Kawasaki Corporation is now under construction for which an area of 138 hectares is needed. A booklet by the Phividec Industrial Estate

Authority describes the objectives of the zone as follows: 'The main objectives of the industrial estate are the inducement of the export oriented industries and the utilisation of indigenous labour and raw materials.'

Along the shores of Northern Mindanao, in the Province of Misamis Oriental, giant earthmoving machinery crawls over what was once the barrio of Nabacaan where 143 families used to live. The scene will be repeated again and again until two whole towns will have given way to 3000 hectares of 'progress' known as the PHIVIDEC Industrial Estate. Meanwhile human rights, comfort, and dignity in all probability, will be steamrolled like so much dirt as they were in Nabacaan.

Misamis Oriental just happens to be far enough from the Muslim rebels and close enough to cheap hydro-electric power from Maria Cristina Falls. Tagaloan and Villanueva just happen to have an ideal topography for industrial development. But Tagaloan and Villanueva also happen to be the home of about 29000 people.

The final site chosen for relocating the people is the barrio Kalingagan. The selection was purportedly based upon the majority's preference, among other factors. Kalingagan is located seven kilometers away from the highway and rises 500 meters above sea level. It is a rolling rocky plateau. As agricultural land, it can only be described as submarginal. The acid land is too sterile to yield even tomatoes. So if Kalingagan was the people's choice, it is indeed very hard to imagine how the seven other proposed sites must be.

The living conditions of the relocated people, however, seem far away from the IATF's [Inter Agency Task Force in the Office of the President] projection. Reporters visiting Kalingagan have found that most of them still cannot find any means to make a living. Even a goat cannot survive on the land.

It is a long way to Kalingagan from the nearest highway. It is a steep climb all the way. No passenger vehicles ply the dirt road up since there is really nothing there until the IATF arrived. The people have been promised first priority in jobs at the sinter plant. Right now many are employed in the construction work. Two buses have been purchased for transporting the people when the relocation area is finally ready for occupancy. But their resolve to resist the arbitrary treatment they are receiving is also strong. Their recent meeting closed on a defiant note: '. . . this is our land . . . and we are not used to work in our lands . . . we are not used to work through employment . . . so we'd rather die now than die later with hunger! May God forbid Kawasaki to expand and reach this area! . . . Our big problem is that many of us are not land owners – in whose lands we work – sell, what shall we do? We must unite – to have strength in our struggle – against what the government and Kawasaki has imposed on us!'[1]

Capital is made available for the development of the industrial site (i.e. preparing it for occupancy) and the provision of services and the construction of other infrastructure such as energy and water, roads, ports, airports. The sources of the capital supplied are (a) the redistribution of the economic surplus generated primarily in agriculture and mining and (b) credits obtained chiefly from

1. Emmanuel O. Fernandez, 'Relocation – Marcos Style', *Japan-Asia Quarterly Review* 1 (1976), pp. 54, 56.

international financing institutions such as the World Bank and the Regional Development Banks. In many countries the capital made available represents a large portion of all the economic surplus which is at the state's disposal for economic development as a whole.

The provision of labour is mediated mainly through government organised recruitment of the specific labour-force required from the industrial reserve army. State mobilisation of the industrial reserve army for world market oriented industry starts with the advertising of the existence of the labour-force which is available in the vicinity of the respective sites on the world labour market; the next step is the placement of applicants in jobs by state recruitment agencies and labour exchanges; this is supplemented by the organisation of schools and the specialised industrial training of the labour-force. Such programmes include the establishment of workers' dormitories and compounds. If necessary recruitment is even made compulsory.

17.3 Minimal domestic social earnings and maximal foreign private profits

An analysis of the impact of world market oriented industrialisation on the socio-economic development of the underdeveloped countries must distinguish between its effects on national income and its effects on corporate profits. Whereas the economic yields for the countries concerned are in most cases slight and in some cases even negative, corporate profits are massive. As a result of the industrial enclave character of world market oriented industry, corporate profits do not even indirectly increase the local national income, for example through re-investment, and conversely negative developments in the local domestic economies have hardly any impact on the rate of corporate profitability.

The 'benefits' which underdeveloped countries derive from world market oriented production in the free production zones and world market factories, as indicated above, include the creation of job opportunities – but only for specific groups of the economically active population. However for the reasons already given, this employment does little to raise national income. Another contribution to national development, though again very slight, may be some transfer of training and technology. Finally, one may add the development of the industrial infrastructure although this is primarily domestically financed.

World market oriented production has practically no multiplier effects which might either increase income or employment in other sectors of the economy. This applies to both the internal economy as well as the, in this instance somewhat misleadingly titled, external sphere.

The integration of world market production with the domestic economy is limited predominantly to the utilisation of the labour-force and infrastructure. Backwards integration occurs only on a very limited scale. With the exception of a few industries backward linkages are limited to the supply of raw materials.[1] Forward linkages, i.e. the local processing of parts and products manufactured in the free production zones and world market factories, are precluded by the nature of the world market orientation of production. Forward and backward linkages exist only in a very rudimentary form even between world market factories located at the same site.[2]

1. The UNCTAD analysis of the electronics industry points the connection between the transfer of single non-complex processes and the virtual absence of forward and backward linkages with the local industries of the respective countries: 'The "spill over" effects of international sub-contracting in electronics depend partly on the nature of the operation and the type of sub-contract involved, and partly on the policy environment in which it is carried out. On the whole sub-contracting of single processes is likely to have the least "spill over" effects. Foreign firms that are transferring such processes to developing countries for the essential purpose of lowering their costs are normally not concerned with forward or backward linkages with local industries of the host country. They are essentially concerned with maintaining the linkages with their own international production and marketing network. It would appear that the assembly of semiconductors – or other highly specialised components – has not led, so far, to many direct linkage effects in developing countries. There are, however, important exceptions: in Hong Kong and Singapore, completely local production of transistors and even some integrated circuits is now commencing.' (UNCTAD, *International Subcontracting Arrangements in Electronics*, p. 26.)
2. 'Since many labour-intensive manufacturing activities using unskilled or semiskilled labour are transferred to export-processing free zones in developing countries by foreign manufacturers for the essential purpose of lowering costs for a specific industrial process, "linked" industrial activities in the zone country are not likely to develop spontaneously (except for those related to finish products, as mentioned above). Within the zone itself, "interrupted" production techniques usually result in an isolation of the different industries and a lack of inter-industrial linkages. In particular, the multinational corporations which operate within the zones are concerned with maintaining the linkages within their own international production and marketing network. To the extent that the industries situated in the zone are free to purchase their inputs wherever they wish, they will not choose locally produced inputs, unless these can be supplied at world prices. Thus, while there have been a certain number of cases – for example in the fields of electronics – in which component assembly has led on to component fabrication, such developments would normally result only from deliberate efforts to this end by the government of the country.' (UNCTAD, *The Use of Free Zones as a Means of Expanding and Diversifying Exports of Manufactures from the Developing Countries*, TD/B/C.2/125, 18 June 1975, p. 11.)

The enclave character of world market oriented production and its lack of connections with the local economy mean, as hinted at above, that this production in fact takes place outside the sphere of the real foreign trade of the country in question. Although statistically and terminologically referred to as exports from the country, they in fact represent economic activities which are largely separate from the domestic economy and foreign trade of the respective country. Exports from the zones and world market factories are not exports from the respective nations but intracompany transactions. Exports can only be said to occur for the host country to the extent that the products exported from the zones and world market factories incorporate raw materials, inputs and services from the domestic economies, and inasmuch as the companies operating in the free zones and world market factories have bought local labour. Even then the exports consist of the exports of a few goods and services and one particular commodity: the labour-power of the local work-force. Furthermore the system of production for the world market can only be said to improve the host country's foreign trade receipts if actual surpluses are obtained from the sale of these goods and services.

As against the very low domestic and foreign trade income, corporate profits are very high. However, these are mostly transferred abroad. Those analyses of the profitability of world market oriented production in the free productions zones and world market factories which are available show without exception the exceptionally high rates of profit to be made in such establishments.

The following analysis[1] of the profitability of export-oriented investments is based on data from eighty plants of transnational companies in the underdeveloped countries, of these twenty-one were export-oriented production units. Six of the export-oriented plants were in Latin America, twelve in South East Asia and three in other regions.

> Export oriented projects tend to be very profitable and use less LDC capital than other projects. Funds are repatriated more quickly and a large percentage of profit is made directly in the home country...Of the two types of investment that took place at the foreigner's initiative, export oriented investments might be termed exploitative. Their high rates of profitability, however, were not so much at the

1. Harold Crookell, 'Investing in development – a corporate view', *Columbia Journal of World Business*, 1 (1975), p. 82.

expense of the host country as they were a result of matching an affluent market to a low-cost production base . . .

Average % return on equity (after tax)	39.2%	(5)*
Internal payback period – actual or latest estimate (years)	3.9	(12)
Estimated time to repatriate foreign capital input (years)	3.8	(10)
% of total capital raised in LDC	31%	
% of total capital raised in form of debt	66%	

* Figures in parentheses indicate number of firms in sample.

Application of earnings	
Reinvested	34%
Paid in dividends	25%
Paid in royalties and fees	1%
Paid in other ways	40%

The DEG and the Secretariat of the United Nations Conference for Trade and Development made the following cost comparison for the manufacture of shoes and of components for the electronics industry.

The following calculation starts from the assumption that 1000 pairs of shoes are produced per day (220000 pairs of shoes per year); in Germany this requires 100, in Tunisia – although productivity is lower – only 93 workers since the number of hours effectively worked annually is much higher. All the primary material is imported. The production costs are as follows:

	Germany		Tunisia	
Total costs per year	(DM)	(%)	(DM)	(%)
Salaries	249600	9.3	241254	26.5
Wages	2125200	79.2	329870	36.3
Depreciation	116250	4.3	135000	14.8
Operating costs	101084	3.8	118864	13.0
Financing costs	91000	3.4	84500	9.4
Total	2683134	100.0	909488	100.0

Total costs per pair of shoes on the basis of these costs adds up to: in Germany DM12.20; in Tunisia DM4.13. Transport costs have to be added to the production costs in Tunisia. Thus, for example, for the transport of 13 tonnes of primary material to Tunisia and 18000 pairs of shoes packed in cartons to Germany the total charge is DM1.10 per pair of shoes.[1]

The next table compares the feasibility calculations for an annual production of 3 million electronic components for the European market.[2]

1. DEG, *Schuhproduktion Tunesien* (Cologne 1975).
2. UNCTAD, *International Subcontracting Arrangements in Electronics*, p. 40.

Cost item	Manufacture in West Europe (Source of material: West Europe)	Manufacture in Far East (Source: West Europe)	(Source: a third country)
	(in US $ per 1000 components)		
Material	378	378	363
Handling/freight/insurance	7	37	30
Duties	—	—	—
Cost of production	670	188	188
Running-in expenses	22	22	22
Coverage for research and development	86	86	86
Ex-factory delivery price	1163	711	689

Although such cost comparisons do not permit the direct conclusion that surplus profits will amount to the cost savings, they are nevertheless an indication of the size of such possible surplus profits.[1]

One of the salient features of the enclave character of world market oriented industrial production is therefore the disparity between social earnings and corporate profits. For the countries in which the enclaves are located this means high costs which must be financed from the surpluses generated by other sectors of the domestic economy in return for minimal benefits. For the companies operating within the new enclaves for world market oriented industrial production it means low costs and maximal profits. Corporate profits from world market oriented production are transferred from the respective production sites abroad; directly, where such transfers are not subject to any limitations, or indirectly, via intra-company transfers (transfer pricing). They are hence largely withdrawn from direct consumption as well as productive consumption in the respective host countries.

1. Regarding profits rates in Brazil and in the Philippines the *Frankfurter Allgemeine Zeitung* reported:

'Even if the investment risks may always be held to be higher in a foreign country, with an amortisation time for investments of three years, which is held to be the general rule by insiders, in view of profits of 15% or more and under conditions of stable growth, the gamble is not too reckless.' (*FAZ/Blick durch die Wirtschaft,* 28 June 1975.)

'On the whole the German firms in Manila consider the investment conditions very good. Particularly for labour-intensive production working with relatively little capital, dividends of 40% are not rare and high capital turnover can be achieved. The transfer of profits as well as of interest and amortisation payments are allowed.' (*FAZ,* 28 March 1977.)

17.4 Dependent and uneven development

The world market oriented industrialisation of the underdeveloped countries, as it occurs via the establishment of free production zones and world market factories, is the development of an industrial structure the reproduction of which is dependent on the reproduction process of capital, which in turn is largely dependent upon the reproduction process in the economies of the industrialised countries. In this sense world market oriented industrialisation is a development which clearly intensifies the historical process of dependent development in the underdeveloped countries of Africa, Asia and Latin America.

The structural dependency of world market oriented industry pervades all sectors of the process of industrial reproduction: the structure of production, supply of capital goods, raw materials, and spare parts, product and process technology, management, research and development and access to markets. In addition, world market oriented industrialisation, as a process of dependent development, intensifies the structural dependence of economic reproduction as a whole – and not merely in a linear manner.

The structure of production is predominantly characterised by the subdivision of the production process into its component operations and by the transnationally organised manufacture of a specific product or product group, with different operations (sub-assembly, final assembly etc.) being allocated to different factories at different sites. Production is integrated into the respective national economy only through the use of particular industrial inputs, services and of the labour-force. In all other respects this type of production is cut off from the local economy and vertically integrated into the world market within the framework of the transnational corporate organisation of manufacture. What is produced in the (world market oriented) industrial sector is determined neither by the respective structure of local needs nor by the local structure of industrial capacity. What is to be produced and how it is to be produced are decisions which are subordinated to the profit maximising calculus and strategies of foreign companies, which for their part are determined by the development of conditions on the world market.

The reproduction of world market oriented industry is only very restrictedly geared to obtaining supplies of raw materials and semimanufactured goods from local sources: it is highly dependent on foreign suppliers from outside. The organisation of production into a vertically structured set of subprocesses means that linkages between industries hardly ever develop, and that the production structure is systematically developed so as to remain dependent on external suppliers.

As far as the underdeveloped countries are concerned world market oriented production does not entail access to modern product and process technology, the organisation and management of large-scale industrial production or export markets.

Research and development, in the sector of product technology as well as process technology, simply does not take place in world market oriented industry in the underdeveloped countries. The actual organisation and control of the production process in the vertically integrated factories is the responsibility of the head offices of the foreign companies or corporations. And whatever superficial appearances might suggest, this system does not provide the respective countries with any lasting access to export markets.

The structural dependency of world market oriented industry in the underdeveloped countries is most clearly visible in relation to markets. The structural dependence on outlets in the industrialised countries (both as far as production and consumption are concerned) results from:

(1) the structure of the subproducts, products, partial or complete manufacture with a market principally only in the industrialised countries;
(2) the exclusive control over outlets and markets exercised by the companies' head offices and their marketing and sales network in the industrialised countries;
(3) the dependence of the market potential of the underdeveloped countries on market trends in the industrialised countries.

How much the reproduction of the world market oriented industrial sector in the underdeveloped countries actually does depend on market trends in the industrialised countries was revealed by the 1974/75 crisis. Hardest hit were the countries in which world market oriented industrialisation was the most advanced, such as Hong Kong,[1] Singapore,[2] South Korea,[3] and Taiwan.[4]

1. 'Hong Kong, which exports 80% to 85% of the goods produced there has been hard hit by the worldwide recession. The textile and garments industries, whose share in exports is about 50% and which also employ almost 50% of all industrial workers, in particular felt the impact of the sales crisis. The capacity of most of the Hong Kong plants is today not used to the full.' (*FAZ*, 17 March 1975.) [Notes 2, 3 and 4 are on page 385.]

The long-term impact of the structural dependency inherent in world market oriented industrialisation is even more serious for production than for sales, as it suppresses any potential tendency towards the development of an alternative structure of production, independent of the world market, and at the same time undermines the basis of residual sectors of autonomous production.

In addition, world market oriented industrialisation in the form of free production zones and world market factories also constitutes dependent development in the political and legal sense, in that it entails the virtual abandonment of a part of national sovereignty over the territorial enclaves which the production zones and export-processing plants represent.

World market oriented industrialisation as the development of a structurally dependent industrial complex is simultaneously a structurally uneven development. The basic structural disproportions are uneven regional, uneven sectoral and uneven social development. Uneven regional development can be seen at the level of world-wide uneven development between underdeveloped countries and industrialised countries, between urban and rural areas, and between the industrial enclaves and the non-industrialised regions. Uneven sectoral development can be discerned between industry and agriculture as well as within the industrial sector itself. Uneven social development is not only confined to the exploitation of the labour-force in production and to the external accumulation of the

2. 'The tropical city-state of Singapore, which has consistently pursued an open-market policy, is finding it difficult to protect itself against the icy draft of the impending international recession...For months labour-intensive manufactures such as electronics, textiles, boat yards for luxury yachts, wood processing industry have been hit by the slackening of international demand, and reports about large-scale redundancies involving several thousand workers in these branches have alarmed the population although since the end of 1973 leading politicians in the government have tried to warn them that hard times were ahead.' (*Handelsblatt*, 11 December 1974.)

3. 'According to Labour Office sources, fifteen foreign controlled companies, mostly US and Japanese electronics manufacturers, have retrenched about 4000 workers in recent weeks.
Hardest hit by the slowdown are the electronics and textile manufacturers which expanded during the 1975 export boom. The authoritarian Administration's determination to restrain wage increases and union activity in order to keep the country's all-important export industries competitive and to attract foreign investment, has meant that labour has had little redress. When workers recently sought wage hikes in the Masan Free Export Zone (South Korea), some Japanese employers closed their factories.' (*Far Eastern Economic Review*, 4 October 1974, 'Growing unrest on the factory floor'.)

4. 'World recession has forced Taiwan, which is about as big as Holland and has a population of 15.8 million, to set lower targets for its foreign trade. Market shares figuring in the five-year plan, which has now had to be recalculated, were lost. This applies primarily to trade with Japan and the USA. The losses sustained by exports here came to 15% and 20% respectively in comparison to 1974.' (*Handelsblatt*, 14 July 1976.)

surplus but also results from the subsumption of other areas of life to the model of world market oriented accumulation. It begins by displacing the rural population from their rural homesteads, and consequently from the residual sectors of autonomous reproduction, and ends with the impoverishment and disintegration of the labour-force once it is finally expelled, physically and mentally exhausted, from the production process.

World market oriented industrialisation reduces industrial development to non-complex, horizontally disintegrated and highly imbalanced partial manufacture. No industrial base which might, in time, provide for the needs of the mass of the population has a chance of developing. World market oriented industrial production to take advantage of a local cheap labour-force is linked to two ways in which the agricultural surplus is drained out of the agricultural sector and pumped into the industrial sector: (a) through financing the construction of the industrial infrastructure, and (b) through permanently bearing a part of the costs of the reproduction of the industrial labour-force, whose wages are insufficient to cover these costs. Any surplus attained in the industrial sector will not be re-invested in industry, but transferred abroad for the most part. The steady outflow of surplus from the agricultural sector leads to the stagnation and underdevelopment of the rural economy. That this surplus is then used to build up an industrial infrastructure leads to a one-sided and unbalanced development of the infrastructure of the economy. While no infrastructure is installed in the agricultural sector, world market oriented industrialisation demands the carrying out of infrastructural projects – primarily water, energy, roads, ports, airports and the respective equipment – the cost of which in many cases by far surpasses the funds available to the underdeveloped countries, even when the entire agricultural surplus is absorbed. The result is growing indebtedness with the international financial institutions such as the World Bank and regional development banks.

World market oriented industrialisation does not terminate but in fact perpetuates the historical process of dependent, uneven and unequal development for the countries of Africa, Asia and Latin America. Reproduction in the industrial sector depends on the reproduction process of the economies of the developed countries. Uneven and unequal development is the result of dependent reproduction and its counterpart – the subsumption of all other areas of life to the dictates of the model of world market oriented accumulation.

17.5 Mobility of firms, competition between production sites

In 1975, seventy-nine free production zones were in operation in twenty-five countries in Asia, Africa and Latin America. In ten of these countries, and in an additional eleven other countries, a total of thirty-nine free production zones were also under construction. In another sixteen countries free production zones were at various stages of planning.[1] These figures are an indication of the pace at which the number of new production sites for world market oriented production is multiplying.[2]

Each site not only contributes to the expansion of the world market for production sites but also leads to an enlargement of the world labour market, given that the site fulfils all the preconditions for the industrial employment of the labour-force available. Both these trends are underlying and immediate factors which figure in the calculations of corporate managements.

World market oriented manufacturing industry has displayed an enormous degree of locational flexibility. In their search for the most profitable production sites, companies no longer simply move from the traditional industrial sites in the industrialised countries to the developing countries, but also relocate production from what have now become 'traditional' sites in the developing countries to an ever increasing number of new sites in other developing countries. What is more, the pattern of this redistribution has come to include shifts from the new manufacturing sites in the developing countries back to traditional sites in the industrialised countries, and back again, if changes in conditions at both the traditional and the new sites and changes in production (especially the possibility of rationalisation) make this profitable.

Two instances of relocation of production reported and commented on by *Business International* provide an illustration of the global mobility of firms.

Delta Brush Co., a subsidiary of Binney & Smith, which was the first company to set up manufacturing operations in La Romana still appears satisfied with its

1. See Chapter 14.3.
2. We have shown in other chapters that this is a development planned and organised by both national agencies and international institutions. (See Chapter 14.1.)

operation. The company produces a wide range of artist and school brushes for which it imports virtually all its raw materials. Delta exports all of its production to the US, roughly $1.5 million last year. The firm employs about 350 workers and pays approximately $3500 a month for rents on its plant, which was expanded in 1972 in order to double its capacity to 31 400 square feet. Delta does not avail itself the tax exemptions offered. The company's decision to locate in La Romana and to expand its Dominican operations was based on the low operating costs offered in the free zone. Until two years ago, Delta had manufacturing operations in Puerto Rico which finally were closed down when the firm decided to expand the Dominican plant and to rationalise Caribbean production in general. Demand was growing considerably for the firm's brushes, and Delta had to make a choice of increasing production at one of its two plants. Since labor availability was not adequate in Arecibo, Puerto Rican wage rates were running high and all goods exported to the US Mainland from Puerto Rico had to be shipped in US vessels, the company thought it more economical and efficient to shift total production to the Dominican Republic. Delta's experience in La Romana has been 'satisfactory'. The company reports no labor problems and only a few power failures.[1]

During the past few years a US firm, National Semiconductor (NS), has evolved a global Asian strategy that, while partly dictated by circumstance, is essentially motivated by a desire to spread growth opportunities as well as risks. The company's most recent initiative in the area is its decision to start production of electronic components in Thailand, thus spreading the firms off-shore bases to a fourth Asian nation (besides Hong Kong, Malaysia and Singapore), and pioneering another location in the Far East for electronics production. NS also considered the Philippines, Indonesia and Taiwan, but found the attraction of Thailand irresistible...[2]

NS's triple-decker reasons for picking a new investment site over expanding in established ones:

– The firm's existing plants in Singapore and Hong Kong were experiencing increasing labor costs and faced prospects of constantly rising wages. NS found that even if it was paying high wages, it was difficult to obtain adequate workers in the two locations, particularly for shift work. In Singapore, the government's stress on high-technology industries and its expressed lack of further interest in such labor-intensive operations as wiring integrated circuits was a clear portent to the US firm that it has to look elsewhere for expansion. In addition, the Singapore government had, over the past two years, been encouraging unionisation of labor (in SILO, the Singapore Industrial Labor Organisation), which has added to upward pressure on wages.

1. *Business Latin America*, 8 May 1974, p. 151.
2. The attractions of Thailand are indicated in the same text of *Business International* as being: 'A major air traffic terminal, essential in the US firm's marketing strategy, since output will be exported by air to Europe, Japan and the US...

An incentives package exempting NS electronics from import duties on raw materials for at least eight years and from the Alien Business and Occupation Laws restricting opportunities for foreign capital and employment. The venture has also obtained Industrial Investment Promotion Privileges, i.e. full waiver of income and business taxes for five years from the date of start of production, as a totally export oriented operation.

Plentiful, trainable, low-cost, non-unionised labor.

Freedom to operate. NS expects minimal government interference in its Thai operations.' (*Business International*, 8 June 1973, p. 182.)

– The US firm also concluded that its ability to grow off-shore was better with a number of smaller plants than with a large one. Once development at any of these off-shore plants is past the initial slow-moving 'nucleus' stage, the rate of growth is usually rapid in relatively small units.[1]

Two factors have greatly enhanced the transnational flexibility and mobility of companies: firstly, changes in world market conditions, such as the availability of modern communications and manufacturing technologies; secondly, production-related factors which enable manufacturing industry to react very flexibly even to marginal modifications in the world market for production sites. Thus, unlike mining, world market oriented production is not restricted by natural conditions, such as the uneven distribution of raw material resources. Production based on cheap labour can find a practically unlimited industrial reserve army throughout the world. Unlike the raw materials industry, the world market oriented manufacturing of even complex products can be undertaken at any site in the world, often with only low initial investments. The specific installations at new sites tend to increase the companies' capacity for flexibility and mobility. This begins with the availability of factory premises (by now standard equipment in many free zones), which enables companies to relocate production from one site to another perhaps thousands of miles away practically overnight, and ends with a large area of financial manoeuvrability in which government subsidies for the costs of relocation have long been regarded as just one more item in the overall calculations of firms.

The mobility and flexibility of the companies has to be seen in relation to the competition between countries on the world market for production sites to attract producers to their respective sites. The efforts to attract world market oriented production, and the exploitation of the competition between sites by companies force the respective sites to offer continually improving and more effective incentives in order to secure new investments and prevent relocation to other sites. This implies chiefly: stronger financial incentives, wage controls and the preparation of new sites.

For example, the Government of Singapore reacted to the relocation of production from Singapore to other sites in Asia by introducing additional fiscal incentives,[2] offering new investment

1. *Business International*, 8 June 1973, p. 182.

2. 'To this end the government has introduced additional fiscal measures which have been well received. The original tax holiday of up to five years for pioneer plants has been increased to 10 years, the period of grace depending on the technology and skill-intensity

credits,[1] and in particular by introducing measures to prevent wage increases.[2] Similarly, reducing social security costs, streamlining customs procedures and opening up new industrial estates were the attempts made by the Mexican government to secure Mexico's position in the competition for locations for world market oriented production.[3] Even subsidising wage costs in world market factories has figured among the incentives offered by governments to keep sites competitive.[4]

However, governmental measures to 'improve the investment climate' at a particular site do not necessarily imply that world market oriented production will continue or expand there, as these measures may well have been 'devalued' in the eyes of companies by developments at other sites. Further, the mere threat that a company will relocate production suffices to obtain concessions from governments and trade unions which will yield high profits. Relocation of production to newer and cheaper sites is not the only threat which is constantly on hand: the possibility of rationalisation and relocation back to the traditional industrial sites can also be deployed.

Hence, competition between sites, and countries and the mobility of the companies contribute equally to the dynamic underlying the

potential which the new plant offers. At the same time, pioneer status is now possible even for new commitments which do not exceed one million dollars each.' (*Financial Times*, 8 October 1976, 'Singapore'.)

1. 'Export promotion is coming in for increasing official support in Singapore as the goverment increases the incentives package for firms to set up export oriented businesses. Recent steps include a scheme for rediscounting of export bills and special export financing to tide firms over the present economic difficulties.' (*Business Asia*, 12 September 1975, p. 291.)
2. 'While the National Wage Council (NWC) has unanimously recommended a wage increase of 7% for all workers, there are so many exceptions and strings attached that it is not clear how much, if anything, the workers will actually receive...

   The NWC recommendation had other limitations welcome to employers. The council especially emphasised that "there are certain export oriented manufacturing industries in the republic in which the labour content is high and where competition from low wage centres in other countries is particularly stiff. For these industries, the guidelines need not be implemented either in part or in full".' (*Far Eastern Economic Review*, 9 July 1976.)
3. 'The Mexicans are competing with Taiwan, El Salvador and Haiti for assembly business. So, to make things more attractive for the in-bond operators, new rulings were effected last month that should streamline the paperwork involved in shipping materials and machinery across the border, facilitate immigration for in-bond personnel, and lower the Social Security taxes paid by in-bond plant owners. In addition, the Mexicans hope to open up new duty-free areas in the interior where unemployment is high and wages low.' (*Business Week*, 23 February 1976, 'Mexico. New duty-free zones that aid US industry'.)
4. 'Puerto Rico has made additional efforts to participate in new direct investments for production for the United States market...Enterprises with 300 employees or more, for instance, in the first two years get a subsidy equal to 25% of the wage-bills.' (*FAZ/Blick durch die Wirtschaft*, 19 May 1976.)

global process. The constant search for new reserves of cheap labour which can be set to work in industrial production results in the spread of world market oriented manufacturing to a constantly growing number of locations in the developing countries. The competition between countries on the world market for production sites results in an increasing number of sites on offer for this purpose. Of course the rationality underlying the global valorisation of capital entails anarchy as far as individual regions are concerned. Whereas, on the one hand, a new international division of labour is emerging and the social character of production is being expressed in an unprecedented new form in the transnational organisation of production, on the other hand, regional development at the respective production sites is more than even before characterised by the anarchy of alternating aggressive and regressive development and by the steadily declining capacity for autonomous reproduction.

18 ❧ Statements by managers, trade union officials and employees

The following extracts reveal what production in the free production zones and world market factories means for the companies (capital) and their workers (labour) better than any abstract analysis could hope to show. As will emerge, exactly how the operations of the world market factories are judged depends on the position within the production process.

The world market factories to which the following statements refer are all located in free production zones in Malaysia. The statements of the managers are taken from the proceedings of an international seminar on investment opportunities in Malaysia organised by the Federal Industrial Development Authority of Malaysia. The statements of the employees and the trade unionists (quoted in indirect speech) were recorded by the author in the course of discussions with the former. The statements of the employees refer exclusively to enterprises other than those cited in the statements of the company managers.

Managing Director Economics, Robert Bosch Malaysia Sdn. Bhd.[1]

The Bosch Group is represented in the fast growing markets of East Asia by a wholly-owned company in Japan, a sales company in Singapore with a branch office in Malaysia and some agencies in other countries. Besides, it holds minor interests in three Japanese companies. Since 1971, the Photokino Division of the Bosch Group has been manufacturing with our Bauer & Sun Optical Co. Ltd in Taiwan high quality zoom lenses for Super 8mm movie cameras – our sister company employs 500 people at present. The need for further production capacity, particularly for movie cameras and electronic products and the business prospects in the fast-growing Far East markets induced our decision to build a plant in this region. Preliminary investigations resulted in the alternative suggestions: Singapore, Malaysia or Hong Kong.

1. Proceedings of International Seminar 'Investment opportunities in Malaysia' (Federal Industrial Development Authority), Kuala Lumpur, 27–29 October 1975, pp. 89–91.

As you know, the basic criteria for the selection of a manufacturing location are:
(1) The market for the product concerned
(2) Manufacturing costs
(3) Availability of manpower
(4) Good infrastructure of the country, especially efficient communication systems and traffic facilities
(5) Purchase possibilities for the required materials and components
Our final choice in January and February 1972 was Malaysia, and there the Free Trade Zone of Bayan Lepas on Pulau Penang because of its decisive advantages, particularly:
(1) The well-prepared industrial Free Trade Zone
(2) The labour resources of Penang
(3) A stable economic situation
(4) No customs problems
(5) The relatively low construction costs
(6) Favourable financing by local banks
(7) And last, but not least, the great readiness of the Malaysian government and its authorities to assist us and to further our project
Favoured by a reliable and unbureaucratic administration, by the efficient assistance of accountants and lawyers and by experienced, flexible architects, our plant was designed, constructed and the necessary machinery installed within five months.
— In February 1972, we filed our investment application with FIDA
— In March, approval and Pioneer Status in principle was granted
— In April, we started construction of our plant in the Bayan Lepas Free Trade Zone of Penang
— In June we began to train our employees
— In July we took up production on our assembly lines on an area of 4000 square metres
Due to the extraordinarily good cooperation with the Malaysian Government and its authorities, we were able to take up production in a new, air-conditioned building half a year after we decided to do so. To begin with, we manufactured 2 types of exposure-meter for our cameras. In November 1972, we expanded operations and began to assemble Super 8 mm cameras under the trade mark 'Bauer'. Today we manufacture in Penang, on an area of 8000 square metres with more than 700 employees, ten different types of movie cameras and, for one of Robert Bosch Automotive equipment divisions, magnetos and flashers. In compliance with our medium term planning, the manufacturing programme of Robert Bosch (Malaysia) will be expanding, although it will not be as fast as in the past. Between the end of 1976 and the middle of 1977, we intend to start manufacturing also high feature cameras which are at present produced in our parent plant in Germany.

Notwithstanding the well-known normal, initial difficulties, the results of our Penang venture turned out to be good so far – I may say this without any restriction. Training our employees, comprising Malays, Chinese and Indians went on smoothly and without problems. The progress of our trainees was remarkable, the high quality of the products they manufacture being equal to that of comparable products manufactured in the Federal Republic of Germany. This fact is a clear evidence of the willingness of the people to learn and the success of our training. Willingness to learn and to work hard on the part of the Penang people were of great advantage to us, especially in the initial phase. However, I should also mention that every foreign investor in Malaysia has to train his employees by himself for highly sophisticated technical professions such as toolmakers, foremen and supervisors if he is going to manufacture products of excellent quality. Although there is still no shortage in the availability of labour force in general one cannot expect an excess of well-experienced highly skilled technical people. On the other hand our skilled employees trained by ourselves have attained good experience. The education programmes for technicians and engineers from universities and polytechnics here are good. One only has to give them time for experience, and tasks to let them show what they can do. For example, in our Development Department the challenge to find new solutions for new problems finally resulted very often in amazingly good answers which were not expected at that time. This obviously is the result of the good theoretical background acquired from the universities and the polytechnics together with their challenge for practice. Or in our Toolmaker Department where we have a training programme under one German instructor for at least 20 local toolmakers. Today we are able to produce most of our own tools, dies and devices.

One more positive aspect of the stormy industrial development in South East Asia is the increasing possibility of buying materials and components even from local manufacturers and, in consequence, reducing the comparatively expensive shipments from Europe. Nevertheless, we must also take into consideration the negative aspect of this industrial development, that is particularly, the inflationary tendencies. The average living expenses increased by 18% from December 1972 to December 1973 and by 12% from December 1973 to December 1974, due especially to increasing cost of food. Unfortunately, prices keep climbing although the rate of increase has been reduced.

Consequently, Robert Bosch (Malaysia) had to raise wages in 1974 by approximately 25% and in 1975 by 16%. This tremendous increase in labour cost cannot completely be compensated by means of rationalisation. Adequate raises of the prices for products manufacture are therefore inevitable. Nevertheless, we hope that the future trend will be in such a way that our products manufactured in Malaysia will remain competitive on the world markets.

Managing Director, Italasia Malaysia Sdn. Bhd.[1]

Our company has set up a joint venture with the Malacca State Development Corporation. This joint venture is 60% foreign owned, is located in the Free Trade Zone and is an export oriented project for the production of shoes. We have an employment capacity of about 600.

We consider that our experiences in Malaysia to date have been both positive and encouraging. This does not mean that we have not had problems to face, nor does it mean that everything has always gone smoothly for our company, but it does mean that in sitting back and evaluating our experiences here in the last two years, we can say that the pros have far outweighed the cons. Our experience here is comparatively short, but in the last two years we have seen our company established and able to produce a real competitive product for the international market. We are now successfully exporting to the United States, Germany, the Scandinavian countries and we are looking towards Australia.

1. 'Investment opportunities in Malaysia', pp. 86–8.

We have been requested by FIDA to give our frank impressions concerning investment in Malaysia, problems encountered in setting-up a factory and exporting from Malaysia. This is what I am trying to do for if it is our considered opinion that the investment climate in this country is good and will remain so in the foreseeable future, it doesn't mean that things cannot become better. Malaysia is a country with a vast potentiality for further development and with a wealth of large resources still to be tapped. From this point of view the country is a most desirable area for investment. However, a note of warning must be sounded here. The speed with which new investment and industrial development have taken place in Malaysia during the last five years is now creating problems and difficulties due to their outpacing the creation of new infrastructure facilities and the expansion of control agencies within the Government Ministries to cope with specific problems encountered or caused by such new industries...

Malaysia has a unique opportunity to control, encourage and assist rapid industrial development of the right kind. It is possible to ensure that the industrial development now taking place, and the future development planned is the right kind of development for the country. In order to do this, there must be a much closer cooperation between departments at both the State and the Federal level, and the investor than what exists at present. Certain difficulties are commonly experienced by companies newly established here – these difficulties stem from many causes – none of them insurmountable. However, in many cases the difficulties have not been foreseen by the departments controlling the particular area concerned and have taken a while to overcome due to lack of coordination and follow-up on the solving of the difficulties. The result can often be expensive in time and money for the company concerned...

Investors invited to Malaysia in future should be given more opportunities to assist in the planning of the industrial estates where their factories will be located. In this way many problems can be avoided right from the beginning and development proceed in a smoother and less costly manner. I would be very much in favour of the establishment of a powerful committee at both State and Federal levels for the follow-up of industrial development in different areas of the country. Such committees could meet periodically in order to discuss problems affecting industrial development in their area, arrive at solutions and recommend the necessary action to the Government department concerned. Such committees should have the power to do so. Positive results could thus be quickly achieved and delay in such problem solving become a thing of the past.

In conclusion I must say that our company is planning further investment in this country, therefore, it means that our original opinion of this country has not changed. We have not had to revise our opinion in any way and that in the final analysis is the most important factor. We therefore recommend investment in Malaysia during the next few years because the general advantages offered to prospective investors are attractive and generous and will continue to make Malaysia a prime development area for years to come. The improvement of co-ordination in the fields I have mentioned earlier will, I'm sure, render Malaysia even more attractive to investors in the future and I expect the economy to continue to grow and expand with the aid of increased investment from overseas.

Manager, Kanematsu–Gosho Ltd[1]

In this speech, I wish to give a brief extract of my experience in the feasibility study and implementation mainly for Malaysian Topmaking Mills Sdn. Bhd., a wool processing industry which was part of the initial performance within my duty and investment of our company. It was late 1972 when I visited South Korea, Taiwan, Hong Kong, Philippines, Thailand, Indonesia and finally Malaysia with the aim of choosing the best location for this project. Wool processing industry which is well established in Japan had been facing or forecasting by then like many other intensive, land and water consuming industries there, shortage of labour and high cost of land and water resources and subsequently difficulties of running factories and maintaining export market.

Our Branch Office in each country gave me preliminary report and data on investment environment and potential site for this project, with support of which I pursued the first detailed studies from country to country spending one to two weeks in most of them and stayed almost one month in Indonesia. However, I could not be fully satisfied with any of them. Besides general and basic conditions like stable politics and sufficient manpower, as a 100% export industry this project requires abundant infrastructure such as port facility with an efficient and skilled shipping, forwarding and transportation service network as well as legislated incentives for export. It also needs power and water at low cost, as well as labour forces with good quality. Some countries can supply cheap labour but no such infrastructure. Some had labour and port of high efficiency but no water. Some could afford all, but incentives for export and administration of authority are very poor. In Malaysia, however, I have found all of them...

This first impression of mine has remained unchanged until today. Besides me, many people have pointed out so many advantages that Malaysia enjoys, such as political stability under parliamentary democracy and neutral diplomacy, economical and monetary stability with rich natural resources and well planned development infrastructure facilities which are as highly developed as those in advanced countries, abundant labour which is quick to learn and willing to work hard, tempting investment incentives which are specially legislated to attract new investors into the manufacturing sectors. In our case, however, because of its particular nature of export oriented industry I must specially emphasise the following aspects:

1. Productivity of manpower

Our industry seeks export to world-wide markets including Europe, Hong Kong and Japan, which means that our products must be competitive enough in these countries. Cost of products depends very much on productivity of manpower. Even with wages which are comparatively low, if we fail to train people here both in technology and administration, within scheduled period and up to scheduled level, our price will never be competitive. If efficiency of work, either in administration of public sectors or in business services of private sectors, is poor, our export business will never cope with international terms and conditions.

2. Incentives for export industry

In addition to legislated export incentives such as Export Allowance, Accelerated Depreciation Allowance and Additional Deductions for Overseas Promotion, Free

1. 'Investment opportunities in Malaysia', pp. 92–4.

Trade Zone is well established for those who import 100% of their raw material and export 100% of products. More attractive incentive provided to our case is the Licensed Manufacturing Warehouse, as our factory site was chosen in less urbanised area to enable us to utilise mining pool for processing water and unemployed young labour in these areas. I understand that LMW is established only in Malaysia in this region and it can be an unique advantage for export industry. This represents, I believe, special and traditional concern to export industry and trade in this country.

3. High efficiency of society

As I have said, some countries provide labour, some countries have labour and infrastructures, but they are yet not satisfactory. As in most practical business of international nature, our desire is quite great and wide also in mental and cultural aspects. In the course of implementation of project and operation of factory we require conditions in our favour given from a multitude of people and society which must be as highly developed as those in advanced countries, especially in the case of export industry which has to penetrate into the market in these countries. High efficiency and moral of Government authorities, labour force full of eagerness to learn and willingness to work hard, well organised services of contractor and distributor and a huge pool of technical skills, all of which we have required for and we have really enjoyed in our implementation and operation so far. All of these may be some of the great inheritances of this country which has traditionally developed a high degree of education system, social morality and civil service administration. These are also very important factors of total package of resources that Malaysia is offering.

Statement by a trade union secretary who was in charge of organising the employees in the electronics plants in the Free Zones of Bayan Lepas, Penang, Malaysia in 1974

The Free Trade Zone of Bayan Lepas had been set up on land which had previously belonged to independent farmers producing both for their own subsistence and for the market (Georgetown), and who had had a decent standard of living. The government had expropriated them and resettled the farmers in remote regions where the land which was usable did not yield as much as the land which had been expropriated. At first the farmers tried to resist expropriation but they were finally forced off the land by a law which allows expropriation in the public interest. The government then paid out a negligible compensation of about 2000 Malaysian dollars per family.[1]

Resettlement had compelled the families concerned to try to make a living by some of the members leaving the agricultural sector and trying to find work elsewhere. The first to do this were the young

1. 2.40 Malaysian dollars = US $1.00.

girls who were among the initial work-force in the Free Zone at Bayan Lepas. Wages in Bayan Lepas when production started – in 1972 – had been lower than at other production sites in Malaysia. On average they came to 1.80 Malaysian dollars a day. By 1974 they had been raised a little but working conditions in Bayan Lepas were still very bad. These included:

(1) generally low wages,
(2) overcrowding of the work-rooms,
(3) long distances from home to factory and high charges for public transport,
(4) high cost of canteen meals (0.80 Malaysian dollars per meal),
(5) work in excess of legal working time. The eight-hour day was observed but the legal annual paid leave was not granted (only three to four days of paid leave instead of the legally prescribed seven days were granted and employees were deprived of the five paid holidays stipulated by law – prior to such holidays the workers were required to work on the preceding Sunday at the normal wage rate),
(6) inadequate public health service in the plants,
(7) bad treatment of the employees in the case of sickness. The doctor's certificate that a worker was ill was not taken seriously but regarded as issued to do the person concerned a favour. Women workers had not succeeded in preventing such charges being made and management did not pay out wages in case of days lost through illness.

Mainly women aged between eighteen and twenty-four years were employed in the plants. One of the reasons for this was that women in this age group were willing to accept any kind of work to free themselves from the constraints of family ties. Another factor was that these women had no political experience and were not organised in the trade unions. The Electrical Industry Workers' Union had tried to organise the workers in the electronics factories in Bayan Lepas. They had distributed leaflets at the factory gates, started discussions and organised a large meeting to which workers were invited. When several thousand women accepted the invitation to the trade union meeting, the Federal Government of Malaysia organised a counter-movement. Notable personalities were sent to hold discussions in Bayan Lepas and intimidated the women, warning them about trade union activities. In spite of these attempts some 3000 workers came to the meeting. The moment the participants began to fill in membership application forms the Registrar stopped them, arguing that the *Electrical* Industry Workers' Union was not entitled to register workers from the *electronics* industry. The Government's intention was to prevent any union being formed in the electronics industry: in new branches of industry employees are only allowed to set up a union after a period of three years. Furthermore, they wanted to divide the trade union movement – in this case into one union for electrical engineering and one for electronics. In Malaysia there already existed 300 such unions based on industrial sub-branches, which weakened the union movement very considerably.

In 1974 companies began to retrench in the Bayan Lepas zone; several firms had introduced short time without adjustment of wages. The trade union was worried that the companies, having run through the period when they enjoyed pioneer status (four to seven years of tax exemption), would wind up operations in Bayan Lepas and restart at new sites. Even if the government would, by offering new incentives, try and counteract such tendencies, there was no reason to count on the companies staying where they were. In the first five years, because of the extremely low wages paid at the beginning, the companies made such vast profits that even new or additional incentives could not compensate for the slow and gradual rise in wages and the corresponding drop in profits.

The mass of the population lives in dire poverty. Many people live with a heavy heart. In the morning they don't know where to get the money to buy the food they need for that day and to be able to send their children to school.

Statement from an assistant supervisor in a plant in which pocket calculators are assembled

The plant in which she worked employed 1900 workers in 1974. Production originally comprised both the assembly of components for the manufacture of pocket calculators as well as their final assembly. The assembly of components had been stopped at the beginning of 1974. Management had not disclosed its reasons for doing this, but it was thought that the assembly of components was to be moved to Mauritius. However, since the assembly of complete calculators was stepped up no redundancies resulted. Only women were used in production. Of the total number of employees

90% were women. Wages as a rule were very low. The employees assumed that the company made very high profits, but they could not hope to have any demands for higher wage rates accepted as management could have reacted by dismissing people. The fear of being fired and the fear of being noticed determined the women's action. The daily wage of the operators came to 3.10 Malaysian dollars on commencement. After six weeks it could be raised to 3.30. An operator who had been working for one or two years might be earning a maximum wage of 6 Malaysian dollars a day. Assistant supervisors received an average maximum daily wage of 4.90 Malaysian dollars. The intensity of work was very high. Workers who failed to make up their score of pieces would get a warning. Further failure to make the prescribed number of pieces resulted in dismissal within two days. The work was predominantly manual, with very few machines in the whole factory. 'The assistant supervisor is in charge of about thirty operators. She has to push them. She gets pushed by the supervisor who gets pushed by an assistant production manager etc.' Trade union activities were forbidden in the plant. Employees' Relations Committees had been organised by the management. They could register complaints and wishes of the employees and present them to the management. The management held monthly discussions with the Committees. Thus management had a source of information and always knew about the workers' feelings and opinions. The following wishes had been accepted: instead of the traditional music programme, piped music in the work-rooms was now mainly pop music. Managements response to the complaint that there were not enough public buses was to make charter buses available.

Statement by a former operator in a semi-conductor plant

The operator had been working in the plant for eleven months in 1974. She had given in her notice because the working conditions were unbearable. 'They have treated us like garbage.' The management kept on trying to push up the pace of work. Each operator had to work on 700 components a day under a microscope. There were no breaks during the working day, and workers were not allowed to leave the job even for a moment. Talking during working hours was forbidden. The operators were subjected to constant criticism: they were always told that they were not working enough or that their work was of poor quality. There were always warnings and dismissals. Anyone who spoke out against the working conditions, in particular against the pace of work, and the low wages, would be fired. Workers who failed to reach the required output would also be fired. Every quarter wages were raised by 0.30 Malaysian dollars per day. One these occasions there would always be half-hour lectures in which management made it very clear to the operators that wage increases could only be granted if output increased too. One day the workers had got fed up with this and a spontaneous strike broke out. The strike resulted in some of the demands being accepted. Work under the microscope is very tiring: eight hours work gave the operators sore eyes and completely exhausted them. Anyone who fell asleep at the microscope on night shift would receive a warning on the first occasion and be dismissed on a second. Training lasted fourteen days and after that there was nothing more to learn, even if the worker wanted to. Average wages for operators were 100 Malaysian dollars per month. In spite of having been forced to sign written undertakings that they were not members of a trade union many operators secretly belonged to a union. 'The companies are here for cheap labour and treat us like garbage.'

A worker in a plant in which machinery was produced who had been trained to be a skilled worker

'We are happy.' According to this worker the manager was a 'fine man'. He had not received any formal vocational training himself, but had been trained on the job to become a skilled worker and worked in quality control. 'We are all really happy at the factory. It's a fine place.'

Extracts from a report of the Electrical Industry Workers' Union in Malaysia[1]

The organising campaign undertaken by our organising committee was one whereby newsletters or literature were circulated to unorganised workers, bringing to their attention their rights as workers and the need for unionisation. On many occasions, employers instructed their security guards to snatch away every circular distributed by our organising committee to their employees. On viewing the behaviour of these anti-union industrialists we reviewed our strategy. The organising committee was requested to distribute newsletters to unorganised Electronic

1. Electrical Industry Workers' Union, Malaysia, Country Report, May 1974, pp. 7–8, 12–14.

Workers only when they were returning home after work, whereby bringing to their attention that general meetings would be conducted to enlighten some on the need for unionisation and the benefit they would derive from union membership.

When the employers came to know of our reviewed strategy, they threatened and intimidated their employees to attend the meeting on pain of dismissal. The employers further confused their employees by advising them that workers engaged in industries granted pioneer status and further, if situated in free trade zones would not be eligible for trade union membership. Workers also gathered in small groups and informed that the policy of the company, is that their workers should not join a trade union and should they join same the 'godfathers' would have no other alternative but to wind up operations and move over to some other neighbouring country.

As most of the workers engaged in electronic companies are fresh from school and mainly from the rural areas and further knowing little about working life and having no knowledge about the trade union movement, are very confused. They are even frightened to speak to our officials and have been motivated to the degree to think that we are persons who bring about insecurity to their employment... It's no secret that the electronic workers are amongst the lowest paid in the country and are subject to the maximum exploitation. Our Union felt that workers should not be led to the altar to be sacrificed in the bid to woo foreign investment. That's the main reason why we made the move for electronic workers although they are reasonably established...

The electronic industrialists who are currently enjoying a tax holiday period in the paradise of the free trade zones of Malaysia have paraded the Asian Region. They started their industries in Japan and subsequently moved to Taiwan, Hong Kong, Singapore and are now holidaying in Malaysia.

The future of these industries is bleak. The main contributing factor to the bleakness in the future of these industries is that they do not recognise labour and treat labour as the slave of capital. Their main aim is to make the maximum of profit with the minimum of investment in the shortest possible period of their holiday. They have also remarked that should there be labour unrest in our country and a demand for higher wages they could within a month wind up operations and go in search of cheap labour to some other neighbouring country in the Asian sphere.

Concluding remarks

The analysis of the world market oriented industrialisation of the underdeveloped countries through the establishment of free production zones and world market factories has shown that this industrialisation process, which is determined by a change in the conditions for the valorisation of capital, actually intensifies the tendency towards uneven and dependent development in the underdeveloped countries.

The more this process of industrialisation oriented to the world market expands and deepens – and there is nothing to suggest that this tendency will diminish in the foreseeable future – the more the development of the underdeveloped countries will manifest itself as continued underdevelopment.

In the classical international division of labour the process of underdevelopment which the countries of Africa, Asia and Latin America have experienced was determined by the development of their economies as plantation agriculture and raw materials economies. Although a new international division of labour has been brought into existence by the new and increasingly dominant process of the world market oriented industrialisation of these countries, this form of industrialisation has not meant any change in the historical process of underdevelopment, but in fact in its deepening. The dependent and uneven development of plantation agriculture and mining, which has up until now typified the socio-economic development of the underdeveloped countries, is now, in addition, being reproduced in the industrial sphere as well.

The extent to which this industrialisation is quantitatively distributed over individual sectors of the economy of particular countries is relatively unimportant. What is decisive is that this new development has the same consequence: underdevelopment. One causal factor is that the effects of the global process of the valorisation of capital continue to be radically different in their impact on the peoples of the underdeveloped countries in comparison to the industrialised countries. The transnational organisation of production is structured in a hierarchy controlled by a small group of industrialised countries. The effect of this is the constantly increasing disparity between the material living conditions of the inhabitants of the underdeveloped and the industrialised countries.

Although it should be recognised that the world market oriented industrialisation of the underdeveloped countries is a process capable of integrating a growing number of the labour-force in these countries into itself, and although it should also be recognised that this process increasingly manifests itself in the relocation of sections of industry and certain production processes from the industrialised to the underdeveloped countries and that an increasing proportion of world industrial production will take place at these new sites, there is nothing to indicate that this process will materially improve the material conditions of the populations of the underdeveloped countries. In fact, the opposite has become apparent, inasmuch as these conditions can get any worse.

Even if large sections of industrial manufacturing were relocated from the traditional industrial centres to the underdeveloped countries, only a relatively small proportion of the potentially economically active population would be drawn into this process. It is a process which lacks the potential to eliminate unemployment and underemployment, but can only absorb a fragment of the hundreds of millions of unemployed, at a minimum wage, with the result that most of these unemployed are condemned permanently to be members of the reserve army of labour.

The implications of the world market oriented industrialisation of the underdeveloped countries are not only that it provides employment only for a very small part of the unemployed and underemployed (at wages which do not even cover these workers' reproduction costs) but outside the immediate bounds of this sector this process also perpetuates those structures which generate dependency and uneven development and the marginalisation of a large part of the population without creating even the most rudimentary preconditions for alternative development.

Since this process does not offer the underdeveloped countries the chance of overcoming underdevelopment why has it met with support in these countries and why do many governments in underdeveloped countries still support it so strongly? We can only hint at an answer to this question. If we disregard for the moment the problem of 'corruption' and 'commissions' one explanation may well be that for many people who are aware that this process entails the direct exploitation of the labour-force, their recognition is still combined with hopes that this very process will develop an industrial structure which will eventually have the potential for autonomous development – that is, a development in the interests of the working population. It is a hope which proceeds from the assumption that unlike the dependent agricultural and raw materials producing economy of the past, this industrial development may from within itself produce an industrial nucleus for further development. The destruction of this illusion, once shared by the authors, could be one of the contributions of the present study.

We have investigated a new development, the emergence of a new international division of labour, and its implications for the industrialised and the underdeveloped countries. These implications are structural unemployment in the former and continued underdevelopment (which also means continuing unemployment on a massive scale) in the latter. We have explained this development as the consequence of a change in the conditions under which the valorisation of capital is taking place; as we have shown, and this is also relevant to the overall thesis and explanation, the issue is not whether corporations act morally or not. In the process of the valorisation of capital companies are not free agents but are compelled to adapt to new conditions. The consequences, in terms of unemployment and underdevelopment, flow from the process of adaptation under these forces.

It is of little use to attribute blame to the companies involved. If the consequences of this development are considered unacceptable and if an alternative path of development is thought necessary, the first step is to seek to understand the structure and the rationality within which companies can only act as they do. Alternative courses of development are therefore a question of an alternative mode of production or an alternative form of society.

In this connection we should refer to what is perhaps the most important effect of the new international division of labour. A working class, disciplined for industrial work, is in the process of formation at the new sites: the organisation of these workers inside the labour process, on the production line, also embraces the possibility of their developing forms of political and social self-organisation with which they can struggle for their own development. Our analysis has shown the immense obstacles which block the way to such organisation. In the final analysis much will depend on the labour movements of the traditional industrial countries as to whether these obstacles can be overcome. In fact the effects of the new international division of labour should make it easier for workers in these countries to discard their role of real or supposed world labour aristocracy and recognise that their fate on the world labour market is inseparably linked with that of their fellow workers in the underdeveloped countries.

The development of the new international division of labour therefore contains the *possibility* of international solidarity between workers. Whether this possibility will become a reality for the conscious transformation of human society is ultimately dependent on whether the world working class allows itself to become divided by the promise of benefits, whether real or supposed, to one particular section within it.

Appendix

Tables III-17 and III-18

Table III-17. *Free production zones in Asia, Africa and Latin America: 1975*

Country	FPZs in operation		FPZs under construction	
	No.	Name	No.	Name
Asia				
Bahrain	1	Industrial Area, Port Mina Sulman	1	Industrial Area Sitra Island
Hong Kong		Free Port Hong Kong		
	2	*Industrial townships*	2	*Industrial districts*
		Kwung Tong		Shatin
		Tsuen Wan/Kwai Chung		Tuen Mun
	5	*Industrial districts*		
		Sam Ka Tsuen		
		San Po Kong		
		Cheung Sha Wan		
		Chai Wan		
		Wong Chuk Hang		
India	2	Kandla Free Trade Zone (KAFTZ)	3	Readymade Garment Export Processing Zone Gurgaon
		Santa Cruz Electronics Export Processing Zone (SEEPZ)		Knitwear Export Processing Zone Ludhiana
				Multi Product Export Processing Zone Dum Dum
Indonesia			2	Bonded Zone Pulo Gadung Jakarta
				Bonded Zone Rungkut Surabaya
Jordan	1	Free Zone Aqaba Port	1	Jordan-Syrian Free Zone
Lebanon	1	Zone Franche du Port de Beyrouth		
Malaysia	8	Prai Free Trade Zone	2	Pasir Gudang Free Trade Zone
		Prai Wharves Free Trade Zone		Senai Free Trade Zone
		Bayan Lepas Free Trade Zone		
		Sungei Way Free Trade Zone		
		Ulu Klang Free Trade Zone		
		Telok Panglima Free Trade Zone		
		Batu Berendam Free Trade Zone		
		Tanjong Kling Free Trade Zone		
Philippines	1	Bataan Export Processing Zone (BEPZ)	1	Phividec Industrial Estate
Singapore		Free Port Singapore		
	14	*Industrial estates*		
		Bukit Timah		
		Jurong Town		

		Redhill		
		Ayer Rajah		
		Tangling Halt		
		Kallang Basin		
		Toa Payoh		
		Ang Mo Kio		
		Chai Chee		
		Bedok		
		Indus Road		
		Woodlands		
South Korea	9	Masan Free Export Zone (MAFEZ)		
		Iri Free Export Zone (IFEZ)		
		Gumi Export Industrial Estate (GEIE)		
		Gurudong, Korea Export Industrial Estate (KEIE)		
		Gurudong KEIE		
		Gurudong KEIE		
		Bupyong KEIE		
		Juan KEIE		
		Juan KEIE		
Syria	1	Old Free Zone Damascus	5	New Free Zone Adra
				Free Zone Lattakia
				Free Zone Tartous
				Free Zone Aleppo
				Free Zone Deraa (Jordan-Syrian Free Zone)
Taiwan	3	Kaohsiung Export Processing Zone (KEPZ)		
		Nantze Export Processing Zone (NEPZ)		
		Taichung Export Processing Zone (TEPZ)		
Thailand			1	Export Processing Zone Klong Toey
Yemen, Dem.			1	Free Zone Port of Aden
Western Samoa			1	Industrial Free Zone Vaitele
Africa				
Egypt	1	Free Zone Port Said	3	Free Zone Alexandria
				Free Zone Cairo
				Free Zone Suez
Liberia			1	Free Zone Monrovia Port
Mauritius	2	Mauritius Export Processing Zone Plaine Lauzun	4	Mauritius Export Processing Zone Curepipe
		Mauritius Export Processing Zone Coromandel		Mauritius Export Processing Zone Vacoas-Phoenix
				Mauritius Export Processing Zone Mer Rouge
				Mauritius Export Processing Zone Mahébourg
Senegal	1	Zone Franche Industrielle de Dakar		
Togo	1	Zone Industrielle Franche du Port de Lomé		
Tunisia	2	Zone Industrielle de Mégrine		
		Zone Industrielle de Ben Arous		
Latin America				
Brazil	1	Zona Franca de Manaus		
Chile			2	Zona Franca de Iquique
				Zona Franca de Punta Arenas

Table III-17 (*continued*)

Country	FPZs in operation		FPZs under construction	
	No.	Name	No.	Name
Colombia	4	Zone Franca Industrial y Comercial de Barranquilla	2	Zona Franca Industrial y Comercial de Cartagena
		Zona Franca Industrial y Commercial de Buenaventura		Zona Franca Santa Marta
		Zona Franca Industrial y Comercial Manuel Carvajal Sinisterra de Palmaseca		
		Zona Franca de Cucúta		
Dominican Rep.	3	Zona Franca de La Romana		
		Zona Franca Industrial de San Pedro de Macorís		
		Zone Franca Industrial de Santiago de los Caballeros		
El Salvador	1	Zona Franca Industrial de San Bartolo		
Guatemala	1	Zona Libre de Industria y Comercio Santo Tomás de Castilla		
Haiti	1	Parc Industriel Metropolitain Port-au-Prince (PIM)		
Honduras			1	Zona Franca Industrial de San Pedro Sula
Jamaica			1	Kingston Free Zone
Mexico		Zona Fronteriza		
	11	*Industrial parks*		
		Tijuana		
		Mexicali		
		Nogales		
		Cd. Juárez (2)		
		Cd. Acuña		
		Piedras Negras		
		Nuevo Laredo		
		Reynosa		
		Matamoros (2)		
Nicaragua			1	Airport Export Manufacturing Zone (APEX)
Panama	1	Zona Libre de Colón		
Puerto Rico	1	Mayaguez Foreign Trade Zone		
Uruguay			2	Zona Franca de Colonia
				Zona Franca de Nueva Palmira
Venezuela			2	Estado Nueve Esparta de Margarita
				Zona Franca Industrial de Paraguaná

Source: Author's compilation.
FPZ: free production zone.

Table III-18. *Free production zones and world market factories in Asia, Africa and Latin America: commencement of operation, size, structure of industry, employment, foreign capital: last available year*

FPZs and WMFs[a]	Commencement of operation	Size (hectares)	Structure of industry: Production	Structure of industry: Employment	Total employment	Foreign capital
Asia						
Bahrain						
Industrial Area, Port Mina Sulman	1968	74	(1975) Aluminium		(1975) 2770	US, GB, FRG
			Aluminium powder			
			Aluminium products			
			Air-conditioning units			
			Metal products			
			Plastic products			
			Rubber products			
Industrial Area, Sitra Island	Under construction (1975)	135				
Hong Kong						
Free Port Hong Kong[b]			(1975) Electronics	24146	(1975) 59607	(1973) 274 million US $; US (119), Jap. (55), GB (30), Thail. (28), Singap. (10), Austr. (9), France (6), Taiw. (3), other (14)
			Textiles, garments	12372		
			Watches	5391		
			Electrical products	3847		
			Chemical products	639		
			Printing/publishing	1182		
			Food processing	1533		
			Toys	4412		
			Construction material	333		
			Metal products	1434		
			Metal rolling, extrusion	889		
			Other	3429		
India						
Kandla Free Trade Zone, Kandla, Gujarat	1965	284	(1975) Electrical appliances, switches	316	(1975) 649	
			Knitting machines	30		
			Textiles	114		
			Pharmaceutical products	8		
			Spectacle frames	30		
			Plastic products	30		
			Food processing	109		
			Typeset film positives	12		

Table III-18 (*continued*)

FPZs and WMFs[a]	Commencement of operation	Size (hectares)	Structure of industry: Production	Structure of industry: Employment	Total employment	Foreign capital
Santa Cruz Electronics Export Processing Zone, Bombay	1974	41	(1975) Electronics	(1975)	600	US
WMFs[a] (bonded facilities)	1976		(1976) Containers Leather goods Porcelain Garments		n.a.	Can., FRG
Readymade Garment Export Processing Zone, Gurgaon	Under construction (1975)					
Knitwear Export Processing Zone, Ludhiana	Under construction (1975)		Textiles			
Multi Product Export Processing Zone, Dum Dum, Calcutta	Under construction (1975)					
Indonesia						
WMFs[a] (foreign offshore manufacturing)	1975		(1975) Electronics Garments	2088 9103 (1975)	11191	(1975) 19 million US $; US (9), Hong K. (4), S. Korea (3), Jap. (2), Thail. (1)
Bonded Zone, Pulo Gadung, Jakarta	Under construction (1975)	n.a.				
Bonded Zone, Rungkut, Surabaya	Under construction (1975)	n.a.				
Iran						
WMFs[a]	1974		(1974) Shoes Leather goods Textiles Garments			US, FRG
Jordan						
Free Zone, Aqaba Port, Aqaba	n.a.	n.a.	n.a.			
Jordan-Syrian Free Zone, Ramtha	Under construction	n.a.				

Table III-18 (*continued*)

FPZs and WMFs[a]	Commencement of operation	Size (hectares)	Structure of industry: Production	Structure of industry: Employment	Total employment	Foreign capital
Lebanon						
Zone Franche du Port de Beyrouth, Beirut	n.a.	n.a.	n.a.	n.a.	n.a.	n.a.
Malaysia				(Factories)		
Prai Free Trade Zone, Penang	1973	348	(1975) Electronics, electrical products	1	(1975) 6823[c]	Jap., Hong K., Taiw., Norway, Denm., GB, Switz.
			Textiles	6		
			Garments	1		
			Optical products	1		
			Rubber boots	1		
			Wood products	1		
				(Factories)		
Prai Wharves Free Trade Zone, Penang	1972	17	(1975) Textiles	1		Jap.
				(Factories)		
Bayan Lepas Free Trade Zone, Penang	1972	203	(1975) Electronics, electrical products	17	15608	US, Jap., FRG, Hong K., Singap., Philipp.
			Textiles	2		
			Medical instruments	1		
			Metal products	1		
			Toys	1		
			Rubber products	1		
			Film cameras	1		
				(Factories)		
Sungei Way Free Trade Zone, Selangor	1972	39	(1975) Electronics, electrical products	8	(1975) 6446	US, Jap., Can., Switz.
			Watches	2		
			Air-conditioning units	1		
			Cameras	1		
			Watch jewels	1		
			Moulds	1		
				(Factories)		
Ulu Klang Free Trade Zone, Selangor	1974	17	(1975) Electronics	6	(1975) 4414	US, Jap., France, GB
			Textiles	1		
			Garments	1		
Telok Panglima Garang Free Trade Zone	n.a.	20	n.a.		(1975) 1918	n.a.
				(Factories)		

Table III-18 (*continued*)

FPZs and WMFs[a]	Commencement of operation	Size (hectares)	Structure of industry: Production	Structure of industry: Employment	Total employment	Foreign capital
Batu Berendam Free Trade Zone, Malacca	1972	12	(1975) Electronics, electrical products	6	(1975) 3307	US, FRG, Jap., Switz.
			X-ray equipment	1		
				(Factories)		
Tanjong Kling Free Trade Zone, Malacca	1972	7	(1975) Textiles	1	n.a.	GB, Italy, FRG
			Garments	1		
			Footwear	1		
			Metal products	1		
WMFs[a] (bonded factories)	1972		(1975) Electronics		n.a.	Jap., US, FRG
			Garments			
			Metal products			
Pasir Gudang Free Trade Zone, Johore	Under construction (1975)	131				
Senai Free Trade Zone, Johore	Under construction (1975)	40				
Philippines				(Factories)		
Bataan Export Processing Zone, Mariveles, Bataan	1973	1300	(1975) Textiles	1	(1976) 8177	(1975) 42 million US $; US, GB, Can., Jap., Hong K., Taiw., Austr.
			Garments	10		
			Footwear	3		
			Plastic products	1		
			Compressors	1		
			Metal products	2		
			Electronics, electrical products	1		
			Car bodies	1		
			Ship building, ship repair	1		
			Wood products	1		
			Sporting goods	1		
				(Factories)		
WMfs[a]	1975		(1975) Electronics	2	(1975) 1650	US, FRG, Hong K., Austr.
			Garments	2		
Phividec Industrial Estate, Misamis Oriental, Mindanao	Under construction (1975)	3000	Iron and steel			Jap.

Table III-18 (*continued*)

FPZs and WMFs[a]	Commencement of operation	Size (hectares)	Structure of industry: Production	Structure of industry: Employment	Total employment	Foreign capital
Singapore						
Free Port Singapore[d]			(1975) Food processing		(1974) 105 000[e]	(1974) 1,178 million US $; US (422), GB (167), Netherl. (162), Jap. (119), FRG (46), others (262)
			Textiles, garments			
			Wood, paper products			
			Leather, rubber products			
			Chemical products			
			Petroleum products			
			Non-metal mineral products			
			Casting products			
			Metal products, machinery			
			Electronics, electrical products			
			Transport equipment			
			Plastic products			
			Precision instruments, optical products			
			Miscellaneous			
South Korea				(Factories)		
Masan Free Export Zone, Masan	1972	175	(1975) Electronics, electrical products	26	(1975) 21 100	(1974) 89 million US $; Jap. (65), US (3)
			Optical products	7		
			Metal products, machines	25		
			Precision instruments	3		
			Bicycles	1		
			Transport equipment	2		
			Construction material, glass products	4		
			Plastic products	4		
			Toys, sporting goods	9		
			Textiles, garments	11		
			Footwear	5		
			Paper products	3		
			Boats	2		
			Miscellaneous	8		
Iri Free Export Zone, Iri	1974	92	n.a.	n.a.	(1975) 90	n.a.
Gumi Export Industrial Estate, Gumi	1973	1 044	(1975) Electronics, electrical products	n.a.	(1975) 11 100	Jap., US
			Textiles, garments	n.a.		
Korea Export Industrial Estates (6), Seoul, Inchon	1966	372	n.a.	n.a.	(1975) 80 000	Jap., US

Table III-18 (*continued*)

FPZs and WMFs[a]	Commencement of operation	Size (hectares)	Structure of industry: Production	Structure of industry: Employment	Total employment	Foreign capital
Syria						
Old Free Zone, Damascus		1	(1975) Garments	155	(1975) 231	n.a.
			Cologne, aromate	18		
			Sugar-candy	30		
			Toothpaste	28		
New Free Zone, Adra	Under construction (1975)	20				
Free Zone, Lattakia	Under construction (1975)	8				
Free Zone, Tartous	Under construction (1975)	3				
Free Zone, Aleppo	Under construction (1975)	10				
Free Zone, Deraa	Under construction (1975)	4				
Taiwan						
Kaohsiung Export Processing Zone, Kaohsiung	1966	68	(1975) Electronic products	17704	(1975) 41017	(1975) 62 million US $; Jap., US
			Metal products	1969		
			Plastic products	2296		
			Machinery	214		
			Furniture	734		
			Handicrafts	2339		
			Electrical appliances	460		
			Leather products	923		
			Toys	571		
			Textiles	3684		
			Garments	9136		
			Others	987		

Table [illegible] 18 (continued)

FPZs and WMFs[a]	Commencement of operation	Size (hectares)	Structure of industry: Production	Structure of industry: Employment	Total employment	Foreign capital
Nantze Export Processing Zone, Nantze	1970	90	(1975) Precision instruments	39 (1975)	13160	(1975) 57 million US $; Jap., US
			Electronic products	6847		
			Optical products	97		
			Metal products	478		
			Plastic products	1107		
			Machinery	187		
			Furniture	309		
			Handicrafts	431		
			Electrical appliances	27		
			Leather products	1011		
			Textiles	445		
			Garments	1007		
			Musical instruments	928		
			Others	247		
Taichung Export Processing Zone, Taichung	1971	23	(1975) Precision instruments	1301 (1975)	7966	(1975) 32 million US $; Jap., US, FRG
			Electronics	4262		
			Optical products	437		
			Metal products	126		
			Plastic products	535		
			Machinery	287		
			Furniture	197		
			Arts & crafts products	55		
			Leather goods	310		
			Garments	300		
			Musical instruments	85		
			Miscellaneous	71		
WMFs[a]	n.a.	n.a.	Electronics	n.a.	n.a.	Jap., US
Thailand						
WMFs[a]	n.a.		(1975) Electronics	3700 (1975)	16700[e]	US, Jap., FRG
			Textiles			
			Garments			
			Paint brushes			
			Plastic products			
			Furniture			
			Shoes, leather goods			
			Wood products			
			Chemical products			
Export Processing Zone, Klong Toey	Under construction (1975)	18				

Table III-18 (*continued*)

FPZs and WMFs[a]	Commencement of operation	Size (hectares)	Structure of industry: Production	Structure of industry: Employment	Total employment	Foreign capital
Turkey						
WMFs[a]	n.a.		(1975) Garments	n.a.	n.a.	FRG
West Somoa						
Industrial Free Zone, Vaitele	Under construction (1975)	40				
Yemen, Dem.						
Free Zone Port of Aden	Under construction[f]					
Africa						
Botswana						
WMFs[a]	Under construction (1975)		Electronics, electrical products			Brazil
Egypt						
Free Zone Port Said	1976	n.a.	(1976) Medical instruments Garments	n.a.	n.a.	France, Italy
Free Zone Alexandria	Under construction (1976)	126	(1976) Tyres			
Free Zone Cairo	Under construction (1975)	84				
Free Zone Suez	Under construction (1976)	n.a.				
Ghana						
WMFs[a]	Under construction (1976)					
Ivory Coast						
WMFs[a]	1976		(1976) Textiles Garments	n.a.	(1976) 2800	France, US, Jap., Netherl., FRG
Lesotho						
WMFs[a]	Under construction (1975)		(1976) Electronics, electrical products			FRG

Table III-18 (*continued*)

FPZs and WMFs[a]	Commencement of operation	Size (hectares)	Structure of industry: Production	Structure of industry: Employment	Total employment	Foreign capital
Liberia						
Free Zone Monrovia Port	Under construction (1975)	32				
Mauritius				(Factories)[g]		
Mauritius Export Processing Zone, Plaine Lauzun, Port Louis	1971	44	(1975) Textiles	4	(1975) 9952[g]	South Africa, Hong K., France FRG, India, Réunion
			Garments	20		
			Electronics	4		
			Plastic products	2		
			Rubber products	1		
			Toys	1		
			Leather goods	1		
			Furniture	2		
			Processed diamonds	2		
			Food	4		
			Eyeglass frames	1		
			Boats	1		
			Miscellaneous	4		
Mauritius Export Processing Zone, Coromandel	1976	25				
Mauritius Export Processing Zone, Curepipe	Under construction (1975)	20				
Mauritius Export Processing Zone, Vacoas-Phoenix	Under construction (1975)	15				
Mauritius Export Processing Zone, Mer Rouge	Under construction (1975)	55				
Mauritius Export Processing Zone, Mahébourg	Under construction (1975)	n.a.				
Morocco						
WMFs[a]			Electronics			France, FRG
			Textiles, garments			
			Car parts			

Table III-18 (*continued*)

FPZs and WMFs[a]	Commencement of operation	Size (hectares)	Structure of industry: Production	Structure of industry: Employment	Total employment	Foreign capital
Senegal						
Zone Franche Industrielle de Dakar	1976	650	(1976) Construction material	150	(1976) 150	US
South Africa						
WMFs[a]	Under construction (1976)		Watches			FRG, Italy
			Textiles			
			Metal products			
Swaziland				(Factories)		
WMFs[a]			(1976) Food	1	(1976) 2500	Finland
			Pharmaceutical products	1		
			Textiles	1		
			Electronics	1		
			Miscellaneous	8		
Togo						
Zone Industrielle Franche du Port de Lomé	n.a.	50	Garments	n.a.	n.a.	
Tunisia						
Zone Industrielle Mégrine, Tunis	n.a.	100	(1974)[h] Food	1400	(1974) 24000[h]	(1974) 206 million US $; FRG (83), Italy (52), Netherl. (28), GB (17), France (15), others (11)
			Construction material, glass	100		
			Electrical products, metal products	2600		
			Chemical products	500		
			Textiles, garments	17700		
			Miscellaneous	1700		
Zone Industrielle de Ben Arous, Tunis	n.a.	200				
WMFs[a]	n.a.					
Latin America						
Barbados				(Factories)		
WMFs[a] (enclave enterprises)	n.a.		(1975) Garments	5	(1975) 3000	US
			Metal goods	1		
			Electronics	7		
			Toys	1		
			Sporting goods	1		
			Pharmaceutical products	1		
			Eyeglass frames	1		
			Miscellaneous	2		

Table III-18 (*continued*)

FPZs and WMFs[a]	Commencement of operation	Size (hectares)	Structure of industry: Production		Structure of industry: Employment	Total employment		Foreign capital
Brazil								
Zona Franca de Manaus	1968	1600	(1975)	Jewelry	n.a.	(1973)	27650	US, Jap., Netherl.
				Textiles, garments				
				Toys				
				Watches				
				Electronics, electrical products				
				Wood products				
				Paper products				
				Food				
WMFs[a] (drawback system, entreposto industrial, entreposto aduaneiro)			(1976)	Cars	n.a.		n.a.	US, FRG, Jap., Netherl., Italy, Sweden, France
				Car parts				
				Machines				
				Chemical products				
				Pharmaceutical products				
				Garments				
				Tyres				
				Office machines				
				Electrical products				
				Casting products				
Chile								
Zona Franca de Iquique	Under construction (1975)	n.a.						
Zona Franca de Punta Arenas	Under construction (1975)	n.a.						
Colombia					(Factories)			
Zona Franca Industrial y Comercial de Barranquilla	1965	100	(1974)	Garments	14	(1974)	5000	US
				Leather goods	5			
				Car parts	2			
				Sewing machines	1			
				Boilers	1			
				Miscellaneous	5			
Zona Franca Industrial y Comercialde Buenaventura	1973	34		n.a.	n.a.		n.a.	n.a.

Table III-18 (*continued*)

FPZs and WMFs[a]	Commencement of operation	Size (hectares)		Structure of industry: Production	Structure of industry: Employment		Total employment	Foreign capital
Zona Franca Industrial y Comercial Manuel Carvajal Sinisterra de Palmaseca	1973	48	(1975)	Footwear Garments Medical instruments Jewelry Chemical products	160 180 100 120 40	(1975)	600	US
Zona Franca Cucúta	1974	25		n.a.	n.a.		n.a.	n.a.
Zona Franca Industrial y Comercial de Cartagena	Under construction (1975)			Chemical products Toys Boats Elevators Food				
Zona Franca Santa Marta	Under construction (1975)							
Costa Rica								
WMFs[a] (drawback system)	n.a.		(1975)	Textiles Garments Food	n.a.		n.a.	US
Dominican Republic								
Zona Franca de La Romana	1969	93	(1975)[i]	Textiles Garments Miscellaneous		(1975)	6500[i]	US
Zona Franca Industrial de San Pedro Macorís	1973	30						
Zona Franca Industrial deSantiago,Santiagodelos Caballeros	1974	60						
Dutch Antilles								
WMFs[a]	n.a.		(1975)	Electronics	(Factories) 3		n.a.	n.a.
Ecuador								
WMFs[a] (drawback system)	Under construction (1976)							
El Salvador								
Zona Franca Industrial de San Bartolo, San Salvador	1975	54	(1975)	Electronics Textiles Miscellaneous	1900 660 3583	(1975)	6143	US

Table III-18 (*continued*)

FPZs and WMFs[a]	Commencement of operation	Size (hectares)	Structure of industry: Production	Structure of industry: Employment	Total employment	Foreign capital
Guatemala						
Zona Libre de Industria y Comercio Santo Tomás de Castilla	1975	n.a.	n.a.	n.a.	n.a.	n.a.
Haiti						
Parc Industriel Metropolitain Port-au-Prince	1974	25	(1975) Garments Electronics Metal products Dental products Furniture Fishing rods Construction material	n.a.	n.a.	US
WMFs[a]			Textiles Garments Electronics Metal products Plastic products Rubber products Toys Sporting goods Electrical products Office machines	n.a.	25 000[j]	US
Honduras						
Zona Libre de Puerto Cortes, San Pedro Sula	Under construction (1975)	40				
Jamaica						
WMFs[a]	1971		(1973) Garments Leather goods Miscellaneous	(Factories) (1973) 11 6 14	(1971) 5 100	n.a.
Kingston Free Zone	Under construction (1975)	n.a.				

Table III-18 (*continued*)

FPZs and WMFs[a]	Commencement of operation	Size (hectares)	Structure of industry: Production	Structure of industry: Employment	Total employment	Foreign capital
Mexico						
Zona Fronteriza[k] Zonas y Perimetros Libres	1966		(1974) Food	(1974) 1633	(1975) 74676	US
			Garments, footwear	13440		
			Furniture	1480		
			Machines, transport equipment	1939		
			Electronics, electrical products	46634		
			Miscellaneous	1612		
WMFs[a] (empresas maquiladoras de exportación, interior de pais)	1972		(1974) Food	(1974) 200	(1975) 9632	US
			Garments, footwear	384		
			Machines, transport equipment	443		
			Electronics, electrical products	3885		
Nicaragua						
WMFs[a] (offshore assembly operations)	n.a.		(1975) Electrical products	n.a.	n.a.	n.a.
			Chemical products			
			Paper products			
			Metal products			
Airport Export Manufacturing Zone Las Mercedes	1975 (under construction)	n.a.				
Panama						
Zona Libre de Colón	1974[l]	48[m]	(1975) Garments	n.a.	(1975) 1300	US, Jap., FRG
			Electronics			
			Pharmaceutical products			
			Bicycles			
			Miscellaneous			
Puerto Rico				(Factories)		
Mayaguez Foreign Trade Zone	1964		(1970) Leather goods	2	(1975) 481	US
			Pharmaceutical products	2		
			Garments	1		
			Precision instruments	1		
WMFs[a]	n.a.		(1975) Petroleum products	n.a.	(1975) 96245	US, France, GB, FRG, Can., Switz., Venez., Jap., Netherl.
			Pharmaceutical products			
			Electronics, electrical products			
			Precision instruments, optical products			
			Textiles			
			Garments			
			Metal products			

Table III-18 (*continued*)

FPZs and WMFs[a]	Commencement of operation	Size (hectares)	Structure of industry: Production	Structure of industry: Employment	Total employment	Foreign capital
St Lucia						
WMFs[a] (bonded factories)	n.a.		(1976) Garments Electronics Metal products Plastic products	n.a.	(1976) 3500	n.a.
Trinidad and Tobago						
WMFs[a] (enclave industries)	n.a.		Garments	n.a.	n.a.	n.a.
Uruguay						
Zona Franca de Colonia	Under construction (1975)	n.a.				
Zona Franca de Neuva Palmira	Under construction (1975)	n.a.				
Venezuela						
Zona Franca Industrial de Paraguaná	Under construction (1975)	n.a.				
Zona Franca de Margarita	Under construction (1975)					

Source: author's calculation
FPZ: free production zone WMF: world market factory
a: World market factories outside of free production zones
b: Free Port Hong Kong: two industrial townships, seven industrial districts; the statistics concerning structure of industry and employees pertain only to foreign companies in Hong Kong. Production for the world market by foreign companies exists since the mid-1960s
c: Including employees in Prai Wharves Free Trade Zone
d: Free Port Singapore: fourteen industrial estates; production for the world market by foreign companies exists since 1967
e: Estimate
f: Industrial zone under construction, free port in operation
g: Including Export Processing Zone Coromandel
h: Free production zones, industrial zones and world market factories outside of free production zones together
i: Including Zona Franca Industrial de San Pedro de Macorís and Zona Franca Industrial de Santiago
j: Including employees in Parc Metropolitian Port-au-Prince
k: Eleven industrial parks
l: Free port in operation since 1948
m: Size of industrial area
n: Employees in manufacturing industry (total number of employees in the zone: 8405)
o: Commercial activities since 1961
p: Commercial activities since 1949
q: Duty-free zone since 1971